MR. X AND THE PACIFIC

MR. X AND THE PACIFIC

George F. Kennan and
American Policy in East Asia

Paul J. Heer

Paul Heer

CORNELL UNIVERSITY PRESS   **ITHACA AND LONDON**

First published 2018 by Cornell University Press

Printed in the United States of America

Library of Congress Cataloging-in-Publication Data

Names: Heer, Paul J., 1959–author.
Title: Mr. X and the Pacific : George F. Kennan and American policy in East Asia / Paul J. Heer.
Description: Ithaca : Cornell University Press, 2018. | Includes bibliographical references and index.
Identifiers: LCCN 2017028411 (print) | LCCN 2017028879 (ebook) | ISBN 9781501711169 (pdf) | ISBN 9781501711176 (ret) | ISBN 9781501711145 | ISBN 9781501711145 (cloth :alk. paper)
Subjects: LCSH: United States—Foreign relations—East Asia. | East Asia— Foreign relations—United States. | Kennan, George F. (George Frost), 1904–2005. | United States—Foreign relations—1945–1953.
Classification: LCC DS518.8 (ebook) | LCC DS518.8 .H34 2018 (print) | DDC 327.7305—dc23
LC record available at https://lccn.loc.gov/2017028411

Cornell University Press strives to use environmentally responsible suppliers and materials to the fullest extent possible in the publishing of its books. Such materials include vegetable-based, low-VOC inks and acid-free papers that are recycled, totally chlorine-free, or partly composed of nonwood fibers. For further information, visit our website at cornellpress.cornell.edu.

For Melissa, Charlie, Kevin, Zane, Brett, and Paulus

Contents

Illustrations

Acknowledgments

This book began in the history department at The George Washington University in 1995. I am immensely grateful to Professor Peter P. Hill, who allowed me to convince him that it was a viable topic; to Ronald Spector and William R. Johnson, who also served on the original research committee; and to Edward Berkowitz, Edward McCord, and Thomas Elmore, who rounded out the final examining committee. I am also indebted to the late Professor Lawrence Gelfand, who was my adviser during my master's program at the University of Iowa, and who let me convince him to check the box on my graduation form that endorsed me for future doctoral study—when he was ambivalent about doing so. Finally, I am eternally grateful to Professor Joan Skurnowicz, who first inspired me at Loras College to become a history major.

Both during the original research and when I revisited the project twenty years later, I received invaluable assistance from the staffs at the National Archives in Washington, DC, and College Park, Maryland; the Washington National Records Center in Suitland, Maryland; the Harry S. Truman Presidential Library in Independence, Missouri; the George C. Marshall Research Foundation in Lexington, Virginia; the MacArthur Memorial Archives in Norfolk, Virginia; and the Seeley G. Mudd Manuscript Library in Princeton, New Jersey. Archival librarians are the caretakers of a priceless segment of our national treasure.

The twenty-year delay in my pursuit of publication was due to my preoccupation with a richly rewarding career as an analyst at the Central Intelligence Agency (CIA). This left me no time to devote to academic publishing, but I never abandoned my dream of turning my dissertation on Kennan's involvement with East Asia into a book. In the meantime, I enjoyed generous support and encouragement for both my doctoral studies and my dream of publication from my supervisors and colleagues in the Intelligence Community and elsewhere in the government, and among many scholars who also became professional colleagues and friends during my years in government service. Their names are too numerous to list, but they know who they are, and I am deeply grateful for their inestimable contributions to my professional and personal development.

It was the Center for International Studies at the Massachusetts Institute of Technology (MIT) that gave me the long-sought opportunity, after I retired from government, to return to the Kennan project by offering me its Robert E. Wilhelm Fellowship. I am deeply grateful to Dick Samuels for the invitation; to

Robert E. Wilhelm for his sponsorship; and to Barry Posen, Taylor Fravel, Phiona Lovett, Laurie Scheffler, and the rest of the faculty, staff, and students at MIT's Security Studies Program for welcoming me into their extraordinary company. They provided me with an ideal environment in which to not only pursue this book project but also learn so much through immersion in the activities and expertise of the Security Studies Program.

During my time at MIT I also received generous cross-town support and encouragement from Graham Allison and Gary Samore at Harvard University's John F. Kennedy School of Government. They provided me with a forum to discuss my Kennan project with faculty and students there, and the opportunity to participate more broadly in Kennedy School events. As at MIT, I benefitted greatly from the wealth of world-class expertise that resides at or is drawn to the Harvard campus.

As the process advanced, I eventually crossed the threshold into the academic publishing world. I am deeply grateful to Roger Haydon at Cornell University Press, who introduced me to both the process and his colleague Michael McGandy, who became my editor. My biggest debt is to Michael, who accepted the project and assumed the task of guiding me to the finish line, thus making possible the fulfillment of my twenty-year-old dream. He served simultaneously as a constructive critic and a sympathetic cheerleader as he walked me through the review and publication processes. I also greatly appreciate the comments and recommendations from the anonymous reviewers that Michael consulted; their input, in tandem with his, was instrumental in prompting me to substantially transform the manuscript from my original concept into the much richer narrative of the final version.

I am also grateful to the CIA Publications Review Board for its thorough review of the manuscript. For the record, this review was done solely for classification purposes and does not constitute an official release of CIA information. All statements of fact, opinion, or analysis in the book are mine and do not reflect official positions or views of the CIA or any other US government agency. Nothing in the book should be construed as asserting or implying US government authentication of information or CIA endorsement of my views.

This book would not exist without the contributions to history made by the late George F. Kennan and John Paton Davies Jr., both of whom I had the enormous privilege and thrill of corresponding with directly while working on the original dissertation. Both men were generous in responding to my queries about their work together during the early Cold War, and both read my dissertation in its entirety and offered me highly gratifying compliments. This book is their story, and it is a great honor to tell it. I also wish to thank Kennan's other biographers, especially John Lewis Gaddis, Wilson Miscamble, and David Mayers, all of whom originally encouraged me that Kennan's role in East Asia policy was a viable and important subject for a book. Special thanks goes to Michael Green for introducing me to Davies's daughter Tiki, and to the Davies family for their support and assistance with the project.

Finally, I must express my profound thanks to my family. My parents Carl and Mary Adele Heer made possible every opportunity I have ever had, and my siblings—Steve, Joel, Dave, Tim, Janet, and Susan—and their families have always provided encouragement for my work, even when they didn't realize it.

MR. X AND THE PACIFIC

George F. Kennan as director of the State Department Policy Planning Staff, 1947.

A STRATEGIC VISION INTERRUPTED

On 21 August 1950, two months into the crisis that was sparked by the outbreak of the Korean War, US diplomat George F. Kennan—then serving as a senior adviser to Secretary of State Dean Acheson (having postponed a sabbatical leave to help the Truman administration deal with the crisis)—wrote a memorandum to Acheson expressing his alarm about the overall direction of American policy in East Asia. "The course upon which we are moving today," Kennan wrote, "is one, as I see it, so little promising and so fraught with danger that I could not honestly urge you to continue to take responsibility for it." Washington's objectives and strategy in Korea, he argued, were not clear and were thus inviting potential escalation of the war. Meanwhile, the apparent decision to retain US military forces in Japan risked undermining the long-term US relationship with Tokyo. Washington's ambiguous position between the rival Chinese regimes on the mainland and Taiwan risked alienating both sides as well as other countries in the region. Finally, Kennan observed, the emerging US support for France in its efforts to thwart Vietnam's bid for independence was almost certainly a losing bet.[1]

Kennan was especially dismayed because he had spent the previous three years, as director of the State Department's Policy Planning Staff (PPS), attempting to avoid precisely these dilemmas by establishing a US strategic approach to East Asia that minimized US commitments and even attention there. As the department's top expert on Russia and the intellectual author of the policy of "containment" of the Soviet Union, Kennan was focused almost exclusively on the Soviet threat to US interests, which he thought was not significant in the Far East and could be readily contained there by a "perimeter defense." The centerpiece of his framework was a revitalized but demilitarized and neutral Japan. His primary recommendation to Acheson thus echoed a position he had formulated during his tenure at the PPS: "We should make it an objective of our policy to terminate our involvements on the mainland of Asia as rapidly as possible and on the best terms we can get." Kennan added the extraordinary proposal that Washington should offer to withdraw militarily from both Japan and Korea in exchange for Russia's agreement to arrange the retreat of North Korean forces from the South.[2]

These recommendations were ignored, as Kennan anticipated in his cover message to Acheson: "I am afraid that, like so many of my thoughts, they will be too remote from general thinking in the Government to be of much practical use to you."[3] Kennan had grown frustrated with his marginalization within the State Department under Acheson (which had prompted his decision to take a sabbatical at the Institute for Advanced Study in Princeton, New Jersey). Many of his ideas had indeed become "too remote from general thinking in the Government" to prevail in policy deliberations. This was particularly the case in East Asia, where Kennan—after playing a profoundly influential role on China and Japan between 1947 and 1949—subsequently saw US policy incrementally shift toward what he considered ill-advised commitments and military strategies in the region. Starting in the summer of 1950, he watched grimly as the Korean War accelerated this trend, which eclipsed and ultimately destroyed Kennan's own nascent strategic vision for US policy in the Far East.

This book chronicles the rise and fall of that strategic vision, and the legacies of Kennan's engagement with East Asian affairs. Although his name is rarely associated with the region, his involvement and influence were by no means limited to the policies toward the Soviet Union and Europe for which he is best known. Indeed, historian Wilson Miscamble has observed that Kennan's impact on East Asia policy "may well have exceeded his influence on American policy in Europe"—which was substantial, given that Kennan is widely credited with a central role in formulating the postwar European Recovery Program (the Marshall Plan).[4] His impact on East Asia was profound even though much of it appears at first glance to have been ephemeral.

Although the book focuses largely on Kennan's tenure as PPS director (1947–50), it also carries the story beyond his time in government—from which he retired in 1953—tracking how his views on East Asia evolved (or in some cases evidently did not) for the remainder of his long life (1904–2005) as a public intellectual. What emerges is a record of surprisingly broad and deep involvement in an area in which Kennan previously had little knowledge or experience, a surprisingly distinct and enduring set of ideas about what he believed was the appropriate scope and direction for US policy there, and some lessons that are applicable to the dilemmas US foreign policy still confronts in East Asia today.

Kennan's substantial involvement with policy toward the Far East coincided with his formulation of the containment doctrine in the early, formative years of the Cold War. During this period, he was one of the primary architects of Washington's decision to disengage from involvement in the Chinese civil war—a role that his "official" biographer, John Lewis Gaddis, has deemed "pivotal."[5] In Japan, he was *the* primary agent of Washington's redirection of its postwar occupation policy away from a punitive approach and toward economic reconstruction. Kennan was less successful in his subsequent efforts to influence policy toward Korea and Southeast Asia, but in both cases he gave advice that was overruled but later vindicated: he played a key bureaucratic role during the US response to the North Korean invasion—where he was almost alone in warning against military intervention north of the 38th Parallel—and he was among the first US officials to warn against a commitment of US resources and inheritance of the French role in Indochina.

Kennan's impact on East Asia policy was almost entirely a product of his role as PPS director. When General George Marshall—who as army chief of staff had been credited as the architect of the Allied victory in the Second World War—was appointed secretary of state in January 1947, he established the PPS to replicate the role of the Army Department's war plans division, as the formulator of strategic policy direction. He selected Kennan as its director. Like most policymakers, Marshall was focused on the emerging Soviet challenge and had been deeply impressed (along with many others in Washington) by a now famous "Long Telegram" that Kennan had written in February 1946—when he was serving at the US embassy in Moscow—assessing the Soviet Union's strategic worldview and objectives.[6] Marshall delegated to the PPS a central role in policy formulation that has never since been replicated, and the influence of which was probably reinforced by his personal stature in Washington as a revered statesman and military hero. As long as Marshall was secretary of state, the policy papers generated by Kennan and the PPS carried Marshall's weight in interagency policy deliberations—which was often decisive—and thus frequently became the foundation for overall US policy direction.

Appropriately for Kennan, the Soviet threat became the prism through which he and other US policymakers viewed the postwar challenges they faced in East Asia. During the war, Soviet leader Josef Stalin had agreed to intervene in the fight against Japan after the defeat of Germany, in exchange primarily for Soviet access

East Asia in 1947.

Source: Bill Nelson Cartography

to ports and railroads in the northeastern Chinese region of Manchuria. He also promised to continue supporting Chiang Kai-shek's Nationalist (Kuomintang, or KMT) regime as the government of China, notwithstanding Soviet links to Mao Zedong's Chinese Communist Party (CCP). The Japanese surrender in August 1945 cut short Russian intervention in the Pacific War, but not before Soviet troops established a presence in Manchuria and the northern half of the Korean Peninsula, pursuant to a US-Soviet agreement to jointly but temporarily supplant Japan's colonial occupation there. This postwar Soviet military presence set the stage for the East Asian component of the Cold War.

In China, neither the Nationalists nor the Communists were wholly comfortable with the Soviet presence—the former because it compromised Chinese sovereignty and created opportunities for Stalin to shift material support to the Communists, which he soon did; and the latter because they too resented Stalin's territorial power play in the region, but also his nominal neutrality up to that point in their rivalry with the KMT. For its part, the United States gradually embraced the Nationalists—as representatives of the ostensibly democratic Chinese with which Americans had a long-standing political and sentimental relationship—while maintaining a pragmatic dialogue with the Communists. Most importantly, President Harry Truman in December 1945 had sent Marshall to China in an attempt to mediate the civil war there, which had renewed immediately after the defeat of Japan. Marshall returned to the United States (to become secretary of state) in January 1947—over a year later—having largely failed in this mission. The Chinese civil war continued to escalate, and the tide was turning in favor of the Communists.

In Japan, the surrender of the imperial government and the totality of the US victory had opened the door for a US-led military occupation under the auspices of General Douglas MacArthur as supreme commander of the Allied powers (SCAP). This was nominally overseen by the interallied Far Eastern Commission (FEC), which included representatives of the Soviet Union and was ostensibly responsible for advising occupation policies in line with the terms of the Japanese surrender. However, Washington's commanding position and leverage allowed it to largely exclude the Soviets from any substantial role. From the outset the occupation administration focused on punishing the Japanese militarists deemed responsible for the war and dismantling Japan's military and industrial capacity to ever wage war again.

In Korea, the peninsula had been divided into two zones occupied by the Allies that accepted the Japanese surrender there: the Soviets in the north, and the Americans south of the 38th Parallel. The plan was to withdraw both occupation forces after establishing a UN trusteeship for Korea as a transitional stage to Korean independence, but Washington and Moscow could not agree on the terms of the trusteeship and the Koreans themselves wanted immediate independence. Through 1946 and into 1947, this stalemate allowed an incremental polarization to develop between the two zones of Korea—and their two occupying powers.

In Southeast Asia, the defeat of Japan had created a vacuum in which indigenous nationalist movements emerged in a bid to preempt the restoration of European colonial rule. Most problematic were French and Dutch efforts in Indochina and Indonesia, respectively, to reestablish their prewar control. During the war, President Franklin Roosevelt had embraced the idea of national self-determination in Southeast Asia; but after his death and the end of the war, Washington was constrained from promoting this by the need for cooperation elsewhere from its European allies—especially the French—and by the emerging fear that nationalist movements in Southeast Asia might be exploited by the Soviets or the Chinese Communists. For its part, the United States tried to set an example in the Philippines—which it had acquired in 1898 after the Spanish-American War—by granting its independence in 1946. But a subsequent bilateral agreement in March 1947 left a substantial US military presence in the Philippines.

This was the security environment the United States confronted in the Far East when Marshall became secretary of state and Kennan the director of the PPS. However, Washington's overwhelming focus was on Europe and the emerging Soviet threat there—as reflected in the promulgation in March 1947 of the Truman Doctrine, which essentially committed the United States to resist efforts by the Soviet Union to extend its influence further into Europe, and the announcement in June 1947 of the Marshall Plan, which aimed at rebuilding the Western European economies to bolster them against any such Soviet efforts. East Asia was a lesser priority, in terms of both attention and resources. Nor was it clear that the United States faced imminent dangers in the Far East comparable to those perceived to be present in Europe. Moreover, to the extent that strategic dilemmas in East Asia were recognized, no quick or easy solutions were apparent. Accordingly, there was little focus in Washington on developing a strategic plan for East Asia and little sense of an urgent need to do so.

When Kennan was able—and soon required—as PPS director to turn his attention to the region, his approach to East Asia predictably drew first and foremost on his focus on the Soviet Union, both because that was the foundation of his expertise and because he—like most policymakers in Washington—viewed the Soviet Union as the primary strategic threat the United States faced. Accordingly, his perspective on East Asia centered primarily on assessing the nature and extent of the Soviet challenge there. Within that framework, Kennan would apply the same realist principles that he applied in other parts of the world to assess what US interests were at risk and where, and what the relative capacity of the United States was to protect those interests. This led to judgments about what

Kennan thought was strategically vital to the United States in East Asia, and where and how Washington should draw the line in defining and securing its position there. What emerged was a strategic concept for US policy in the region that was based on Kennan's assessments of the relative power—and importance to the United States—of the key countries in East Asia, the limits on the resources and attention Washington could devote to the region, and the ability of the United States to influence developments there.

As will be seen, Kennan was inconsistent in both his application and his advocacy of the strategic concept he devised for the region. Moreover, his policies toward East Asia—like many of the policies he developed toward the Soviet Union and other parts of the world—were not always well developed, realistic, consistent, or politically viable. They sometimes reflected a condescending and even racist attitude toward Asian peoples. Nor were his recommendations for East Asia policy uniformly accepted by his superiors and colleagues—especially after Marshall was replaced as secretary of state by Acheson. Perhaps most importantly, Kennan was never able to resolve some of the dilemmas posed by his own strategic calculus in the region—especially the tension between his assessment of what was strategically important to the United States and his simultaneous view that US credibility and prestige should not be compromised.

Nonetheless, it is remarkable how often Kennan's advice on East Asian affairs was validated, both in those cases where it was followed (as in China and Japan) and in those where it largely was not (as in Korea and Indochina). He was sometimes right about East Asia when his bosses and some of the Asian experts were wrong. And even when he didn't have the answers, Kennan usually focused on the right questions, which are equally valid today: How should the United States define its interests and goals in East Asia? What capability does the United States have to pursue those interests and to influence developments there? What are the implications of the limits on those capabilities? And based on those elements of the equation—especially the limits—what policies should the United States be pursuing in East Asia that are most realistic and most likely to maximize achievement of US strategic goals?

ENCOUNTERS WITH EAST ASIA
Inheritance of a Strategic Perspective

Kennan had almost no experience with East Asian affairs before he became director of the Policy Planning Staff (PPS) in May 1947. He had never been in the Far East, nor, by his own account, had he ever been particularly interested in it. Even after he left the PPS in 1951, he claimed he had "no personal familiarity with that part of the world" and had "read no more [about it] than a busy person, not an expert on Far Eastern affairs, can contrive to read in the face of other interests and obligations."[1] Kennan nonetheless had forged elements of a strategic perspective on East Asia—and some preconceived notions—that were largely derived from professional colleagues who greatly influenced his initial thinking about the region.

He was aware that his distant relative and namesake George Kennan (1845–1924)—whose career the younger Kennan emulated in part—had some experience with the Far East. The elder Kennan (the first cousin of George F.'s grandfather) was an explorer and writer best known for his travels in Russia, especially Siberia, but was also engaged as a journalist during the Russo-Japanese War of 1904–5. Citing the similarities between their careers, George F. Kennan noted in his memoirs that both he and his distant cousin "had occasion to plead at one time or another for greater understanding in America for Japan and her geopolitical problems vis-à-vis the Asian mainland."[2] But this influence on Kennan's perspective on the region was superficial at best, and his own pleading on Japan's behalf came only later.

The MacMurray Memorandum

Of more profound importance in framing Kennan's mind-set toward East Asia was the influence of a senior US Foreign Service colleague and fellow Princeton graduate, John Van Antwerp MacMurray (1881–1960), who had served as US minister to China from 1925 to 1929. MacMurray was a generation older than Kennan, but they briefly served together abroad in 1933, when MacMurray was appointed minister to the Baltic States, resident in Riga, Latvia—where Kennan was then serving in his first diplomatic assignment. Almost immediately, however, Kennan was transferred to the newly opened US embassy in Moscow.[3]

Washington, meanwhile, was grappling with the crisis in East Asia that had been sparked by the Japanese invasion of Manchuria (northeastern China) in 1931. In 1935, MacMurray was tasked by the State Department to contribute an assessment of the situation there, based on his long-standing experience and expertise on the region. The memorandum he produced—"Developments Affecting American Policy in the Far East" (1 November 1935)—was largely neglected at the time it was written but was later recognized both inside and outside the State Department as a seminal document.[4] Indeed, MacMurray's memorandum and Kennan's own February 1946 "Long Telegram" from Moscow assessing Soviet foreign policy were considered by some to be the two best analytical reports ever produced within the department.

Although it is not clear precisely when Kennan first encountered the MacMurray memorandum, records show that it was circulating among State officials involved with East Asia policy during the years 1947–50, when he was PPS director; Kennan shortly thereafter told MacMurray he "stole" a copy as an "indispensable aid" when he left the department. Kennan later acknowledged that the memorandum made a "deep impression" on him, and it became an enduring foundation for his approach to East Asia.[5]

The central thesis of MacMurray's memorandum was that the Far Eastern crisis of the 1930s was largely the result of China's failure to abide by its commitments in the framework for regional security cooperation that had been embodied in the Washington Naval Conference treaties of 1922, and Washington's failure to press China to do so.[6] Those commitments included China's obligation to avoid discrimination in "dealing with applications for economic rights and privileges from Governments and nationals of all foreign countries."[7] In MacMurray's view, Japan had acted militarily to secure its interests in northern China only after repeatedly but unsuccessfully seeking the help of the United States and other Western powers in forcing the Chinese to act responsibly. In his prescient conclusions, MacMurray predicted that war between the United States

John Van Antwerp MacMurray as assistant secretary of state, 1924. MacMurray was the primary source of Kennan's assessment of the relative strategic importance of China and Japan.

Source: Library of Congress / Prints and Photographs Division

and Japan was inevitable if Washington chose to oppose Japanese domination of China.

Many of the themes outlined by MacMurray in the 1935 memorandum would later be echoed repeatedly in Kennan's own thinking and writing. Foremost among these was MacMurray's characterization of US attitudes toward China and the extent to which the Chinese exploited them. He observed that Americans harbored strong sentimental attitudes toward China that were "based upon rather naive and romantic assumptions" whose "vigor and intensity seemed out of all proportion to the average citizen's concern with Chinese affairs." This popular attachment to the Chinese was "based in part upon a somewhat patronizing pride in the belief that our Government had borne the part of China against selfish nations, but still more upon the fact that our church organizations had through several generations cultivated a favorable interest in China in support of their missionary enterprises therein."[8]

MacMurray considered the missionaries and other adherents of a sentimental attachment to China to be dupes for the Chinese inasmuch as they became a powerful lobby pressuring the US government to defend China's interests. The Chinese, for their part, were more than willing to accept the favor—but without incurring any obligations or showing any gratitude. Indeed, MacMurray felt that the Chinese had virtually asked for whatever pain they suffered at the hands of Japan and other outside powers:

> The Chinese . . . had been willful in their scorn of their legal obligations, reckless in their resort to violence for the accomplishment of their ends, and provocative in their methods; though timid when there was any prospect that the force to which they resorted would be met by force, they were alert to take a hectoring attitude at any sign of weakness in their opponents, and cynically inclined to construe as weakness any yielding to their demands. Those who sought to deal fairly with them were reviled as niggardly in not going further to satisfy them, and were subjected to difficulties in the hope of forcing them to grant more; so that a policy of appeasement and reconciliation, such as that with which our own Government attempted to soothe the hysteria of their elated racial self-esteem, brought only disillusionments.[9]

Nor did MacMurray believe that US efforts to extract Japan from China would endear the Chinese to the United States:

> The Chinese always did, do, and will regard foreign nations as barbarian enemies, to be dealt with by playing them off against each other. The most successful of them might be respected, but would nevertheless be regarded as the one to be next put down. . . . If we were to "save" China from Japan and become the "Number One" nation in the eyes of her people, we should thereby become not the most favored but the most distrusted of nations. It is no reproach to the Chinese to acknowledge that we should have established no claim upon their gratitude. . . . They would thank us for nothing, and give us no credit for unselfish intentions, but set themselves to formulating resistance to us in the exercise of the responsibilities we would have assumed.[10]

Strategically, MacMurray believed that US policy toward China, starting with the "Open Door Notes" of then Secretary of State John Hay in 1899–1900, had been based on a specious assumption of the potential value of US trade with China and on Washington's consequent but unenforceable support for China's territorial integrity as a prerequisite for ensuring free access to trade with it. This, in MacMurray's view, overestimated China's strategic importance and underestimated

the risks of engaging with it by failing to recognize that China was not a consequential nation but instead "a mere congeries of human beings, primitive in its
political and economic organization, difficult and often troublesome to deal with
in either aspect, and by its weakness constantly inviting aggressions that threatened such interests as we might have or hope for." As far as US interests were concerned, Washington needed to recognize that China had "ceased to be, for us, a
field of unlimited opportunity, and seems in the way of becoming a waste area"
and "an almost negligible factor" in East Asia.[11]

In contrast, MacMurray insisted that Japan was the consequential nation in
East Asia and should be the center of US policy there: "a working theory of the
relative importance of the various objectives in our Far Eastern policy" would
dictate that "Japan has come to be of paramount interest to us." Accordingly,
Washington needed to "write off our claims to leadership" in China and acknowledge that the "virile people" of Japan were the strategic key to the region.
MacMurray acknowledged that Japan itself was potentially volatile and that a
precipitous US abandonment of China "would buy us no reconciliation with the
Japanese, gain us no respect, and ease none of our difficulties." Accordingly,
he advised that Washington should "be meticulously careful not to lose the
wholesome respect with which the Japanese at heart regard us, by any attempt to
ingratiate ourselves with them by compromising our own national power or dignity or principles." Nonetheless, MacMurray's bottom line was that the United
States needed to "write down our interest in China to its present depreciated
value," adjust US policies to accommodate the real balance of power in East Asia,
and acknowledge the limits of US interests and influence there.[12]

The central themes and the analysis contained within MacMurray's memorandum have been the subject of persistent debate among historians, particularly
those focused on the origins of World War II in East Asia.[13] However, an assessment of the validity of his judgments about Chinese and Japanese policies during
the 1920s and 1930s is beyond the scope of this book. In any event, much of his
analysis was overtaken by subsequent events and the Pacific War itself.

Nonetheless, when Kennan encountered the MacMurray memorandum, probably more than a decade after it was written, he was wholly won over by Mac-
Murray's analysis and the power of his prose. He considered the memorandum
"extremely thoughtful and prophetic" and wrote to MacMurray: "I know of no
document on record in our government with respect to foreign policy which is
more penetrating and thoughtful and prescient than this one. It was an extraordinary work of analysis and of insight into the future; and it is a disturbing reflection on the ways of our government that it failed to leave a deeper mark than
it did on the minds of those to whom it was presented and who had access to it
at the time. It has done a great deal to clarify my own thinking on Far Eastern

problems."[14] Decades later Kennan wrote that he "would put M[acMurray]'s paper among the rare great state papers of this century, comparable to Sir Eire [sic]
Crowe's famous memorandum of 1907 in the British Foreign Office documents—
but even better."[15] He quoted MacMurray on multiple occasions, and ideas and
even language traceable to the MacMurray memorandum are clearly evident in
Kennan's analysis and commentary on East Asian affairs from the beginning of
his tenure as PPS director and indeed through the rest of his life. His own analytical and writing style may even have been influenced by MacMurray's.[16]

    Kennan first cited MacMurray publicly in his 1951 lecture "America and
the Orient"—later published in *American Diplomacy*—which borrows multiple
themes from MacMurray's 1935 memorandum. In assessing the evolution of US
policy toward China from the Open Door Notes forward, Kennan highlighted
what he considered an ill-advised emphasis on moral principles and emotional
sentiment rather than strategic calculations in dealing with East Asia in general
and China in particular. In criticizing the Open Door Notes—none of which, as
he had observed in an earlier lecture, "had any perceptible practical effect"—
Kennan lamented that the "tendency to achieve our foreign policy objectives by
inducing other governments to sign up to professions of high moral and legal
principle appears to have a great and enduring vitality in our diplomatic practice." In the Far East, he observed, this "seems to have achieved the status of a
basic diplomatic method, and I think we have grounds to question its soundness
and suitability."[17]

    Echoing MacMurray, Kennan argued that the Open Door Notes' principled
emphasis on upholding China's territorial and administrative integrity was bound
to conflict with valid Japanese interests in China—and thus risked alienating
Japan in favor of China, which did not merit US patronage and protection. He
thus credited MacMurray with predicting the war with Japan, which might have
been avoided: "I can only say that if there was a possibility that the course of events
might have been altered by an American policy based consistently, over a long
period of time, on a recognition of power realities in the Orient as a factor worthy of our serious respect . . . then it must be admitted that we did very little to
exploit this possibility."[18]

    Both Kennan and MacMurray appear to have somewhat misperceived or mis-
calculated the drivers of US policy toward China prior to World War II. As historian Warren Cohen has observed, the Open Door Notes were largely prompted
by a desire to sustain and maximize US trading opportunities in the Far East,
rather than any sentimental attachment to China or particular concern for China's own interests or its territorial integrity. It was only during negotiation of the
Washington Conference treaties that the United States began to invoke a commitment to upholding Chinese sovereignty, which in any event it was never in a

position to enforce. Moreover, Kennan's criticism of a US emphasis on "high moral and legal principle" in dealing with China overlooks the fact that Mac-Murray himself insisted that China needed to comply with its treaty obligations before the United States would surrender its extraterritorial privileges there. Finally, the eventual decision by the United States to go to war with Japan was almost certainly driven more by "a recognition of power realities" and a calculation of US strategic interests than by an altruistic desire to protect and defend China.[19]

Notwithstanding these flaws in their perspective, Kennan absorbed MacMurray's assessment of the weaknesses and failures of the US approach to East Asia in the prewar period. He also adopted several other core elements of MacMurray's thinking. Most fundamental among these was MacMurray's assessment of the relative strategic importance of China and Japan—the former being marginal, and the latter crucial. Kennan's later contributions to East Asia policy would consistently reflect this view; indeed, his internalization of MacMurray's view of China as a "waste area" may be one of the reasons Kennan later in his life continued to downgrade China's strategic importance well after it was realistic to do so. He also adopted MacMurray's cynical attitude toward both the Chinese and the Americans who did their bidding, as well as his relative respect and admiration for the Japanese. As will be seen, these too would be recurring themes throughout Kennan's involvement in East Asian affairs.

John Paton Davies

Whereas Kennan may have derived many of his fundamental ideas about the Far East from MacMurray, it was another Foreign Service colleague—John Paton Davies Jr.—who would become the greatest and most sustained influence on Kennan's approach to East Asia policy. Davies (1908–99) was the primary Asian affairs expert on the PPS during Kennan's tenure as its director. Accordingly, most—but not all—of Kennan's contributions to Far Eastern policy drew heavily on Davies's expertise. Indeed, Kennan has described Davies as having been his "mentor" on Asian affairs during this period.[20] Their personal and professional relationship was unusually close and was characterized by a high degree of mutual respect and admiration—and a sense of loyalty that would endure the destruction of Davies's career at the hands of McCarthyism.

Davies was one of the State Department's "China hands"—the small group of China experts in the Foreign Service (including John Carter Vincent, John Stewart Service, Owen Lattimore, and O. Edmund Clubb) who became the scapegoats for the supposed "loss of China" by the United States because of their allegedly

John Paton Davies Jr. as a member of the Policy Planning Staff. Kennan had a very close professional and personal relationship with Davies, whom he later called his "mentor" on East Asian affairs.

Source: Courtesy of the Davies Family

pro-Communist reporting from China during the late 1930s and early 1940s.[21] Davies, who had been born in China to missionary parents and studied in Beijing, served in several posts in China after joining the Foreign Service in the early 1930s. After the outbreak of World War II, he was a political adviser to General Joseph Stilwell in the China-Burma-India Theater before being assigned to the US embassy in Chungking.[22]

Davies's personal experience with and in China generated a perspective that echoed MacMurray's, both in its attitude toward the Chinese and in its assessment of China's strategic importance. Summarizing it later in his autobiography, Davies characterized the US approach to China during World War II as "largely subjective."

> It was a product of one hundred years of missionary compulsions and involvement, spiritual and emotional, of a sense of guilt that the United States had not gone to the rescue of China under attack from Japan . . . and of propaganda portraying the Chinese as heroically fighting on our behalf and wanting only American arms and know-how to drive the enemy into the sea. . . . The widespread mythology about China meant that more than facts and logic went into the making of American wartime policy toward China. The surcharged sentimental attachment to the Chinese raised the importance of China in strategic planning all out of proportion to its real military and immediate political worth.[23]

This was the context in which Davies became immersed in the Chinese war against Japan and eventually the civil war between the Chinese Nationalist regime (Chiang Kai-shek's Koumintang, or KMT, government) and the Chinese Communist Party (CCP). He became a central player in Washington's efforts to navigate between the KMT and the CCP when he was sent from Chungking in July 1944 as a member of the "Dixie Mission" of US observers to CCP headquarters at Yenan in northern China.

Even before going to Yenan, and largely because of his involvement with Stilwell's dealings with Chiang, Davies had developed a profound skepticism about the reliability of the KMT and the utility of US engagement with it. In February 1944 he assessed that "a strong, independent, and democratic China" would be a valuable asset for the United States in the event of postwar tensions in the region. But he had little confidence in that prospect: "We must recognize that while China is at present independent it is neither strong nor democratic; that the Chiang regime is unsound and unstable; that it has been singularly uncooperative with us in prosecuting the war against Japan; [and] that counting on American help, it threatens to engulf China in a calamitous civil war against the Chinese Communists." Davies concluded that "we therefore have little to gain from supporting the Chiang regime in its present attitude."[24] Based on this experience and assessment, Davies advised flexibility in Washington's approach to China, and especially avoidance of an exclusive attachment to Chiang, which might leave the United States "discredited and our ends defeated" if Chiang was overthrown by another coalition that had popular Chinese support.[25]

Davies was already speculating that the CCP might lead such a coalition. Yenan gave him the opportunity to compare firsthand the relative strengths of the KMT and the CCP. His assessment was contained in a series of reports in November 1944 that described the Communists as "the toughest, best organized and disciplined group in China." Moreover, unlike Chiang's KMT, the Communists had widespread popular support because their local governments and armies were "genuinely of the people." Davies concluded that "the Communists are in China to stay. And China's destiny is not Chiang's but theirs."[26] Nonetheless, he was obliged to suggest a tactical approach: "We should not now abandon Chiang Kai-shek. To do so at this juncture would be to lose more than we could gain. We must for the time being continue recognition of Chiang's Government and give him nominal support. . . . But we must be realistic. . . . We must not indefinitely underwrite a politically bankrupt regime."[27] In the meantime, Washington should try to "capture politically" the Chinese Communists—partly to prevent them from falling completely under the influence of the Soviet Union—by bringing them into a coalition government with the Nationalists.[28]

These reports came back to haunt Davies during the "who lost China?" debate that erupted in 1950 and focused in part on the alleged pro-Communist inclinations of Davies and other State Department China hands who—according to the conspiracy theory—had willfully undermined the Chiang regime and facilitated its defeat by the Communists in the civil war. Davies later acknowledged mistakes in his analysis of the CCP and attempted to clarify its intentions:

> I obviously underestimated the commitment of the Chinese Communist Party at that time to ideology and the dexterity with which Mao and company manipulated it. At the same time, if I was correct in my supposition that in the [CCP] oligarchy two latent factions existed— doctrinaires headed by Mao and pragmatic moderates potentially under some of the generals—an American policy of collaboration with the Communists would probably at least have exposed the schism and strengthened the moderate elements. . . . In retrospect, the idea of politically capturing the Chinese Communists was unrealistic. . . . Better grounded was the calculation that American aid to the Chinese Communists, who I assumed would take over China in any event, could free them of materiel dependence on the Soviet Union and thereby reduce the Kremlin's influence on them.[29]

These subtleties, however, did not protect Davies from the political buzz saw.

Davies's ideas in 1944–45 about the relative strengths of the Nationalists and Communists—along with similar observations by other China hands—ran afoul of General Patrick Hurley, then ambassador to China and an unwavering advocate for the Nationalist regime. Hurley had taken it upon himself to mediate cooperation between the KMT and the CCP and traveled for that purpose to

Yenan—where Davies warned him "against expecting the Communists to agree to what was acceptable to Chiang." The ambassador balked at Davies's advice and sent him back to Chungking. Predictably, Hurley's efforts to forge a working relationship between the two parties accomplished little. Instead, he became "thoroughly entangled and exploited by both sides," as Davies described it unsympathetically: "Driven by vanity, ignorance, gullibility, and recklessness, Hurley would not withdraw to a detached position."[30]

Back in Chungking, Davies—unwilling to work for an ambassador whose "approach to the problem was both uninformed and deluded"[31]—contacted friends in Washington for help in arranging a transfer. Hurley, who was already under pressure from Chiang's foreign minister and brother-in-law, T. V. Soong, to have Davies replaced, was more than willing to let Davies go. Their parting, in January 1945, was less than warm: "In my farewell call to the Ambassador I wished him luck in his endeavors. As I recall on that occasion, I also said that I hoped that he would not be entrapped by Chinese intrigue in case his negotiations failed. His career had been so distinguished that this would be a deplorable culmination. Hurley flushed, then turned florid and puffy. He would break my back, His Excellency warned. 'You want to pull the plug on Chiang Kai-shek,' he shouted over and over again. Indignantly I remonstrated with him. But Hurley was in no mood for reason, the tantrum had to run its course. It did and ended with a civil handshake."[32] Ten months later, Hurley resigned as ambassador, publicly blaming his failure to negotiate a CCP-KMT coalition on Communist sympathizers within the State Department—thereby planting the seeds of the "who lost China?" debate five years later.

Davies, in the meantime, had been transferred to the US embassy in Moscow, where he had begun working for Kennan. The two men had first met in Moscow in 1937, during one of Kennan's earlier assignments to the embassy there. Davies was transiting the Russian capital en route to home leave in Washington via the Trans-Siberian railroad. On that occasion, Kennan had described to Davies over lunch the proceedings of the Stalinist show trials then under way. "This was the first lesson in Russian psychology and Communist politics that I was to receive from an extraordinarily gifted colleague, teacher, and friend," Davies later wrote.[33] By 1945, Kennan was minister-counselor at the Moscow embassy, and Davies's primary responsibility working under him—as the only East Asia specialist at the embassy—was to help analyze Soviet relations with China and Japan; Davies, however, eventually assumed responsibility for "all political reporting, including on internal Soviet developments."[34]

It was in Moscow during the years 1945–46 that the Kennan-Davies partnership was forged, and the two men's mutual admiration and close friendship developed. Davies recalled that working for Kennan was "an exhilarating experience, for his was an intuitive and creative mind, richly stored with knowledge, eloquent in expression, and disciplined by a scholarly respect for precision"; he was also "an exceptionally illuminative teacher" whose "intellectual zest and his subtle insights, penetrating the Soviet phenomenon, found expression in fluent, stylish communication, both in writing and conversation."[35] For his part, Kennan described Davies as "a rock of strength to us at that time in the Moscow embassy." Referring to both then and later years, Kennan wrote: "I owe largely to him whatever insight I was able to muster in those years into the nature of Soviet policies toward the Far East. He was a man of broad, sophisticated, and skeptical political understanding, without an ounce of pro-Communist sympathies, and second to no one in his devotion to the interests of our government."[36]

The issue that brought Kennan and Davies together, appropriately, was the strategic mystery of Sino-Soviet relations. At the beginning of 1945, little was known but much was feared about the relationship between the Soviet and Chinese Communist parties. The Cold War had not yet begun, nor was a Communist victory in the Chinese civil war a foregone conclusion; nonetheless, policymakers in Washington were already uncertain about postwar policy in China and skeptical about Soviet intentions there. They were particularly uncertain about whether the Communists in Yenan were inclined to take orders from the Communists in Moscow.

The first opportunity Kennan and Davies had to address these questions was thrust upon them in April 1945—only a few months after Davies's arrival in Moscow—when Hurley himself, as Davies later described it, "blew in" to take the matter up directly with Stalin. On the eve of Hurley's visit, Davies prepared a memo for Ambassador Averell Harriman assessing the nature of the Sino-Soviet relationship. He began by reiterating his view of the Nationalist regime as "venal, inefficient, and stale" and probably incapable of reforming itself. As for the Chinese Communists, Davies believed they had started out as an instrument of the Kremlin but had "been left pretty much to shift for themselves" after Moscow advised them to accept a united front with the KMT in the late 1930s. In Davies's estimation, Chinese Communist leaders "would scarcely be human if they did not feel some resentment" at the "shabby treatment" that they had since received from the Kremlin.[37]

Hurley, accompanied by Harriman, met with Stalin and Soviet Foreign Minister Molotov on 15 April. The latter assured Hurley that Moscow did not support the CCP; indeed, when Hurley said he interpreted remarks Molotov had made previously to mean that Moscow did not consider the Chinese Communists to be Communists at all, Molotov assented. Molotov also said the Soviet Union did not want civil war in China. Stalin himself assured Hurley that Moscow fully supported the "National Government of China" under Chiang, as well as Washington's policy of unifying all Chinese military forces—including the Communists—under Chiang's leadership. Hurley accepted these assurances at face value and cheerfully reported them back to Washington.[38]

Kennan and Davies were deeply troubled by Hurley's report on his meeting with Stalin, which was drafted and transmitted after Harriman himself had left for a trip to Washington. "It did not check at all," Kennan later wrote, "with the view of the Soviet outlook on Chinese matters" that he and Davies had formed. Hurley's assessment was "much more optimistic than anything warranted by the situation as we knew it," and Kennan and Davies suspected that it conflicted with Harriman's views as well. Consequently, the two men prepared a follow-up telegram for Harriman after Hurley left Moscow for Chungking.[39]

The Kennan-Davies commentary was intended as a corrective to Hurley's report. "In Ambassador Hurley's account of what he said to Stalin," they wrote, "there was of course nothing to which Stalin could not honestly subscribe, it being understood that words mean different things to the Russians than they do to us. Stalin is of course prepared to affirm the principle of a unification of the armed forces of China. He knows that such unification is practically feasible only on terms acceptable to the Chinese Communists. . . . Russia [similarly] is entirely ready to support the principle of a 'united' China, knowing that this could be achieved in reality only if the demands of the Chinese Communists, which would ultimately amount to domination of the government, could be realized."[40] Kennan predicted that the Soviets would in fact persist with a "fluid, resilient policy, aimed at the achievement of maximum power with minimum responsibility" in East Asia. To that end, Moscow probably would be willing to work either through surrogates within a nominally independent national Chinese government—such as that proposed by Washington—or through dissident local elements, where necessary.[41]

Perhaps more problematic than Soviet intentions and tactics in East Asia, however, was the corresponding question of where the Chinese Communists placed themselves with regard to the Soviets. This became a crucial policy issue in December 1945, when Marshall began his mission to China to mediate a settlement to the civil war and the establishment of a united Chinese government. Here Davies's expertise was fully brought to bear. In another telegram from Moscow, sent over Kennan's signature in January 1946, the two men again examined the nature of the Sino-Soviet relationship, this time from the Chinese perspective. They stated frankly that the evidence was inconclusive on whether Yenan took orders from Moscow. Most Communist parties were subservient to the Soviet Union, but the Chinese Communists' relations with Moscow were "more subtle and obscure" than those of any other Communist party. Accordingly, Kennan and Davies were willing to entertain the possibility of a surprising degree of independence for the CCP.[42]

They gave four reasons for this judgment. First, the Chinese Communists owed little to Moscow; on the contrary, they had "survived and grown not because of but despite relations with Moscow," which had in the past given them orders that led to disaster. Second, the Chinese party was the "most mature of all Communist parties," having developed its own strain of Marxism-Leninism. Third, the Chinese Communists "are no fugitive band of conspirators"; they had years of experience operating a de facto regime with its own army and bureaucracy. Finally, they had made nationalism a key element of their ideology. Nevertheless, Kennan and Davies cautioned that Yenan had little latitude in its foreign relations and that events had tended to keep it within the Soviet orbit. They calculated that Moscow thus retained "enormous" possibilities for exercising decisive influence over the Chinese Communists.[43]

Acheson later wrote that "brilliant as this analysis was, it failed as a prophecy" because Moscow ultimately did not persuade—or even try to persuade—the Chinese Communists to enter a coalition with the KMT.[44] But it was only Kennan and Davies's concluding caveat that failed as a prophecy. The thrust of their analysis—that the Chinese Communists were largely independent of Moscow—later proved to be correct. Kennan's identification with this view is particularly noteworthy. Referring to the ideas expressed in the January 1946 telegram, W. Walton Butterworth—one of Kennan's closest associates in the Foreign Service, who had extensive experience in both European and Asian affairs—later said Kennan was an exception among the State Department's European experts, "including most of our Russian specialists," in understanding that the CCP—unlike the Communist parties of Western Europe—was a functioning government and had to be dealt with as such. Butterworth similarly credited Kennan with recognizing that both nationalism and xenophobia were ingrained Chinese characteristics.[45]

Kennan, of course, owed much of what he understood about China to Davies, and many of his ideas about the Far East in general grew out of his collaboration with Davies in Moscow. (Butterworth, as a close personal associate of both, no doubt recognized this.) As 1946 began, however, that chapter in their partnership was about to close, and each of the two men's careers was about to take a dramatic turn. For his part, Davies parried the first assault in what would become a long battle to save his professional career. In December 1945, as noted above, Hurley appeared before the Senate Foreign Relations Committee to assign blame for his failure to preempt civil war in China; Davies was among those Hurley singled out and accused of pro-Communist sympathies. Davies was inclined to "roar on back home and shoot the works" in his defense. His wife Patricia and Kennan, however, dissuaded him: "They told me to wait and see how the thing shaped up."[46]

Prelude to the PPS: The National War College

Kennan, meanwhile, experienced the big breakthrough of his career. His "Long Telegram" of February 1946 assessing Soviet foreign policy had an effect in Washington that was, in Kennan's own words, "nothing less than sensational. . . . My reputation was made. My voice now carried."[47] It led to his assignment in April as the first "deputy for foreign affairs" at the newly established National War College (NWC) in Washington.

Kennan's year as a lecturer at the NWC gave him an opportunity to expand his reputation and influence and to flesh out his ideas for national security policy. During this year, as with the rest of his career, his efforts were focused primarily on interpreting Soviet foreign policy and how the United States should address it. (This led, at the end of his NWC tenure, to the July 1947 publication in *Foreign Affairs* of Kennan's famous "X" article, "The Sources of Soviet Conduct," which introduced the doctrine of containment.)[48] But developments in East Asia did not escape his attention, and his lectures at the War College occasionally revealed elements of his emerging strategic approach to East Asia, especially China.

Kennan's experience with Davies had dovetailed with his reading of MacMurray's 1935 memorandum and led him to develop strong doubts about the rationale behind Washington's involvement in China. Recalling themes from MacMurray's memorandum, he began to ask whether China was really strategically important to the United States, and thus whether it was worth either the heavy commitment of political and economic resources or the frustration of dealing with the Chinese themselves. Kennan concluded that it was not. As an illustration, in March 1947 he told NWC students that three criteria were then driving US involvement in Greece and Turkey—where the recently announced Truman Doctrine had justified a US commitment to support anti-Communist political forces in those countries. The three prerequisites were (a) solving the problem at hand was within US capabilities, (b) failure to act by the United States would result in clear benefits to "our political adversaries" (understood to be the Soviet Union), and (c) positive US action would have favorable long-term consequences not just for the region at stake but for the free world as a whole. Kennan suggested that none of these conditions was met by the situation then prevailing in China. He expanded on this theme in another NWC lecture two months later. "China," he said, "could take all of the national budget we could divert to it for the next 25 years, and the problems would be worse at the end of that time than they are today."[49]

His NWC lectures also drew on his work with Davies in Moscow analyzing China's relationship with the Soviet Union. In May 1947 he speculated that the Chinese Communists would "dance to the Moscow tune" only as long as they remained "a little minority movement fighting for its life." On the other hand, "if they were to become a majority, if they were to come to control, let's say, a large portion of the territory of China, I am not sure their relations with Moscow would be much different than those of [the Nationalists] today because they would be much more independent, much more in a position to take an independent line vis-à-vis Moscow." Eventually, Kennan said, the Russians—no less than the Americans—probably would "come a cropper" in China "just as everybody else has for hundreds of years."[50]

He similarly told an audience at the University of Virginia that the Soviet Union probably would have a difficult time maintaining any influence over Beijing. Borrowing from Davies's analysis, Kennan said the Chinese Communists almost certainly were "made of sterner stuff" than the Nationalists and were less corrupt—and thus were likely to expand their sphere of control in China. Even if they came to dominate all of China, however, they were unlikely to be Soviet puppets. On the contrary, he thought, Moscow "would suddenly discover that this fluid and subtle oriental movement which they thought they held in the palm of their hand had quietly oozed away between their fingers and that there was nothing left there but a ceremonious Chinese bow and a polite and inscrutable Chinese giggle."[51]

Kennan also opined at the NWC on the situation in Japan and Southeast Asia, again speculating on the Soviet perspective. He saw little possibility of Moscow using military force in an effort to expand its influence in East Asia because the Russians had "little hope of accomplishing radically important objectives at an early date in the Asiatic sphere," and because conditions there were arguably already conducive to Soviet interests: "The people in Moscow can be quite content . . . with the situation that exists in Japan, which they must figure is going to leave a Japan after the occupational period more vulnerable to their [own potential pursuit of Soviet] occupation than the Japan that existed before. They can be content with the situation in the colonial countries where a sort of groundswell of social revolution is doing their work for them and sweeping out the European powers."[52]

Kennan addressed the latter situation in Southeast Asia after the Viet Minh insurgents under Ho Chi Minh launched a major attack on French forces in Indochina in December 1946. Analyzing the insurgents in the context of the international Communist movement, he described Ho as "an old Moscow Comintern figure" who probably was still influenced by the Kremlin, although Kennan suspected that Ho's ties to the Chinese Communists may then have been stronger and more direct. Indeed, he doubted that Moscow was behind the Viet Minh's decision to fight the French because the Kremlin's public response to the attack had apparently been one of embarrassment and confusion.[53]

Kennan was asked by a member of his NWC audience what US interests were at stake in Indochina. Some officials and observers, he responded, believed that Washington should offer to mediate the conflict because French colonial rule had been "oppressive and unworthy" and that it behooved the United States to establish a "favorable reputation" with the native population rather than be identified with Paris. Kennan, however, was reluctant to see Washington play such a role, although he recognized the problems inherent in doing nothing: "So far our position has been the usual one; all we want is sweetness and light. We don't want anybody to win, we hope they will compose their differences, and we want everybody to be happy. It is as though we said we hoped that neither the Army nor the Navy would win the Army-Navy game. I am afraid the time is going to come pretty soon in international politics when this government is going to have to make political choices in the world whether we like to or not." He nonetheless concluded that the United States could and should defer making a choice in Indochina until the circumstances there were clarified. First and foremost—in an early hint of his dismissive and subtly racist attitude toward at least some Asians—he was not convinced that the Vietnamese were "fit to govern themselves." It was always dangerous, Kennan argued, to support a nationalist movement that had not demonstrated the ability to resist becoming the instrument of a foreign power— and he was skeptical about the willingness and capacity of Ho and the Viet Minh to do so.[54]

These intermittent comments on East Asian affairs during Kennan's tenure at the NWC reflected both the impact on his thinking of MacMurray and Davies, and Kennan's own assessment of Soviet strategic ambitions and capabilities as they pertained to the Far East. They also foreshadowed key elements of his subsequent approach to the region as PPS director—particularly his view that China was strategically expendable, his concern about Japan's vulnerability to Soviet influence, and his belief that the United States should resist entanglement in Indochina.

In any event, Kennan's tenure at the War College was cut short when Marshall— who had initially offered the PPS director position to Kennan in January 1947— told him in late April that he was needed immediately. Kennan quickly set about the task of organizing the PPS. In a memorandum to then Undersecretary of State Acheson, he requested that only two persons be permanently assigned to the staff in addition to himself. One was an experienced State Department administrative officer, Carleton Savage, who would serve as PPS executive secretary. The other was John Paton Davies.[55]

CHINA
"Minimum Aid" and "Maximum Flexibility"

As noted earlier, Marshall had become secretary of state and chosen Kennan as director of the Policy Planning Staff (PPS) immediately after spending a year in China trying without success to mediate the civil war there. During that year, the tide had started to turn in favor of the Communists, and policymakers in Washington began to grapple with the advisability of their commitment to the Koumintang (KMT) and their uncertainty about what commitment—if any—Moscow had to the Chinese Communist Party (CCP). Accordingly, when Kennan took charge of the PPS the overriding dilemma for US policy in East Asia was how to deal with the Chinese civil war.

This challenge was considerably complicated by the US domestic political environment in which Washington confronted China policy in the late 1940s. Davies later summarized this in terms that echoed MacMurray and were absorbed by Kennan. The diminishing prospects for the Chiang government, "whom Americans fancied as the true Chinese—our Chinese," fueled anxiety that was "preyed upon" by three groups: the Chinese Nationalists themselves, who launched a public relations campaign aimed at garnering US aid and support "in their decrepit and doomed struggle against the Communists"; the "China Lobby," which Davies described cynically as "a mixed, unstructured, freewheeling, variously motivated lot of American publicists, businessmen, military officers, politicians, churchmen and apostate Communists" who advocated for the KMT; and the sympathetic "China bloc" in the US Congress. "It was, then," Davies wrote, "in a national mood of mounting public apprehension, suspicion, and anxiety, exacerbated by Chinese agitators, American lobbyists and hostile members of Congress, that we China specialists of the Foreign Service went about our business during the decade following World War II."[1]

The PPS Confronts the China Problem

This was Kennan's perspective on China when he inaugurated the PPS on 5 May 1947. Davies, although his transfer to the staff had been approved, was still in Moscow and would not officially take up his duties with the PPS until the end of July.[2] China policy, however, would not wait—even though the foreign policy community was preoccupied in the spring and summer of 1947 with the promulgation of the Truman Doctrine and formulation of the Marshall Plan. The failure of Marshall's mission to China had only intensified the debate within the administration and with Congress over US policy toward the Chinese civil war. The State Department had taken the lead in arguing that aid to the Nationalist regime should be reconsidered and limited if possible. The Joint Chiefs of Staff (JCS), however, believed this approach was premature and insisted that military and other economic aid be continued. This divergence of views was precisely outlined in a memorandum to Marshall from John Carter Vincent, then director of the State Department's Office of Far Eastern Affairs:

> The fundamental difference in viewpoint between our Far Eastern Office and the JCS . . . lies in the answer each would give to the following question: Is it good and feasible American policy to give direct and substantial military assistance to Chiang Kai-shek in his attempt to eliminate Communism from China by force?
>
> The answer of the Far Eastern Office has been and is "no" because such a course (1) would lead inevitably to direct intervention in China's civil war; (2) would provoke the USSR to similar intervention on the side of the Chinese Communists; (3) would be inconclusive unless we were prepared to take over direction of Chinese military operations and administration and remain in China for an indefinite period; [and] (4) would invite formidable opposition among the Chinese people . . .
>
> The JCS answer would seem to be "yes" (1) because Chiang can be assured of success in his campaign against the Communists by American military and economic assistance and (2) because failure to assist Chiang would result in USSR domination of China. With regard to the second point . . . it is the opinion of the Far Eastern Office that a USSR-dominated China is not a danger of sufficient immediacy or probability to warrant committing ourselves to the far-reaching consequences which

would ensue from our involvement in the Chinese civil war on the side of the National Government.[3]

Marshall, eager to resolve this disagreement and to devise a positive course of action, began soliciting widely for suggestions on what to do about China.[4]

The PPS's initial response to Marshall's request took the form of a 23 June memorandum from Kennan to Undersecretary of State Robert Lovett. Kennan acknowledged that the staff had not yet had time to address East Asian issues and did not expect to do so for several months; he nonetheless was prepared to forward some of his "personal views." First and foremost, Kennan believed that de facto Russian control over Manchuria was a foregone conclusion of the Yalta accords; consequently, the United States had already surrendered that portion of China to Soviet Communism. Moreover, Kennan considered the territorial expansion of Chinese Communism itself to be "inevitable" in the absence of large-scale US support to the KMT. He added, however, that he thought the CCP was unlikely to take over all of China, or—if it did—to "retain the ideological fiber of their movement or the present degree of their dependence on Moscow" as their strength and power grew.[5]

Kennan, no doubt drawing on ideas gleaned from Davies in Moscow, recommended that US policy toward the CCP be directed at "splitting" the party "in such a way as to leave the hard core . . . on one side and the genuine agrarian reformers on the other." As for the KMT regime, he said he had "great misgivings as to the advisability of placing funds or goods at [its] disposal." He believed a better approach would be to "support specific and limited projects having a clear social-economic purpose and to see that these are carried out with American technical supervision and assistance."[6]

Marshall was either unwilling or unable at this stage to make a ruling on the basis of the advice and recommendations he received from Vincent, Kennan, ambassador to China John Leighton Stuart, the military, and others. He agreed with Vincent that the JCS approach was "not quite realistic" and that the military's recommendations were "somewhat impracticable." But he was not ready to commit himself to completely disengaging from the Nationalists. As a result, he opted to defer the issue for further study. He forwarded the matter to President Truman for his consideration and simultaneously decided to send General Albert Wedemeyer on a mission to China "to make a survey of the situation."[7]

Wedemeyer left for China on 16 July and returned to Washington on 18 September; he delivered a report to Marshall the following day.[8] In his conclusions, he declared that China was disintegrating and facing the threat of Soviet Communism. The country's most urgent needs included internal reform of the KMT government, reduction of the military budget, and external assistance. Wedemeyer

George C. Marshall. Kennan's influence on US foreign policy was largely attributable to Marshall's delegation of policy formulation—during his tenure as secretary of state (1947–48)—to Kennan's Policy Planning Staff.

believed that a "program of aid, if effectively employed, would bolster opposition to Communist expansion, and would contribute to gradual development of stability in China." Accordingly, he recommended that Washington provide "moral, advisory, and material support" to the KMT as long as the regime formally requested it through the United Nations and accepted US military and economic advisers to supervise its use.[9]

Marshall apparently did not find Wedemeyer's recommendations to his liking and opted to suppress the general's report—forwarding it to Truman but not releasing it to a wider audience. Instead, the secretary of state renewed his search for a viable China policy. It was at this stage that Kennan and the PPS became centrally involved. Kennan attended a China policy review meeting in Marshall's office on 21 October and broached the idea of a full-scale PPS study of the China problem—an idea Kennan had been considering but had deferred pending PPS access to the Wedemeyer report. Marshall expressed his interest in a PPS paper on China, and Kennan instructed Davies—who by then had arrived in the PPS—to take the initiative in drafting.[10]

By 29 October Davies had prepared a short memo on the problem of defining US policy toward China. In it, he reiterated the view—which he and Kennan had come to share—that it was doubtful the Nationalist regime was capable of implementing the kind of systemic reforms that would be required for the effective use of US aid. As a result, Davies suggested that the PPS recommend to Marshall "that the US should extend the minimum aid necessary to satisfy American public opinion and, if possible, to prevent any sudden and total collapse of the Chinese Government." It was "not within the realm of feasibility" to ensure a total Nationalist victory.[11]

From the outset, Kennan was eager to coordinate the PPS's views on China with the State Department's Office of Far Eastern Affairs (FE). Fortunately, the PPS and FE were then in the process of forging an unusually close and cordial relationship, based on strong personal ties. In September, Vincent was replaced as FE chief by W. Walton Butterworth, who had been serving as head of the US Mission in China. Butterworth, however, had originally been a European specialist and was an old friend of Kennan's; the two had been classmates at Princeton University and had served together in Portugal in 1942–43.[12] Davies later recalled that Kennan and Butterworth held each other in high regard and worked very well together. The relationship between the PPS and FE, however, was made especially strong by Davies's own connections: whereas Kennan personally knew only Butterworth—who was himself relatively new to East Asian affairs—Davies had many "friends of long standing" in FE, especially the China experts, and he routinely coordinated PPS efforts on the Far East with them and with the East Asian specialists in the department's intelligence and research divisions. This personal rapport effectively prevented the PPS and FE from developing the kind of adversarial relationships the PPS had with other geographic offices in the State Department, many of which resented the PPS poaching on their turf—an attitude Davies described as "quite acute" in some cases.[13]

Borrowing heavily from Davies's draft memo, Kennan prepared a short summary of PPS thinking on China that he showed to Butterworth[14] before forwarding it to Marshall on 4 November as his personal "off-hand views." Despite its informality, this memo was the first detailed expression of Kennan's approach to China policy, and it established the framework within which the PPS addressed the issue through 1948. Kennan began by reaffirming his belief that, even if the Nationalist government were to collapse, it was unlikely that the Communists could assume effective control over all of China and still remain under Soviet control. Consequently, Kennan argued, a Nationalist collapse "probably would not be a catastrophe for American interests in China." As for the Nationalists themselves, Kennan was not optimistic. "The National Government of China," he wrote, "cannot under present conditions hope to achieve its objective of decisively defeating the Chinese Communists." This would require both fundamental reform of its politics, economy, and armed forces and extensive foreign aid. It was impossible to estimate how much of the latter would be required. Kennan nonetheless observed that the amount would certainly not be small and that there was no foreseeable end to the regime's needs. As for internal reform of the KMT, this would require the government to "change the very bases of its existence." Moreover, the regime had already resisted US pressure to reform for several years. Quoting the Davies memo, Kennan judged that the Nationalists were probably incapable of "carrying out the reforms which would be essential to the effective utilization of any considerable American aid."[15]

Kennan cited Manchuria as a "special problem" because of its strategic significance to the Soviet Union. Moscow was probably confident that the Chinese Communists would ultimately prevail in the region and be subservient to the Kremlin there; consequently, the Soviets were unlikely to intervene in the Chinese civil war *unless* US aid to the Nationalists threatened this scenario. But Kennan suggested that Manchuria was not important enough to be the chosen site for a US showdown with Moscow.[16]

After outlining these arguments against providing aid to the Nationalists, Kennan acknowledged that there were "strong traditional ties of sentiment between the US and China and a highly vocal body of opinion in this country advocating US aid to the National Government"—neither of which could be ignored. Thus, he clearly recognized that US public opinion would need to be reckoned with if the administration moved to distance itself from the KMT. Moreover, he was keenly aware, as was Marshall, that the China Bloc in Congress was threatening to hold hostage the European Recovery Program (ERP)—the Marshall Plan—unless a comparable aid package was promised to China. Being himself one of the Marshall Plan's primary architects, Kennan arguably had as much at stake in its success as did Marshall himself. Finally, Kennan accepted that "a certain amount of aid" to China was justifiable as "moral support" to the regime, whose collapse would at least appear to be contrary to US interests.[17]

The problem Kennan confronted was that of balancing these political requirements against his strategic assessment that China did not merit a substantial US commitment. He appears to have viewed the issue of public opinion itself as merely a tactical problem, and even as a nuisance. China's avid supporters among the US public and in Congress, Kennan believed—in an echo of the 1935 Mac-Murray memorandum—were emotionally attached to that country on the basis of misguided notions. Moreover, he thought their support might easily prove fickle if confronted with a realization of the depth of commitment and volume of resources that would be necessary for the United States to successfully defend the Nationalist regime against the Communists. In addition, Kennan believed not only that it was not feasible for the United States to set its sights on a Nationalist victory but also that any such attempt might lead to conflict with the Soviets "in an area of dubious strategic advantage to the US."[18] Kennan summarized the situation in his diary:

> The dilemma is this: . . . We are obliged to put [a China aid] bill before Congress by virtue of our past commitments and of the pressures that exist in favor of aid to China. If, in presenting it, we tell the truth, which is that the Nanking Government is doomed by its own inadequacy regardless of our aid, we demolish at one blow its remaining prestige in China, hasten enormously the process of disintegration, and lay ourselves open to the charge of having treacherously undermined Chiang's prestige and killed his government by our own action. If, on the other hand, we hold out any hope to Congress that the bill can accomplish anything positive from the standpoint of US foreign policy, we will only be faced a few months hence with incontrovertible evidence that this objective has not been achieved and with renewed approaches for having urged Congress into another "operation rathole."[19]

Borrowing Davies's bottom line, Kennan ultimately concluded that Washington should provide only the "minimum aid necessary to satisfy American public opinion" and hopefully prevent a sudden collapse of the Nationalist government. This, as historians Wilson Miscamble and William Stueck have observed, was Kennan's and Davies's first and perhaps most substantial contribution to the China policy debate: the idea of the "minimum aid" required to placate US public opinion.[20]

Kennan, however, also took it largely upon himself and the PPS to carry the burden of justifying this approach, and with it the drawdown of Washington's commitment to Chiang. Thus, having provided Marshall with a new policy toward China, Kennan subsequently played a key role in supporting the secretary of state's efforts to sell it to Congress and the public.

The China Policy Debate: Justifying the Retreat from the Mainland

Marshall began preparing a China aid package in late 1947 and early 1948. In late January, Butterworth asked Kennan to draft a statement for the secretary of state to deliver to Congress along with the aid proposal. In preparing his response, the PPS director consulted both with Butterworth and with Charles Bohlen—a fellow Soviet expert and Kennan's closest friend in the Foreign Service, who was then serving as State Department counselor. The three men agreed that the presentation should be particularly designed to avoid problems with the ERP; specifically, they advised that Marshall's presentation be made to as many Congressmen as possible, in executive session, and that it provide "a frank appraisal of the political and strategic realities which underlie our policies with respect to foreign aid and which explain the difference between Europe and China in the aid picture."[21]

In Kennan's view, the key difference was that China simply was not strategically important to the United States. Communist advances there, he argued, would be unfortunate but tolerable, whereas any Communist expansion into Europe was a vital threat to the United States. This in essence reflected the emergence of Kennan's view that his doctrine of containment was not applicable or relevant to China. Davies supplemented this with the argument that East Asia, unlike Europe, was undergoing a "profound political, economic, and social revolution" to which World War II had been largely incidental; under those circumstances, the United States could only play a constructive role "insofar as the Far Eastern people are willing and capable of helping themselves"—and Davies was skeptical of their capacity to do so. Perhaps more importantly, Davies wrote, the Marshall Plan in Europe was "a calculated economic risk. A similar approach to the Far East as a whole or to China alone, is not possible. They represent an incalculable economic risk."[22]

Marshall was skeptical of using these arguments with Congress. He feared that spelling out reasons why Chinese Communist successes were no threat to the United States would only lend credence to the China Lobby's claim that the administration had deliberately delayed aid to the KMT in the hope that the situation would become irretrievable. Kennan, however, felt strongly that China's strategic irrelevance to the United States needed to be acknowledged: "In my thinking, this is the crux of the whole problem, and I see no way of hitting it except by the head-on assertion that the Communists will probably not take over all of China and could not make a dangerous military power out of China if they did."[23] Marshall either did not agree or was unwilling to make such a bold and politically volatile assertion. As a result, when he presented the China aid package to the House Foreign Affairs Committee on 20 February, his statement sidestepped any assessment of the Communists' long-term prospects or of China's strategic importance to the United States. The gist of Marshall's presentation, according to Defense Secretary Forrestal,[24] was simply that the China problem, under the prevailing circumstances, was "practically insolvable" and that Washington could afford neither to withdraw entirely from China nor to "be drawn in on an unending drain upon our resources."[25] Marshall's approach was sufficient to carry the day, especially since much of Congress was beginning to entertain doubts about the wisdom of funding what was increasingly being recognized as a hopeless cause. The China Aid Act was approved by Congress on 2 April 1948 and signed by Truman the next day; indeed, the amount actually appropriated was significantly less than the $570 million Marshall had requested.

By that time, however, the legislative debate over aid to China was becoming less important than the debate developing within the administration itself over long-term policy goals there. In this regard, Kennan had been prescient in focusing on the question of China's strategic significance—particularly its ability to pose a threat to the United States. By the end of 1947, he had concluded that because China was not vitally important to the United States, Washington should avoid policy decisions or commitments that were based on the assumption that it was. In the meantime, he thought, the administration should keep its options open and let the dust settle in China. As he wrote in a PPS global survey in November 1947, "There is not much we can do" in China "but to sweat it out and to try to prevent the military situation from changing too drastically to the advantage of communist forces."[26]

Kennan—again channeling MacMurray—had essentially decided that the United States should simply disengage from China altogether. He began to build a case for this course of action, focusing on his belief that Washington not only had little at stake in China but also had little hope of controlling events there. This idea became prevalent in his thinking early in 1948. On 14 January, he told Navy Secretary John Sullivan that the United States was "unable to achieve anything useful either for ourselves or others" in Asia; in China in particular, Kennan recommended a "grimly neutral attitude" based on the idea that the Chinese "cannot threaten our security by themselves and cannot assist any Russian threat."[27]

He incorporated this line of thinking into another PPS review of US foreign policy in late February. Both the administration and the American public, Kennan said, were "greatly over-extended in our whole thinking about what we can accomplish, and should try to accomplish," in the Far East:

> It is urgently necessary that we recognize our own limitations as a moral and ideological force among the Asiatic peoples. . . . We will have to dispense with all sentimentality and day-dreaming; and our attention will have to be concentrated everywhere on our immediate national objectives. . . . It is not only possible, but probable, that in the course of this process many people will fall, for varying periods, under the influence of Moscow. . . . All this, too, is probably unavoidable; and we could not hope to combat it without the diversion of a far greater portion of our national effort than our people would ever willingly concede to such a purpose. In the face of this situation . . . we should stop putting ourselves in the position of being our brothers' keeper and refrain from offering moral or ideological advice. We should cease to talk about vague and—for the Far East—unreal objectives such as human rights, the raising of the living standard, and democratization. The day is not far off when we are going to have to deal in straight power concepts.[28]

The bottom line, Kennan said, was that Washington should decide which parts of East Asia were "absolutely vital to our security" and concentrate on ensuring that those parts "remain in hands which we can control or rely on"—in effect, pursuing a policy of containment only in those areas. China, in his view, was not one of those areas. Accordingly, the administration's goal should be "to liquidate as rapidly as possible our unsound commitments in China and to recover, vis-a-vis that country, a position of detachment and freedom of action."[29]

Needless to say, Kennan's views were heretical to those within the administration—especially in the military establishment—and in Congress who believed that the United States had to retain its commitment to the Chinese Nationalists and prevent a Chinese Communist victory. Forrestal was in the forefront of those who, from late 1947 on, insisted that the National Security Council (NSC) confront the problem of China and develop a viable and proactive policy. Kennan, however, feared that any such policy review would only result in a renewal—or even an expansion—of Washington's obligation to prop up the KMT. He argued against NSC consideration of the China question, but without success. On 15 January, Forrestal sent through the NSC a formal request that the State Department submit a policy statement on China. Kennan reluctantly agreed that the PPS would assume the task of drafting one.[30]

Over the next several weeks, Davies spearheaded the PPS's efforts to prepare a comprehensive assessment of the situation in China and of US policy options there. He consulted with several academic China specialists[31] and also broached the subject of China's long-term future in his correspondence with John Melby, a longtime friend and fellow China hand then serving in Nanking. Davies asked Melby in particular for his assessment of the idea that China was vitally important to the United States—an idea he told Melby had been "accepted as axiomatic in US government thinking." Challenging this assumption, Davies asked rhetorically: "Strategically, is China a springboard or a morass?"[32] Both Davies and Kennan believed it was the latter, as MacMurray had asserted over a decade earlier.

The PPS had not yet completed its China paper when the NSC met on 24 March to discuss a draft prepared independently by the NSC staff on options for Chinese aid—NSC 6, "The Position of the United States Regarding Short-Term Assistance to China." The NSC paper listed four options: (1) to stop delivery of economic and military aid to China altogether, (2) to provide extensive economic and military aid for the purpose of helping the Nationalists defeat the Communists, (3) to furnish limited economic and military aid, and (4) to furnish only limited economic aid. The army, navy, and air force representatives at the meeting favored option (3) on the grounds that only direct US military assistance would allow the Nationalists to maintain the struggle against the Communists, which was a prerequisite to worthwhile investment of economic aid. The State Department, however, supported option (4), believing it would limit the drain on US resources and keep the burden of fighting the war on the Nationalists, where it belonged.[33]

The PPS's failure to have its China paper ready by the end of March was probably due in part to the absence of Kennan, who spent part of the month in Japan and was hospitalized with duodenal ulcers for several weeks after his return.[34] Marshall himself was abroad from mid-March through early April. Fortunately for Kennan and Davies, the NSC agreed on 2 April—the day the China Aid Act was approved by Congress—that its China aid policy paper (NSC 6) had been overtaken by events, and deferred any further action on China until the State Department completed its China paper. Kennan and Butterworth, taking advantage of the opportunity, made the deliberate decision to stall on completion of the PPS paper; Kennan thought "it would be preferable to wait on the persuasive influence of events in China to demonstrate the validity" of State's analysis. Accordingly, he instructed Davies to suspend work on the China paper.[35]

Kennan and Davies enjoyed a respite of nearly four months before the China policy debate was renewed and went into full swing.[36] The catalyst for reenergizing it was NSC 22, "Possible Courses of Action for the US with Respect to the

Critical Situation in China," submitted in late July by Secretary of the Army Kenneth Royall. Royall, who had witnessed with dismay the progressive collapse of KMT forces and Washington's failure to respond, submitted the paper in an attempt to force a policy decision. After identifying what he considered the broad objectives of US policy—which included helping the Chinese develop an effective army and navy—and listing the critical questions that needed to be addressed, Royall outlined four alternative courses of action: (1) increasing US aid "to the maximum extent feasible," (2) withdrawing it altogether, (3) continuing US aid "on the basis of programs now authorized," and (4) shifting US recognition and aid from the KMT government to "appropriate regional regimes that may arise" in the event of its collapse.[37] Not surprisingly, Royall dismissed the first option as unaffordable, the second as inconsistent with the will of Congress, and the fourth as inadvisable if it risked actually encouraging separatist movements. In Royall's view, the remaining option—maintaining aid at current levels—was not a long-term solution, but it served the purpose of "buying time until the overall world situation is clarified."[38]

Kennan and Butterworth swung into action. The PPS notified Marshall that the time was "now about ripe" for completion of its China policy paper; as for NSC 22, the PPS agreed with Royall's preferred option but nonetheless denigrated his paper, saying there was no useful purpose in "raising the questions of increasing or withdrawing aid only to dismiss them and conclude that our present policy of aid is correct." Kennan's staff added that the option of aiding regional regimes would "obviously be inappropriate."[39]

Butterworth, meanwhile, provided Marshall with an update of the situation on the ground in China. The picture was decidedly bleak. Reports from the field indicated "a growing feeling among the Chinese people in non-Communist areas that the present government must go"; many of them would accept "even a Communist government if this would bring peace." Political, military, and economic conditions were deteriorating quickly, and the situation could be rescued only by "inspired leadership"—something of which Chiang appeared increasingly incapable. In the meantime, regional regimes were already beginning to emerge and were likely to solicit US recognition and assistance. In an indication of the central role that Kennan and his staff were playing on the China issue on FE's behalf, Butterworth directed Marshall's attention to the forthcoming PPS China paper and recommended that it, upon completion, serve as the basis for the State Department's submission to the NSC in response to the Army's NSC 22.[40]

The JCS, meanwhile, soon weighed in—concurring, predictably, in Royall's recommendation for continued military and economic aid. In defense of this view, the JCS admitted that a Nationalist collapse was possible and that massive US aid to prevent it was "out of the question," but still insisted that it was "not correctly a foregone conclusion that it is too late for worthwhile continuation" of US aid. "The situation is worse than it was," according to the Joint Chiefs, "but it is not . . . so bad that any further effort on the part of the United States would be useless." Accordingly, the JCS recommended "well-supervised assistance to the Chinese Nationalist Government, with safeguards against misuse of such assistance."[41] Davies privately characterized this "seemingly virile call to action" as "sophistry" because its requirements that the aid be well supervised and include safeguards were unrealistic. He did, however, cynically credit the Pentagon with having finally recognized that "the Chinese conflict was not a musical comedy."[42]

At this juncture Ambassador Stuart in Nanking issued a plea to Marshall for guidance, giving Kennan an opportunity to forestall consideration of what he viewed as premature or ill-advised courses of action. He was fortuitously assisted by indecision at the embassy itself. On 10 August Stuart sent Marshall not one but two messages. The first stated plainly that there was only a "faint glimmer of hope" for the Nationalist regime. US policy in China was at a crossroads, and long-term policy decisions needed to be addressed. The embassy, for its part, recommended that a coalition government that included the Communists be avoided, and that this could best be done through "continued and, if possible, increased support" to the Nationalists. At the same time, the embassy admitted that "it may already be too late for our support to change the course of events."[43]

Stuart, however, sent a second, accompanying message specifying that he had approved the embassy telegram "because it represents the unanimous views of the senior officers on my staff," and "I am in complete agreement with their analysis of the situation as it stands today." Nonetheless, Stuart added, "I cannot agree with the conclusions they reach as to the course of action the United States should follow if our analysis proves correct." On his own behalf, Stuart argued that Washington should consider dealing with, or even helping to create, a coalition government—something Marshall had tried but failed to foster during his mission to China in 1946—if such a development appeared inevitable. If China disintegrated, on the other hand, Stuart thought Washington had the choice of either maintaining its sponsorship of the KMT or "keeping the door open" to whatever regime rose from the ashes. In any case, both he and his senior officers were eager to see "an expression of the Department's views in at least general terms on the policy which the United States is likely to follow in the event of a major change."[44]

Even before receiving Stuart's two 10 August messages, Marshall had prepared a terse policy directive for the embassy proscribing any expression of support for a coalition government involving the Chinese Communists. He had recognized the futility of seeking such a coalition at the end of his mission to China. The secretary of state's directive, which was transmitted on 12 August, also made it clear that Washington had "no intention of again offering its good offices as a mediator in China." Marshall cautioned Stuart against giving Chiang any reason to believe that US intercession in the civil war or unlimited aid was forthcoming; they most emphatically were not.[45]

In the meantime, Marshall received Stuart's 10 August messages and asked that the PPS provide an assessment of the situation.[46] Kennan immediately consulted with Butterworth and set Davies to work on a response to Marshall's request. Davies agreed with the embassy that a KMT collapse appeared inevitable; he cautioned, however, that whatever the circumstances when it occurred, any attempt by the United States to influence the course of events would be highly problematic and could easily backfire. Consequently, he had little comfort or constructive advice to offer, concluding that "the shape of things to come is not sufficiently clear to make a positive decision." Davies was certain only that "the longer the civil war in China continues the worse our interests are served"—and the greater the chances that the Communists would ultimately win.[47]

Kennan responded to Marshall on 12 August. He concurred with a draft response to Stuart that had been prepared by Butterworth's office, but, drawing on Davies's assessment, added the suggestion that Stuart effectively be told that "it is not likely that the situation will make it possible for us at this juncture to formulate any rigid plans for our future policy in China." It was "really impossible," Kennan insisted, to foresee the impending course of events there. He warned against repeating the past mistake of making commitments that restricted Washington's freedom of action and ignored its overall objectives. He claimed that passage of the China Aid Act had eliminated room for argument: "The dimensions and general character of our aid to China until next summer are no longer a subject for deliberation here. They have been determined by the existing legislation. The only important question is whether we wish to switch some of this aid to local commanders. This question is now being actively explored as an operational matter."[48] Complete freedom of action, Kennan argued, was imperative: "We must retain maximum flexibility, and make our decisions as we go along."[49]

Marshall wholly embraced Kennan's suggestion and forwarded the message to Stuart—verbatim—in a telegram the following day: "While [the] Department will keep actively in mind [the] questions raised [in your messages] it is not likely that [the] situation will make it possible at this juncture to formulate any rigid plans for our future policy in China. Developments in China are obviously entering into a period of extreme flux and confusion in which it will be impossible with surety to perceive clearly far in advance the pattern of things to come and in which this Gov[ernmen]t plainly must preserve a maximum freedom of action."[50] This statement, which originated with Kennan and Davies, became the basis of US China policy for the next several months. Marshall repeated it to Stuart—again verbatim—

in late October, after the ambassador sent yet another urgent plea for policy guidance as the KMT's position continued to deteriorate.[51] In effect, this approach put the administration in a holding pattern on China policy, but Kennan saw this as wholly preferable to the only alternative then under consideration, that of deepening the US commitment to the Nationalist regime.

Kennan was in part trying to buy time until the PPS could complete its China paper for the NSC—"the definitive paper on China," as Davies, its drafter, later described it. Davies had been working in full consultation with his China colleagues in FE, including O. Edmund Clubb and Philip Sprouse, who had been the political officer on the Wedemeyer mission the year before. The paper, PPS 39, "United States Policy toward China," was completed on 7 September. Kennan forwarded it to Marshall on 15 September.[52]

Kennan later described PPS 39 as a completely "analytical" paper that avoided making any policy recommendations simply because "we found it almost impossible to do so."[53] In fact, PPS 39 was designed to provide the rationale for doing nothing in China, on the grounds that there was nothing that could be done to salvage the situation, and that China was simply not strategically important enough to warrant the effort. The paper began by building its case for the latter point around the idea that China—for social, demographic, and economic reasons— was incapable for at least the foreseeable future of industrializing into a major world economy or a military power. As a result, China, except for its coastal fringe areas, was destined to "more closely resemble a strategic morass than a strategic springboard"—answering Davies's rhetorical question to Melby of the previous spring.[54]

PPS 39 went on to summarize the recent history of the Chinese civil war and to assess prospects for the Nationalist regime, whose performance on the battlefield was progressively deteriorating despite at least $2 billion in US aid since the end of World War II. Davies spelled out the reasons for this:

> The National Government is continuing to lose the civil war because it has been unable to cope with a profoundly revolutionary situation . . . the Kuomintang revealed during the war with Japan its loss of dynamism. . . . Since then the decay has eaten more deeply. . . . The Government's economic position has continued to deteriorate until it is now at a stage of acute crisis. Incompetence and corruption have increased, leading to a general lowering of morale and of confidence in the Government. These same defects afflict the armed forces whose weaknesses lie within themselves rather than in their weapons. It is not so much equipment which the Nationalists lack as generalship, morale and the affirmative support of the population in whose midst they must operate.[55]

The Communists, on the other hand, were winning the war because they were an "organized revolutionary force." In contrast to the KMT, they were economically self-sustaining, administratively efficient, well-disciplined, and militarily effective.[56]

The paper said US policy toward China, for its part, had been based on idealistic US notions of the country "as a perennial international underdog"—a view reminiscent of MacMurray. As such, US policy had fallen short of its aims because China was not what the myth suggested, nor had Chinese leaders—particularly Chiang—lived up to US expectations. Instead, Chiang had extracted an open-ended commitment from Washington that remained intact even though it had become clear that he could not win the war. This "exclusive commitment to Chiang," Davies observed, was "understandable, but it is not good diplomacy." It bound Washington to a losing cause and constrained its options; "we need the freedom to tack, or perhaps even to lie at anchor until we are quite sure of our bearings."[57]

PPS 39 assessed that the Nationalist government was no longer capable of saving itself; only "all-out aid" from the United States had a chance of rescuing the regime. But this was out of the question because it would be prohibitively expensive, amount to overt intervention in the war, politically strengthen the Communists, and offer no guarantees and no end in sight. Washington, therefore, must resign itself to the probable disappearance of the Nationalist regime; meanwhile, the administration could at least derive some consolation from the expectation that the Communists—who were likely to dominate a successor regime—would be confronted with the myriad problems facing the Chinese polity, which could easily overtax the Communists' capabilities and undermine their ideological vigor.[58]

Davies's bottom line was that US policy goals were, for the time being, not "susceptible of achievement." Washington needed a "pragmatic guide through the Chinese maze" that avoided any attempt at a detailed course of action: "The current situation is so chaotic and that which would follow the disappearance of the present National Government would be so fluid that any definite prescription for action would be bogus." PPS 39 therefore concluded that the administration should continue to recognize the KMT but prepare for the eventuality of its collapse and withhold judgment on recognition of any successor regime until the time for decision came. More to the point, Washington simply had to acknowledge that the "salvation or destruction of China lies essentially with the Chinese" and that "for some time to come China will be a chaotic and undependable factor on the Far Eastern scene." Davies later summarized the paper as saying "the future of China is chaos or authoritarianism."[59]

Because it resonated with his own experience in China, Marshall fully endorsed PPS 39, expressing only a few minor problems with its contents and some concern over the "mode of expression" of some of its conclusions. Before leaving on a trip to Europe, he delegated responsibility for the paper to Lovett, who forwarded it to the NSC virtually intact. On 13 October, PPS 39 was circulated to council members as NSC 34.[60]

Conflict immediately erupted in the NSC when Forrestal and Royall took exception to the State Department's approach—as enunciated in the PPS paper—and made an all-out push for a more proactive China policy. On 2 November, spurred on by the rapid deterioration of the situation in China as reported by Stuart, the NSC staff circulated "as a matter of urgency" a draft of specific policy options for China, including contingencies to be considered in the event of a collapse of the Nationalist regime. A special meeting of the NSC was called for the next day.[61]

In preparation for Lovett's attendance at the meeting, Butterworth provided him with FE's assessment of the NSC draft. He began by recalling Marshall's 13 August message to Stuart—which had been inspired by Kennan and repeated in another message to Stuart in late October—to the effect that the situation was too fluid to allow for detailed policy planning, and that "maximum freedom of action" was necessary. The NSC paper, on the contrary, "appears to plot very rigidly and specifically the course of action we should take in the immediate future." Butterworth reiterated the view expressed earlier by Kennan that Washington could have little decisive influence on developments then unfolding in China and thus should avoid committing itself to a course of action that might prolong the civil war there.[62]

Forrestal and Royall, of course, came to the 3 November NSC meeting with the opposite view, thereby provoking heated debate. In response to their calls for a more clearly defined China policy, Lovett reportedly "deplored the tendency of always looking to this country to save China." He drew the military leaders' attention to the statement in NSC 34 (PPS 39) that "nobody could save the Chinese except themselves."[63] Forrestal and Royall were not dissuaded. Instead, they increased the pressure, openly accusing the State Department of having "no policy" toward China; they also forged ahead with the NSC paper on alternative policy options.

Kennan, upset with the negative reaction to NSC 34, launched a full-scale counteroffensive. Addressing a conference at the Pentagon on 8 November, he drove home the point that the problem in China was not what the United States *should* do but what it *could* do. Most observers, Kennan stated, vastly overrated what US aid to China could accomplish and vastly underrated the extent of the problem: "It is just unbelievable what amounts of stuff you can pour into that country and still have it spread too thin to really accomplish much, even if it were well used, but actually an awful lot of it seems to get out of control. . . . Once delivered to a Chinese port and turned over to the Chinese, [US aid] is in the hands of the gods."[64] On 16 November, Kennan prepared a draft public statement in defense of the State Department's approach to the China problem. In it, he acknowledged that recent dramatic setbacks for the Nationalists had "startled and shocked American public opinion." The resulting flood of congressional and public questions about US policy, however, made it clear that the government was faced "not with the normal measure of intellectual disagreement with US policy toward a complicated situation, but with a widespread lack of understanding for the elementary facts by which that policy is governed."[65]

Among these facts, Kennan argued, were that China had not been a unified or stable nation for over fifty years, and that the US government really knew very little about China and was "sadly lacking . . . in yardsticks to measure that which we know." Among the things we did know, however, was that China "could never become a first class military power"; its culture and traditions were "not conducive to any rapid technical or economic development." Kennan then folded in several additional ideas and ethnocentric attitudes he had similarly absorbed, at least in part, from MacMurray:

> Over and against these weaknesses, we find a political personality in China which is complex and puzzling in the extreme. The Chinese people are unquestionably a people of great spiritual and intellectual power. . . . Yet we also know that there exists in China a powerful xenophobia and even a profound sort of arrogance with respect to a foreigner. And we know that the history of China's relationship with the Western world has not been exactly a happy chapter in international affairs. The West, to be sure, has not always shown its best side to these observant people of the Orient. But they in turn have demonstrated a marvelous capacity for corrupting not only themselves but those who have to do with them. The result is that in China's relations with the West, including this country, things have rarely been clear and easy to understand and there has always been much that remained unsaid.[66]

Kennan observed in conclusion that the persistence of Americans in viewing China "as a nation and as a friendly nation" only complicated efforts to adopt a rational policy approach.[67]

Kennan composed yet another draft public statement designed to counter Forrestal's charge that the State Department had "no policy" with regard to developments in China. In it, he argued that the US government was under no obligation to have "a policy" with respect to the internal affairs of another country. As far as China was concerned, the US government had always been and still was prepared to do what it could to help the Nationalist regime, but Marshall had made it abundantly clear that the administration would avoid assuming direct responsibility for the conduct of the Chinese government or its military affairs. The US government certainly favored a strong, independent, united, and non-Communist China, but the primary responsibility for pursuing that goal had to be carried by the Chinese government itself.[68]

Neither of these draft statements appears to have ever been used with the public. Indeed, neither of them could have been expected to solve the administration's problem. A well-reasoned argument for "doing nothing" in China, however correct it might be, was unlikely to placate the congressional and public demands—reinforced by the military establishment—that something be done to rescue the situation. Instead, Kennan simply refocused his attention on trying to influence the policy debate within the administration itself. Accordingly, he prepared a lengthy version of his response to the "no policy" charge to use with the NSC staff in his efforts to counter both Forrestal's criticism and the NSC's attempts to draft an elaborate China policy paper. This document, which was designated PPS 39/1 on 24 November,[69] expanded on Kennan's argument that "there is no requirement either in United States diplomatic tradition, or in the general rules which govern intercourse between states, that a government have 'a policy' with respect to internal events in another country." Nonintervention in other countries' affairs, Kennan stated, was standard practice, and anyone who proposed breaking that practice was obliged to prove "(a) that there is sufficiently powerful national interest to justify our departure in the given instance from a rule of international conduct which has been proven sound by centuries of experience and which we would wish others to observe with respect to ourselves, and (b) that we have the means to conduct such intervention successfully and can afford the cost in terms of the national effort it involves."[70] Neither of these criteria was applicable in China, Kennan argued. The success of the Chinese Communists was regrettable and prejudicial to US interests, but it was not likely to be catastrophic in its effects. In any event, Washington did not have the means to intervene successfully in China because it would require the United States to assume the primary burden of fighting the war on the KMT's behalf. The Nationalists could not do it themselves, and anyone who believed the regime's deficiencies could still be remedied was making "obviously gross oversimplifications which can only stem from ignorance or naiveté." Kennan pulled no punches in his effort to discredit the critics of the State Department's approach to China: the idea that US aid could make a difference, he said, was "unrealistic and indefensible," and any attempt to commit the administration to enhanced aid was "frivolous and irresponsible" because it was obvious "even to the casual inquirer" that neither the Congress nor the public would support full-scale intervention in the Chinese civil war. In conclusion, Kennan returned to the accusation that the State Department had "no

policy" toward China: "We cannot have 'a policy' toward China as a whole, except to favor authorities which take a relatively cooperative view toward United
States interests and to disfavor those which do not. Such a policy must be translated into action on a day by day basis in accordance with the changes of the moment. It cannot be explicitly defined on paper in a form which can serve as a guide
for months and years ahead."[71] The latter, of course, is what Kennan saw Forrestal and Royall trying to do.[72]

Kennan forwarded this document—PPS 39/1—to Marshall and Lovett with a
memo informing them that he intended to call a meeting of the NSC consultants
at which he would raise his concerns about the NSC staff's draft China paper.
Accordingly, he also sent PPS 39/1 to Admiral Sidney Souers—the NSC's executive
secretary—for circulation at the consultants' level. Simultaneously, Kennan sent
Lovett a copy of the NSC China paper, which, in Kennan's view, "seeks to achieve
the impossible—a clear-cut prescription of what our operational tactics in China
should be from now onward." Kennan, however, was reluctant to antagonize the
military by formally rejecting the paper at the consultants' level. Instead, he requested Lovett's authorization to inform Souers that the State Department wanted
the paper discussed at a meeting of the full NSC, which Lovett would attend.[73]

At this juncture, however, Marshall himself seized the reins and decided to take
the China question directly to the president. He asked Kennan and Butterworth
to provide him with a "digest of Chinese developments" and recommendations
for presentation at the next meeting of Truman's cabinet, on 26 November. The
PPS and FE responded, in collaboration, with PPS 45, "United States Policy toward
China in the Light of the Current Situation."[74]

PPS 45, for the most part, reviewed old ground. Butterworth's office drafted
the summary of recent developments, referring back to the substance of the
president's own message to Congress transmitting the China aid bill the previous
February. Truman had said then, and the State Department had insisted ever since,
that the Chinese government was primarily responsible for its own fate. Congress, moreover, had "clearly indicated its desire to avoid commitments and
responsibilities in China" by reducing both the period and the amount of the State
Department's proposed aid program. In any case, deliveries made since then under
the China Aid Act had had minimal effect. In the meantime, Stuart and US military advisers in China continued to report on the KMT's loss of public support
and the general ineffectiveness of its military forces. Stuart, in fact, had reported
that "the bulk of the Chinese people and virtually all officials are resigned to an
early Communist victory and believe that the immediate cessation of fighting
would be in the best interest of all concerned."[75]

Kennan contributed PPS 45's recommendations, which largely repeated those
of PPS 39 (NSC 34): the administration should continue to recognize the Nation-

alist government for the time being but should be prepared for its imminent collapse and for the possibility of shifting US recognition to a successor regime. Kennan, however, added a bold new suggestion, based on his judgment that the biggest problem then facing the administration's China policy was public confusion about the reasons behind it. "It is now less important," he argued, "to cover up the inadequacies of the Chinese Government than it is to regain the understanding confidence of the American public, without which we cannot effectively implement China policy." Accordingly, Kennan proposed that Truman make a public statement reiterating the theme of his February message to Congress and stating plainly that developments in China could not have been averted, and could not in the future be significantly affected, by any feasible action of the US government. Kennan had drafted just such a statement, which he forwarded to Marshall along with PPS 45.[76]

More important, however, was Kennan's final and related recommendation: "All of the facilities of the Executive Branch of the Government should be used to get before the public, and keep before the public, a uniform and consistent presentation of the background of US-Chinese relations. The Department of State should take the lead in preparing the necessary materials."[77] This proposal, which eventually gave birth to the "China White Paper" the following summer, had originated with Davies and his fellow China expert John Melby. The two men, Melby later recalled, had discussed the idea of publishing an article on China policy—inspired, specifically, by Kennan's own "X" article in *Foreign Affairs* on Russian foreign policy. Melby had actually tried drafting such an article but had quickly concluded that "China was a much too big and difficult subject for a mere article." Davies, who was "keenly aware of the beating the State Department was taking" on China and believed it was not responding "out of courtesy to Chiang Kai-shek," agreed. He took the idea to Kennan, who immediately approved it and incorporated it into his proposals to Marshall in PPS 45.[78] Kennan perhaps saw this as an opportunity to update and promulgate elements of MacMurray's account of US-Chinese relations.

On 26 November, Marshall read Kennan's recommendations to the cabinet, whose members were "horrified—appropriately," as Davies later recalled. Although Truman agreed that public understanding of both the history of US policy and the failures of the Nationalist regime was "extremely important," a public accounting at that time would "in effect, virtually destroy the influence of Chiang Kai-shek" and "administer the final coup de grace" to his government. Kennan, for his part, appears to have been willing (or even eager) to accept this consequence, but Marshall was obliged to consider the political repercussions. According to Forrestal's account of the cabinet meeting, the secretary of state conceded to the president that such an effect had to be avoided. As a result, Truman decided to at least postpone any publication or public statement in defense of the administration's China policy.[79]

With the cabinet's rejection—for the time being—of his proposal for a white paper, Kennan resumed the struggle over China policy at the NSC level. As promised, he notified Souers that he could not accept the NSC staff's China paper because "the whole idea of attempting to define the course which we should follow . . . by means of a paper of this sort is theoretically unsound and impossible of practical application." At the same time, Kennan, who still felt the need to preempt any effort by the military to expand the US commitment to the KMT, suggested to Marshall that the secretary continue to push the State Department's China paper (NSC 34) at NSC principals meetings. Coincidentally, Kennan provided Marshall with talking points for an early December meeting with Madame Chiang Kai-shek, who had arrived in Washington to lobby for increased aid. Kennan felt there was "little use in talking to Madame Chiang about anything but fundamentals"; even she should be made to understand that "China's cause will not really be served by our indulging ourselves in . . . over-simplified panaceas."[80]

The NSC debate on China began anew in mid-December, when Forrestal formally asked the NSC to again review the question of aid to China and offer guidance on whether it should continue "and, if so, at what priority and under what conditions." For its part, the JCS, as scripted, recommended that the current aid program be continued; its priority and tempo could be relaxed if necessary, but it should be suspended only after an actual collapse of the Nationalist regime. Butterworth, reacting on behalf of the State Department, gave lip service to the JCS position that no change to the status quo was necessary pending dramatic changes to the situation on the ground in China. Meanwhile, he advised Lovett to essentially stall for time by recommending to the NSC that the Pentagon solicit the views of the Joint US Military Advisory Group (JUSMAG) in China; State would similarly consult with the embassy.[81]

This proposal was accepted at the NSC meeting of 16 December; it was also agreed that the NSC should consider the possibility of diverting to Taiwan aid then destined for the mainland. Stuart soon thereafter weighed in with his own assessment that stopping aid deliveries to the KMT would be taken as confirmation that Washington had abandoned Chiang and favored a coalition with the Communists. He recommended that any aid diverted to non-Communist forces other than the KMT—which the NSC paper was suggesting—be sent to those in Canton rather than on Taiwan, where it would only increase the island natives' concern about the growing incursion of mainland refugees. JUSMAG chief General David Barr, for his part, responded that the Nationalist regime would, in his estimation, lose the civil war "in the immediate future" and that further military or economic aid thus would have little effect; he recommended, however, that it not be withdrawn abruptly.[82]

The NSC met on 3 February 1949 to discuss Forrestal's request for a review of the China aid situation in the context of the reports that had been submitted from the field. Acheson, who had replaced Marshall as secretary of state on 20 January, argued—in line with Kennan's thinking—that continued deliveries of aid to the Nationalists on the mainland would be a waste and ran the risk of falling into Communist hands. Under Secretary of the Army William Draper and Air Force Secretary Stuart Symington recommended that current deliveries be diverted elsewhere; Acheson agreed. The NSC decided to recommend to Truman that he advise Congress that further military aid shipments to China would be suspended pending clarification of the situation on the mainland. Truman, however, overruled this and declared that shipments not be suspended. At the next NSC meeting, Forrestal, citing the conflicting views on the appropriate pace and method of aid deliveries, recommended that the president be requested to direct that his decision be fully implemented, and to designate Acheson as the "coordinator of such implementation." Forrestal's proposal was approved.[83]

In addition to addressing the aid question, at the 3 February meeting the NSC also revisited—in an attempt to bury—the debate over long-term China policy, as reflected in the contest between the PPS's original China paper of the previous September (PPS 39/NSC 34) and the Forrestal-inspired NSC draft of early November, which had tried to outline specific policy options. Two months of bureaucratic hand-wringing had produced NSC 34/1 of 11 January 1949, a document essentially representing the lowest common denominator between the two earlier papers—and as such, a very brief document. It stated only that Washington's goal was a "unified, stable, and independent China friendly to the US," that this goal appeared unlikely of accomplishment for the foreseeable future, and that the US government should focus its efforts for the time being on preventing China "from becoming an adjunct of Soviet power." No specific plan was offered on how the latter goal was to be accomplished. In any case, it was to be done while "avoiding irrevocable commitments to any one course of action" and assigning China a lower priority than other areas "where the benefits to US security are more immediately commensurate with the expenditure of US resources."[84]

It was readily apparent to NSC participants at the 3 February meeting that this paper was virtually meaningless and that the debate over long-term China policy—at least within the administration—had largely exhausted itself. Acheson admitted that the document was "general and somewhat obscure in its phraseology" but added that "the house appeared to be falling down and there was not much to be done until it had come down."[85] Treasury Secretary John Snyder also reluctantly acknowledged that the policy "could not be any more definite than it is, in spite of the feeling of dissatisfaction with it." Accordingly, the council voted to approve NSC 34/1, which was in turn approved by Truman the following day.[86]

In an effort to seal their case, Kennan and Davies in late February submitted one more paper on long-term China policy. This memorandum, designated PPS 39/2, was essentially a status report on developments in China, which Kennan and Davies believed had vindicated the State Department's approach as spelled out in the original PPS 39. The Communists, as predicted, had all but destroyed the Nationalist government and inherited the bulk of its power. Here Kennan acknowledged for the first time that "eventually most or all of China will come under Communist rule."[87] Washington, however, could take some consolation in recognizing the problems the Communists would face in administering the spoils of victory. Indeed, those problems loomed even larger than they had when PPS 39 was written the previous September. Moreover, the Communists sooner or later would create their own opposition: "That force will take time to appear and develop; but inevitably it will, simply because a China under the Communists will breed it just as surely as Chiang's Koumintang was the forcing ground of the Communists."[88]

In the meantime, any effort by the United States to salvage the KMT regime would be futile or counterproductive: "It is now beyond question of doubt that any further military program for the Chinese mainland will in the foreseeable future (a) be ineffectual, (b) eventually contribute to the military strength of the Communists and (c) perhaps most important of all, solidify the Chinese people in support of the Communists and perpetuate the delusion that China's interests lie with the USSR."[89] Kennan and Davies recommended anew that the administration's position be one of waiting for the dust to settle. Until that time, nominal recognition of the Nationalist government should continue, support for any other non-Communist groups should be avoided, and any viable opportunity to exploit rifts between the Chinese Communists and Moscow should be seized on.[90]

PPS 39/2, redesignated NSC 34/2, was discussed at an NSC meeting on 3 March. Royall relayed comments from Wedemeyer, who took exception to the paper and argued that Washington should try to bolster anti-Communist groups in eastern China. Butterworth, however, countered that such support would constitute a decisive change in policy that would again "commit us on the mainland and would give the Communists a real propaganda issue just when the mass of Chinese wanted peace at any price." The NSC ultimately agreed that the recommendations contained in NSC 34/2 were "our only possible policy at the moment."[91]

With the approval of NSC 34/2 in March 1949, the case was essentially closed on the question of aid to the Nationalist regime in mainland China. The policy of minimal aid and gradual disengagement recommended by Kennan and Davies, beginning in late 1947, had finally prevailed—with the help of Butterworth and the support of Lovett and Marshall. Moreover, Kennan's policy of essentially "doing nothing" in China—notwithstanding the political and bureaucratic factors that had suggested such an approach was impractical or even impossible—was basically the course that the administration settled on. It generated much congressional and public criticism, but it was nonetheless the best way out—the lesser of several alternative evils, as Kennan had claimed. Kennan and Davies had not been the only advocates of disengagement from the Chinese civil war, but they had been its most aggressive and persistent bureaucratic proponents—and they prevailed over the Pentagon by taking advantage of its lack of a viable alternative approach. Thus, it was the PPS that provided Marshall, and later Acheson, with the justification for the decision to withdraw the US commitment from the Chinese mainland.

The China problem, however, was far from resolved, and the China policy debate was far from over. The focus was merely shifting from the mainland, where a KMT defeat was a foregone conclusion by the beginning of 1949, to Taiwan, where a new set of dilemmas had seized Washington's attention. Here again, Kennan and Davies would play a crucial role.

JAPAN
"The Father of Reverse-Course Policy"

While the China policy debate was playing out under Marshall's tenure, Kennan had similarly and simultaneously taken the lead on Japan policy, with even more consequential effect. Having concluded that China was strategically expendable to the United States, the director of the Policy Planning Staff (PPS) saw Japan as the centerpiece of American policy in the Far East. His starting point with Japan was one he had adopted from MacMurray: Japan, not China, was the important strategic power in East Asia, and US policy there should be centered on Japan. MacMurray had predicted in 1935 that alienating Japan and obstructing its reasonable claims to influence—and access to resources—in China would lead to war and primarily benefit the Soviet Union. Kennan believed that MacMurray had been proved correct and that the US preoccupation with China at Japan's expense from the Open Door policy through the 1930s had unnecessarily antagonized Japan. In 1951 he wrote emphatically that "most of our problems" in the Far East since 1945 had been self-imposed and "stem from our insistence on the elimination of Japanese power from areas for which no other satisfactory political arrangement was visible."[1] Years later Kennan still lamented that the United States "should have encouraged the Japanese to pursue their own interests on the Asian mainland in preference to their seeking increased power and influence in the island world" of Southeast Asia.[2]

By the time Kennan became PPS director, this was all water under the bridge. Japan had launched its bid for a western and southern empire and had been defeated and occupied. But the question remained of how to fit Japan into a stable balance of power in East Asia that would secure US interests and prevent any renewal of conflict.

In his memoirs, Kennan wrote that he considered his involvement with Japan to be "the most significant constructive contribution I was ever able to make in government," next to his role in devising the Marshall Plan. "On no other occasion, with that one exception," he wrote, "did I ever make recommendations of such scope and import; and on no other occasion did my recommendations meet with such wide, indeed almost complete, acceptance." Miscamble has described Kennan's involvement in Japan policy as "an intervention so consequential in its implications that it alone richly warrants his inclusion among the important policymakers of the postwar era."[3]

Kennan's contribution to Japan policy was that of spearheading, primarily during late 1947 and early 1948, a change in the purpose and direction of US occupation policy so that Japan could become the linchpin of Washington's forward defense posture in East Asia. Since the Japanese surrender of 1945, occupation policy had focused on demilitarizing and democratizing the country to prevent Japan from ever again posing a military threat to the West. Given the structure of Japanese society, however, this approach required dismantling or at least reorganizing key sectors of the Japanese economy, which consequently began to collapse. Kennan, among others, recognized this as a threat to Japan's political stability—the maintenance of which was widely understood to be in Washington's best interests over the long term. Accordingly, he launched an effort to shift the goal of US policy toward that of stabilizing and rebuilding Japan so that it could sustain itself, resist potential Soviet influence or control, and serve as the center of US interests in the region. To do so, Kennan had to overcome strong bureaucratic inertia—especially the resistance of General Douglas MacArthur, who since World War II had exercised near-autocratic authority over occupied Japan, largely independent of Washington's control. It was MacArthur himself who set the stage for Kennan's initial foray into Japan policy.

A Peace Treaty for Japan

In March 1947, MacArthur told the Tokyo press corps—without consulting Washington, as was his wont—that the time was ripe for negotiation of a peace treaty that would allow the United States to withdraw from Japan. MacArthur's announcement sparked a prolonged debate over whether either Japan or the international community was ready for the former to be left on its own. In the meantime, the State Department began tentative planning for peace negotiations, and in July 1947 even invited the eleven nations that were members of the Far Eastern Commission (FEC)—which nominally supervised the occupation of Japan—to attend a preliminary peace conference. The conference was soon postponed indefinitely—because of Soviet opposition, resistance from other Allies, and scheduling conflicts—but the State Department nonetheless completed an initial draft of a peace treaty.[4]

The PPS received a coordination copy of the draft treaty—which had been prepared by a Japan specialist in the State Department's Office of Far Eastern Affairs (FE)—on 6 August 1947, and Kennan the following day assigned Davies to "look [it] over informally." Davies soon reported back to Kennan that he found the draft "preoccupied with drastic disarmament and democratization" and thus probably counterproductive in terms of promoting Washington's overall goal, which Davies presumed was "a stable Japan, integrated into the Pacific economy, friendly to the U.S. and, in case of need, a ready and dependable ally of the U.S." Davies argued that Japan was no longer a military threat to its neighbors and that "democratization" under international supervision that included the Soviet Union, as the draft treaty stipulated, was a tenuous prospect at best. Accordingly, Davies recommended that the PPS confer with FE on "harmonizing the treaty with fundamental American objectives" in the Far East.[5]

Kennan forwarded Davies's comments to Lovett with the observation that Washington had yet to enunciate a long-term policy for Japan; "Until we know precisely what it is we are trying to achieve" there, Kennan argued, peace negotiations were highly inadvisable and even dangerous. Lovett fully concurred. He remanded the draft peace treaty to FE as "wholly inadequate" and asked Kennan to prepare a full-scale PPS assessment of the Japan problem. Kennan again assigned the task to Davies.[6]

The PPS spent much of the next two months immersed in an interdepartmental and interagency study of Japan's readiness for a peace treaty. The central question during this initial period appears to have been whether a peace settlement and subsequent US withdrawal from Japan were prerequisites for the country's economic recovery, or vice versa. For its part, FE—which had started preparations for a peace conference and did not want to lose momentum—argued that a peace treaty should come first. James Penfield, FE's acting director in late summer 1947 (between John Carter Vincent's departure and Walton Butterworth's arrival), notified Kennan that FE thought it important to avoid any delays in the peacemaking process while the PPS's Japan policy review was under way. Penfield enclosed a memo that argued the case for an early peace settlement, primarily on the grounds that the occupation had reached the point of diminishing returns and that it was "impracticable to attempt measures to revive the economies" of Japan and its neighbors until after peace was declared.[7]

The military establishment quickly weighed in with an opposing view that added another key consideration to the policy debate: the US military presence in Japan. Senior officers argued that it was premature to consider an early peace treaty before it was decided whether Washington wanted or needed to retain military bases in Japan after a settlement was reached. Indeed, the question of a long-term military presence in Japan had not been confronted or resolved, and would need to be before the occupation itself could end.[8]

Kennan and Davies, for their part, viewed the Japan problem in a still larger context: that of the emerging conflict between the United States and the Soviet Union. Japan, they argued, could not be expected to remain neutral in that conflict; either it would gravitate into the Soviet orbit or it would remain in the American sphere of influence. Washington should commit itself to preventing the former and actively ensuring the latter, given Japan's strategic significance relative to China, which Kennan was prepared to let the Soviets control if Moscow was inclined and able. In contrast, he viewed Japan as being to Asia what Germany was to Europe: the strategic and economic center of its region, whose recovery was crucial to the restoration of regional stability and the international balance of power. In order to ensure that its resources were used "for constructive purposes," Kennan considered it essential that Japan be kept out of Communist hands. In short, he saw Japan—unlike China—as an area where his doctrine of containment was not only applicable but pivotal. As for the peace treaty issue, Kennan and Davies were concerned only that the peace process serve this overarching goal.[9]

Davies, in his first draft of a PPS memo on the peace treaty issue, tried to accommodate the views of both FE and the military—which he argued were not irreconcilable—and to incorporate them with his own. He acknowledged that "economic considerations within Japan dictate that we should reach a peace settlement at the earliest possible date"; at the same time, in an attempt to placate "the military desire for delay," he predicted that the peace process itself would take at least a year to complete. Davies also presented his own solution to the long-term military problem by suggesting that the peace treaty be immediately followed by a bilateral security treaty that provided for US military bases in Japan. He acknowledged that the Soviet Union and perhaps other US allies might balk at such an approach. Davies recommended, however, that Washington not hesitate to seek a bilateral settlement with Tokyo if the Allies' support was not forthcoming. Japan was simply too strategically important for the United States to surrender any control over deciding its fate.[10]

This and successive drafts by Davies evoked a flurry of responses from FE, other State Department offices, military representatives, and other Japan experts with whom PPS consulted through September 1947. FE from the outset took exception to Davies's suggestion that Washington consider unilateral action, insisting that any approach that was not at least nominally multilateral would unnecessarily antagonize the Soviets and probably alienate other US allies and friends in Asia and elsewhere.[11] The Army Department, meanwhile, was not reassured by Davies's claim that peace negotiations would last long enough to give Washington time to resolve the question of long-term military bases. On the contrary, both the Plans and Operations Division of the General Staff (P&OD, the powerful military equivalent of PPS) and the chief of naval operations argued that the international situation remained so volatile that it was impossible to foresee when a US withdrawal from Japan would be safe.[12] Finally, the State Department's economic bureau (OE) weighed in with a view that flatly contradicted FE's. The economists argued that peace treaty negotiations should be postponed until more progress had been made toward Japanese economic recovery; in the meantime, and for that purpose, OE recommended that the occupation be "civilianized," with authority over it being transferred from the Army Department to the State Department.[13] Given the inherent conflict between these myriad views, no consensus emerged. The only apparent point of agreement was that, pending completion of the PPS's study of the Japan problem, preparations for a peace conference would be neither halted nor hastened.[14]

Kennan, however, had already concluded on his own that Japan was not ready for a peace treaty. He agreed, in effect, with the military planners' argument. "It was simply madness," Kennan believed, "to think of abandoning Japan to her own devices in the situation then prevailing." The country had been rendered totally defenseless and was surrounded by areas of Soviet control; despite this, "no provision of any sort had been made for her future defense; nor could we discover that anyone in our government or in any of the Allied governments had given any thought in their planning for a peace treaty to the question of how this need was to be met in the post-treaty period."[15] Nor, Kennan believed, was Japan prepared to defend itself against potential Communist subversion in the wake of a US withdrawal. This would require, in Kennan's view, a semblance of economic security and political stability—neither of which Japan had at that time. In this respect, Kennan agreed with OE that progress toward Japanese economic recovery was a prerequisite to a peace settlement.

The PPS's review of Japan policy simultaneously led Kennan to the conclusion that the occupational administration of Japan was itself part of the problem. From what he was able to learn, the occupation had served only to aggravate Japan's plight. Not only had it reached the point of diminishing returns, it was not advancing the fundamental goal of strengthening Japan economically and politically. On the contrary, Kennan thought "the nature of the occupational policies pursued up to that time by General MacArthur's headquarters seemed on cursory examination to be such that if they had been devised for the specific purpose of rendering Japanese society vulnerable to Communist political pressures and paving the way for a Communist takeover, they could scarcely have been other than what they were."[16] Kennan concluded, in short, that what was needed was "a thorough re-examination of our occupation policies."[17]

This, Kennan recognized, would be futile without input from the supreme commander of the Allied powers (SCAP), General MacArthur himself. Unfortunately, MacArthur too was part of the problem. The primary difficulty with SCAP, Kennan judged, was his autonomy. Washington had essentially left the general to his own devices as proconsul of Japan; MacArthur had responded by administering the country with little accountability to his superiors back home. Neither the Army Department nor the State Department's Office of Occupied Areas exercised more than nominal control over SCAP's activities, and occupation policy itself was devised and implemented largely from within SCAP headquarters in Tokyo. As a result, Kennan had "very little idea of what General MacArthur and his headquarters were really doing with the Japanese. And it did not take me long . . . to realize that the Department of State as a whole knew no more than I did about this (nor, it appeared, did General MacArthur want it to)."[18]

Consequently, Kennan decided that the PPS's review of Japan policy had, for the time being, reached its constructive limits. As a result, when he forwarded the results of the staff's inquiry to Marshall and Lovett on 14 October, in a memorandum designated as PPS 10, his first conclusion was that "we do not have before us here in Washington the facts which would enable us to make firm and sound judgments on some of the most important points at issue." Kennan therefore advised that "some high official of this Department" be designated to travel to Tokyo for consultations with MacArthur and his staff. The PPS would withhold a final paper on Japan policy until such a mission could be completed.[19]

Marshall and Lovett approved PPS 10 and its recommendations, effectively suspending preparations for a peace conference. From the beginning of November 1947, the State Department's approach to Japan focused instead on a reassessment of occupation policy. Kennan became the driving force in this regard, launching what often seemed a personal crusade. Davies later recalled that after the submission of PPS 10—even though Davies had originally drafted the paper— Kennan "picked up the ball and ran with it" on Japan policy, taking it "directly across the upper echelons" of the administration without again significantly involving Davies, or anyone else in the PPS. Kennan himself acknowledged that, in the weeks following PPS 10, the direction of Japan policy was the subject of "several oral discussions" he had with Marshall alone. Other divisions of the State Department, particularly FE and OE, were concerned enough to specifically request that they be kept in the loop.[20]

The Economic Imperative

In reassessing the occupation, Kennan was operating neither exclusively nor originally. As historians Michael Schaller and Howard Schonberger have noted, Kennan had not been the first in Washington, or even at the State Department, to recognize the need for rebuilding the Japanese economy and redirecting occupation policy. His efforts were "partly anticipated," in Schaller's words, by the work of civilian and military economic planners both inside and outside the government, starting at the beginning of 1947, even before Kennan became director of the PPS.[21] This prehistory to Kennan's involvement with Japan helps explain how he became the agent of a strategic economic policy initiative despite his limited understanding of and attention to economics.

Early in the year, Forrestal—when he was still secretary of the navy—had latched onto the idea that Japan's economic recovery, like Germany's, was crucial to restoring the global balance of power. He raised the issue repeatedly with fellow cabinet members.[22] At about the same time, State Department economists in OE and "O" (the designator for the office of the assistant secretary for occupied areas, General John Hilldring) began formulating a detailed economic program for Japan that was designed to increase its contribution to the economic recovery of East Asia and "create a viable Japanese economy such as would be conducive to the emergence of a peaceful and democratic Japan." This reflected the same underlying goals Kennan would later emphasize: the strategic reorientation of Japan and the restoration of political and economic stability in East Asia.[23]

Hilldring strongly supported the idea of a positive economic program for Japan, and he foreshadowed Kennan by becoming its leading bureaucratic proponent during the late spring and through the summer of 1947. In May he urged Marshall to take up the matter with Truman, with the eventual purpose of "getting General MacArthur interested now" in Japan's economic problems. Hilldring and his colleagues were responding in large part to the adoption that same month by the FEC of a policy paper, designated FEC-230, which MacArthur had received several months earlier from the Joint Chiefs of Staff (JCS) as an interim directive. The centerpiece of occupation economic policy, FEC-230 was based on the assumption that Japan's lack of political and economic freedoms and its militarism had been the product of the country's excessive concentration of economic power. FEC-230 ventured to remedy this by dissolving the zaibatsu, the industrial and banking conglomerates that controlled most of Japan's economy.[24]

Hilldring and the State Department economists, however, considered this approach counterproductive to their goal of rebuilding the Japanese economy. Accordingly, they launched an effort to block implementation of FEC-230 and to replace it with their own constructive economic program for Japan. In addition to lobbying Marshall, Hilldring raised the issue at a cabinet-level meeting of the State-War-Navy Coordinating Committee (SWNCC, the forerunner to the National Security Council [NSC]) in June 1947. Finally, on 22 July, he submitted to the committee a paper designated SWNCC 381, "Revival of the Japanese Economy," which became known as the "crank-up" plan. Hilldring simultaneously notified his military counterpart that the State Department believed SWNCC 381 should be treated "as a matter of the highest priority within the United States government." Again anticipating Kennan—this time the PPS director's suggestion that a senior official take up the matter directly with MacArthur—Hilldring advised that "an executive of unquestionable stature and ability" be appointed to coordinate a new policy toward Japan based on the economic program contained in SWNCC 381.[25]

Although Hilldring's efforts were thus in progress before Kennan and the PPS were first drawn into the Japan issue in mid-August, the initiative nonetheless shifted to the PPS for a variety of reasons. First, Hilldring resigned as assistant secretary for occupied areas and was replaced by Charles Saltzman on 15 August. Saltzman, for his part, later acknowledged that he was largely unfamiliar with the situation in Japan when he took office, and was slow to focus on it. As a result, even though he picked up the baton on SWNCC 381 and advised Marshall and Lovett to pursue it, the momentum generated by Hilldring was largely lost.[26] The Office of Occupied Areas subsequently took a back seat to Kennan and the PPS in the State Department's deliberations on Japan policy. Kennan, however, inherited the economic rationale for reviewing occupation policy in Japan because it coincided with and served his goal of strategically stabilizing and bolstering Japan.

The second important development affecting Japan policy in August 1947 was a trip to Japan by James L. Kauffman, a New York–based lawyer with extensive experience in Japan who traveled there to provide his business clients with an assessment of Japanese economic conditions and investment prospects. Kauffman was aghast at what he found, particularly with plans for implementation of FEC-230. As Schonberger has described, Kauffman decided to make FEC-230 the "focus of a sweeping and vitriolic attack on the whole reformist orientation of the occupation." He drafted a trip report that essentially characterized SCAP's economic program as socialistic and certain to destroy the Japanese economy. Kauffman's report "quickly found its way to top Washington policy makers," where its impact was "staggering."[27]

The policymaker on whom the Kauffman report had the greatest impact was General William H. Draper, whose appointment to the newly created position of undersecretary of the army on 30 August 1947 was the last, but certainly not the least important, of the developments affecting Japan policy that occurred that month. Draper was a well-connected Wall Street banker, having been a member—along with Forrestal—of New York's Dillon Read investment firm. Like Saltzman, Draper "knew nothing about Japan" when he took office, having served as a senior economic adviser in occupied Germany. Dillon Read, however, was one of the clients of Kauffman, whose Japan trip report reached the desks of Forrestal and Draper shortly after the latter became under secretary. Draper immediately went to Japan on his own fact-finding mission. He returned in late September with "grave concern" over the country's economic future and promptly launched his own campaign for a "major reorientation" of occupation policy—at precisely the time Kennan was doing the same at the State Department.[28]

By October 1947, then, Japan policy was being driven, in roughly the same direction, by Kennan at the State Department and Draper at the Army Department—although the two men were still operating quite independently. Some officers in the State Department, at least, were content to keep it that way, pending completion of State's own Japan policy review, and also to avoid the possibility of the Army foreclosing any direct channel between State and SCAP.[29] The two departments, in fact, were essentially at odds over how to proceed, and neither had yet fully worked out its plan of action.

Draper initially was a step ahead of Kennan and State. Within a week after he returned from his trip to Japan, his office had prepared SWNCC 384, "Economic Recovery in Japan," which was submitted for interagency consideration on 3 October. Schonberger considered this paper to be "the first explicit formulation linking economic recovery to a 'reverse course' in other occupation programs" inasmuch as SWNCC 384 argued that a "shift in emphasis" in overall occupation policy was a prerequisite to restoring Japan's economy. Kennan himself would later identify with this argument. At this stage, however, the State Department went on record as opposing Draper's approach. Saltzman, who represented the department on the interagency coordinating committee, said State saw no need for SWNCC 384 because it had already tabled a paper on the subject—SWNCC 381, Hilldring's paper of the previous July. Saltzman invited the Army to withdraw SWNCC 384 and instead propose amendments to State's paper.[30]

Draper balked at this suggestion, provoking an interagency debate that centered on the implications of a "shift in emphasis" in occupation policy. What was essentially at stake was the international framework within which the occupation was nominally administered. Draper, for his part, believed that the FEC—through which all economic policy directives for Japan were required to pass—was hindering rather than helping Japanese recovery because many of the wartime allies that sat on the commission remained focused on democratizing and demilitarizing the country. The FEC, Draper argued, was more interested in squeezing

reparations out of the defeated nation, and dissolving the zaibatsu, than in see-
ing Japan's economic vitality restored. Draper judged that the only way to pursue
the latter, which he saw as urgent, was to somehow bypass the FEC and assert
Washington's de facto unilateral control over Japan. To that end, he intended
SWNCC 384 as an "interim" directive from Washington to SCAP, which the
FEC would be allowed to review only after the fact.

The State Department shared the Army Department's feeling that the FEC was
an obstacle to rapid economic recovery in Japan.[31] State, however, was nervous
about supporting unilateral action that might arouse US public and congressional opinion (which retained a punitive attitude toward the Japanese) or antagonize US allies on the FEC and thus undermine support for Washington's proposed
new policy direction. The department instead favored a more cautious and diplomatic approach, as Saltzman spelled out in a letter to Draper in mid-November.
State fully agreed, Saltzman wrote, that SCAP, the public, Congress, and the FEC
should be notified that

> the US Government desires to accelerate the processes of economic re-
> covery in Japan. There is agreement also that any statement of US pol-
> icy on this subject should be formulated in such terms as to make clear
> the desirability of a "shift in emphasis" toward a more positive atti-
> tude. . . . Such a statement, it is believed, should be worded as to mini-
> mize fears that this "shift of emphasis" implies in any way reversal or
> repudiation of the broad principles and policies which have underlain
> long term occupation objectives. It should seek to elicit maximum sup-
> port of allied countries in the Far East . . . [and] should be sufficiently
> specific and clear in its intent to assist in obtaining Congressional sup-
> port for the financial assistance required to attain our ends.[32]

Accordingly, Saltzman prepared a draft statement to be delivered by the US representative on the FEC that would announce the new policy direction in terms
that downplayed its significance while nominally reaffirming the jurisdiction of
the FEC. SWNCC 381, meanwhile, would serve the purpose of giving SCAP the
necessary policy guidance while avoiding an explicit "shift in emphasis" announcement, which State viewed as unnecessary and problematic.[33]

Saltzman and Draper, however, were unable to reach a meeting of minds on
what, if any, instructions to give the FEC. Deliberations over SWNCC 381 and
SWNCC 384 thus dragged on through the fall and into January of 1948, with
the two departments repeatedly offering counterproposals on their respective
papers.[34] In the meantime, however, several developments gradually undermined Saltzman's position. Draper, for his part, was actively promulgating the
Kauffman report, which he leaked to *Newsweek* magazine, along with a copy of

FEC-230, in late November.[35] MacArthur, meanwhile, was forging ahead with his de-zaibatsu program—making preemptive action by Washington more urgent. Finally, and perhaps most importantly, the initiative on Japan policy within the State Department shifted from the economists in O and OE to the PPS and FE—where Kennan and Butterworth had teamed up in pursuit of a common agenda.

The tide turned in early January, when Butterworth told OE that he thought State's impasse with Army was a product of the two sides' "infatuation with words and phrases such as 'shift of emphasis' " rather than a "serious matter of substance." Butterworth, moreover, was much less concerned than the department's economists about offending the FEC. On the contrary, he felt the greater threat was that Washington would reduce its freedom of action in Japan by kowtowing to the commission. Butterworth said bluntly that, in order to pursue urgent US interests in Japan, "we may need to ride rough-shod over the other FEC countries on certain matters."[36]

On 6 January 1948, the same day Butterworth made these comments, Army Secretary Kenneth Royall, who had joined his deputy Draper in the Japan crusade, gave a public speech in which he effectively announced a reassessment of Japan policy and the impending "shift in emphasis" in the occupation. He told the Commonwealth Club in San Francisco that Washington had decided it was necessary to rebuild Japan into "a self-sufficient democracy, strong enough and stable enough to support itself." This, he said, would require serious reconsideration of plans to radically decentralize the Japanese industrial sector—referring to MacArthur's de-zaibatsu program.[37]

Thus, by the time the SWNCC met again in mid-January, the die was cast. Saltzman tried again to block Draper's efforts to issue a "firm, unequivocal policy directive" to MacArthur that bypassed the FEC, arguing that Washington would be sending an order that, without the necessary details, would be only a "meaningless gesture" at the expense of inevitably antagonizing the commission. Royall, however, had given the SWNCC a fait accompli, and Butterworth and Kennan were prepared to give the Army Department's position their tacit approval. In a gesture of compromise, Draper invited Saltzman to draft "the strongest general statement that represented State's views." The result was the effective suspension of State's paper (SWNCC 381) in favor of agreement on an amended version of the Army's paper (SWNCC 384), which referred to "more emphasis" on, rather than a decisive "shift" toward, Japanese economic recovery. This was approved by the SWNCC on 21 January and immediately sent to Frank McCoy, Washington's representative to the FEC, who read a formal statement to the commission announcing the decision; the directive was also delivered to the JCS for transmission to MacArthur.[38]

The stage was thus set for unilateral US action to reexamine Japanese economic policy. Kennan had not initiated this element of the process; indeed, he does not appear to have been particularly conversant with the economic factors that necessitated a review of occupation policy. He had, however, incorporated them into his own approach to the Japan problem, and he seized the initiative in the process. Draper's efforts and the SWNCC debate over Japan policy, as important as they were in setting the stage for a "reverse course" in Japanese economic policy, were essentially a prelude to Kennan's own pivotal involvement, which dovetailed with Draper's work before eventually eclipsing it. By the end of 1947, the economic policymakers who had first suggested a new approach in Japan were following Kennan's lead.

Kennan Meets MacArthur

Through the fall of 1947, while Draper was lobbying his case, Kennan was doing the same, and in some of the same channels. Kennan, in fact, was arguably as influential as Draper in bringing the urgency of the Japan problem to the attention of Draper's own bosses, Forrestal and Royall. Although Forrestal shared Draper's concerned reaction to the Kauffman report, it was not until after a discussion with Kennan on the topic of Japan that the defense secretary mobilized his bureaucratic resources for a reassessment of occupation policy. On 31 October, shortly after Marshall's approval of PPS 10 (Kennan's preliminary Japan paper), Kennan had lunch with Forrestal, Royall, and NSC Executive Secretary Sidney Souers. According to Forrestal's own account, Kennan was eager to discuss the need for new occupation policies: "With respect to Japan, he said it had become clear to him at the end of the summer that the socialization of Japan had proceeded to such a point that if a treaty of peace were written and the country turned back to the Japanese it would not be possible, under the present economic machinery, for the country to support itself. This would mean it would go through a period of economic disaster, inflation, [and] unbalanced budgets, resulting possibly in near anarchy, which would be precisely what the Communists would want. The social policy . . . was of such a character that it was totally impossible for any business in Japan to plan for the future."[39] Kennan here was promulgating the economic arguments that had been developed by others within both the State and Defense Departments. He went on to describe several of the "vicious features" of MacArthur's "de-zaibatsuing process."[40]

The next day, Forrestal sent a memorandum to Royall instructing him that "we should do everything possible to get the State Department to reexamine its economic policy in Japan." Echoing Kennan's comments, the defense secretary said that the evidence that had come to his attention from various sources—including the Kauffman report—indicated "a degree of socialization in Japan which would make it totally impossible for the country's economy to function if it were put on its own." Forrestal asked Royall for a memorandum on the status of Japanese economic developments, a copy of FEC-230, and a recommendation as to whether he should take the matter up directly with Marshall or submit it to the NSC.[41]

One product of Royall's involvement was a recommendation that Washington send a "top-flight man" to Japan to investigate "whether there is indicated the necessity for a change in direction or course." Royall and Forrestal were both thinking in terms of a prominent businessman whose focus would be on Japanese economic conditions. They thus appear to have viewed such a trip as something separate from Kennan's recommendation in PPS 10 that a senior State Department official be sent to discuss the full range of Japanese issues with MacArthur. When the matter was raised in the NSC on 17 December, however, Lovett made no such distinction. He told the NSC that State had "long ago" concurred in such a mission; the problem, he said, was that of choosing "a qualified man."[42]

Marshall and Lovett indeed were slow in choosing a "qualified man" for the mission that Kennan had recommended in PPS 10. Lovett, when he approved the PPS paper, had commented that the idea was "only as sound as the man we send." He wanted to send either Kennan himself or Charles Bohlen but suggested that Butterworth make the trip because the first two men for some reason were "not available" for such a mission.[43] For the next two months, however, no decision was made on who would go. Butterworth revived the matter in a 31 December memo to Marshall on the peace treaty question. The FE director requested that, in accordance with Kennan's earlier recommendation, arrangements be made "at an early date" for a State Department representative to confer with MacArthur on the treaty issue as well as matters involving overall US security needs in the Pacific and Japanese economic recovery. Marshall again approved the idea in principle, but again inexplicably failed to take action for another month.[44]

Kennan and Butterworth in the meantime grew nervous that the delay was not only squandering valuable time but also giving the Army Department the opportunity to seize the initiative. The SWNCC, as already seen, was about to approve the Army's paper calling for a "shift of emphasis" in occupation policy—partly because of Butterworth and Kennan's own efforts to reverse State's opposition to the paper. Kennan and Butterworth probably were also worried that Royall would carry through on his plan to send his own mission to Japan. Ironically, however, Royall himself appeared to have been waiting for the State Department to make the first move. In mid-January, Kennan was informed that Royall was eager to send an Army representative to accompany whoever Marshall selected from State for the mission to Tokyo.[45]

Under the circumstances, Kennan and Butterworth renewed their efforts to get the secretary of state to make a decision as quickly as possible. In a late January memo to Marshall, Butterworth emphasized the urgency of the matter: "We are now faced with the necessity of making decisions on several phases of policy regarding Japan, including steps which might now be taken to achieve our purposes despite the Japanese peace treaty deadlock. All these matters are dependent upon the exchange of views with General MacArthur contemplated by [our earlier] recommendations. It is therefore believed that prompt implementing action should be taken."[46] At this point, Butterworth recommended that Kennan be designated to make the trip, that he be directed to go "as soon as he is able to assemble the necessary background on subjects to be discussed," and that MacArthur be formally notified of the mission. On 9 February, Kennan was informed that Marshall had accepted all of Butterworth's recommendations, including the selection of Kennan to make the trip.[47]

Kennan immediately began to mobilize for his mission to Japan. He asked Lovett to instruct all offices in the department—especially those involved with the SWNCC and the FEC—to suspend all actions on Japanese matters until after he had returned from his consultations with MacArthur. Moreover, after consulting with Draper, Kennan recommended that FEC-230 be formally withdrawn from consideration by the commission on the grounds that it no longer reflected Washington's policy goals. By taking this step, Kennan argued, "the decks will be cleared for a basic reexamination of our policy with regard to the Japanese economy," which he said should follow his visit to Japan and that of any Army Department delegation. Finally, Kennan dictated the substance of the telegrams that should be sent to both MacArthur and William Sebald—SCAP's political adviser and the senior State Department officer in Tokyo—notifying them of the mission and its purpose.[48]

Kennan was particular about who would accompany him on the trip because, as he told Butterworth, he wanted to "avoid giving the impression of this being a high-powered mission." When he notified the military establishment that he had been selected for the trip, he requested that Forrestal select a working-level officer who could represent all three services without a large retinue. "This, fortunately," Kennan later wrote, "turned out to be a highly competent, intelligent, and reasonable officer"—P&OD chief General Cortlandt Schuyler. Kennan meanwhile asked Butterworth to recommend a "younger officer" from FE who could accompany him. Butterworth selected Marshall Green, whom Kennan similarly described later as "a congenial companion and effective aide" whose knowledge of Japan and "tactical effectiveness in liaison with the intermediate levels of SCAP" were to prove invaluable. Saltzman, for his part, suggested to Kennan that he include in the delegation one of the State Department economists who was familiar with

General Douglas MacArthur as supreme commander of the Allied powers (SCAP). Kennan's redirection of US occupation policy in Japan required him to confront MacArthur in Tokyo in March 1948.

the SWNCC and FEC deliberations on Japan policy. Kennan parried this request—effectively excluding OE and O from the process—probably in an effort to retain full control of the agenda. The final delegation thus consisted of Kennan, Schuyler, Green, two colonels from P&OD, and Kennan's long-time secretary Dorothy Hessman.[49]

To pave the way for Kennan, Marshall sent a personal telegram to MacArthur, through Army channels, nominally requesting concurrence for Kennan's mission, and saying that it was an offshoot of State's close work with "Forrestal's and Royall's people" on the Japan problem.[50] On 19 February, Marshall met with Kennan to advise the PPS director on how to deal with SCAP. Marshall's own relationship with MacArthur at the time, Kennan later observed, was "remote and, I sensed, not cordial" inasmuch as the secretary of state "seemed reluctant to involve himself personally in any attempt to exchange views" with MacArthur.[51] At the very least, Marshall's advice to Kennan suggested previous experience with SCAP's imperious personality. He recommended that Kennan let MacArthur do the talking "as long as he cared to talk" before raising the State Department's concerns. Marshall then warned the PPS director about dealing with MacArthur's entourage: "The Secretary cautioned me strongly about what I might say to others in Japan besides General MacArthur. He emphasized that what would be reported to General MacArthur was not what I really said but what people wished to make out that I had said. He felt that I would be on much sounder ground to make directly to General MacArthur any statements I had to make which could possibly be interpreted as critical of SCAP. At the same time, I would have to try not to appear to the others to be cryptic or mysterious."[52]

On the eve of his departure for Tokyo, Kennan submitted a PPS paper summarizing the "current trends" of US foreign policy that included a concise summary of his perspective on the Japan problem as he prepared to confront it head-on. Kennan placed Japan within the framework of Washington's need to focus its Asia policy on identifying those areas that were vital to US security and ensuring that those areas were in friendly hands. He speculated that Japan would emerge as one of the cornerstones of a "Pacific security system." To that end, it was necessary "to devise policies with respect to Japan which assure the security of those islands from communist penetration and domination as well as from Soviet military attack, and which will permit the economic potential of that country to become again an important force in the Far East, responsive to the interests of peace and stability in the Pacific area."[53] Among all the US objectives in Asia, Kennan argued, those regarding Japan possessed "the greatest need for immediate attention . . . and the greatest possibility for immediate action."[54]

With this overarching goal in mind, Kennan and his entourage left for Japan on 26 February. For his part, Kennan saw himself as conducting the mission "very much on my own"—given Marshall's reluctance to become personally involved, the "unconcealed skepticism" of FE about Kennan's chances of success, and the fact that the Army probably "licked its lips as they watched a civilian David prepare to call on this military Goliath." As for the task ahead, Kennan described this, his first trip to East Asia, as essentially that of "an envoy charged with opening up communications and arranging the establishment of diplomatic relations with a hostile and suspicious foreign government." Marshall Green, his assistant on the trip from FE, later concurred that Kennan was essentially received in Tokyo as "a spy from the State Department." Such was the nature of both the State and the Army Departments' relations with SCAP.[55]

Green, who described his role on the delegation as that of Kennan's "amanuensis," later recalled that on the flight to Tokyo, Kennan did not bother to read his background papers. Instead, the PPS director spent his time "looking dreamily out the window writing poetry" and reading *Siberia and the Exile System*—the 1891 opus of his distant relative, namesake, and fellow Russian expert. As a result, Green said, Kennan arrived in Japan mentally "from Vladivostok."[56]

Kennan's initial experience there was not encouraging. After a grueling and troubled thirty-hour flight that arrived in Tokyo during a snowstorm at 4:00 a.m. on 1 March, he and Schuyler—having been deprived of sleep for two days—were summoned to SCAP's residence for lunch with MacArthur and his wife. At the end of the meal, MacArthur, turning his back to Kennan and addressing himself exclusively to Schuyler, "embarked on a monologue" that lasted two hours. Kennan described the episode in his memoirs: "Oppressed by weariness, I sat motionless in my humble corner. Unable of course to take anything in the nature of notes, I could not make any detailed record of this discourse. I suspect that it was much the sort of thing he was in the habit of saying to all manner of visitors from Washington. Caesar's experience in the military occupation of Gaul was cited, I remember, as the only other historical example of a productive military occupation. The Japanese were thirsty for guidance and inspiration; it was his aim to bring them to both democracy and Christianity. They were now tasting freedom. They would never return to slavery. The Communists were no menace in Japan."[57] Following this "ritual humiliation" of Kennan, as Schaller described it, MacArthur then delivered his visitors into the hands of subordinates, presumably for the duration of their stay in Japan. As Kennan was later told, MacArthur had been "furious" about the news of Kennan's trip and had chosen to have the PPS director "briefed until it comes out of his ears."[58]

Recognizing MacArthur's ploy, Kennan sent a note to SCAP the following day deferentially requesting another audience. "I must make sure," Kennan wrote, "that in enjoying these briefings and the local hospitality I do not neglect my official mission."[59] Green, meanwhile, started pulling strings on Kennan's behalf.

He took up the matter with Stanton Babcock, a military officer on SCAP's staff whom Green knew from an earlier tour in Japan. Babcock, as Green later recalled, shared Green's concerns about the importance of Kennan's mission and his lack of access to MacArthur. The two men arranged for Kennan to give a briefing to SCAP personnel on Soviet history and politics. The brilliance and effectiveness of Kennan's presentation "unlocked the door," according to Green. MacArthur himself was not present at the briefing, but he apparently heard about it from several of his assistants—including his intelligence chief and confidant, General Charles Willoughby, who was deeply impressed with Kennan. MacArthur, who "respected brains," subsequently invited Kennan to a private meeting on 5 March.[60]

In preparation for the meeting, Kennan sent MacArthur a brief set of talking points outlining the key questions his mission was designed to answer. Negotiation of a peace treaty, Kennan stated, was now temporarily on hold, implying an indefinite extension of the occupation. The original purpose of the occupation, however, had already been served. Under the prevailing circumstances, Washington was prepared to suggest that the objective of the occupation shift "from here on out" to that of achieving the "maximum stability of Japanese society." This would require, Kennan speculated, a long-term US commitment to Japanese security, an intensive economic recovery program, and a relaxation of SCAP control that gradually gave the Japanese greater responsibility over their own affairs.[61]

Kennan and MacArthur finally met one-on-one for several hours on the evening of 5 March. During this session, Kennan recalled, the two men "discussed—without exception, I think—all the leading problems of occupational policy as well as the problems of relations with our former allies in matters affecting the occupation and the peace treaty." MacArthur was especially preoccupied with the latter, claiming that the FEC was the key impediment to any change in the direction of occupation policy that Washington might wish to make. Kennan responded with a bold solution: inasmuch as the FEC's authority over the occupation was technically based on its responsibility to oversee implementation of the terms of the Japanese surrender, that authority had effectively lapsed with the completion of the first stage of the occupation. Accordingly, Kennan argued, "we would be entirely within our rights in declining to agree to FEC directives which attempted to go beyond" the terms of surrender. Washington could not eliminate the FEC, he said, but it could "easily render it quiescent, and permit it to languish as long as we pleased."[62]

This suggestion—which was consistent with Draper's agenda—appears to have been made at Kennan's own initiative, and without consulting his State Department colleagues. Indeed, Green speculated that many officials in Washington would have been shocked to learn that Kennan was presenting it to MacArthur. For his part, SCAP was "much impressed with the suggestion," which he thought was "exactly the right line" to take. According to Kennan, MacArthur "slapped his thigh in approval."[63]

On the subject of Japanese economic recovery, MacArthur told Kennan he acknowledged the goal but did not know what else SCAP could do beyond what it was already doing to achieve it. He agreed with Kennan that the reparations program had been excessive and counterproductive and should be ended as soon as possible. As for SCAP's regime of control, MacArthur insisted that it was much less extensive and onerous to the Japanese than was generally supposed in Washington. It was not true, he stated, that zaibatsu dissolution threatened to eliminate the influence of Japan's most competent administrators. On the contrary, MacArthur argued, the "brains of Japan" had been in the armed forces; accordingly, it was the military purge that SCAP had been ordered and obliged to conduct that had sidelined Japan's bureaucratic expertise.[64]

In response to Kennan's talking point on the long-term security of Japan, MacArthur postulated that the "strategic boundaries" of the United States, in the wake of World War II, "lay along the eastern shores of the Asiatic continent." The primary strategic goal of the United States was to prevent the Asian mainland from posing a military threat into or across the Pacific. This could be done by stationing an air and naval striking force along the chain of islands stretching from the Aleutians to the Philippines, with Okinawa serving as the "most advanced and vital point." Under such a framework, MacArthur suggested, US bases on the Japanese home islands themselves would not be necessary, as long as Japan was denied to any other power. This, however, made it all the more crucial that the United States retain unilateral and complete control of Okinawa and the southern Ryukyus.[65]

After this meeting, Kennan later wrote, "things went very well." MacArthur insisted on seeing the PPS director again before he left Tokyo, and arranged for a private railway car to carry Kennan and his delegation on an inspection tour of outlying areas of the country. Kennan reported back to Butterworth that he had found MacArthur's views "much closer to my own than I dared to hope" and that SCAP appeared more than ready to cooperate with Washington as long as he was kept in the loop and given "the wide latitude which he needs to implement future policies in his own way."[66]

The Army Catches Up: Draper's Mission to Japan

On 10 March, after preparing and forwarding to Butterworth a summary of his meetings in Tokyo and his tentative findings, Kennan made a weeklong side trip to Okinawa and the Philippines (which will be discussed in the next chapter). He then planned to return to Washington as soon as possible, but he was instructed to stay on in Tokyo to consult with Draper, who would soon be arriving there himself as head of an Army Department delegation. Royall, who had recommended to the NSC in December that a purely economic mission be sent, apparently had failed to recruit the businessmen he had selected for the trip. In the meantime, he had perceived the need to build a stronger case for his and Draper's economic program for Japan in order to secure congressional approval. Accordingly, he hastened his efforts to pull together such a mission. In a letter to MacArthur hand-carried by Schuyler, Kennan's military escort, Royall had told SCAP that he himself wanted to follow Kennan to Tokyo along with several prominent businessmen who could reexamine Japanese economic conditions. Subsequently, however, Royall opted to send Draper in his place.[67]

The State Department reacted with suspicion to the announcement of the Draper mission. In preparation for the trip, Royall and Draper had requested that State send one of its experts on the Japanese economy to accompany the Draper group. Lovett parried the request and instead authorized Kennan to meet with Draper in Tokyo, calculating that inclusion of a State officer on the Draper delegation might commit the State Department to whatever policy recommendations Draper made upon his return. Indeed, Frank Wisner, Saltzman's deputy in the office of occupied areas, suspected that behind Royall's request was "a desire to have the Department share the responsibility in case of an unfavorable reaction on the part of General MacArthur."[68]

For his part, Kennan was anxious to leave Tokyo. As he wrote to Butterworth, he considered his original mission to be concluded, and he did not want to "outwear my welcome or to incur unnecessary risks." Echoing the advice he had been given by Marshall, Kennan was afraid that the longer he stayed in Japan the greater the risk he would say or do something—"or be reported as having said or done something"—that might upset MacArthur and thus jeopardize the positive accomplishments of his visit. Kennan was greatly discomfited by the environment in which SCAP operated. The atmosphere around MacArthur, he wrote to Butterworth, had "that fragile psychic quality peculiar to the immediate entourages of great rulers."[69] MacArthur's overpowering personality, moreover, had combined with SCAP headquarters' remoteness from Washington and its autocratic authority over the Japanese to create "a certain stuffiness of atmosphere, a didactic quality of opinion, a sensitiveness to criticism, and a degree of internal intrigue which reminds me of nothing more than the latter days of the court of the Empress Catherine II, or possibly the final stage of the court of the regime of Belisarius in Italy."[70] Kennan was similarly expressive in his comments to Butterworth on the impact the occupation—particularly the resident US community—was having on the Japanese people:

There is something about the habits of this dependent population—its peculiarly American brand of Philistinism, its monumental imperviousness to the suffering and difficulties of the population around it, its unblushing readiness to monopolize for itself everything that smacks of comfort or elegance or luxury in a strange land, plus the idleness and boredom of its members and their dreary preoccupation with the acquisition of new possessions—which fills me with despair when I see it superimposed upon the struggles and problems of a defeated and semi-ruined country. The monotony of contemporary American social life: its unbending drinking rituals, the obvious paucity of its purposes, and its unimaginative devotion to outward convention in the absence of inner content or even enjoyment—all these things are pathetic at home; but here they are profoundly out of place and misleading. Perhaps I am abnormally vulnerable to these impressions; I am certainly not ungrateful for the hospitality I have received; but as I prepare to leave Japan the shrill cackling of these gatherings still rings in my ears. And I ask myself whether it could really have been true that we went through all the miseries and sacrifices of this recent war in order that Mrs. X, whose home was on a farm in Nebraska, might have six Japanese butlers with the divisional insignia on their jackets—that Mrs. Y might have a black lacquer dining table made by Japanese carpenters—and that Miss Z might learn her skiing in the mountains of Hokkaido at the expense of the Japanese Government.[71]

Draper arrived in Tokyo on 20 March with a delegation so "casually thrown together," in the words of historian and former SCAP official Theodore Cohen, that "it was doubtful" whether any of the businessmen in the group "had given much detailed thought to occupation facts or policies." The undersecretary was accompanied by four businessmen, of whom Chemical Bank Chairman Percy Johnston reluctantly agreed to serve as nominal chairman—hence the group's designation as the "Johnston Committee."[72] The group's agenda was almost exclusively economic. SCAP was notified in advance of the delegation's five areas of interest: the de-zaibatsu law, reparations, Japanese budget and currency problems, the viability of reducing US governmental appropriations to Japan, and export stimulation.[73]

While Johnston and the businessmen began their economic investigation, Draper met with Kennan and Schuyler on the morning of 21 March, before all three men had a conference with MacArthur that evening. The first topic of discussion at the morning session, surprisingly, was the rearmament of Japan—an idea that was growing in currency within the Army Department. Kennan at this meeting was prepared to give lip service to some version of Draper's rearmament agenda even though most of his State Department colleagues opposed it—and he himself was ambivalent, as will be seen. Kennan and Draper tentatively agreed that the future defense of Japan (implicitly against the Soviet threat) would require either the indefinite retention of US military forces there or the rebuilding of an indigenous Japanese defense force. The two men further agreed that the latter option was the more logical approach; indeed, they suggested that Washington needed to "find an incident," such as Communist advances in Europe, that would justify the rearmament of Japan to the US public and to US allies.[74]

Draper then outlined the key points of his economic agenda. Every effort should be made, he said, to expand Japanese foreign trade, and reparations should be reduced to the bare minimum. On the latter point, Draper recommended acceptance of the proposals regarding reparations that had been submitted by the Overseas Consultants Inc. (OCI)—a group that the Army Department had commissioned several months earlier to study the reparations question. Kennan agreed—again in conflict with the views of most of his State Department colleagues, who saw Draper's efforts to stop reparations as another move that would antagonize the allies in the FEC.

Kennan and Draper were of one mind on the need to reverse zaibatsu dissolution and to drastically ease up on the purge of Japanese militarists, in the interests of economic and political stability. Draper was in the process of commissioning a "Deconcentration Review Board," which he hoped would do for zaibatsu dissolution what the OCI had done for reparations—namely, examine the problem and submit preordained recommendations that justified reversing existing policy.[75] Kennan, surprisingly, was willing to go further than Draper, who had suggested that a few of the zaibatsu might still be dissolved; the PPS director thought that "even this might involve too much interference" and that the Japanese should simply be allowed to work the matter out themselves. Draper's response was that MacArthur was constrained by existing directives, on both deconcentration and the purge, which proscribed a dramatic and immediate reversal in either policy.[76]

In the end, Kennan and Draper agreed that, regardless of the details, the overarching need was for new and explicit directives that set in motion the desired "reverse course." To that end, "it was agreed that Mr. Kennan would write up a basis of a broad policy paper regarding Japan, and that he would discuss this within the State Department; but that a formal State Department position would not be taken prior to Mr. Draper's return to Washington. At that time, Mr. Kennan's paper or a paper developed by Mr. Draper (or a combination of both) should be put up to the NSC at once, in order that appropriate directives could be issued to SCAP and the government agencies concerned. . . . Mr. Kennan stated that he felt this was the most important thing that he should tell Secretary Marshall as a result of his trip to Japan."[77]

That evening, Draper and Kennan, accompanied by Schuyler, met MacArthur in their only joint session with SCAP. The meeting was essentially Draper's opportunity to evoke the general's response to the key elements of the Army's agenda, as Kennan had done with his own agenda two weeks earlier. The result was mixed. MacArthur spoke "most emphatically" on the subject of reparations, taking Draper's proposal one step further. He said the requirements of Japanese recovery made it "utterly fantastic" to consider further undermining the country's economic potential through continued removal of industrial equipment for reparations, as had been the practice. A "decision should be made now," MacArthur insisted, "to abandon entirely the thought of further reparations" after deliveries then in process were completed.[78]

Draper and Kennan, however, hit a brick wall on the subject of Japanese rearmament. MacArthur said he was "unalterably opposed to any such plan" because it would constitute a violation of "many of our most solemn international commitments" and would alienate most of the other countries of the region, which still feared Japanese militarism. Moreover, it was contrary to the principles that had guided SCAP's administration of Japan since the surrender. Finally, the Japanese themselves, in MacArthur's view, could neither afford to rebuild their military nor were willing to support another armed force. Instead, MacArthur reiterated his view that the United States could provide for Japan's long-term defense by placing it under the umbrella of the "defensive perimeter," centered on Okinawa.[79]

On balance, Kennan's and Draper's respective consultations with MacArthur had produced an apparent consensus that the occupation had fulfilled its initial purpose and that Washington could and should reassess the direction of US policy in Japan. MacArthur's concurrence in that assessment, however, was tentative. At the very least, it involved little commitment on his part. Moreover, several key issues were still unresolved, including the details of the reparations program, the requirements of Japanese defense, and the future of the US military presence in Japan. These matters had yet to be addressed decisively back in Washington.

PPS 28: Kennan's Japan Policy Paper

Kennan left Tokyo immediately after fulfilling his obligation to consult with Draper. On 25 March he formally submitted PPS 28, "Recommendations with Respect to US Policy toward Japan," along with a lengthy memorandum summarizing the findings of his trip and thus explaining his proposals for the redirection of occupation policy.[80] Kennan began by outlining the framework within which the "reverse course" would be implemented. First and foremost, he observed, it was fortunate that negotiations toward a peace treaty had made little progress, since there was "no important respect in which Japan is really prepared today to bear the responsibilities of renewed independence in a manner fully satisfactory to US interests. And with the possible exception of the question of military security, there is no important respect in which it could not become better prepared during a further period of occupation, if US policy were shaped to that purpose."[81] Accordingly, Kennan recommended again that peace negotiations be put off to give Washington time to focus its efforts on preparing Japan for the eventual removal of US authority. Indeed, as many issues as possible should be resolved before peace negotiations proceeded, so that the ultimate peace treaty itself could be as brief and general as possible.[82]

The timing of an eventual peace settlement, Kennan argued, ultimately depended on resolving the problem of Japan's long-term security. He saw only two alternatives: Washington either had to commit itself to maintaining US forces in Japan after conclusion of a peace settlement, which Kennan viewed as "psychologically unsound," or had to accept "a certain degree of remilitarization" of the country—something that he thought would shock or alienate most of the Allies. MacArthur, Kennan reported, was of the view that neither option was necessary, that Japan could be demilitarized without inviting Communist attack or subversion. The PPS director, however, was skeptical—and was formulating alternative ideas on the subject of Japanese security (which will be discussed in the next chapter). In the meantime, he thought the most viable option was continued deferral of a peace treaty.[83] Although Kennan acknowledged that the question of Japanese security would have to be postponed, he nonetheless thought Washington could and should "make up its mind at this point" to permanently retain Okinawa—as MacArthur had advocated—and to do so by establishing a US trusteeship over it. The US Navy's needs, moreover, could be met by developing Okinawa as an advance operating base and simultaneously making arrangements to retain the ship repair and other facilities at Yokosuka, at the mouth of Tokyo Bay, on a commercial basis. Finally, he recommended that the Japanese "police establishment" be strengthened and reinforced with the creation of a "strong and effective coast guard" and a civilian Japanese intelligence agency equivalent to the Federal Bureau of Investigation (FBI).[84]

Kennan then focused on the "reverse course" and its administrative requirements. The problem here was twofold, involving both the difficulties of working through the FEC and the troublesome aspects of SCAP headquarters itself. Kennan observed that there was an "unhealthy tendency" among SCAP personnel to overstep the bounds of engagement in the actual operations of the Japanese government, and thus make SCAP's presence in Japan self-perpetuating. This, he insisted, was an "evil" that needed to be reversed before any plans could be made for the eventual transfer of administrative authority to the Japanese government. Kennan thus recommended that SCAP begin a process of gradually reducing both the scope of its operations and the number of its personnel. He noted that Washington alone could mandate this process, since SCAP was unlikely to take the initiative voluntarily.[85]

As for the FEC, Kennan saw no need for a dramatic shift in Washington's fundamental policy toward the commission. He believed, however, that the FEC should be discouraged from considering any policy papers not directly related to the terms of the surrender, or from passing judgment on SCAP activities that could be considered outside the commission's jurisdiction. On those matters, Kennan argued, Washington could and should issue unilateral directives to MacArthur in his capacity as commander in chief of US forces in the Far East.[86]

Finally, Kennan outlined his proposed framework for occupation policy, essentially codifying the "reverse course." The central objective was to prepare Japan for an eventual US withdrawal. The occupation's existing policy direction, however, was almost entirely counterproductive in this respect. The "reform program," under which Japan was being democratized and demilitarized, was based on Western models and Western ideas that "the more mature students and observers of Japan" doubted were fully applicable there. Because of the confused and arbitrary manner of their implementation, the land reform and deconcentration programs and the purge were creating "considerable bewilderment" among the Japanese at the expense of political stability. Kennan thus recommended that the main reform programs be "steadily but unobtrusively" relaxed.[87]

In their place, Kennan stated, "economic recovery should be made the prime objective of United States policy in Japan for the coming period." This should include a long-term aid program—on a declining scale that would gradually wean Japan off dependence on the United States—and a concerted US effort to eliminate obstacles to, and promote the revival of, Japan's foreign trade. Kennan specified that the details of the economic recovery program would be worked out between the Army and State Departments following Draper's own return from Tokyo. He addressed the problem of reparations in the same context, warning that its resolution was critical to Japan's economic recovery. Heavy reparations had been justified on the grounds that they would help the recipient countries with their own recovery while preventing Japan from again posing a military threat to the region. This, Kennan argued, was shortsighted to the point of absurdity; on the contrary, continuation of the reparations program would "license the squandering of the wealth of the one country in the Far East capable of producing goods upon which that whole area must so heavily depend."[88]

Washington, Kennan recommended, must drive this point home with the other FEC countries because "it is we who are responsible for the occupation of Japan. It is we who pay in dollars and cents for its failures and its inconsistencies. It is mainly upon our future foreign relations that any frivolities of occupational policy will eventually wreak their revenge. This being the case, the realistic thinking and leadership in matters of the occupation must come from us, if it is to come from anywhere. The others have neither the incentive nor, in most cases, the sense of responsibility, to view these things incisively and dispassionately from the standpoint of an enlightened comprehension of the longterm needs of peace and stability in the Far East."[89] Kennan acknowledged that other FEC countries might issue "outraged complaints" against the new policy direction he was proposing, but he insisted that it was necessary and could be managed through "careful diplomatic preparation."[90]

Having taken up the Japan issue as a personal crusade, Kennan maintained a proprietary attitude toward the recommendations he included in PPS 28. Indeed, according to Paul Nitze, Kennan always considered the reports he wrote personally to be "etched in steel" and was reluctant to see them altered in any way.[91] Accordingly, when Kennan submitted PPS 28 to then Acting Secretary Lovett, he emphasized in his cover letter that the paper's recommendations represented a "unified concept" that he believed was consistent with the views of both MacArthur and the Army Department. Any tampering with those recommendations within the State Department might "ruin the concept as a whole"; at the very least, Kennan argued, it would increase the possibility of disagreements with the military establishment over Japan policy. In an effort to prevent this from happening, Kennan suggested that the State Department fully coordinate its position internally before Draper's return from Tokyo in mid-April.[92]

Kennan was hospitalized with duodenal ulcers immediately after he returned to Washington at the end of March 1948; he did not return to the PPS until 19 April.[93] In his absence, however, his State Department colleagues generally obliged him in expediting the review of his paper. John Allison, then head of the Japan desk in FE, reported to Butterworth that he was in "entire agreement" with "the Kennan report"; Allison recommended not only that it be "adopted at once" but that "all subsequent action with regard to Japan, the Far East as a whole, and the Far Eastern Commission . . . be brought into line with the recommendations" in PPS 28. Hugh Borton, the FE Japan specialist who had drafted the initial version of a peace treaty the previous summer, largely concurred with Allison's view, raising only minor reservations.[94]

The department's economists, however, were more skeptical. The sticking point proved to be Kennan's proposals with regard to reparations, which Assistant Secretary of State for Economic Affairs Willard Thorp believed were ill advised. "No reparation formula," Thorp argued, "can meet the tests suggested by Mr. Kennan." Similarly, Saltzman disagreed with Kennan's claim that the removal of Japanese "war industries" would hamper the country's economic recovery; he insisted that the industries being dismantled had in fact been excessively developed before the war and were simply "unnecessary to the Japanese economy." In any case, Saltzman argued, the reparations question required much further study before it could be finally resolved.[95]

By 16 April, the State Department was ready to forward PPS 28 to Draper and the Army Department, who for their part had been willing to let State take the lead but were eager to weigh in on Kennan's recommendations and claim their role in crafting the new Japan policy. Kennan himself acknowledged that coordination with the military establishment was necessary before the paper could be submitted to the NSC, but he was anxious to avoid any delays that might undermine his "unified concept." From his hospital bed, Kennan told NSC Executive Secretary Sidney Souers that he hoped the council would take "quick, almost automatic" action on the paper when it was ready for consideration.[96]

The Army Department, given its well-established view that Japan's economic recovery was urgent, was no less desirous than Kennan that PPS 28 be rapidly approved and implemented. Several of Kennan's recommendations, however, were unacceptable to various elements of the military establishment. The P&OD, for example, was uncomfortable with the vagueness of Kennan's suggestion that Washington put off negotiations for a peace treaty "at this time." The P&OD wanted to say explicitly that a peace treaty would not be signed until Japan had become stable enough "to allow her to carry out her responsibilities in a manner satisfactory to the US" and until Washington could be assured against a power vacuum in Japan. Similarly, the P&OD was unwilling to support what was then perceived to be Kennan's suggestion that Washington aim at demilitarization of Japan. On the contrary, the eventual peace treaty should allow Japan "to maintain armed forces . . . of a strictly defensive character and in limited numbers" for the purposes of internal security.[97]

The two issues, however, that proved to be the greatest sources of contention between the State and Army Departments were reparations and the role of the FEC. Whereas Thorp and Saltzman had objected to Kennan's reparations proposal within the State Department because they believed it had gone too far toward abruptly ending the reparations program, Draper and the Army Department argued that Kennan's proposal did not go far enough. In the same vein, the military thought Kennan had not gone far enough toward eliminating the problem of coordination with the FEC. The P&OD wanted Kennan's paper to say explicitly that Washington's long-term goal was to see the commission abolished altogether. In the meantime, US actions with regard to the FEC should be based on the explicit premise that the commission's policymaking functions had, "in effect, been terminated" inasmuch as the initial surrender terms had been implemented. The P&OD thus recommended that PPS 28 be amended to say that Washington would henceforth "resist all attempts by other [FEC] members to introduce and secure passage of further policy proposals within the Far Eastern Commission."[98]

Ironically, the Army's positions on reparations and the FEC (as on Japanese rearmament) essentially coincided with Kennan's personal views, but he had been obliged to moderate the language of his proposals to obtain the concurrence of his State colleagues. State and Army officials, in any case, spent most of May trying to settle these differences and produce a fully coordinated version of PPS 28 for submission to the NSC. For his part, Kennan observed that the Army's desire to rearm Japan, however modestly, would require the concurrence of the other FEC countries; without commenting on the goal itself, Kennan argued that the language in the paper would at least have to acknowledge this requirement. As for the FEC itself, he believed the Army's reference to the goal of "terminating the existence" of the commission was too extreme. Kennan recommended "something more modest" in language such as "eliminating the FEC from the control of decisions going beyond implementation of the terms of surrender."[99]

By far the most complex and troublesome issue dividing State and Army was the matter of reparations. The Johnston Committee, which had accompanied Draper to Japan, had submitted its final report on 26 April. In conclusions probably preordained by Draper, the committee found that continued uncertainty over the reparations issue was suppressing Japanese industries' incentives to rebuild; moreover, the industrial capacity "that can be spared without affecting Japan's useful peacetime productivity is not great." Consequently, the committee recommended that the removal of only "excess capacity" be authorized—thus setting even lower targets for the amount of plant equipment that would be available for reparations than had been suggested by the OCI, the previous reparations mission Draper had sent to Tokyo.[100]

Draper incorporated these findings, predictably, into his response to the reparations proposals Kennan had included in PPS 28. Needless to say, Kennan's colleagues within the State Department—who, unlike Kennan himself, were unwilling to antagonize the FEC allies by drastically reducing their expected shares of Japanese reparations—rejected Draper's new reparations proposal out of hand. Allison described the Draper plan as "so extreme as to be wholly impractical and ill-advised." Draper, according to Allison, was recommending "a reparations program which completely ignores the rights and interests of the claimant nations, and which would bring down upon the head of the US Government the outraged wrath of every country whose cooperation we must have if Japan is to regain a self-supporting status."[101] The State Department further accused Draper of trying to constrain SCAP's authority to determine the appropriate level of industry for retention in Japan, of misstating MacArthur's own position on the reparations question, and of trying to impose procedural requirements on reparations decisions that would effectively block any deliveries from being made.[102]

The State and Army Departments soon became hopelessly deadlocked on the reparations issue. At the end of May, it was deemed necessary to simply remove the relevant paragraph from PPS 28—pending coordination of a mutually acceptable position—so that the paper could move forward for consideration at the NSC principals' level.[103] Kennan and Butterworth thus submitted the paper—minus the reparations section—to Marshall for his approval, emphasizing that it had been coordinated both inside the State Department and with the military, with only minor changes having been necessary.[104]

Marshall was already fully on board. The secretary of state had mentioned Kennan's Japan policy paper at a cabinet meeting on 30 April, describing it as "a very closely reasoned and persuasive document" that he was eager to submit to the NSC and the president in turn.[105] On 1 June, PPS 28/2 was sent to the NSC, where it was redesignated NSC 13. Draper, on behalf of the Army Department, forwarded the text of the paper to MacArthur on 7 June to solicit SCAP's comments.[106]

The general responded on 12 June, concurring on many aspects of Kennan's paper but raising troublesome objections to others. MacArthur flatly rejected as "entirely unrealistic and fallacious" the implication that the number of SCAP personnel could and should be reduced. In his view, US tactical forces in Japan had already reached a "dangerously low" level. Nor could the Japanese police establishment be strengthened without drawing increasingly harsh criticism from the other FEC countries. As for the FEC itself, MacArthur privately agreed with the Army Department that the commission's elimination was preferable; he added, however, that this might be impossible to attain. Overall, MacArthur's view was largely that the underlying goals of NSC 13 were already implicit in the guiding principles of the occupation; he thus appeared to deny that approval of Kennan's recommendations would require any dramatic actions on his part. Butterworth and his subordinates in FE analyzed MacArthur's comments and interpreted them as an indication that the general had simply missed the fundamental "underlying concept" of Kennan's paper, which was that circumstances dictated the beginning of a new phase in the occupation.[107]

Kennan had already recognized the need to proselytize this view, not only with MacArthur but throughout Washington and also with the Allies. He told a National War College audience on 19 May that the occupation had "passed the point of maximum return" under policies that now ran counter to the goal of economic stability. In a nod to MacArthur, he asserted that "SCAP should not be blamed for this" because those policies had originated in Washington. In any event, Kennan argued, "fairly extensive modifications" were necessary if Japan were to be left capable of handling its own affairs. He also interjected a larger point to drive home the nature of the problem: "I think it is no exaggeration to say of all the deficiencies of our national policies in recent years, none has been so grievous and potentially dangerous as our failure to think through to the end the realities of our position as a victor nation and above all as an occupying nation, which has commanded and received unlimited scope of action through the formulation of unconditional surrender."[108]

In late May, Kennan separately launched a diplomatic lobbying effort designed to facilitate international acceptance of Washington's "reverse course" on Japan policy. Within days after his initial return from Tokyo, Kennan had recommended that the British and the Canadians be recruited to help sell the new policy to other FEC member states.[109] Accordingly, Kennan and Butterworth met in Washington on 26 May with M. E. Dening, the British Foreign Office's senior Far Eastern expert, to brief him on Washington's reassessment of its policy toward Japan. Kennan outlined for Dening the rationale for postponing a peace treaty until Japan could be strengthened internally. He suggested that SCAP would be encouraged to exercise greater initiative in areas that, in the past, Washington itself had incorrectly left under the FEC's authority. Kennan also foreshadowed changes in the area of reparations, observing that deliveries from Japan of capital equipment from "obsolescent industries would be uneconomical and perhaps of no real benefit to recipient countries." Summarizing the new approach, Kennan said Washington was embarking on "a program of recovery as opposed to reform, of stability as opposed to uncertainty," which was designed not to prevent a peace treaty but rather to ultimately facilitate one. A few days later, Kennan traveled to Ottawa to deliver essentially the same presentation to senior Canadian officials.[110]

Kennan's efforts to smooth the way for implementation of the more dramatic elements of NSC 13 proved somewhat premature. Because of the deadlock on the reparations issue, the Army's persistent concerns about other sections of the paper, and uncertainty about MacArthur's receptiveness to the new policy direction, NSC deliberations on the Kennan paper quickly bogged down and dragged on through the summer of 1948. This no doubt was also due to the administration's preoccupation during the same period with the implications of the Communist takeover of Czechoslovakia, the establishment of the state of Israel, and the

Soviet blockade of Berlin. In the meantime, Saltzman assumed primary responsibility on the State side for working out a compromise plan on reparations, without which Draper was determined to withhold Army's approval of NSC 13. The Army Department also continued to insist on language declaring that the FEC's functions had been exhausted. Kennan personally was prepared to concede on the latter issue, but Butterworth, Saltzman, and Nitze (who was then working in the economics division for Thorp) were standing firm.[111]

MacArthur, in Tokyo, remained surprisingly and perhaps deliberately oblivious to the debate in Washington over Japan policy. Attempts to solicit his input on the reparations question apparently produced no definitive response. In late July, Butterworth and Kennan learned that MacArthur had never consulted on the subject of NSC 13 with William Sebald, the State Department's senior representative in Tokyo; Sebald, who was at the mercy of SCAP's communications channels, had never even received a copy of PPS 28 or of the subsequent FE memorandum analyzing MacArthur's initial response to NSC 13. The general's lack of substantive engagement seemed to be confirmed by a letter from Sebald to Marshall in mid-September relaying MacArthur's praise for a recent State Department policy statement on Japan—a statement based largely on NSC 13, which SCAP had criticized three months earlier. An exasperated Butterworth saw this as evidence that SCAP's 12 June comments on the Kennan paper may have been written by SCAP subordinates rather than MacArthur himself.[112]

The debate finally came to a head at the end of September, when NSC 13/1 (basically NSC 13 with two alternative reparations proposals) was placed on the agenda for a 30 September meeting of the NSC principals. The meeting focused, predictably, on the FEC and reparations issues. Royall chastised the State Department for its "deferential attitude" toward the FEC, claiming that the commission's oversight of US policies in Japan had resulted only in delay and compromise of urgent policy directives. He stated frankly that the Army Department wanted to "render the FEC impotent." Similar discussion of the reparations problem produced little agreement.[113]

In order to prevent contentious side issues from indefinitely delaying progress on overall policy, the NSC ultimately decided to temporarily remove from the paper the paragraphs on reparations and the FEC, as well as one dealing with the future disposition of Okinawa and the Ryukyus, which had also emerged as an additional source of disagreement between the State and Army Departments. Consequently, Kennan's paper—now redesignated NSC 13/2—was quickly approved by the NSC on 7 October and signed by President Truman two days later.[114]

This, of course, was far from the final victory for Kennan's crusade to redirect Japan policy. Not only did the most contentious issues remain temporarily unresolved, but MacArthur himself had yet to be brought on board. Nonetheless, Truman's approval of NSC 13/2 represented presidential affirmation of Kennan's "reverse course" in occupation policy. "If any one event is to be designated as the turning point in America's postwar policy toward Japan," wrote historian Frederick Dunn, "it should be this National Security Council decision."[115]

The Final Hurdles: Reparations and MacArthur

After the approval of NSC 13/2, the State and Army Departments were able to arrive at mutually acceptable positions on the FEC and the Ryukyus relatively quickly. In late October, Lovett forwarded to the NSC both compromise language on the Ryukyus and what was to be the final version of NSC 13/2's paragraph on the FEC. On the latter, the two departments simply agreed to delete the language suggesting that the commission's policymaking functions had been substantially carried out.[116]

Resolving the reparations problem required substantially more effort. Appropriately, the responsibility for working out an interagency compromise was assigned to Kennan and Draper. The PPS director, drawing heavily on technical advice from his colleagues in FE, OE, and O, immersed himself in frequent discussions with the undersecretary of the army throughout October and November. Kennan again found himself caught in the middle because his personal views on the reparations question were closer to Draper's than to the consensus within the State Department. Perhaps as a ploy to resolve this dilemma, Kennan in mid-October suggested that State simply accept the Army's reparations proposal but advise the NSC that State was doing so in protest and would not be responsible "for the unfortunate consequences for our foreign relations which we anticipate from the plan."[117]

Kennan and Draper eventually reached agreement between themselves, but the State Department apparently was unwilling to sign on to the deal. The Army Department subsequently reverted to one of its own earlier proposals, which State was willing to consider, but the negotiations still dragged on for several more weeks. In late November, following a series of exchanges between Lovett, Royall, and Forrestal, the two sides signed a "memorandum of understanding" on implementation of the reparations paragraph that would be submitted to the NSC for inclusion in NSC 13/2. In effect, the issue was again substantially deferred, pending working-level deliberations that resolved the problem—essentially on the Army's terms—in May 1949.[118]

State and Army similarly went back and forth, also during October and November 1948, on the text of the directives that would be sent to MacArthur instructing him on the implementation of NSC 13/2. Kennan, sensitive to the Allies' concerns about dramatic unilateral action in Japan by the United States, suggested advising MacArthur "that he should do this in as quiet and routine a way as possible, and should use his influence, if necessary, to discourage a sensational exploitation of the measures by the Japanese or foreign press. If there is press curiosity, the measures should be portrayed by SCAP as perfectly normal evolutions of an operation which it was always understood would require gradual modification as the events of the war recede into the past."[119]

A more immediate problem emerged, however, in getting the Army Department to sign off on the instructions to MacArthur for which approval of NSC 13/2 had given the green light. Army leadership, after having insisted for months that urgent action was necessary, now began to drag its feet when it came to issuing orders to the general that he might not be eager to receive. Indeed, Kennan himself had observed even before his trip to Japan that the military establishment in Washington was generally reluctant to arouse the wrath of SCAP. "They were intimidated by MacArthur," Kennan wrote, "even more than people in the State Department."[120]

In late October, Butterworth warned Lovett that the Army was showing signs of opposing "prompt and forceful implementation" of certain sections of NSC 13/2, such as that on the purge of militarists, which MacArthur had consistently refused to moderate. Because Kennan's original proposals had already been "considerably watered down" to gain Army concurrence, to the point where NSC 13/2 represented State's minimal position, Butterworth argued that it was essential that the final version be implemented "to the fullest extent." He advised Lovett to make this approach personally to Royall. On 10 November, the acting secretary of state forwarded directly to the army secretary, for transmission to Tokyo, two telegrams containing MacArthur's new instructions.[121]

Controversy arose two weeks later when the State Department learned that the telegrams had not been sent. According to the Army Department, "the delay was occasioned because the original cables as presented were unsuitable in form and content for dispatch and had not received prior coordination with the Department of the Army." The Army Department essentially accused State of trying to transmit instructions to MacArthur that had not been fully coordinated with the military establishment in Washington. Following some interagency wrangling, the telegrams to SCAP were finally sent on 30 November and 1 December. Subsequently, the two agencies saw it necessary to negotiate a "memorandum of understanding" on their respective obligations with regard to implementation of NSC 13/2. Needless to say, a certain amount of mistrust and miscommunication lingered for months thereafter.[122]

By this time, however, the focus of resistance to NSC 13/2 had finally shifted to SCAP himself. MacArthur reacted to his new instructions from Washington by claiming that he was a supranational official representing the Allied powers, and thus that Washington did not have the authority to give him orders unilaterally. On 4 December, the general informed the Army Department that he was "not empowered as CINCFE [US Commander in Chief in the Far East] to alter policies . . . carried out in his capacity as SCAP pursuant to Allied directives." In any case, MacArthur added, most of the policies reflected in his new instructions "had long been in effect"; his objections to those that were not had been enunciated in his 12 June response to the initial version of NSC 13.[123]

It was now Draper's turn to seize the bull by the horns. From the beginning, the undersecretary of the army's agenda had focused on developing a detailed new economic program for Japan. Approval of NSC 13/2, having been the prerequisite, had set the stage for Draper to launch his plan. On 10 December, the NSC met to discuss the "economic stabilization" directive that would essentially flesh out the details of the "economic recovery" paragraph in Kennan's NSC 13/2. This directive, of course, would require even greater obligations on MacArthur's part. Draper flatly told the NSC that SCAP would be required "to direct, not suggest" a wide variety of specific actions by the Japanese government. Draper also said he was planning to assign SCAP an "economic deputy" with stature and real authority, and that he was considering Detroit Bank president Joseph Dodge for the job. The NSC approved Draper's economic directive and authorized him to transmit it to MacArthur.[124]

MacArthur responded as he had to the State Department's telegrams: "The purport of your message is not understood. Few of the policy decisions contained in NSC 13/2 and none of those referred to for report are within the field of responsibility of CINCFE. . . . The international character of SCAP . . . renders him subject solely to Allied policy either formulated by the FEC or under specific limited circumstances by the United States, if transmitted as an interim directive. . . . NSC 13/2 has not rpt not been conveyed as an order to SCAP by appropriate directive . . . and SCAP is not rpt not therefore responsible in any way for its implementation."[125] Draper, working in conjunction with the State Department, prepared a firm rebuke for MacArthur that was couched in terms that would simultaneously undermine the basis of his resistance while flattering his ego. The general was expected, Draper wrote, to implement NSC 13/2 in his capacity both as CINCFE and as SCAP, the latter position in which MacArthur possessed "considerable latitude in the interpretation and execution of FEC directives." Invoking the idea that Kennan had first introduced to MacArthur during their meetings in Tokyo, Draper's message said the FEC had no basis on which to contest this:

> The State Department considers that there is full international recogni-
> tion of primary US interest in the conduct of the executive authority and
> responsibility in Japan. . . . It would [thus] be utterly unreasonable to
> contend that the US could not advise SCAP in the exercise of his execu-
> tive authority within the limitations of existing policy decisions of the
> FEC. . . . In preparing NSC 13/2, it was recognized that, in many in-
> stances, in light of previous policies and commitments, it posed no easy
> task for you. The National Security Council felt, however, that you would
> find, in the authority that you possess and in your wide background of
> experience, means for seeing that progress is made, gradually and with
> a minimum of disturbance of public opinion, in the direction of the goals
> outlined in the NSC paper.[126]

To drive home the point that MacArthur was receiving instructions based on NSC
unanimity, Draper added that the JCS and the acting secretary of state had coordinated on the telegram.[127]

MacArthur, seeing a unified front in Washington, at last relented. In a message
to Draper on 26 December, he reported that he was "in complete accord with your
conclusion as to the clearly delineated area of SCAP responsibility."[128] This, of course,
did not necessarily mean that the general was now prepared to enthusiastically
embrace the "reverse course" policies of Kennan's NSC 13/2 and Draper's economic stabilization program. Kennan himself observed that MacArthur "had am-
ple means of delaying, if not frustrating, their execution. For these reasons the effect
of the decisions in Japan was probably a gradual and to many an almost imper-
ceptible one." Indeed, MacArthur dragged his feet on, or successfully resisted implementation of, many elements of NSC 13/2, such as those dealing with the purge
and the strengthening of the Japanese police force. Nevertheless, MacArthur could
not and largely did not obstruct the nucleus of the "reverse course"—the economic recovery program. December 1948 also saw the appointment of Dodge as
SCAP's economic deputy and—in a move that represented the symbolic end to
SCAP's original economic program—the formal withdrawal of US support for
FEC-230, the commission's de-zaibatsu program.[129] With these developments,
economic historian William Borden wrote, "The period of policy development had
finally ended, the FEC was stilled, and the drama shifted to Japan."[130]

Kennan and Draper: Allocating the Credit

In characterizing Kennan's role in postwar US policy toward Japan, John Dower—
one of the preeminent historians of modern Japan—described Kennan as "the
father of reverse-course policy."[131] In *Aftermath of War*, however, Schonberger

claims that it was Draper who was "singled out by his contemporaries as the American policymaker most responsible for launching and setting the direction of the Japanese economic recovery program." Draper, according to Schonberger, had been "the first to directly link the Japanese economic recovery program to a 'reverse course'" in occupation policy. Schonberger adds, moreover, that NSC 13/2, "while based primarily on George Kennan's PPS 28 paper, represented the consensus in Washington on the relationship of recovery to reform that Draper, more than any other policymaker, articulated and implemented throughout his tenure as Army Under Secretary." Schonberger does not deny that Kennan played a pivotal role in the redirection of occupation policy that was set in motion in 1948. He does suggest, however, that Draper deserves at least as much credit as Kennan for engineering the "reverse course," that Kennan to a large extent was following Draper's lead, and that Draper played perhaps a larger role than Kennan in actually implementing NSC 13/2. In addition to Schonberger, other historians have characterized Kennan and Draper as having worked as a team to foster the new policy direction in Japan.[132]

Draper does deserve a large measure of credit for spearheading the economic recovery program, which was the operational heart of the "reverse course" and thus its most visible and dramatic element. In that sense, he did play a greater role than Kennan in actually implementing NSC 13/2. The economic recovery program, however, was only one component of Kennan's "unified concept" for a new strategic approach to Japan, the goal of which was a stable and sovereign Japan that was friendly to the United States and not vulnerable to Communist subversion. In essence, Kennan's goal was that of applying his containment doctrine to Japan—an area that, unlike the mainland of Asia, he viewed as being of vital strategic importance to the United States. Historian Bruce Cumings has characterized this as the "Kennan Restoration": Kennan wanted Japan "restored as a regional power . . . thus to butt up against the Soviets, to establish a balance of power like that at the turn of the century, and to save the needless spillage of American blood and treasure."[133]

Draper's agenda, self-admittedly, was much more limited: his goal was primarily that of freeing Washington of the financial burdens of the occupation. He appears to have paid little attention to the broad strategic outlook that motivated Kennan. Indeed, Schonberger quotes Draper as telling a press conference in Tokyo during his second trip there, in March 1948, that Washington "was not attempting to build Japan into a base against the Reds and that his mission was 'purely economic.'"[134] This was clearly reflected in the text of the Johnston Committee report, which exclusively discussed Japan's economic conditions and prospects.

In the same way that Draper paid little attention to Kennan's strategic rationale for the "reverse course," Kennan was relatively uninterested in the details of

Draper's economic recovery program. According to Nitze, Kennan had little knowledge of economics, understood his limitations in that area, and thus generally left economic policy to the experts. Borden concurs that Kennan was "less economically astute" than Nitze. Moreover, as a planner rather than an operational officer, Kennan was more than willing to cede control when it came to implementation of many of his policy initiatives.[135]

These observations help explain the division of labor between Kennan and Draper on Japan policy. For example, Draper's goal of expanding Japan's trading relationships in Southeast Asia—which Schaller, Schonberger, Borden, Cumings, and others have emphasized as a key element of occupation policy under the Dodge Mission—was not a major preoccupation for Kennan, even if it was for some of his colleagues at the State Department. He barely mentioned it in PPS 28 (his Japan policy paper), referring only briefly to "the revival of Japan's trade with other countries" and making no specific reference to Southeast Asia. He was not averse to the idea, and occasionally endorsed it, most notably at a State Department conference in October 1949 when—as other historians have highlighted—Kennan cited the "terrific problem of how . . . the Japanese are going to get along unless they again reopen some sort of empire to the South" and said, "Japan's industrial strength has got to operate in a realm much wider than the Japanese islands themselves." But on these occasions Kennan was endorsing an idea that was more strongly held and advocated by policymakers other than himself. Decades later Kennan could "not recall that the possibility of expanding the Japanese trading block was a factor in my thinking at that time," and Davies recalled only that it "might have been" an issue for the PPS at the time.[136]

Draper no doubt got a head start on Kennan in pursuing a "reverse course" in Japanese economic policy. His first trip to Japan, in September 1947, and his sponsorship of SWNCC 384—the "shift in emphasis" paper—came months before Kennan's mission to Tokyo and his drafting of PPS 28; they even predated PPS 10, the initial PPS study of the Japan problem. Kennan, however, does not appear to have been particularly aware of Draper's earlier efforts. Although Schonberger suggests that Kennan was in "regular contact" with and was "deeply influenced by" the Japan lobbyists associated with Draper—including Kauffman, the author of the September 1947 report that attacked the zaibatsu dissolution program—Kennan himself later could not recall ever having had "anything to do with" the group.[137]

Draper's efforts, crucial as they were, were essentially eclipsed by Kennan's trip to Japan in February 1948, and by the deliberations over PPS 28 that flowed from it. From that point until the final approval of NSC 13/2 in early October, the initiative and the focus of decision making were with Kennan. Indeed, Schonberger acknowledges that it was Kennan and the PPS that "developed the geopolitical rationale for a full-scale revision in policy for Japan that closely dovetailed with the work of Draper." Schaller has accurately characterized the subsequent relationship between the two men's efforts: "As Kennan steered a new strategic agenda through the national security bureaucracy, Draper expanded his campaign to unleash Japanese industry by promoting an export-oriented economy." Thus, it was largely Kennan who mobilized what Schaller has described elsewhere as the "coalition against MacArthur," and it was Kennan who was the driving force at the highest levels of the government behind the strategic reassessment of US policy in Japan.[138]

Nor did Kennan and Draper ever really function as a team. Kennan himself later could not recall "that there was any consultation between myself and Bill Draper either before or after my submission of PPS 28" except on the reparations issue. The record shows that his recollection was faulty in this regard, given the two men's interaction both in Tokyo and subsequently in Washington. Kennan readily acknowledged that his memory decades later may have been deficient, but he almost certainly would have had a stronger recollection of partnership with Draper if he had perceived it at the time. Similarly, both Davies and Nitze—who were closely connected at various times with Kennan's work on Japan—later had no recollection of the PPS director working closely with Draper. Finally, Kennan's and Draper's respective trips to Japan in March 1948, although they briefly merged, were largely independent, according to Marshall Green, the FE officer who accompanied Kennan on his mission.[139]

For his part, Draper told the story of the "reverse course" as he remembered it in a 1972 interview: "The Draper plan . . . this report that . . . Paul Hoffman and Percy Johnston and the rest of the businessmen made after we spent a month in Japan . . . resulted in the President changing the policy, on the recommendation of the Secretary of State. . . . And it was then that I recommended . . . that Joe Dodge . . . be invited to go to Japan as a kind of economic czar. . . . We adopted a new policy which was sent by cable to General MacArthur, which made it possible for the economy to be revised."[140] Like Kennan's, Draper's recollection was not entirely accurate. Truman changed the policy "on the recommendation of the Secretary of State" largely as a result of the Kennan paper rather than the Johnston report. Draper, however, accurately recalled—and deserves full credit for—his pivotal role as the architect of the economic stabilization directive to SCAP that followed approval of NSC 13/2, and the subsequent Dodge mission. Finally, Colonel Trevor Dupuy, the policy aide who accompanied Draper on the March 1948 trip to Japan that linked up with Kennan, described the simultaneity of the trips as "completely fortuitous." In Dupuy's recollection, the two missions were separate and largely unrelated, and there was no sense of either cooperation or competition between them. Here too the archival record indicates otherwise, because the memo Kennan and Draper jointly prepared after their meeting with MacArthur clearly reflects cooperation and even shows their plans to coordinate actions upon their return to Washington.[141] Nonetheless, the way the principal players subsequently remembered and characterized their respective roles strongly indicates that Kennan was the central player—especially from the NSC perspective—and Draper's involvement was vital but subordinate.

On balance, Kennan cannot be denied primary credit for devising the strategic rationale for the "reverse course" in Japan and for serving as its leading proponent. It was his advocacy with Marshall and Forrestal, and his mission to Japan, that drove the process and made possible the adoption and implementation of Draper's economic program. Gaddis attributes Kennan's success in large part to his "agility" in devising an effective approach to MacArthur that won the general's trust, framed the policy issues in a way that facilitated MacArthur's concurrence, and negated MacArthur's concerns about the FEC. Thus, it was Kennan's central role that allowed Washington in the end to reclaim control of Japan from MacArthur, and to begin the new policy direction that would lead to that country's political and economic reconstruction.[142]

EBB TIDE

Acheson Takes the Helm

The final approval in October 1948 of NSC 13/2 (Kennan's Japan policy paper that outlined the "reverse course" in US occupation policy) and in March 1949 of NSC 34/2 (the PPS China paper that affirmed the policy of minimum aid to the Koumintang [KMT] and US disengagement from mainland China) represent the high-water mark of Kennan's impact on US policy in East Asia. Working with the high level of autonomy and initiative delegated to him by Marshall, Kennan played a central role in formulating and executing major shifts in the strategic direction of Washington's approach to both China and Japan. Inspired by this process and his exposure to East Asian issues, he seized the opportunity to devise and propose an ambitious "strategic-political concept" for American policy toward the region as a whole.

Kennan's strategic framework for East Asia, however, had a short shelf life. This was due in part to the inconstancy of his promotion of that framework, which—in varying measures—faced bureaucratic obstacles, included problematic or impractical elements, and was ultimately overtaken by events. It also faced competing demands on Kennan's attention elsewhere in the world, as the Berlin blockade and other developments in Europe fueled the emerging Cold War with the Soviet Union. Perhaps more importantly, not long after Kennan formulated his strategic framework for the region, his decisive influence on US policy in the Far East—as on other issues—began to erode in 1949. This was primarily a result of Marshall's departure as secretary of state and his replacement by Dean Acheson, under whose tenure Kennan's role in policymaking was gradually diluted and eventually marginalized. As a result, the strategic vision for East Asia he had developed under Marshall started to fade soon after its conception.

Kennan's "Strategic-Political Concept" for US Policy in Asia

Kennan's proposal for a strategic framework for the region was a product of the side trip he took to Okinawa and the Philippines during his March 1948 trip to Japan. Contemplating the problem of US defensive strategy in the Far East, Kennan had been intrigued and encouraged by MacArthur's comments in Tokyo about the "strategic boundaries" of the United States in the western Pacific, particularly the general's exclusion of the East Asian mainland and his emphasis on the offshore islands as constituting that boundary. Prior to his trip to Japan, the director of the Policy Planning Staff (PPS) had come to similar views about the country's future security needs and about US strategic goals in the Far East.[1] His thinking on this subject derived in part from MacMurray, who had argued in his 1935 memorandum that, over the long term, Japan rather than China would be the strategic cornerstone of the Far East, and that the United States was best advised to make a "strategic retreat" from the Asian mainland.[2] Both of these ideas had been reiterated by Kennan in PPS 23, the summary of US foreign policy objectives that he had submitted immediately before his departure for Tokyo.[3]

Accordingly, while in Manila, Kennan drafted an unusual memorandum for Marshall addressing the problem, as Kennan saw it, of the lack of an "overall strategic concept" guiding US policy in the region. In Japan—as has been seen—he thought the occupation was quickly becoming counterproductive, while there was as yet no plan for the country's long-term security. The future of the US presence on Okinawa was also unresolved. Likewise in Korea, the "international mandate" that governed the presence of US troops had proven "unrealistic." Finally, in the Philippines, Washington had "the worst of all possible worlds"—bases large enough to anger the Filipinos but too small to be militarily decisive in the event of war. Washington, Kennan asserted, needed to address these problems while keeping in mind the limitations that were imposed on US policy by financial, logistical, and administrative constraints.[4]

Having outlined the problem, Kennan proceeded to recommend his own "strategic-political concept" for US policy in Asia. He apologized to Marshall at the outset "for being so bold, as a civilian, to offer suggestions on matters which are largely military," but added that he was doing so only after consultation with "a number of competent officers" in the region, and even then only tentatively.

His proposal was merely "something to be shot at by the experts when the proper time comes."[5]

Kennan's "strategic concept" rested on three principles: (1) the mainland of Asia was not strategically vital to the United States, (2) Okinawa would become the center of a "US security zone" stretching from the Aleutians to Guam, and (3) Japan and the Philippines would remain outside this zone and be completely de-militarized and neutralized. Most of these ideas, Kennan observed, were shared by MacArthur. In particular, the supreme commander of the Allied powers (SCAP) did not consider bases on Japanese territory to be essential as long as the country was neutralized. On the other hand, Kennan acknowledged that his suggestion for Philippine neutrality was subject to debate and that the US Navy might be-lieve that its needs were being overlooked in his plan. He argued, however, that his framework was based on a balanced assessment of both military and political considerations:

> My interest in this concept stems directly from the fact that it would pro-vide us with the basis of a political program for this area. If we knew that these proposals, or something like them, constituted our longterm strategic concept, we . . . could then approach the immediate questions of the Japanese peace treaty, the Ryukyus, and our base difficulties with the Philippines, in a confident and consistent manner; and I think we could avoid most of the pitfalls which now seem to me to loom across our path. But without such a concept, we cannot move at all. . . . I need hardly stress the desirability of an early clarification of our policy in this area in view of the trend of world events and the necessity of having all our hatches battened down for the coming period.[6]

This memorandum by Kennan was essentially an outline of what came to be known as the US "defensive perimeter" or "offshore island defense" plan. Although many of the ideas in it were not wholly original to Kennan, the memorandum "did much to stimulate thinking within the government" on the concept, according to Gaddis.[7]

However, it does not appear that this thinking ever coalesced, let alone con-verged, toward an "early clarification of our policy" in East Asia. Although the defensive perimeter concept became a de facto basis for US security planning in the region—in large part because key elements of it were consistent with the views of both MacArthur and the Defense Department—Kennan himself does not appear to have actively considered the concept after his return to Washington in March 1948.[8] His subsequent activities suggest that it remained on a back burner while he focused his efforts on winning support for the "reverse course" and post-poning a peace treaty with Japan. Nor did he focus either his own attention or that of others on several unresolved and potentially problematic elements of the concept, such as where South Korea fit into the equation, and how to define and defend US interests in Southeast Asia. Per his initial memorandum to Marshall, Kennan most likely saw these issues, and the concept itself, as largely the purview of the military establishment and thus left the initiative to the Pentagon. No doubt he knew from his conversations with Draper in Tokyo that many there were already advocating the retention of US military forces in Japan.

In any event, the "defensive perimeter" concept had a short history—at least as a policy orientation—that ended two years later with the outbreak of the Korean War, as will be seen. Nonetheless, Kennan continued to invoke elements of his "strategic concept"—including years later—even though he increasingly found himself swimming against the tide.

Changing of the Guard: Kennan and Acheson

In the meantime, Kennan's involvement and influence as a policymaker evolved considerably due to the significantly altered bureaucratic environment that resulted from Acheson's appointment as secretary of state in January 1949. Although Kennan remained a key player until his departure from the State Department in August 1950, his relative weight and voice began to diminish—along with his morale.

Marshall had created the PPS, defined its mission, and chosen Kennan as its director—although Acheson himself, ironically, as undersecretary of state during the first half of 1947, had played a central role in recruiting Kennan for the job.[9] Acheson, however, had left the State Department almost immediately thereafter to return to private law practice. Kennan subsequently enjoyed almost a free hand under Marshall, who used the PPS as he had originally conceived it: as the primary source of policy formulation on the full range of front-burner issues. Kennan's access to Marshall, moreover, was unparalleled. From May 1947 to the end of 1948, "I had the only office adjoining his own, and enjoyed the privilege (which I tried never to abuse) of direct entry to him, through our common side-door," Kennan wrote. Most importantly, perhaps, Marshall and Lovett solicited Kennan's advice and recommendations directly, without requiring the PPS to coordinate its papers with the geographical and functional offices of the State Department. Kennan staunchly defended this practice against attempts by the operational divisions to secure the right to pass judgment on PPS papers.[10]

Kennan and Marshall were not personally close, but their professional relationship appears to have been one of deep mutual respect and interdependence.

Dean G. Acheson as secretary of state. Kennan's influence on US foreign policy waned after Acheson succeeded Marshall as secretary of state in January 1949.

Source: U.S. Department of State / Wikimedia Commons

Kennan, who greatly admired Marshall for the many traits for which the general was widely revered, told Marshall in 1950 that their association was "the greatest of the privileges I have known" in government service. Kennan certainly owed the bulk of his influence as PPS director to Marshall's and Lovett's willingness to delegate authority and policy development to him. Marshall, for his part, once told Kennan that he found the latter's "calm and analytical approach" to problem solving "most comforting" and his professional judgment "a source of great confidence."[11]

This working environment for Kennan changed after Acheson returned to the State Department as secretary. Even before then, Kennan was beginning to grow frustrated with the bureaucratic hassles of foreign policymaking, which were consuming much of his energy and attention. Kennan had become increasingly intolerant of what he viewed as constraints imposed on foreign policy experts—such as himself—who he believed best understood the long-term challenges the United States faced in its international affairs, and should be allowed to formulate responses to those challenges unhampered by partisan political considerations and organizational turf battles. This attitude, no doubt, was partly Kennan's response to those within the administration who disagreed with his policies. But his frustration with the policymaking process appears to have been genuine. At the beginning of 1949, Kennan addressed this problem in a letter to Acheson—just before the latter's appointment as secretary was announced: "I am really not interested in carrying on in government service unless I can feel that we have at least a sporting chance of coping with our problem: that we are not just bravely paddling the antiquated raft of US foreign policy upstream. . . . The members of this top executive level [in the State Department] must have some degree of mutual intellectual intimacy, and must work together as a team. . . . [Otherwise] I'd rather be . . . any place where I could sound off and talk freely to people . . . than in the confines of a department in which you can neither do anything about it nor tell people what you think ought to be done."[12] This letter almost certainly reflected, at least in part, Kennan's disappointment with the departure of Marshall—and Lovett with him—and Kennan's fear that his own unique access and influence would diminish as a result. This fear proved to be justified.

Acheson himself later wrote that the PPS, under Kennan and Nitze (who succeeded Kennan as director in January 1950), was of "inestimable value as the stimulator, and often the deviser, of the most basic policies."[13] Kennan nonetheless believed that after Marshall's departure, the PPS "was never used in the same way again and I don't think Mr. Acheson ever fully understood it." Although Kennan respected and admired Acheson's integrity, and enjoyed his friendship, in his view the new secretary was "a man who dealt, in his inner world, not with institutions but with personalities; and he was not always . . . a good judge of the latter."[14] Kennan's friend and colleague Charles Bohlen shared this assessment of Acheson's leadership,[15] which had a direct impact on the role of the PPS and, by extension, Kennan's influence as a policymaker. Kennan later wrote:

> Although it was in the position of director of the Planning Staff that [Acheson] asked me to remain, he saw me only as an individual—as one, in fact, of a group of individuals whom he had around him and with whom he liked to explore ideas. . . . The thought of consulting the staff as an institution and conceding to it, as did General Marshall, a mar-

gin of confidence within which he was willing to respect its opinion even when that opinion did not fully coincide with his own—the thought, in particular, of conceding to the staff a certain function as the ideological inspirer and coordinator of policy, bringing into coherent inter-relationship the judgments and efforts of the various geographical and functional divisions of the department—all this would have been strange to him.[16]

For his part, Acheson found Kennan's intellectual style frustrating. Davies recalled that the secretary was "impatient with some of George's theorizing," and Charles Burton Marshall—who joined the PPS in 1950—quoted Acheson as saying that Kennan "knows everything except what to do about anything." This view, apparently, was widely shared throughout the State Department: according to another contemporary Foreign Service officer, "the common saying around the Department at the time was that George was not only in an ivory tower, but the fog had closed in so he couldn't see the ground."[17] Clearly Kennan's tendency to intellectualize and his frequent neglect of domestic political considerations hampered his utility as a policymaker.

Acheson wrote that Kennan and Bohlen approached policymaking "from a different angle from the rest of us. . . . Insofar as their wisdom was 'noncommunicable,' its value, though great in operations abroad, was limited in Washington." Equally if not more important, Acheson and Kennan came to disagree substantively on a variety of key foreign policy questions, including the future of Germany, international control of nuclear weapons, and strategy toward the Soviet Union. As a result, Kennan reached the point where he sometimes felt "like a court jester, expected to enliven discussion, privileged to say the shocking things, valued as an intellectual gadfly . . . but not to be taken fully seriously when it came to the final, responsible decisions of policy."[18]

For Kennan, the writing on the wall appeared in September 1949, when Lovett's successor, Undersecretary James Webb—a former Budget Bureau director who, in Kennan's view, lacked any foreign affairs experience and "didn't understand the staff problem at all"—instructed that all PPS papers would henceforth require coordination with the relevant geographical or functional divisions of the department prior to their submission to the secretary. From Kennan's perspective, "it was perfectly clear what was involved in this procedure: the staff was to be deprived of direct access to the Secretary of State in the presentation of its views." This, he believed, defeated the purpose of the PPS. Indeed, Kennan interpreted it as the failure of his efforts to foster a systematic and intelligent means of devising and executing foreign policy. This was reflected in a series of entries in his diary in the fall of 1949:

The whole *raison d'etre* of [PPS] was its ability to render an independent judgment on problems coming before the Secretary or the Under Secretary through the regular channels of the Department. If the senior officials of the Department do not wish such an independent judgment, or do not have confidence in us to prepare one which would be useful, then I question whether the Staff should exist at all. [19 September] . . . Pondering today the frustrations of the past week, it occurred to me that it is time I recognized that my planning staff . . . has simply been a failure, like all previous attempts to bring order and foresight into the designing of foreign policy by special institutional arrangements within the Department. . . . The reason for this seems to lie largely in the impossibility of having the planning function performed outside the line of command. [19 November] . . . Pondering further the reasons for my own sense of frustration in my present position, I realize that the heart of the difficulty lies in the fact that my concept of the manner in which our diplomatic effort should be conducted is not shared by any of the other senior officials of the Department, and that the Secretary is actually dependent on these officials, for better or for worse, for the execution of any foreign policy at all. [22 November]

Kennan had gotten used to the autonomy and influence he enjoyed under Marshall, but his preferences for how the planning function should be exercised and his "concept of the manner in which our diplomatic effort should be conducted" had apparently reached their limits, perhaps inevitably so. He always balked at having to subject his views to routine bureaucratic coordination and competition, but ultimately this could not reasonably be avoided. Resigned to being marginalized, on 29 September 1949 Kennan informed Webb that he wished to be relieved as PPS director as soon as possible, and to leave the State Department the following June.[19]

The Taiwan Dilemma

In the meantime, however, Kennan remained in Acheson's inner circle, where—although his relative influence began to diminish—he continued to play a key role in most major policy issues, including those related to East Asia. The first such problem Acheson was forced to confront—after the issue of aid to the KMT on the Chinese mainland had been largely resolved—was that of Taiwan. As the Chinese civil war continued to advance in favor of the Communists, the political and strategic relevance of Taiwan as a potential offshore redoubt or buffer came to the fore.

Kennan had first weighed in on policy toward Taiwan early in 1948, addressing it in the "strategic concept" memorandum that he prepared for Marshall during his trip to Japan, Okinawa, and the Philippines. Although Kennan's concept emphasized the islands offshore from mainland China as key to the US defensive perimeter in the western Pacific, he originally excluded Taiwan from this security zone, suggesting that the United States should "leave the place alone as long as no power other than a genuine Chinese Government showed an interest in it." He added, however, that this approach would have to be reassessed "if there is any final disintegration of [Nationalist] Government authority there or any sudden access of communist influence."[20]

By late 1948, both of these conditions appeared imminent, and Washington was scrambling to reconsider its position with regard to Taiwan. Kennan inserted himself in the process in late October by consulting with Butterworth on the advisability of taking the matter to the National Security Council (NSC). Davies, for his part, suggested that the State Department's Office of Far Eastern Affairs (FE) prepare an urgent memo on alternative courses of action. Lovett subsequently asked the Joint Chiefs of Staff (JCS), through the NSC, to provide a military assessment of the strategic implications of a potentially Communist-dominated Taiwan. The JCS responded on 1 December that such a development would be "seriously unfavorable" to the United States. The Communists' success on the mainland had increased the potential value of Taiwan as a base for US military operations in wartime; "unfriendly control" of the island could have grave consequences. The Joint Chiefs thus considered it advisable to prevent Communist domination of Taiwan "by the application of such diplomatic and economic steps as may be appropriate."[21]

This JCS recommendation conspicuously avoided any mention of possible military action—essentially passing the buck to the State Department. Accordingly, while Kennan, Davies, and their State colleagues began to explore various policy options that might prevent a Communist takeover of Taiwan, they insisted that the Joint Chiefs were also obliged to spell out what they were willing to do in support of that goal.[22]

The problem was addressed as a matter of urgency by the NSC on 6 January 1949. The principals agreed that keeping Taiwan away from the Communists was "of the utmost importance," but Lovett said the difficult question was how best to do it. Given the international commitment to seeing Taiwan—which had been a Japanese colony from 1895 until Tokyo's defeat in 1945—returned to "Chinese" control, he added that any direct US intervention on the island would be highly inadvisable. The NSC staff was instructed to prepare a paper on possible options, drawing on the JCS paper of 1 December, subsequent proposals from the Army and Navy, and a forthcoming paper from the State Department.[23]

Kennan's PPS and Butterworth's FE, which worked together to prepare the State Department's contribution, saw the Communist threat to Taiwan as coming not from a military invasion but rather from political infiltration and the "classic Chinese deal at the top." The best way to forestall this was not by sending in the US Marines—which would be counterproductive—but by fostering the development of a native, non-Communist local government that could itself successfully resist the Communists. If this should fail, however—and that possibility was fully recognized—the central problem, as Davies saw it, was finding a way to isolate Taiwan and its outlying islands from the mainland "without ourselves taking any open unilateral responsibility for or power over them." To that end, if US military intervention became necessary, it should be based "not on obvious strategic American interests but on principles which are likely to have support in the international community, mainly the principle of self-determination of the Formosan people." Butterworth forwarded these ideas to Lovett, who passed them on to Truman along with a recommendation that the Joint Chiefs be asked to decide whether they judged Taiwan to be strategically important enough to warrant the United States going to war to prevent a Communist takeover of the island.[24]

As submitted to the NSC on 19 January as NSC 37/1, the State Department paper observed that Taiwan's legal status was that of a portion of Japan's prewar empire awaiting disposition according to a treaty of peace, which was then still pending. Its native population was increasingly anti-Chinese, having suffered since the end of the Japanese war under a government of KMT officials exiled from the mainland who exhibited all the weaknesses of the Nationalist regime there. The local Communists, meanwhile, were as yet a negligible presence. Given these circumstances, Washington could either (a) simply occupy the island under the terms of the Japanese surrender, an option that was unlikely to gain acceptance in the international community; (b) negotiate basing rights with the KMT, which would not prevent and may even invite Communist infiltration, and would in any case depend on Chiang Kai-shek's tenuous reliability; (c) support the Nationalist regime on the island as the recognized government of China, which would antagonize both the Communists and the native Taiwanese; or (d) support local non-Communist control of the island, an approach that maximized US freedom of action but was problematic because a viable native, non-Communist element did not yet exist.[25]

The department acknowledged that opting for any one of these alternatives would merely be choosing the least of several evils. Nevertheless, the paper recommended that the administration pursue option (d) while simultaneously delivering clear messages to the Nationalist regime on Taiwan that it should clean up its act, be fully responsive to the needs of the native population, and try to minimize both the number of refugees from the mainland and the KMT's military buildup on the island. Washington should especially discourage Chiang from "building up Formosa as his final stronghold," as he apparently was planning.[26]

Meanwhile, the State Department continued its efforts to extract a commitment—or even a clear position—from the Joint Chiefs on possible military actions with regard to Taiwan. Butterworth informed Acheson on 2 February that field reports from Ambassador John Leighton Stuart and Joint US Military Advisory Group (JUSMAG) chief General David Barr suggested it was increasingly unlikely that diplomatic and economic measures could prevent Communist domination of Taiwan. At an NSC meeting the following day, Acheson stated that if those efforts failed, the question would center on the strategic value of the island; the JCS would then have to decide whether the use of force was advisable. The Joint Chiefs agreed to reexamine the issue and report back on any steps they might be willing to take. The State Department simultaneously agreed to provide its own "statement of specific and immediate steps which the US should take" on Taiwan.[27]

The JCS responded in mid-February with a memorandum reiterating that "any overt military commitment in Formosa would be unwise at this time." This judgment was based on the calculation that a major military effort would be required to defend or occupy the island, which was not "directly vital to our national security" and thus not worth a major investment of military resources. Equivocally, however, the Joint Chiefs added that Taiwan's "strategic importance is, nevertheless, great" and thus merited some level of military support—in the form of a small number of fleet units stationed at ports in Taiwan—aimed at fostering the goal of a native, non-Communist government. The State Department disagreed, arguing that any US military presence on Taiwan would be a political liability and was unlikely to prevent Communist infiltration of the island. For its part, the department recommended strengthening US diplomatic representation on Taiwan and approaching the Nationalist government there with offers of economic assistance. The NSC later agreed to stand down on the JCS idea of stationing minor fleet units on the island.[28]

Acheson nonetheless remained irritated at the Joint Chiefs' evasion of the basic question of whether US military action should even be retained as a future option. At an NSC meeting on 3 March, he asked the JCS to explicitly confirm that they did not recommend overt action either then or "under any foreseeable future circumstances." Forrestal turned the question around by asking what the State Department's reaction would be if the JCS recommended such action. Acheson, drawing on Davies's earlier suggestions, responded that any US move to occupy Taiwan would best be done under the guise of international action, such as seeking a UN trusteeship—although the United States could help lay the groundwork by covertly encouraging a local autonomy movement. Such an approach, Acheson argued, would avoid the possibility of "having things go to pieces underneath us if we took direct control."[29]

On 2 April, Secretary of Defense Louis Johnson, who had succeeded Forrestal, responded to Acheson's request for a clarification of the JCS position. The Joint Chiefs, however, were no more ready to make a commitment—indeed, they were even more equivocal—than they had been in February. They confirmed that, in their view, military action on Taiwan was inadvisable under any circumstances, "subject to the following considerations": "The Joint Chiefs of Staff do not believe that the strategic importance of Formosa justifies overt military action at this time or in the event that diplomatic and economic steps prove insufficient to prevent Communist domination so long as the present disparity exists between our military strength and our global obligations. However, it should be pointed out that there can be no categorical assurance that other future circumstances extending to war itself might not make overt military action eventually advisable from the overall standpoint of our national security."[30]

Clearly, neither State nor the JCS had a solution to the administration's dilemma. Both agencies were stalling for time. Developments on Taiwan and on the mainland, however, only enhanced the apparent urgency of the problem. In late April the Chinese civil war escalated when the Communists crossed the Yangtze River. The flow of refugees to Taiwan accelerated, dissension within the Nationalist leadership increased, and Chiang moved closer toward transferring his regime to the island. On 25 May, Livingston Merchant—one of FE's China hands, who had been sent to Taiwan to survey the situation—wrote a memo for Butterworth stating that these developments made it necessary for the NSC to once again review its Taiwan policy. "We find ourselves faced on Formosa," Merchant observed, "with a situation very similar to that which confronted us on the mainland a year ago." The government on Taiwan was corrupt, incompetent, and locally despised, and there was little prospect of its reforming itself or being replaced by a viable non-Communist alternative. As for US policy options, neither strong support for the Nationalist regime on the island nor the commitment of military forces would be useful. Again, some combination of international action and support for local autonomy was advisable. In any case, urgent action was required.[31]

All the relevant offices in the State Department scrambled to devise a workable plan. Butterworth, drawing on Merchant's advice, recommended to Deputy Undersecretary of State for United Nations Affairs Dean Rusk that the department propose to the NSC that the Taiwan problem be forwarded immediately to the UN. Before the General Assembly, Butterworth suggested, the United States would propose that the UN supervise a plebiscite in which the people of the island would decide whether they wanted a return to Chinese rule, independence, or a UN trusteeship. Such a step would involve revoking in part the 1943 Cairo Declaration—under which the wartime Allies agreed that Taiwan would be restored to China—but Washington would frankly state that the Nationalists had "forfeited the right to a perfunctory confirmation of sovereignty" over Taiwan through their "misrule" of the island since the Japanese surrender.[32]

While Butterworth and Rusk worked to refine this approach, Kennan jumped boldly into the fray.[33] By this time the PPS director had nothing but contempt for Chiang and the KMT, whom he held responsible for drawing the United States into the Chinese civil war and complicating Washington's subsequent efforts to get out. Moreover, Kennan considered the Allies' commitment in 1943 to eventually return Taiwan to Chiang to have been extremely ill advised; indeed, he recalled "being told by someone that it flowed . . . simply from something Harry Hopkins once said at a cocktail party in Cairo." He later decried "this thoughtless tossing to China of a heavily inhabited and strategically important island which had not belonged to it in recent decades, and particularly the taking of this step before we had any idea of what the future China was going to be like, and without any consultation of the wishes of the inhabitants of the island."[34] Accordingly, Kennan set Davies to work drafting an alternative course of action that completely dispensed with the KMT and instead relied on a local separatist regime. Davies agreed with Kennan that the Nationalists could not be allowed to take over Taiwan, where they would only repeat "the egregious errors made on the mainland." The "only way out we could see," Davies recalled, was to replace the Nationalists on the island with a competent native government—which unfortunately was still not available—or to "repulse them in their plans."[35]

In his original draft for Kennan, Davies proposed that Washington consider simply removing the Nationalist government on Taiwan and assuming de facto US administration of the island. Acknowledging that such a move would implicitly require underwriting by the US military, Davies cautioned that this recommendation was "suggestive rather than definitive." In Davies's view, "The general course of action being proposed here is so complex and full of unpredictable elements that, if accepted, it should be implemented with intelligent flexibility. . . . During the take-over and the subsequent administration of the island, we should avoid so far as possible a conspicuous role. We should always remember that our aim is more to deny the islands to the Communists than to acquire responsibility for them and that our influence can be far more effectively exerted through indirect and discreet means rather than through unilateral heavy-handed measures."[36] After extensive discussion within the PPS, Davies devised yet another, more legalistic approach. Because Taiwan's status technically remained subject to completion of a peace treaty with Japan, and because the Chinese civil war necessitated keeping the island under stable authority in the meantime, Washington and the

Allies could declare that SCAP—General MacArthur in Tokyo—was prepared to extend his administrative control over Taiwan.[37]

Davies's final paper, completed on 23 June and designated PPS 53, outlined an elaborate plan of action. He recommended first that the JCS be asked whether they were "able and willing to provide the requisite force to subdue and eject, if necessary, the Nationalist troops" then on Taiwan. Meanwhile, the Philippine, Australian, and Indian governments would be quietly sounded out on their willingness to take the diplomatic lead in calling for international action in the UN to organize a plebiscite on Taiwan. If those governments responded positively by taking the public initiative—and the JCS was willing to commit troops—Washington would immediately propose an international conference, at which the United States would state publicly that the Cairo Declaration had been invalidated by the Nationalists' misrule of Taiwan, and that Washington was willing to support international occupation of the island and supervision of a plebiscite there. The United States would agree to "carry the main weight of the military phase of the operation," although token Allied forces would be required to "minimize [its] unilateral appearance." The top Nationalist leaders on the island, finally, would be given incentives to cooperate, and Chiang himself would be offered the status of a political refugee.[38]

Davies's plan appears to have died on the shelf. It probably was never workable, given the military's reluctance to commit troops to Taiwan. Moreover, the plan was too dependent on the diplomatic assistance of other Asian countries, and on the cooperation of Chiang himself, to be a safe bet for Washington. Finally, it is unlikely that the "international" character of the proposed action would ever have been more than a tenuous facade.

Kennan, in any case, had ideas of his own. He had grown increasingly impatient with the administration's inability and reluctance to confront the Taiwan problem head-on, and its preoccupation with avoiding any action that might be perceived internationally as imperialistic or belligerent. Now, reversing his earlier exclusion of Taiwan from the US "defensive perimeter"—which he had made subject to the reliability of Chinese governance of the island—Kennan asserted that Taiwan was too strategically important to be left to either the Communists or the Nationalists, and that Washington should be prepared to do whatever was necessary to prevent the island from falling into the hands of either regime. For example, he was more than willing to throw US support behind a native Taiwanese insurrection against the KMT, which had brought its corruption with it from the mainland and had massacred local anti-government demonstrators in the 228 Incident of February 1947. In a note to Davies, Kennan asked: "What would you think of the following statement with respect to Formosa if there were to be a native insurrection on the island?"

It cannot be reasonably assumed that the hitherto expectant attitude of the United States will be indefinitely maintained. . . . When the inability of China to deal successfully with the insurrection has become manifest . . . a situation will be presented in which our obligations to the sovereignty of China will be superseded by higher obligations which we can hardly hesitate to recognize and to discharge. . . . The United States is not a nation to which peace is a necessity.[39]

This language, Kennan observed, was "well-founded in US diplomatic usage. It occurred in President Cleveland's annual message to Congress of December 7, 1896, but where the term China is used, he said 'Spain.' "[40]

Kennan basically felt that the administration was being overly cautious and was not facing up to reality. In this regard, he doubted that even Davies's proposal was feasible. As a result, when he forwarded PPS 53 to Acheson, he sent it under cover of a separate memorandum containing his own views with regard to Taiwan—a memo later regarded as one of the most curious and uncharacteristic documents Kennan ever wrote. In it, he began with the same premise as Davies: that the only "reasonably sure chance" of denying Taiwan to the Communists and separating it from the mainland was to remove the KMT government there and replace it with a provisional government—under international or US auspices—dedicated to the principle of eventual self-determination for the island. There were two ways of accomplishing this, Kennan argued. One, as outlined in Davies's paper, was to induce other governments in the region to take the lead in initiating international action. The other, in Kennan's view, was simply to temporarily assert unilateral authority over Taiwan on the grounds that regional stability and the interests of the Taiwanese people necessitated US intervention.[41]

Kennan stated frankly that he believed Davies's option would entail a diplomatic operation requiring such sensitivity, subtlety, and timing that it would "surpass the framework of experience and capabilities of the many people, both here and abroad, who would have to participate in it." The second option, on the other hand, "would offend the sensibilities of many people in the Department on legal and procedural grounds, and we would probably have to cut some legal corners to justify it." As a result, the consensus within the State Department, Kennan observed, was that neither course of action was acceptable and that Taiwan should be considered lost to the Communists. Kennan, however, refused to accept this judgment: "I personally feel that if the second course were to be adopted and to be carried through with sufficient resolution, speed, ruthlessness, and self-assurance, the way Theodore Roosevelt might have done it, it would be not only successful but would have an electrifying effect in this country and throughout the Far East."[42]

Kennan admitted that he had "nothing to support this view except my own instinct" and thus "cannot put it forth without reservation as a measured and formal staff recommendation." Nevertheless, he recommended that Acheson discuss both options with Truman and the NSC—reminding them that there appeared to be no other alternatives to Chinese Communist control of Taiwan. If they agreed that the island was of sufficient strategic importance, and if they were prepared to assume responsibility for dramatic action, "then my personal view is that we should take the plunge." If not, Kennan argued, the NSC should be prepared to accept the probability that Taiwan would fall to the Communists, and all the political and strategic consequences thereof.[43]

Kennan has been harshly criticized and even ridiculed by historians for making this proposal. Evan Thomas and Walter Isaacson called it a "remarkable and harebrained scheme from a man who fancied himself a realist and nonmilitarist," and wrote that Acheson "wisely chose to ignore [Kennan's] call to send in the marines." Among other historians, Warren Cohen said the episode "revealed Kennan at his most absurd"; Nancy Bernkopf Tucker referred to Kennan's "cowboy-style tactics"; and David Mayers observed that Acheson "let the plan succumb to a quiet and deserved death." According to Gaddis—who observed that "Theodore Roosevelt, of course, never did anything like this"—Kennan later attributed the idea to Davies, who in turn denied responsibility for such a "totally implausible plan." However, Kennan's attribution to Davies more than 30 years later may reflect faulty recollection of the distinction between Davies's proposal in PPS 53 and Kennan's proposal in the cover memorandum that he sent to Acheson; in any event, it would be highly uncharacteristic of Kennan to blame Davies for any misjudgment of his own.[44]

In retrospect, Kennan's scheme does appear to have been untenable and premature. Yet in the context of the policy debate at the time—with a Communist takeover of Taiwan viewed as imminent, the administration grasping at straws, and no agency willing to commit itself to what appeared to be a hopeless cause— Kennan's proposal was simply a call for serious thinking and, if necessary, decisive action. And it served that purpose, to the extent that it could. "Electrifying or not," according to historian Robert Messer, it "did shock other sources of policy advice into a consideration of what to do about Taiwan."[45] Historian David Finkelstein noted that Kennan's proposal "represented the frustration many in State were probably feeling in their quest to save Taiwan."[46] Moreover, Kennan's idea was not dismissed out of hand, particularly since no other positive plan was offered as a way of keeping Taiwan out of Communist hands. Three weeks after Kennan delivered his memo to Acheson, the secretary asked his inner circle for an assessment of "why we didn't do anything about the Formosan situation in line with Mr. Kennan's recommendations."[47]

In late July, Rusk suggested that the JCS be asked yet again to reassess the US position on Taiwan in light of recent developments, and specifically to address the question of whether the strategic significance of the island was sufficient to warrant either the use of US forces to seize it or the establishment of US bases there. Kennan—who, as has been seen, had concluded that Taiwan was inside the US defensive perimeter even though he placed mainland China outside it— concurred with this suggestion, which was incorporated into another State Department paper for the NSC. The Joint Chiefs replied on 17 August, reiterating once more their equivocal position that Taiwan was strategically important to the United States, but not important enough to justify overt military action—unless, of course, future circumstances made it advisable "from the overall standpoint of national security."[48]

This represented no real progress at all. Indeed, the administration had essentially failed to agree on any policy aimed at significantly altering the course of events on Taiwan. Two months later, Chiang had hoisted his flag there, effectively ending the civil war on the mainland and making KMT control over the island a fait accompli. In early October, Butterworth's office forwarded to the NSC what was essentially a postmortem on Taiwan, recommending that the existing policy—such as it was—be continued; FE specifically advised against any significant program of economic or military aid, or any use of US military force in a last-ditch effort to prevent a Communist takeover of the island, which was deemed "probable." Acheson and his senior advisers subsequently agreed that no further effort would be made to separate Taiwan from the mainland. Kennan disagreed with this judgment, emphasizing in his diary that "I cannot agree that we ought to make ourselves a party to the formal assignment of Formosa to China, when we know that this means only injustice and misgovernment to the natives of the island for decades ahead." But he had given up the fight on Taiwan—as well as his struggle to retain influence as director of the PPS, which, as already seen, he had decided to leave. He declined to comment on FE's report for the NSC.[49]

Kennan's involvement with the Taiwan issue had reinforced his thorough disgust with Chiang and the Nationalist regime—and with the administration's failure to prevent Chiang from installing himself on the island. At a briefing for Central Intelligence Agency (CIA) officers in mid-October 1949, Kennan described the generalissimo as "sitting on Formosa with a group of extraordinarily stubborn and demoralized and selfish and rather pathetic people around him."[50] Although Kennan was vindicated in part less than a year later when the administration quickly committed itself to the defense of Taiwan in the wake of the outbreak of the Korean War, this required Washington to once again guarantee the Nationalist regime, a necessity that Kennan lamented.

The White Paper and the Recognition Issue

While the debate over Taiwan policy was exhausting itself, Kennan continued to play an important role in US policy toward mainland China. Most importantly, the Truman administration in early 1949 began moving toward acceptance of Kennan's suggestion—which had been rejected the previous November—of publishing a record of US-China relations that would justify the drawdown of US support for the Nationalist regime. Acheson began to contemplate such a project soon after he became secretary of state. In February, after Truman received a letter from a group of Republican congressmen assailing the administration's China policy, Acheson volunteered to meet with them and suggested that the time might be right for a public explanation and defense of that policy. He acknowledged—as Truman and the cabinet had in November—that it would "pull the rug out" from under Chiang and probably benefit the Communists, but he personally doubted whether it was necessary to "shore up the Nationalist Government to the extent that we had in the past." Accordingly, Acheson asked for a study of the probable consequences for the Chiang regime of a full public disclosure of the rationale behind US policy.[51] At about the same time, he raised with Truman the idea of having the department prepare a "thorough account of our relations with China" that would be published "when the collapse came." Truman gave his assent, and Butterworth's office set to work compiling the relevant documents.[52]

Appropriately, it was Kennan and Davies—who had originally proposed a white paper on China—who ultimately prompted Acheson's decision to authorize its publication. On 28 June, Kennan—drawing on a memorandum drafted by Davies—told the secretary that the "magnitude and strength of the Congressional offensive" against the administration's China policy had reached the point of requiring a counteroffensive. The time was ripe for release of the white paper, and the considerations that dictated Truman's reluctance to publish one the previous fall were "no longer operative." In addition, Kennan recommended that Truman simultaneously deliver a speech on the subject of China, built around the theme that the administration's China policy had been "a triumph of good sense over a proposed gamble with our deepest national interests and security."[53] Acheson decided almost immediately to expedite the completion of the white paper and the preparations for its publication. On 30 June he informed his senior staff that he had assigned Philip Jessup—then ambassador to the United Nations—the responsibility for supervising the project and editing the final paper.[54]

Jessup's appointment was symptomatic of Kennan's waning influence with Acheson, particularly on East Asia policy. The congressional offensive against the administration's approach to China, combined with the rapidly deteriorating situation on the Chinese mainland (and elsewhere in the region), had convinced many in the administration that Washington's overall policy toward East Asia needed to be reassessed. This set off a flurry of interagency activity, beginning with Defense Secretary Johnson's proposal in June that the NSC begin a full-scale review of the US position in Asia. Acheson, who was determined not to lose the initiative, responded by appointing Jessup as a special adviser on Asian affairs and putting him in charge of coordinating overall China policy.[55] When Acheson released the China White Paper to the public in early August, he also announced that two academics, Everett Case and Raymond Fosdick, would be joining Jessup to serve as consultants to the State Department on Asian affairs. These appointments essentially took policy planning toward East Asia away from the PPS and assigned it to Jessup and "the Consultants." Although Kennan and Davies remained actively involved in East Asia policy deliberations, they—and to a certain extent even Butterworth—were often relegated to simply advising Jessup and the Consultants on what issues they should be addressing in their work.[56]

The most immediate issue facing the Consultants in the fall of 1949—after the KMT fled to Taiwan and the Communists established the People's Republic of China—was whether Washington should recognize the Chinese Communist regime or support its membership in the United Nations. Kennan and Davies were actively involved in addressing both questions. Truman, for his part, believed that Washington "should be in no hurry" to recognize Beijing, having waited over twelve years to establish relations with the Soviet Union.[57] Nonetheless, recognition was the primary topic addressed at a special conference of China experts hosted by Jessup and FE at the State Department in early October. Among the participants at the conference were the Consultants, Marshall, Stuart, Kennan (who had been reluctant to participate),[58] and a variety of prominent academics and businessmen with interests in China. With only two dissenting votes, the conference overwhelmingly favored US recognition of the Communist regime.[59] Kennan subsequently participated—and played a key role—in the Consultants' discussions with Acheson on the recognition question.[60] Acheson opted for a wait-and-see approach, believing that diplomatic recognition should not be viewed "as a major instrument for showing our interest in the Chinese people or for winning concessions from the Communist regime." Washington, it was decided, should adopt a realistic but not an eager stance.[61]

Kennan and Davies, however, expressed a dissenting view after the Communists in late October arrested and incarcerated Angus Ward—the US consul general in Manchuria—and several members of his staff.[62] Davies later admitted that he used the opportunity to write a memo justifying recognition of the Chinese Communist regime, and that Kennan had concurred in it.[63] The memo argued that Ward's arrest was almost certainly engineered by the Russians—who appeared to be the dominant presence in Manchuria—in retaliation for the arrest a few days earlier in the United States of several Soviet trade officials. Davies and Kennan believed that Moscow was deliberately trying to sour Sino-US relations, specifically to derail any chances for normalization between Beijing and Washington, which the Soviets probably feared as a threat to their own influence in China. On the contrary, Davies wrote, there was "no solid reason why we should not now recognize the Communists"; indeed, "all of the reasons why the Kremlin is opposed to our recognizing Peking are decisive reasons why we should."[64]

Ward subsequently was released without any decision having been made by Washington on recognition, despite the fact that most other nations had moved to normalize with Beijing.[65] Kennan, by now in the process of disengaging himself from the PPS, adopted an ambivalent attitude toward the matter. In early January 1950, he wrote to Acheson that the problem of recognizing Communist China was "less important than one would think" from the public attention being devoted to it: "Really important developments in China will not be much affected by whether we recognize or don't recognize; nor is there any compelling need for uniformity in timing, as among western powers. Everyone has his own particular problems. . . . We will not assure any benefits to ourselves just by recognition. . . . But we will also not gain anything by withholding recognition for sentimental reasons alone, if realistic considerations indicate desirability of maintenance of diplomatic contact."[66] In any event, the outbreak of the Korean War in June 1950 derailed any consideration of recognizing the Chinese Communist regime. The Truman administration opted not to do so—a decision that was upheld for nearly thirty years.

Kennan's advice on recognition of the Chinese Communist regime had nonetheless fallen on deaf ears. Indeed, his voice on China policy had been pushed to the sidelines by the end of 1949. After his recommendation that the White Paper be published, his participation in East Asian affairs began to wane. As noted earlier, this was merely symptomatic of his diminished influence under Acheson, which led Kennan to step down as PPS director in January 1950.

Moscow Revisited: Targeting Fault Lines in Sino-Soviet Relations

Before leaving the PPS, however, Kennan became involved with the other key question regarding China that Washington confronted in late 1949. This was the same problem that had originally brought Kennan and Davies together in 1945: Beijing's relationship with Moscow. By 1949, with the Chinese Communists having effectively conquered the mainland, Washington's attention shifted to the question of whether it was possible for the United States to undermine Sino-Soviet relations by encouraging Chinese "Titoism"—the shorthand given to Communist independence from Moscow. Various strategies for doing so were examined, but none was effectively implemented—at least during the time that Kennan and Davies remained at the State Department—for reasons ranging from skepticism that Soviet and Chinese Communists were anything other than intimate bedfellows, to the operational limitations on Washington's ability to carry out any such plan.[67]

Kennan and Davies, of course, were particularly well qualified to assess the possibilities. As already seen, they had been among the first to foresee the inevitability of Sino-Soviet tensions, when they worked together in Moscow. In the memo Davies prepared for then Ambassador to the Soviet Union Averell Harriman in advance of then Ambassador to China Patrick Hurley's infamous meeting with Stalin in April 1945, Davies had stated that the Chinese Communist Party (CCP) had begun its life as "an instrument of Moscow's policy of world revolution," but that its members had been "left pretty much to shift for themselves" after the Kremlin's apparent abandonment of that policy in the mid-1930s. The Chinese Communists had every reason to resent the "shabby treatment" they had since received from Soviet leaders. Kennan, moreover, had expanded on these ideas in a message to the secretary of state in January 1946, arguing that the CCP had "survived and grown not because of but despite relations with Moscow."[68]

As noted earlier, this theme had been reflected in Kennan's lectures at the National War College during 1946–47. It had also been incorporated into the PPS's work on China from the beginning. In Kennan's first, preliminary look at Far Eastern policy as PPS director, he opined to Lovett that the CCP was unlikely to retain its "present degree of dependence on Moscow"—let alone its ideological fervor—if it succeeded in taking over most of the country. Early in 1948, Kennan suggested that Soviet leaders probably were reluctant to see the CCP take over China because "a united Communist China would be much more dangerous to Russia than the present sort of China" by potentially threatening the Kremlin's strategic interests and its control over the Communist movement.[69]

Kennan and Davies initially used the prospect of Chinese Titoism to rationalize withdrawing the US commitment to the KMT government on the mainland. In August 1948, when Ambassador Stuart in Nanking was seeking guidance from Washington on how to deal with the KMT's deteriorating position on the battlefield, Davies cited the promise of Titoism as one reason to hasten the end of the Chinese civil war. "If Titoism is latent in the Chinese communist movement, as we strongly suspect," Davies wrote, "it can only become openly active with a cessation of hostilities."[70]

Davies expanded on this idea in PPS 39 of September 1948—the first China-focused PPS paper, discussed earlier. Even if Moscow was confident of Mao's loyalty, Kremlin leaders were bound to be uneasy about the prospect of a CCP victory, given China's massive size and population and Mao's strident nationalism. As their fortunes improved, Mao and his colleagues—having risen to power on waves of xenophobia—could be expected to distance themselves from any hint of subservience to a foreign power. This, Davies observed, would redound to Washington's benefit: "It is a nice piece of irony that at precisely the time the Chinese Communist leadership is most likely to wish to conceal its ties with Moscow, the Kremlin is most likely to be exerting utmost pressure to bring the Chinese Communists under complete control. The possibilities which such a situation would present us, provided we have regained freedom of action, need scarcely be spelled out."[71] Indeed, Davies soon saw evidence of growing Soviet frustration with the Chinese Communists. He wrote to Kennan in January 1949 that he detected "a strong odor of bad fish . . . emanating from Sino-Soviet relations." Moscow had expressed no great enthusiasm over the rapid advance of CCP forces; in the meantime, the Kremlin was maintaining close and continuing relations with the KMT. In Davies's estimation, Mao had "succeeded too quickly and on too massive a scale for the Kremlin's liking." Soviet leaders were probably disturbed by "the specter of a great autocephalous competitor" in East and Southeast Asia.[72]

The idea that the United States could exploit the situation by trying to drive a wedge between the Soviets and the Chinese Communists appears to have reached practical consideration early in 1949. Even then, however, the possibilities were limited. In PPS 39/2 of February 1949, Kennan and Davies acknowledged that the "natural points of conflict between the Chinese Communists and the USSR have not yet developed." As a result, an operational plan for aggravating them was not yet feasible, or even advisable. Washington nonetheless should be prepared for any opportunities that might arise: "While scrupulously avoiding the appearance of intervention, we should be alert to exploit through political and economic means any rifts between the Chinese Communists and the USSR and between Stalinist and other elements in China both within and outside of the Communist structure."[73] This tentative strategy lost much of its currency on 30 June 1949, when Mao delivered his famous "lean to one side" speech, in which he declared that Beijing would align itself with the Soviet Union. One month later, Acheson, in his "Letter of Transmittal" that accompanied publication of the China White Paper, equated Mao's speech to a public announcement of China's "subservience to a foreign power."[74]

Neither Mao's nor Acheson's statements, however, completely ended consideration of a "wedge" strategy to encourage Chinese Titoism. Acheson's Letter of Transmittal, in fact, had expressed the hope that the Chinese would eventually "reassert themselves and throw off the foreign yoke"; the letter had also advised that Washington should "encourage all developments in China which now and in the future work toward this end."[75] But the priority of any such efforts had greatly diminished, and Chinese Titoism became a back-burner issue. Acheson and his key Asian advisers—by now Jessup, Rusk, and the Consultants—were instead preoccupied with the China White Paper and its aftermath, and with the question of whether to recognize the Chinese Communist regime.

Kennan and Davies kept the idea of a Sino-Soviet rift alive, while acknowledging its limitations. "It is dangerous to talk about a Chinese Titoism," Kennan told a Pentagon audience in September 1949; "Parallels of this sort are always more misleading than clarifying." At the same time, he reiterated his view that Moscow's authority in Beijing was "only a moral one," which could be easily inflamed by a difference of opinion between the two Communist Parties.[76] He believed, moreover, that the possibility of Sino-Soviet tensions was perhaps the only leverage the United States had over the Chinese Communists. Accordingly, he and Davies told Acheson and the Consultants in late October that Washington should try to do what it could "to make life unpleasant for Communist China within the framework of Soviet domination."[77]

Kennan and Davies soon imagined possible opportunities. In January 1950, Kennan interpreted the inordinate length of Mao's visit to Moscow to forge an alliance with Stalin as an indication of possible tension between the two Communist regimes. He thought the talks between the two leaders might be going slowly because of serious differences of opinion, or because Stalin was trying to stall Mao in Moscow while using his minions to undermine Mao's support back in Beijing.[78] Davies, meanwhile, claimed to have seen repeated indications of a split within the CCP itself—specifically, the existence of a faction that was more nationalistic, and thus presumably more "Titoistic" than Mao. This was his reading, for example, of an alleged overture to US officials from senior Communist Chinese official Chen Yi early in 1950. On that occasion, Davies repeated the admonition that Washington should "be ever on the alert for symptoms of such a break-away and should judiciously do all within our power to foster such a split."[79]

The outbreak of the Korean War a few months later largely suspended such wishful thinking, and symptoms of such a breakaway would only emerge nearly a decade later. However, Davies's efforts in 1949–50 to formulate a scheme to foster such a split set in motion the events that ultimately led to his own professional downfall.

PRELUDE TO THE KOREAN WAR

Applying the "Strategic Concept"
on the East Asian Periphery

Having judged that China was strategically expendable to the United States, Kennan focused his strategic framework for US policy in East Asia on establishing a defensive perimeter in the western Pacific, and thus on clarifying Washington's relationship with and presence within the countries on China's periphery. This essentially involved Kennan's prescription of how his doctrine of containment should be applied in the Far East. Indeed, how to contain Communism in the region became a central policy question over the course of 1949 as Washington reconciled itself to the impending victory of the Chinese Communist Party (CCP) in the Chinese civil war. Although his role in policymaking was starting to diminish, Kennan remained actively involved in addressing this question.

On 6 June 1949, Kennan forwarded to Butterworth an unusual memorandum prepared by the Policy Planning Staff (PPS) in response to a query from Acheson, Webb, and Rusk on "where we should draw the line in Asia" and "what specific actions we might take which would contribute to the containment of communism in those areas." The PPS summarized the situation as follows:

> The Communists will sweep, no matter what we do: All of China.
> The Communists will probably, notwithstanding all practicable efforts by us, emerge in control of: South Korea; Indochina.
> The Communists may possibly, no matter what we do, emerge in control of: Burma.

> Provided that we make a major and persevering effort, it is probable that the Communists can be denied supremacy in: Japan; Indonesia.
> Provided that we assert ourselves to a somewhat lesser degree, the Communists probably can be denied supremacy in: The Philippines; Siam; Malaya; Formosa.[1]

This clearly reflected Kennan's readiness to largely accept Communist control of the East Asian mainland.[2] It also reaffirmed his emphasis over a year earlier—in his "strategic concept" memorandum for Marshall—on Japan and, to a lesser extent, the Philippines as the notional strongpoints of the US defense posture in the western Pacific.

This assessment from the PPS was soon folded into the East Asia policy review that Jessup and the Consultants launched on Acheson's behalf, and that initially considered "drawing the line" further inland than Kennan. In mid-July, Acheson gave Jessup his line of march: "You will please take as your assumption that it is a fundamental decision of American policy that the United States does not intend to permit further extension of Communist domination on the continent of Asia or in the southeast Asia area. Will you please draw up for me possible programs of action relating to various specific areas not now under Communist control in Asia under which the United States would have the best chance of achieving this purpose? These programs should contain proposed courses of action, steps to be taken in implementing such programs, estimate of cost to the United States, and the extent to which United States forces would or would not be involved."[3] This directive essentially took policy planning toward the Far East away from Kennan and the PPS and assigned it to Jessup. Moreover, it effectively gave Jessup responsibility for implementing in Asia a policy—containment—that Kennan had devised.

Kennan and Davies nonetheless contributed ideas to Jessup's effort. On 8 July, Kennan forwarded to Jessup, Webb, Rusk, and Bohlen—then serving as State Department counselor—a memo prepared by Davies entitled "Suggested Course of Action in East and South Asia." In this memo, which had originally been drafted as part of the PPS response to Acheson's query on "where should we draw the line in Asia," Davies argued that a "change of climate" was needed to restore US public support for Washington's Asia policy, and the Asian countries' confidence in it. Because there was little that could be done concretely, however, he recommended a series of tactical public gestures—such as inviting the Philippine president to Washington, extending aid to the Indonesian and Thai governments, and moving toward a peace treaty with Japan—that would show Washington seizing the initiative in the region. These gestures, Davies suggested, should be performed "with a real sense of theater" so as to capture public attention and create the impression of confidence and momentum.[4]

Kennan, however, does not appear to have aggressively promoted or invested much bureaucratic capital in Davies's memorandum. Indeed, he was prepared to shelve the paper after it met with some criticism from FE, and he sent it forward only after Rusk and Acheson expressed an interest in seeing it. Even then, Kennan emphasized that the memorandum was not a formal PPS paper and did not represent any formal recommendations. Instead, he said, it was merely illustrative of "the sort of program" the PPS considered advisable; its specific suggestions would "obviously require careful study and airing before they could be seriously considered."[5]

Kennan's ambivalence about Davies's "Suggested Course of Action" memo almost certainly reflected his recognition and frustration that the PPS was being marginalized, particularly on East Asia policy. From July 1949 on, Acheson not only relied primarily on Jessup; he also began to consult more frequently on Asian affairs with Rusk, who responded with his own list of recommended steps to bring about a "change in climate" in Asia.[6]

Nonetheless, Kennan remained substantially engaged on East Asian issues, especially those that were relevant to pursuing his "strategic concept" for the region, which he had not abandoned. On the contrary, his efforts to put it in practice drove his approach to Japan, Southeast Asia, and Korea in the year leading up to the outbreak of the Korean War.

The Question of Japanese Security

In order to expedite the "reverse course"—and particularly to obtain the concurrence of the military establishment—NSC 13/2 (Kennan's Japan policy paper) of October 1948 had deferred the question of a Japanese peace treaty, as well as the issue of Japan's long-term security. Both of these issues, however, returned to the front burner in 1949. The successful launching of the Dodge Mission, and Draper's resignation in March 1949 to return to the private sector, facilitated a gradual shift in the focus of Japan policy deliberations from economic to military and political issues.

Kennan, in the meantime, had grown increasingly ambivalent and even equivocal on the subject of Japan's security. As already seen, he had recommended as part of his "strategic concept" for East Asia that Washington consider as a long-term goal the complete demilitarization and neutralization of the country. He had heard this idea expressed by MacArthur. Under Kennan's version of this scenario, Japan's defense would be the responsibility of an enhanced Japanese "police force" and coast guard, and the country would be included under a regional US defense umbrella, which would operate from Okinawa but ideally would not require US military bases on the Japanese home islands. However, opposition to this view within the military establishment, and MacArthur's own shifting stance on the issue, led Kennan to adopt more ambiguous rhetoric when addressing the question. He was soon suggesting that the only viable alternative to rearming Japan, for the foreseeable future, was an indefinite commitment of US military forces in the country.

Kennan had told a National War College (NWC) audience in May 1948 that although Washington was committed to demilitarization in Japan, people should not "make a fetish of commitments." "Like any sensible individual," he said, the United States "sometimes has to change its mind." At the same time, he acknowledged that Washington's commitment on this particular matter was unusually deep and should not be altered without long and careful deliberation. Under the circumstances, Kennan saw no alternative to retaining a US military presence in Japan for the foreseeable future. He simultaneously reiterated his view—perhaps the only view he had on the subject that was to remain consistent—that Japan's internal security forces should be beefed up.[7]

By the end of 1948, Kennan began to recognize and acknowledge that the question of Japan's security needs could not be deferred indefinitely. The Japanese, he assessed, both resented the US military presence in their country and took it for granted. This, in Kennan's view, was counterproductive, problematic, and unhealthy. Japanese resentment over the occupation would only intensify if such a military presence continued indefinitely, and especially if it remained after the occupation itself had ended. Washington's goal of a stable Japan that was friendly to the United States would not be well served if the process of stabilizing the country itself increased Japanese hostility toward the United States. Accordingly, Kennan told another War College audience in December 1948 that, although Japan was then "in our hands" and thus could be discounted as a threat to US interests, "someday we are going to have to deal with it very seriously."[8]

The same theme was reflected in a memorandum Butterworth sent to Webb in May 1949 introducing State's new leadership team to problems that required action with regard to Japan. The Japanese, Butterworth reported, had grown "increasingly restive under conditions of indefinitely continued military occupation"; this had produced a "gradual souring of popular attitudes" toward the US presence. Desire for a peace settlement had become widespread. As the policy debate of 1947 and 1948 had shown, however, progress toward a peace treaty was contingent on a decision regarding Japan's future security. Acheson and Webb consequently brought the issue back to the front burner by formally asking Johnson for an assessment of US security needs in Japan and a report on implementation of NSC 13/2 that addressed whether the supreme commander of Allied powers (SCAP) had taken the steps required to prepare Japan for withdrawal of the occupation.[9]

The military establishment, for its part, was already interested in relieving itself of some of the burden of defending Japan. In a document later designated NSC 44, the Joint Chiefs of Staff (JCS) advised Forrestal in March 1949—just days before Johnson replaced him as defense secretary—that Japanese rearmament was desirable but "not practicable and advisable at this time" because it would require an amendment to the Japanese constitution and would play poorly both in the region and internationally, and might adversely affect Japan's economic recovery program. The Joint Chiefs instead recommended that Washington proceed with plans to strengthen the Japanese police force—as Kennan had proposed in PPS 28 (NSC 13)—with the "secret goal" of eventually turning the police into a Japanese self-defense force. The National Security Council (NSC) in late April circulated a highly sensitive paper on the need to begin planning such an approach.[10]

Kennan by now was not only a strong advocate of enhancing Japan's internal security apparatus; he had also decided that the time was finally ripe for negotiations leading toward a peace treaty. He told participants at two Pentagon conferences in mid-1949 that the occupation had not allowed the Japanese "an adequate development of their national life," which now only a peace settlement and the withdrawal of US forces could give them. He acknowledged that this would involve risks and problems, but argued that indefinite postponement of a treaty at that stage would be an even greater risk. There were no long-term guarantees. In a distant echo of MacMurray, Kennan said it was "hard to see where the seething, virile population of these overcrowded islands will turn its hopes and its energies." Given the conditions there, the Japanese were likely to "fall into a state of extreme economic hardship and national frustration," perhaps leading again to authoritarianism. Kennan's judgment, however, was that it would be decades before Japan was remotely capable of again threatening the outside world. As a result, the United States could afford to do what he thought it should do: get out of Japan.[11]

Military leaders, notwithstanding their willingness to surrender their responsibility for defending the Japanese, disagreed. On 15 June, Johnson forwarded to the NSC the Joint Chiefs' response to the State Department's request for an assessment of Japanese security needs. This paper, which was designated NSC 49, showed that the military shared Kennan's view that Japan was of vital strategic importance to the United States and should at a minimum be denied to the Soviet Union. The Joint Chiefs, however, argued that US bases on Okinawa and elsewhere in the Ryukyus would not be sufficient to meet "our essential needs." At the very least, the Navy required continued use of its base at Yokosuka in Tokyo

Bay. More importantly, a peace treaty with Japan "should not be such as to preclude bilateral negotiations for base rights" elsewhere on the Japanese home islands. Nor should any peace treaty include a strict schedule for withdrawal of occupation forces. In any event, the military argued, consideration of a peace treaty was still "premature" because Japan's orientation toward the West was not yet ensured. Time was also needed for the Japanese to improve their self-defense forces.[12]

Acheson, however, seized the initiative and began actively pursuing a peace settlement with Japan. It is not clear from the historical record precisely what motivated the new secretary to do so, particularly in the face of resistance from the military. But a Japanese peace treaty appears to have been considered as part of the overall review of Asia policy within the State Department that was prompted by the Republican assault on Truman's China policy and Acheson's appointment of Jessup and the Far Eastern Consultants. Kennan hinted at an explanation in his diary after attending a meeting of the Consultants: "It is ironic that our principal reason for wanting a peace treaty with Japan at this time is that it appears to be the only way of solving internal administrative difficulties within our own government." Citing this diary entry later in his memoirs, Kennan—who could not fully recall the context—speculated that renewed interest in a peace treaty was prompted by the administration's inability to use the "occupational machinery" in Japan, "with its heavy involvement of the military side of the Washington bureaucracy, as an effective instrument of policy." Acheson and his State colleagues may also have simply concluded that the occupation had completed its purpose and was now at increasing risk of becoming counterproductive. In any event, by mid-summer 1949 the Consultants, Rusk, FE, and the PPS all concluded that an early peace treaty was desirable.[13]

There could be no peace treaty, however, without new security arrangements, and there was no consensus in Washington on what those should be. The military establishment, unwilling to liquidate its interests in the Far East, was taking advantage of the uncertainties of the situation by dragging its feet on the issue. Under these circumstances, the State Department may have calculated that its only option was to force the issue by threatening to put the cart before the horse. Acheson apparently judged that, by accelerating diplomatic discussions of a peace treaty, he could force the military to confront the issue and reach a compromise with the State Department that would allow the administration to come to closure on the question of Japanese security. This might also dampen some of the Republican charges that the administration had no compass for its Asia policy.

The signals coming from MacArthur himself probably reinforced State's view that some sort of change in Japan was overdue. SCAP's resistance to change only encouraged Washington to pursue it. In June 1949, apparently reacting to press reports drawing attention to language in NSC 13/3 that called on Washington to concentrate on preparing the Japanese for "the eventual removal of the regime of control" in Japan,[14] the general sent Acheson and Kennan a letter expressing his grave concern about any possible plans to radically alter the organizational structure of SCAP. The occupation, MacArthur claimed, had given the United States a "unique position in the hearts" of the Japanese: "It is a position of respect bordering on reverence and veneration. . . . To some Japanese the presence of troops, with its connotations of order and discipline, has had greatest appeal and most far-reaching influence. But to most, the bestowal and safeguard of human rights, and the social reformation to enhance individual dignity have made a penetrating and lasting impression. But the combination of both has brought to the great masses of the Japanese people a sense of confidence and faith and a feeling of complete security in the American effort and purpose."[15] MacArthur told Kennan in particular that it would be "a source of great comfort" for the general to know that the PPS director was "alive to the disastrous psychological impact" any relaxation of the occupation would have "upon the oriental masses."[16]

Acheson assured MacArthur, when he responded to him in early September, that reports of a change in SCAP's "regime of control . . . so far as I know do not reflect any trend of thought in official circles—certainly not in the Department of State."[17] This statement was true only inasmuch as the State Department was by that time inclined to bypass the "regime of control" question in favor of moving directly forward with plans for a peace treaty—which by definition would ultimately entail dismantling SCAP. Ironically, Acheson was encouraged in the direction of a peace treaty by MacArthur himself, who on several occasions in late summer and early fall of 1949 advised the State Department's representatives in Tokyo that Washington should again seize the initiative and issue invitations to a peace conference. MacArthur was willing to suggest this on the condition that US forces remained in Japan until their withdrawal became "feasible." The general was confident that it would take at least two years before peace negotiations and such a withdrawal could be completed.[18]

Acheson was also encouraged by a report Kennan issued during a trip to London in July; the British, Kennan said, appeared willing to accept a bilateral US-Japan security arrangement as a complement to a multilateral peace settlement. Accordingly, he concluded, "I think it will not be hard to arrive at agreement with them on any program we may work out for progress toward [a] Japanese peace treaty."[19] British Foreign Secretary Bevin and M. E. Dening, his top Asian adviser, confirmed both this and London's desire for an early peace treaty in meetings with Acheson and Butterworth in Washington in early September. Indeed, on the latter occasion, Acheson—eager to seize the opportunity—promised Bevin that, by the end of 1949, the State Department would have a draft peace treaty ready for consideration by

Great Britain and its Commonwealth partners at a meeting scheduled for January 1950. On 16 September, Acheson notified Truman of these "exploratory discussions."[20]

Acheson's scheme quickly ran into serious trouble, predictably from within the Defense Department.[21] The secretary of state had told Bevin that progress toward a peace treaty presupposed that the State Department could "line up our military and other elements of our Government" so Acheson could tell his British counterpart "what sort of treaty we wanted."[22] No progress had been made, however, in resolving the pivotal question of Japan's long-term security. The Joint Chiefs' assessment of the minimum US security requirements in Japan—NSC 49, which had declared a peace treaty "premature"—had been submitted in June, but the State Department had not yet responded. FE had assigned action to the PPS, where Kennan and Davies had been studying the issue.[23]

On 30 September, Kennan submitted a formal PPS paper that was sent to the NSC as the State Department's official response to the Joint Chiefs' paper. In this paper, which was designated NSC 49/1, Kennan agreed with the military that Washington's goal should be that of denying Japan to the Soviets and maintaining its orientation toward the West. He disagreed, however, with the JCS argument that, because neither of these conditions was then ensured, a peace treaty was premature. Kennan argued that denying Japan to the Soviets was a problem of fighting "not overt attack and invasion, but concealed aggression" in the form of domestic subversion. This required the development of "indigenous resistance" to Communism, which in Kennan's view could be achieved only by strengthening Japan politically and economically and making it self-sufficient (in accordance with the original formula for containment). This was unlikely to happen as long as the Japanese were subject to the occupation. Indeed, indefinite retention of the US presence risked alienating the Japanese from, rather than endearing them to, the West. In any case, Kennan observed, it was simply not possible for the United States ever to be completely assured of Japan's "western orientation," as the Joint Chiefs had recommended. Kennan saw all these as compelling arguments for early conclusion of a peace settlement.[24]

On the fundamental question of military forces in Japan, Kennan refuted the JCS claim that a post-treaty US military presence would be a stabilizing force. On the contrary, he argued, "the continued dispersal of American forces in many Japanese cities and towns would constitute an irritating and not a stabilizing influence on the Japanese population." He concurred, however, in the Joint Chiefs' recommendation that preparations be made for limited Japanese rearmament. Indeed, the State Department "has ever since the issuance of NSC 13 persistently pressed for an expansion and strengthening of the Japanese police establishment." Webb followed up on this report to the NSC by asking the Defense Department yet again to reexamine the situation and provide an up-to-date assessment of Washington's security requirements for a peace treaty. The State Department, meanwhile, accelerated the drafting of a treaty so that it might be ready for Bevin and his Commonwealth colleagues by the end of the year. Kennan and Davies were actively involved in the drafting process.[25]

The Defense Department, however, continued to drag its heels and even to block progress toward a peace treaty. Johnson delayed his response to Webb's latest request for nearly two months while he and Tracy Voorhees—Draper's successor as undersecretary of the army—lobbied against an early peace settlement. Acheson later described Voorhees as "infinitely resourceful in discovering obstacles, legal and military, to what the State Department regarded as a just and practical course."[26] When Johnson finally responded in late December to the State Department's request, he forwarded to Acheson a new memorandum by the Joint Chiefs that essentially restated the position the military had taken in June. According to the JCS, the "minimum military requirements" of the United States in conjunction with any peace treaty included exclusive US military access to Japan, strategic control of most of the Ryukyus, naval and other facilities at Okinawa and Yokosuka, and "Army and Air Force bases generally as at present" on Japan's main islands. In addition, the Joint Chiefs stated that a peace treaty could not be considered acceptable unless both the Soviet Union and Communist China were signatories. Given these requirements, which the Joint Chiefs acknowledged were "probably mutually exclusive," they opted to "reaffirm their previous view that negotiations now, leading toward a peace treaty with Japan, are still premature."[27]

A meeting on Christmas Eve between Acheson and General Omar Bradley, the chairman of the JCS, confirmed that the State and Defense Departments were hopelessly deadlocked. Acheson told Bradley it was a "masterpiece of understatement" for the Joint Chiefs to conclude that the requirement for Soviet and Communist Chinese concurrence on a peace treaty made plans for one premature. In the end, the secretary of state was forced to concede that a draft peace treaty would not be ready for Bevin and the Commonwealth any time soon. Acheson so notified the British ambassador in Washington that same day.[28]

This stalemate essentially persisted through the first half of 1950. Acheson made several efforts during this period to break the impasse and hasten negotiations for a peace treaty. In preparation for yet another meeting with Bevin and French Foreign Minister Robert Schuman in May, the secretary of state in late April again confronted Johnson and Bradley, castigating them for their complacency. He told them that "the choice with which the United States was faced was not a choice between the situation we now have and an alternative, but rather a choice between a deteriorating situation and an alternative. The situation in

Japan was not stationary. . . . There were increasing signs that the Japanese wished to regain their freedom from the controls of the military occupation. . . . Therefore, it does not solve the political problem simply to decide to do nothing. . . . The lack of a peace treaty would be acceptable if the present situation could be maintained indefinitely, but this simply was not the case. . . . The Secretary said that the position that a peace treaty is premature is not adequate to meet his needs."[29] This meeting, according to Acheson, "shook the Chiefs up" but produced little more than an agreement that the two departments would study the issue anew.[30]

Shortly thereafter, however, the secretary took a dramatic step that shook up not only the JCS but the entire process, and helped to facilitate a breakthrough. Acheson, as he later wrote, had been consulting with Rusk and Butterworth about who might be assigned responsibility for "writing a paper asking for presidential authority to prepare a Japanese peace treaty and, if it was given, to negotiate it. We all agreed that John Foster Dulles was the man." Dulles, a veteran diplomat and one of the Republican Party's leading spokesmen on foreign affairs, had been brought into the State Department in early April in an attempt to deflect Republican criticism of Truman's foreign policy, particularly in East Asia. Acheson calculated that Dulles, in that capacity, could handle the ambitious task of brokering a peace treaty both in Washington and among the Allies. On 18 May, Dulles was appointed a special adviser to Acheson on the Japanese peace treaty issue. In early June, Dulles and Johnson traveled separately to Tokyo to survey the situation and to confront the question of Japan's security needs. Shortly thereafter, according to Acheson, the military's "filibuster" ended.[31]

Notwithstanding the importance of Dulles's appointment, this break in the impasse was largely due to Washington's receipt—at long last—of MacArthur's definitive views on the subject of a Japanese peace treaty. The general's ambiguity and equivocation on the problem of Japan's long-term security had contributed to the stalemate between the State and Defense Departments. This was exacerbated by the infrequent access policymakers in Washington had to MacArthur, which produced only fragmentary and often conflicting reports of his thinking on post-treaty US security requirements in Japan. In early 1948, as already noted, MacArthur had told Kennan and Draper that he saw no need for a permanent US military presence in Japan as long as it was possible that the Soviet Union would acquiesce to, and respect the neutrality of, a completely demilitarized Japan. As of July 1949, the general still advocated such an approach, but only two months later he told Sebald that he had "completely changed his views regarding post-treaty controls for Japan." Because such a Soviet guarantee of nonaggression against Japan either was unlikely or could not be relied on, MacArthur told Sebald in September 1949 that "some arrangement must be made," preferably in a separate agreement outside the actual peace treaty, "to continue a protective military force in Japan for the indefinite future, such force to comprise United States troops." In April 1950, however, MacArthur apparently reversed himself again, telling Sebald that he had always opposed a US military presence in Japan after conclusion of a peace treaty, but that he had "agreed to keeping a small number of bases [there] under pressure from the Pentagon."[32]

MacArthur, in any case, had not involved himself in the debate between State and Defense over Japan policy. This began to change in early 1950, when the various players in Washington traveled to Tokyo to solicit the general's input and, hopefully, his support. What brought MacArthur off the fence, and essentially onto State's side, was his frustration with Defense's obstruction of a peace treaty, regardless of its terms. The general told Jessup, who visited Tokyo during a tour of East Asia in January 1950, that he was "outraged" at the Joint Chiefs' efforts to postpone a peace treaty and that he hoped Acheson would "take the matter up with the President and have the Joint Chiefs overruled."[33] A month later, shortly after hosting a delegation from the Joint Chiefs themselves, MacArthur told the visiting Butterworth that he believed he had successfully modified the Joint Chiefs' views, although they "should be given a little time so as not to lose face in the process of reversal." SCAP could not say the same about Voorhees, who had accompanied the Joint Chiefs to Tokyo. According to Butterworth's characterization of MacArthur's comments: "Mr. Voorhees would fanatically oppose any treaty in the immediate future. He felt that Mr. Voorhees entertained such exaggerated views about this matter that he would doubtless resign rather than be party to a peace treaty. He took this occasion to refer disparagingly to Mr. Voorhees."[34] MacArthur thus appears to have shared Acheson's personal assessment of the army undersecretary.

Finally, in mid-June 1950, Dulles's and Johnson's respective trips to Tokyo prompted MacArthur to confront the issue head-on and to issue two memoranda containing his personal views on the peace treaty and security issues. Claiming that the bureaucratic conflicts between the State and Defense Departments had "only recently come to my attention," SCAP declared that the JCS had raised objections to a peace treaty that were either invalid or surmountable: "My observation of passing events in Asia and understanding of Oriental psychology have long convinced me that it has been a fundamental error to do nothing pending assurance that we could accomplish all. . . . We should not allow ourselves to be deterred from moving invincibly forward along a course which we ourselves and the entire world recognize to be morally and legally right. We should proceed to call a peace conference at once."[35]

Echoing Kennan's observations the previous September in NSC 49/1, MacArthur claimed that it was more important for Japan to be denied to the Soviets than for it to be a military ally of the United States: "Such denial can best be assured through a firm political alignment resting upon the good will and faith of the Japanese people, with our access to military and naval bases and other available facilities adequate to meet the needs of our security services."[36] This, the general argued, was not inconsistent with the goal of eventual Japanese political neutrality. In the meantime—also reflecting Kennan's recommendations—the Japanese police force should be strengthened "to a size and character adequate for internal security."[37]

Two days after MacArthur sent the second of these memos, North Korea attacked the South across the 38th Parallel. This, combined with MacArthur's pronouncements, effectively closed the debate over the need for a continued US military presence in Japan and a long-term US commitment to Japanese security. From that moment, the question became one not of whether there should be such a presence and such a commitment, but instead what their nature and terms should be. Dulles immediately set to work preparing a draft peace treaty with Japan, based in part on the assumption that it would provide for US basing arrangements. For Kennan, this long overdue movement toward a treaty was gratifying, since he had recommended it a year earlier. But he was less comfortable with the idea of US bases in Japan, because he had been hoping that a long-term US military presence there would not be necessary.

The Limits of Southeast Asian Nationalism

Whereas Kennan had made Japan the centerpiece of his strategic framework for the Far East—and the linchpin of US policy there—he had adopted a dualistic and somewhat ambivalent approach to Southeast Asia. He nominally included maritime Southeast Asia—the Philippines in particular—within his defensive perimeter concept, but he was inconsistent (as he was with Japan) in his explanation of what US interests were at stake or at risk there, and in his advocacy of how to operationalize the US defense posture in the region. In contrast, Kennan judged as early as the end of 1947 that mainland Southeast Asia, and especially Indochina, had little if any strategic value to the United States. Accordingly, he advised the Truman administration to limit US involvement and commitments there, particularly in response to the dilemma Washington faced as France's efforts to retain its control over Indochina faltered. This would become Kennan's most tortuous experience with East Asia policy.

Southeast Asia was certainly among the least of his interests and concerns when he became PPS director. But as nationalism in the developing world became a growing force in the early years of the Cold War, and as the Communist takeover of China focused attention on where to "draw the line" in East Asia, Kennan was gradually drawn into a strategic assessment of US policy toward Southeast Asia. He quickly became aware of the fundamental postwar problem confronting the region: the conflict between the various European colonial powers' efforts to reassert their authority in the wake of the Japanese surrender, and the emerging belief among the native populations that the time was ripe for their independence. Davies himself had anticipated this problem during World War II, when his engagement with the European Allies in the war effort in Southeast Asia revealed the Allies' determination to reclaim their colonies from the Japanese. Davies had advised then that Washington avoid attaching itself to these European ambitions because "the historical dynamics of nationalism throughout Asia will sooner or later bring about the downfall of colonial imperialism."[38]

French Indochina was viewed as the most important country in this respect because of its strategic location and the importance of France as a US ally. In late 1945, after a brief joint occupation of the country by Chinese Nationalist and British troops, French military forces and civilian authorities began to restore their control there. In the northern part of the country, however, the Communist Viet Minh—led by Ho Chi Minh—had effectively filled the vacuum left by the Japanese, making it difficult for the French to reestablish more than nominal authority. Efforts to negotiate a peaceful coexistence between France and the Viet Minh failed, and by the end of 1946 the French were engaged in a full-scale war against the nationalist resistance in Indochina.[39]

As noted earlier, Kennan's initial views on the French war in Indochina were revealed during his tenure at the NWC, just before he became PPS director. On that occasion, he had discussed the Viet Minh in the context of the international Communist movement, speculating that Ho was probably closer to Beijing than to Moscow. He had also recommended then that the United States try to avoid getting deeply involved in Indochina, partly because it was unclear whether the Vietnamese were "fit to govern themselves."[40]

Kennan's skepticism about the capacity of the Vietnamese for self-government reflected more than just his fear that they would become puppets for the Soviet or Chinese Communists. His apparently dismissive attitude toward Southeast Asians in general revealed the most pronounced evidence of the racism that historians and other commentators have detected in Kennan's approach to the developing world.[41] The Eurocentric Kennan certainly had a tendency to generalize about the world's nonwhite peoples. On many occasions, he appeared fundamentally dubious about their native political capabilities. At a meeting with the secretary of the navy in January 1948, he said Asians were especially vulnerable to the "lies" on which Communist infiltration was based because "lies are more effective than the truth with the people of the area who are, for political purposes, emotionally volatile children."[42] Moreover, Kennan observed in a PPS paper a month later that American political values were not applicable to "Asiatic peoples." Those values and institutions "may be all right for us, with our highly developed political traditions running back into the centuries and with our peculiarly favorable geographic position; but they are simply not practical or helpful, today, for most of the people in Asia." Consequently, he said, "we should cease to talk about vague and—for the Far East—unreal objectives such as human rights, the raising of the living standards, and democratization."[43]

These attitudes were only reinforced by the impressions Kennan received during his first visit to East Asia in March 1948, when he toured parts of Japan, Okinawa, and the Philippines in conjunction with his mission to Tokyo to discuss occupation policy with MacArthur. Toward the end of his trip, Kennan wrote to Butterworth that he was thankful for the opportunity to see the region firsthand: "But it is instructive rather than gratifying to get a glimpse of this vast oriental world, so far from any hope of adjustment to the requirements of an orderly and humane situation, and to note the peculiarly cynical and grasping side of its own nature which Western civilization seems to present to these billions of oriental eyes, so curious, so observant, and so pathetically expectant."[44]

Kennan's ideas about Southeast Asia in particular were even more striking, especially in contrast to his occasional and relatively complimentary but nonetheless stereotypical characterizations of the cleverness of the Chinese and the industriousness of the Japanese. In a lecture at the NWC in October 1948, he interjected a climatic theory of political development that he acknowledged as crude but considered especially applicable to the region. In Southeast Asia, Kennan stated, "[You] come up against realities, which perhaps, we may not like to speak of it [sic] sometimes because it involves a certain international tactlessness, but which I think we have to face when we deal in strategic problems. Those are the realities of climate and its effect on human beings. I think we have to face the fact that it is only the temperate climates of this earth which have been able to produce a really vigorous hard-hitting civilization capable of developing the resources of the earth in a formidable way. . . . I think we may as well recognize that in most tropical areas of the earth there is no great likelihood of a vigorous civilization springing up within our time."[45] Kennan cited this theory in support of his argument that Indochina, like China itself, could be effectively ceded to the Communists because it would pose no threat to the United States for the foreseeable future.

It is perhaps disturbing that Kennan could have been so condescending toward the forces of nationalism in Southeast Asia, and thus so dismissive of the region's capacity for "civilization" and its relative importance in the world. Some of his strategic judgments almost certainly were shaded by his ethnocentric and racist views. Although these attitudes were typical of the old-school Eurocentric diplomats and policymakers who dominated the State Department at the time, Kennan may have been more cynical than most in his judgments about what areas and peoples of the world merited US attention—and in his frank recommendations about ignoring those that did not.

Kennan's evolving strategic perspective toward Southeast Asia was reflected more broadly in his approach to those peripheral parts of the world that were subject to the threat of Communist incursion. In PPS 13, the global survey he prepared in November 1947, he recommended that the best way for the United States to counter Soviet expansionism, given that it could not do so single-handedly worldwide, was by "strengthening local forces of resistance" and getting them to shoulder part of the burden. "Only if they show signs of failing," Kennan argued, "do we have to consider more direct action." For the time being, he was prepared to let the French carry the burden of "local resistance" to Communism in Indochina, observing that the task of "bringing some order out of the chaos and uncertainty" there "probably exceeds our capacity." Under such circumstances, he advised, Washington should make a careful study of the possibilities, and then do only "what we *can* conceivably do." Given these criteria and his earlier assessment of the situation in Indochina, Kennan probably would have excluded that country from those worthy of a US commitment.[46]

This view became more explicit in Kennan's thinking in 1948, when he began to formulate his view that the United States had no vital strategic interests on the Asian mainland—least of all in the marginal area of Southeast Asia. In February he foreshadowed his "defensive perimeter" strategy in PPS 23, another "Review of Current Trends" in US foreign policy, in which he stated that Washington was "greatly over-extended in our whole thinking about what we can accomplish, and should try to accomplish," in the Far East. It was a mistake, Kennan argued, to assume that the United States could solve all of Asia's problems, or should even try:

> It is urgently necessary that we recognize our own limitations as a moral and ideological force among the Asiatic peoples. . . . We need not deceive ourselves that we can afford today the luxury of altruism and world-benefaction. For these reasons, we must observe great restraint in our attitude toward the Far Eastern areas. . . . It is not only possible, but probable, that in the course of this process many peoples will fall, for varying periods, under the influence of Moscow. . . . All this, too, is probably unavoidable; and we could not hope to combat it without the diversion of a far greater portion of our national effort than our people would ever willingly concede to such a purpose. In the face of this situation . . .

we should stop putting ourselves in the position of being our brothers'
keeper and refrain from offering moral and ideological advice.[47]

Kennan again called for a "careful study" of which areas in the East Asian region
were absolutely vital to the United States, followed by concerted efforts to secure
only those.[48]

Within a month, Kennan had conducted a semblance of such a "careful study"
during his trip to Japan that included side trips to Okinawa and the Philippines
and produced his "strategic concept" memo for Marshall. The memo implicitly
addressed Southeast Asia at two levels. As already noted, one of its basic principles was that the United States "would not regard any mainland areas as vital to
us." Kennan made no exception for Indochina; indeed, he did not mention it at
all, indicating that he considered it expendable and perhaps even irrelevant.[49]

Kennan, however, addressed the Philippines at length. There, he said, the
United States had "the worst of all possible worlds" after granting the country its
independence in 1946 and signing a military basing agreement in 1947: military
bases that were large enough to annoy the Filipinos but not strong enough to ensure their security, and a military assistance program that was "being only half-
heartedly implemented." The fundamental problem, in Kennan's view, was that
the strategic rationale for the US presence was not at all clear: "As far as I can
learn, we have not made up our minds whether the islands constitute for us (a)
territory which, by virtue of our past commitments, we are morally obligated to
defend from invasion as we would our own; (b) territory which is important as
the location for advance or staging bases useful to US security but which is otherwise of no great military interest to us; or (c) territory which is of little or no
strategic importance to us and where our interests do not warrant the maintenance
of base facilities, but where we see ourselves committed by past political engage-
ments and moral considerations to maintain some show of military power."[50]
Kennan's own view was essentially (c). He judged that the only goal the United
States needed to pursue in the Philippines was keeping it out of hostile hands,
and he saw no motive for any real or potential US adversary to attempt to seize it.
Accordingly, framing the US choices as "going in with all four feet on a full-fledged
program of military assistance and base development," on the one hand, and
withdrawal of US forces but maintaining a small military assistance program, on
the other, he recommended the latter. The Philippines—like Japan—would thus
be excluded from the US security zone as long as it remained "entirely demilitarized
and that no other power made any effort to obtain strategic facilities" there. Kennan acknowledged that there would be diverging views in Washington on this
proposal, and he anticipated that the US Navy would resist it; but he thought
the current US military commanders with whom he had met in Manila would

agree with him.[51] In any event, Kennan appears never to have substantially followed up on his recommendations regarding the Philippines, probably because he recognized that the issues he had raised were largely the purview of military planners.

Nonetheless, the defensive perimeter concept became central to his approach to US policy in Southeast Asia. He was disinclined to support any substantive US involvement there—although he had vaguely conceded in his "strategic concept" memo that Washington would still "endeavor to influence events on the mainland of Asia in ways favorable to our security."[52] This presumably meant only that the United States, even in those areas that Kennan considered strategically unimportant, would work on the margins to encourage developments that were most compatible with US interests. Kennan, however, offered no definition that would have distinguished between what he deemed advisable as marginal efforts and actions that implied a greater commitment in the region than he was willing to support. This distinction became crucial when Kennan and the PPS were drawn into the State Department's deliberations on how best to respond to events in Indochina.

Davies and PPS 51

In June 1948, the State Department organized a conference in Bangkok to address the many questions confronting US policy in Southeast Asia. Representatives from all of the US diplomatic posts in the region attended, along with country and regional experts from the State Department. Davies, who attended on behalf of the PPS, also visited Indonesia, Singapore, Indochina, Hong Kong, and the Philippines.[53] Davies later recalled that he found a "seething situation" in the region—one he recognized from his experience in the China-Burma-India theater during World War II. That experience had brought him "smack up against the colonial problem" in Southeast Asia, which he recognized as the region's fundamental challenge. Now, in the wake of the Japanese surrender, the European colonial powers were "maneuvering clumsily, militarily and politically, to retain as much authority as they could." Local nationalist groups, however, were eager to seize the opportunity to push for independence—which Davies was inclined to support.[54]

Even before Davies returned from his trip, Kennan had decided that he wanted him to write a PPS paper addressing the major issues relating to Southeast Asia. By the first week of August, Davies had completed an initial draft memorandum that closely mirrored Kennan's own thinking. Southeast Asia, he argued, was of secondary strategic importance to the United States, and was characterized by chronic political instability. Only in Thailand and the Philippines, moreover, did there exist responsible and effective native leaders. The local Communist movements, Davies suggested, were more heavily influenced by Beijing than Moscow, although he believed the Soviets were beginning to focus increasing attention on the region. The bottom line for Davies, however, was that even Southeast Asia's non-Communist nationalists were anti-Western in varying degrees. "Anti-white sentiments" were "profound and widespread," posing a serious challenge to the European colonial powers that were attempting to turn back the clock. Davies's judgment—as in 1944—was that Washington should dissociate itself from the Europeans' efforts to do so, and instead encourage them to accommodate the forces of native nationalism.[55]

Davies's point of view was generally shared by the Southeast Asian experts in FE, many of whom were old friends and close colleagues. His suggestions, however, soon confronted the more entrenched and influential views of the department's Europeanists, who according to Davies were "not only in the majority but also in the senior positions." Unfortunately for Davies and his colleagues on the Southeast Asia desk, Butterworth—the director of FE—was among these, having served most of his career in Europe before being assigned to China in 1946. Butterworth, as Davies later recalled, was "very European-oriented" and saw Western Europe as "the center of everything." Predictably, the FE director shared the predilections of the department's Office of European Affairs (EUR), which generally resisted any policies that might antagonize or alienate the continental Allies. Since these Allies included the colonial powers in Southeast Asia, Butterworth and his fellow Europeanists were reluctant to support pressure on those countries to liquidate their colonies there.[56]

Under these circumstances, intradepartmental coordination of Davies's Southeast Asia paper dragged on for months. The draft was initially circulated within FE and EUR at the beginning of September 1948, and the record shows that changes from Butterworth and others were still in the process of being incorporated in mid-December. Much of this delay, however, appears to have been occasioned by unfolding developments in Southeast Asia itself, which made the region a moving target for analysts and policymakers. In the second half of 1948, Washington was especially preoccupied with events in Indonesia, where the Dutch government was trying futilely to reclaim its authority from the non-Communist nationalists who had declared an independent Republic of Indonesia after World War II.[57]

Kennan himself latched onto the Indonesian case after the Republican government successfully quashed a Communist revolt in October. In a 17 December note to Marshall, he surprisingly identified Indonesia as "the most crucial issue of the moment in our struggle with the Kremlin." Washington's response to the crisis there, Kennan believed, could seal the fate of the region "for decades to come." Because the Dutch had no hope of successfully reasserting their control, the only two alternatives he saw were "Republican sovereignty and chaos"—the latter of which would be "an open door to communism." Kennan thus recommended that Washington pressure the Dutch to reach a settlement with the Republic, which should then be granted US diplomatic recognition.[58]

Although previously inattentive to Indonesia, Kennan was willing to get Washington involved there diplomatically for several reasons, none of which he considered applicable in Indochina. First and foremost, Kennan had been impressed with the effectiveness of the Republican government of Sukarno and Mohammed Hatta—especially their success against the local Communist rebellion, which burnished their anti-Communist credentials. Kennan thus calculated that this was both a viable and a relatively attractive native nationalist leadership. The same could not be said about Ho Chi Minh. At the same time, Kennan almost certainly judged that the Dutch, for better or worse, were destined to fail in Indonesia, and that Washington could afford to put pressure on the Netherlands—whose alienation would be far less problematic than that of France, whose support was vital to the Western alliance. Finally, Kennan had decided to assign Indonesia a role in his defensive perimeter concept. In his note to Marshall, he said: "Indonesia is the anchor in that chain of islands stretching from Hokkaido to Sumatra which we should develop as a politico-economic counter-force to communism on the Asiatic land-mass and as base areas from which, in case of necessity, we could with our air and sea power dominate continental East Asia and South Asia."[59] Kennan had not initially addressed Indonesia within his proposed strategic concept, nor did the country ever achieve such a role in US strategic planning. In December 1948, however, it served his purpose—that of encouraging US support for Indonesia's Republican government—to characterize the country in this way.

Two days after Kennan wrote this note to Marshall, Dutch forces seized Jakarta and arrested much of the Republican leadership in a large-scale "police action." Addressing an NWC audience on 21 December, Kennan described the Dutch move as "profoundly ill-advised and unjustified," saying it had greatly complicated the challenge of establishing a "workable balance of power" in the region. The following day, Kennan and his PPS colleagues agreed that Washington should take a strong stand against the Dutch move, but that the PPS itself could do no more with the issue for the time being.[60]

Davies, however, worked to incorporate the developments in Indonesia into his Southeast Asia paper, which was ready for another round of intradepartmental review at the end of February 1949—by which time Acheson had taken over as secretary of state. Jessup, who was then assuming his role in East Asia policy, thought the paper at that stage to be "excellent."[61] Unfortunately for Davies, developments in the region again upset the schedule. This time it was in Indochina itself. On 8 March, the French government signed an agreement in Paris that restored former emperor Bao Dai as head of a newly unified Vietnamese state within the French colonial union. Paris subsequently delivered a formal request to Washington for economic assistance to the new government.[62]

Davies spent the rest of March again reworking his paper to include an assessment of the new situation in Indochina, and of Washington's options for responding to it. In the meantime, he continued to receive conflicting suggestions on how to characterize the Indonesia problem. On 29 March, at long last, the paper was "generally accepted" and ready for submission to Webb—but not before Kennan, who had spent much of March on a trip to Germany, made some minor alterations of his own to the paper's section on Indonesia.[63]

The final paper, designated PPS 51 ("United States Policy toward Southeast Asia"), was one of the longest papers the PPS produced during Kennan's tenure. It began with a lengthy analysis of the region as a whole, and of its relevance to the international balance of power, followed by an assessment of the situation in each of the individual countries, and finally by a comprehensive set of recommendations—again, both general and country-specific.[64] Given the duration and difficulty of the interdepartmental coordination process, PPS 51 shows signs of being drafted by committee, and of incorporating ideas that were not generated by Kennan and Davies themselves.

Southeast Asia, the paper argued, had been severely disrupted, both politically and economically, by the impact of World War II. The region's prewar role as a source of food and raw materials for the rest of the world needed to be revived, but its role as both a market and a source of revenue for the European colonial powers needed readjustment. "Nineteenth century imperialism [was] no longer a practicable system" in Southeast Asia, Davies observed. Long-term stability could come only through diversification of the regional economy. This process itself, however, would be complicated by the "extreme nationalist passions which now inflame much of the region."[65]

Davies argued that the "historical trend" in Southeast Asia was "away from colonialism and in the direction of nationalism." Colonial rule was becoming "unnatural" as the native peoples of Southeast Asia—like those in other parts of the world—irreversibly developed a political consciousness and a militant nationalism. Local nationalist leaders varied widely in substance, motives, and effectiveness, but their capacity for successful indigenous government appeared almost irrelevant: "The real issue would seem to be whether the colonial country is able and determined to make continued foreign rule an overall losing proposition for the metropolitan power. If it is, no rational justification can be advanced by the metropolitan power for continued imperial rule and the colonial country may be considered ready for independence, even though misgovernment eventuates."[66] The Communist powers, both Beijing and Moscow, were eager to capitalize on these conditions. The Soviet Union in particular, Davies stated, had recently identified the region as a primary target for infiltration.

Even though the region "possesses itself no important power potential," it was imperative, according to PPS 51, that the United States prevent Southeast Asia's resources and its trade and communications routes from falling under Communist control. Southeast Asia was "a vital segment on the line of containment" from Japan to India, a line that would be greatly weakened by a break in its center. This essentially invoked Kennan's defensive perimeter concept and specified where maritime Southeast Asia fit into that concept. But it should also be noted that PPS 51 mentioned "containment" primarily in terms of the threat of Soviet rather than Chinese influence; the US objective was "denial of Southeast Asia to the Kremlin."[67]

This would require an "effective counter-force" to Communism in Southeast Asia in the form of a constructive alliance between the local populations and the Atlantic community, with the burden falling on the countries involved rather than the United States. Unfortunately, the colonial period had produced an "essentially pathological relationship" between the Southeast Asians and the Europeans; moreover, the former largely identified the United States with the latter. "The heart of the problem," Davies argued, lay "within the Atlantic Community itself," and particularly with the French and the Dutch, who were pursuing policies in Southeast Asia that were counterproductive in virtually every respect and doomed to failure. Merely advising them to alter their ways and to reach settlements with the Indochinese and the Indonesians, respectively, would seem the appropriate solution if the two colonial powers were "of an acquiescent turn of mind in these matters," Davies stated. "This, however, is not the case." Pressure on Paris and The Hague was more likely to harden their positions, provoke domestic political problems in each country, and threaten the cohesion of the alliance itself—and thus Washington's agenda in Europe. It was thus important not to "ride roughshod over Dutch and French sensibilities."[68]

In its country-specific assessments, PPS 51 said the situation in Indochina was "in an advanced stage of deterioration." It had "simply not been in the realm of practicability" for the French to defeat the Viet Minh, and direct US aid to France was allowing Paris to squander its own resources in Indochina "on a mission which can be justified only in terms of Gallic mystique." Meanwhile, the Bao Dai regime was incapable of drawing nationalist support away from the Viet Minh. Only if France yielded its claim to sovereignty would "the false issue of French imperialism, which cements communists and non-communists in unity, be dissolved." In Indonesia, the Dutch had exhibited "neurotic symptoms of frustration, inferiority, and over-compensation" and had removed "the only Indonesian elements in whom we have confidence." The prevailing chaos there was "ideally suited to the Kremlin's design for capturing control."[69]

PPS 51 acknowledged that, even if sovereignty was transferred to the local nationalists in Southeast Asia, there was no guarantee that the indigenous governments would meet Washington's expectations and goals. Both "chaos in Indonesia and communism in Indochina" might be inevitable. "But the choice before us for the immediate future is not between hostile tumult and friendly stability. It is between two evils and our task is to estimate which is the lesser." It would not do to postpone the question, Davies argued, because the Soviets were already at work in the region, and Washington's image in the developing world was at stake: "We must with resolution and skill steer our way between Scylla and Charybdis, between exasperation and resignation, between the rocks of undue pressure and the whirlpool of letting events take their present course."[70] The paper advised that Washington pursue a multilateral approach, soliciting the support of the British in presenting the problem to the French and the Dutch "in candor, detail, and with great gravity." India, Pakistan, Australia, and the Philippines would subsequently be brought into a cooperative effort to find solutions. Ideally, these fellow Asian states would take the lead in public, with Washington and London offering "discreet support and guidance."[71]

PPS 51 also recommended that the United States "seek vigorously to develop the economic interdependence" between Southeast Asia, on the one hand, and Japan, Western Europe, and India, on the other—"with due recognition, however, of the legitimate aspirations" of the Southeast Asian countries for economic diversification. This idea probably was inserted into the paper during the interdepartmental review process, almost certainly by State's economists and Europeanists. Although it was a key element in the thinking of the economists who focused on the financial aspects of postwar reconstruction, the occupation of Japan, and Europe's colonial empires, at no point does it appear to have been a major factor in Kennan's or Davies's thinking about the Southeast Asian region or about Japan. As noted earlier, both men later indicated that it was not.[72]

Notwithstanding its cogent analysis of the situation, the central flaw in PPS 51 was its equivocation on the same issue on which Kennan had earlier been self-contradictory. Both Davies and Kennan had declared Southeast Asia to be marginal in strategic importance while at the same time stating that Washington should still do what it could to prevent a Communist takeover there. However, they failed to specify how far the United States should go in pursuit of that goal, especially if pushing the European colonial powers toward granting independence might have unacceptable consequences for the Atlantic alliance. Moreover, any deeper engagement was bound to involve Washington in Southeast Asia in ways that were incompatible with the idea that the United States could and should stay out of it.

This dilemma, however, was not yet manifest in early 1949, and it did not prevent PPS 51 from going forward. But it ultimately diluted the paper's potential impact. Kennan sent the paper to Acheson and Webb on 1 April, noting that it had been fully coordinated with all the relevant offices within the department. He recommended that, after its scheduled consideration at a meeting chaired by Webb, the paper be submitted to the NSC for the council's "information" and that appropriate sections of it be shared with the Economic Cooperation Administration and with the British government. PPS 51, however, "fell flat" in its first appearance at Webb's meeting on 6 April. Kennan's old friend Bohlen, then serving as counselor to the department and a staunch Europeanist, criticized the suggestion that the Indians, Pakistanis, Australians, and Filipinos be used in pressuring the French and the Dutch. Bohlen thought it important to deal directly with Paris and The Hague, at least at the outset. Butterworth said his subordinates in FE had earlier raised the same concern with Kennan and Davies. Nitze, another Europeanist who was then still working in the department's economic division, said he thought the paper did not sufficiently emphasize the many obstacles to creating effective indigenous governments in Southeast Asia. Following Nitze's lead, Butterworth used the opportunity to suggest a more gradualist approach than PPS 51 had recommended in advocating sovereignty in Indonesia. The PPS paper was put on hold pending consideration by Acheson himself.[73]

Davies's paper was destined to hang in the balance for another three months. It reached Acheson's office on 29 April, but the discussion on that occasion apparently failed to resolve the many questions about its contents and recommendations. Consequently, as Butterworth reported to Webb on 15 May, no diplomatic initiatives had been launched in line with PPS 51, and the relevant offices of the department continued to study the "comparative advantages" of the paper's various recommendations.[74] On 19 May, Kennan—no doubt frustrated with the various geographic offices' foot-dragging on the paper—resubmitted it to Acheson after incorporating some changes that had been raised in the 29 April meeting. He added the following comment: "Although I am afraid you may have gotten a contrary impression from the recent discussion of this subject in your office, this paper does contain concrete suggestions for action at this time with respect to Southeast Asia. . . . I recommend that you approve the paper as broad guidance to Departmental thinking on the subject and as a strategic concept from which tactical planning by the operational offices should flow."[75] On the day he received this message from Kennan, however, Acheson left Washington for a month-long trip to attend a Council of Foreign Ministers meeting in Paris.[76] PPS 51 would have to wait until his return.

Acheson ultimately approved the paper, and Kennan's recommendations, on 1 July 1949 (just as Jessup was assuming responsibility for the East Asia policy review). As Kennan had requested, the secretary instructed that PPS 51 be transmitted to the NSC for its "information," and that it be used within the department as a "strategic concept from which tactical planning" would flow. Acheson also authorized discussion of the paper's substance with British and French officials, as well as transmission of the text to all appropriate diplomatic posts overseas—but without the section containing the PPS's specific recommendations.[77]

Kennan and Davies, having already seen their recommendations alternately chiseled away and watered down by both EUR and FE, were by this time all but ready to shelve the paper. On 5 July, Kennan told Bohlen and Rusk that he and Davies would rather not have PPS 51 disseminated at all than have it sent out without its recommendations. Kennan added: "I leave it to you. This is no longer a planning responsibility. But if nothing at all is to be done with the paper, I wish a decision would be made to that effect and the paper filed as a record of the views of the Staff."[78]

In the end, Kennan and Davies won a Pyrrhic victory. On 11 July, PPS 51 received its final hearing in Acheson's office. Rusk told the secretary that the suggestion to disseminate it minus its recommendations section was due to a "confused understanding" of the results of the discussion of the paper at Webb's level; Rusk said he wished to send PPS 51 to the field in its entirety. Acheson concurred, but Bohlen added the suggestion that the paper be accompanied by a message to the respective diplomatic posts stating that its recommendations need not be acted on.[79] Thus, the paper was subsequently sent to the field with the following cover note: "The desirability of a clarification and synopsis of United States policy toward Southeast Asia, such as this report represents, constituting a strategic concept upon which tactical decisions will be based, will be well understood and is abundantly attested by the material contained in the report. It is expected that the matters presented in the report will at an early date be discussed by representatives of the United States and those of the United Kingdom and France. The report is, however, transmitted to you with the intention that for the present it will serve only as a source of information and not as the basis for any action on your part."[80]

Davies himself later lamented that the PPS 51 exercise had ended "rather mushily"—so mushily, in fact, that years later he could not remember the ultimate fate of the paper he had worked on for nearly a year. In the end, the Europeanists in the department who were unwilling to put pressure on France and the Netherlands had successfully diluted its impact. They had been assisted in part by some of the Southeast Asian hands, both within FE and at diplomatic posts in the region, whose parochial recommendations and predisposition to support local nationalism no doubt had hampered the paper's review process and helped to water down its results. In hindsight, Davies could say only that his recommendations in PPS 51 obviously were not followed.[81]

Yet this is not entirely accurate. Historian Robert Blum correctly observed that PPS 51 "contained no bold prescriptions for an American containment policy backed by large amounts of money, arms, technical assistance, or prestige" despite the "growing concern that something needed to be done to prevent the region from falling under communist control."[82] Nonetheless, several of the fundamental ideas expressed in PPS 51—if not its specific recommendations—were reflected in Washington's subsequent response to developments in Southeast Asia. Although historian Michael Schaller overstated the case in saying that PPS 51 "formed the basis of Asian containment doctrine for the next two decades," the paper's cogent analysis of the forces operating and the stakes in Southeast Asia provided the rationale for Washington's continued interest in and attention to the area.[83] Unfortunately for Kennan, however, the depth of US engagement in the region that was deemed worthwhile and advisable subsequently began to diverge from the principles of PPS 51—and from his personal thinking on Southeast Asia.

Kennan and the US Commitment to Indochina

As noted earlier, the final months of the bureaucratic process that ultimately produced PPS 51 coincided with the establishment of the Bao Dai regime and France's request for US aid to that regime. Washington thus came under growing pressure to clarify its position toward developments in Indochina. PPS 51 had recommended the adoption of a wait-and-see attitude. "Because we are powerless to bring about a constructive solution of the explosive Indochinese situation through unilateral action," the paper advised, Washington should hold off on any decision regarding Indochina pending the results of the paper's recommendation to multilateralize the issue.[84] This judgment was reaffirmed in mid-May—just before Acheson left for the Council of Foreign Ministers meeting in Paris—at a State Department meeting that included representatives from the Southeast Asia and European divisions, and Davies from the PPS. The SEA officers said the French agreement with Bao Dai was unlikely to attract genuine support from Vietnamese nationalists—and thus was unlikely to succeed—because it left Paris with decisive control over Vietnam's foreign affairs and military. The EUR officers, meanwhile, said there was "no chance whatsoever" that the French would make additional concessions, and that any attempt by the United States to pressure Paris would be counterproductive.[85]

In early June, in the "where to draw the line in Asia" memo cited earlier, Kennan included Indochina among those countries in which "the Communists will probably, notwithstanding all practicable efforts by us, emerge in control." A week later, he told a Pentagon audience that there was "no military line that you can draw in Southeast Asia that would mean very much today." Echoing PPS 51, Kennan argued that the main problem in the region was not a military but a political one that could be confronted only if the native non-Communists joined forces with the resident European powers against their common enemy of Communism. The greatest obstacle to this, however, was the residual colonial mind-set of France and the Netherlands—a mind-set which Kennan thought the local nationalists were bound to view as an even greater enemy than Communism.[86]

The memo that Davies had drafted, "Suggested Course of Action in East and South Asia," which Kennan delivered to Acheson and Jessup in early July, had made no mention of Indochina, suggesting that Kennan and Davies were increasingly inclined to write off that country. It did, however, suggest that Jessup tour the region to discuss "issues of mutual interest" with local leaders.[87] By the end of August, after he and the Consultants had completed their initial review of policy options in East Asia, Jessup included such a trip in his own set of preliminary recommendations to Acheson. He also included the suggestion that Washington issue "a public statement of policy along the lines of [PPS 51] espousing the cause of nationalism."[88]

Jessup's advocacy of the PPS approach to Southeast Asia, however, eventually led to results contrary to those Kennan and Davies had intended. Indeed, during the last quarter of 1949, under Jessup's influence, US policy toward Southeast Asia drifted decisively away from the direction Kennan considered advisable. Not surprisingly, this coincided with Kennan's growing frustration with Acheson's bureaucratic style and his gradual disengagement from the decision-making process. As already seen, Kennan in late September 1949 announced his plans to step down as PPS director at the end of the year.

In the meantime, Jessup and the Consultants took the initiative that ultimately led to the commitment of US economic and military aid to the French effort in Indochina. In late October, in preparation for a meeting with the president, Acheson met with Jessup and the Consultants to summarize the findings of their review of East Asian policy. At that point, the group was still maintaining an ambivalent, wait-and-see attitude toward Indochina. Truman, however, was keen on the idea of a tour of the East Asian region by Jessup—the trip that Kennan and Davies had suggested in July. Consequently, on 15 December Jessup began a three-month junket that included stops in Saigon and Hanoi, even though Indochina was not on the itinerary originally proposed by Kennan and Davies. Impressed by Bao Dai and by the arguments being made in support of economic aid to the region, Jessup returned to Washington in mid-March 1950 as a strong proponent of US assistance to the French-backed regime in Indochina.[89]

Acheson, meanwhile, had gradually come to support the same position for a variety of reasons, as other historians have outlined. These included the need for French support for Washington's agenda within the European alliance—especially the rearmament of Germany; the Indochinese war's severe financial drain on the French treasury, which was destabilizing the government in Paris; the escalating Republican charges that the Truman administration's East Asia policy was soft on Communism; the British government's inclination to recognize the Bao Dai regime; and the recognition of Ho Chi Minh's Democratic Republic of Vietnam by Moscow and Beijing in January 1950. On 7 February 1950, Washington recognized the French-backed governments in Vietnam, Cambodia, and Laos. By the middle of 1950—even before the outbreak of the Korean War—the United States had committed both economic and military aid to Indochina.[90]

Acheson's later justification for this decision is worth noting for its implicit criticism of the approach Kennan (and others) had advocated:

> Both during this period and after it our conduct was criticized as being a muddled hodgepodge, directed neither toward edging the French out of an effort to re-establish their colonial rule, which was beyond their power, nor helping them hard enough to accomplish it or, even better, to defeat Ho and gracefully withdraw. The description is accurate enough. The criticism, however, fails to recognize the limits on the extent to which one may successfully coerce an ally. . . . So while we may have tried to muddle through and were certainly not successful, I could not think then or later of a better course. One can suggest, perhaps, doing nothing. That might have had merit, but as an attitude for the leader of a great alliance toward an important ally, indeed one essential to a critical endeavor, it had its demerits, too.[91]

Needless to say, Kennan viewed these developments with dismay, having concluded that the United States could do little more in Indochina to rescue the country from Communism than it had been able to do in China. He told another Pentagon conference in mid-September 1949 that Southeast Asia was then under the shadow of engulfment by Communism: "There appears to be, as of today, no force which would withstand that power except the fanatical and childish passion of native nationalism. Even this is not a certainty; but it looks like the best bet."[92]

Kennan clearly had little faith in the Southeast Asians' ability to save themselves, and he saw no vital US interest that merited intervention to save them. In this respect, he viewed most of the anti-Communists in the region much as he viewed Chiang Kai-shek's Nationalist Chinese. Regarding a US role, Kennan said "the means at the disposal of this Government for influencing the outcome are far fewer and less significant than many people imagine."[93] Kennan thus believed that in Indochina, as in China, Washington should simply acknowledge that the situation was beyond its power to save.

Kennan reiterated and attempted to rationalize this view in a briefing paper he prepared for Acheson in January 1950 for an appearance before the Senate Foreign Relations Committee. What the French were doing in Indochina, Kennan argued, was "too little and too late"; at the same time, pressuring them to do more would only "get their backs up" and cause problems in Europe. As for the Southeast Asians themselves, Kennan stated that Washington should try "to help [only] people who are seriously trying to help themselves." The people of Southeast Asia, he bluntly judged, were lacking in that regard because of a combination of "immaturity and corruption" in their politics and a variety of "deep seated demographic and social problems." This made it unlikely that any outside power could help. "We must realize," he wrote, "that we cannot metamorphize [sic] life" and that the challenge instead was to identify those areas "where our help really can serve useful and constructive purpose[s]" while "combatting the foolish and dangerous assumption" that Washington "can and should take upon itself basic responsibilities which [the] peoples of [the] area must bear for meeting their own problems."[94] Southeast Asia, Kennan observed, may or may not fall into Communist hands; the point was that "no one in this country can guarantee anything." If Indochina did fall, it would be a "definite deterioration" in world affairs. But "it would not necessarily be fatal or irreparable, from our standpoint, and no cause either for despair or lack of self-confidence on our part."[95] In short, Indochina ultimately was expendable, as Kennan thought of China.

Kennan mustered what other arguments he could against a US commitment to Indochina. To that end, he retreated from his earlier assumption that the Chinese Communists were the real threat in Southeast Asia. There was no evidence, he said, that Beijing was planning to move into the area militarily—a threat that many observers were citing as reason enough for US military involvement there. Kennan, moreover, thought it unlikely that the Chinese would do so. A few months later, he repeated the idea that there were "no really reliable elements with which we can really work" in Southeast Asia to resist Communism. Most importantly, he observed, the Soviet Union probably would like nothing more than to see the United States "tangled up" in a war in Vietnam; Washington should thus avoid a commitment in Southeast Asia if only to deprive Moscow of that pleasure.[96]

Korea: Before the Invasion

As with Indochina, Kennan in June 1949 included South Korea among those countries over which "the Communists will probably, notwithstanding all practicable efforts by us, emerge in control."[97] By all indications he was prepared to let this happen, having concluded that the mainland of East Asia was strategically expendable to the United States, and making no exception for the Korean peninsula.

In his memoirs, Kennan wrote that he was never involved in any official decisions involving Korea prior to the North Korean attack in June 1950. Most of those decisions were made within the military establishment, he claimed, and to the extent that the State Department was consulted, "the resulting deliberations were not ones in which I had been asked to participate."[98] This actually was not correct. Shortly after he became PPS director in 1947, Kennan not only was consulted but also deliberately inserted himself into the policy debate at the time over what was to be done about South Korea. After the Japanese surrender in 1945, the Korean peninsula had been divided into Soviet and US zones of occupation. For the next two years, plans for reunifying and granting independence to Korea were repeatedly stymied by procedural and tactical disagreements between Moscow and Washington. In the interim, the two occupying powers set up their own de facto governments in North and South Korea, respectively. In September 1947, Washington announced that it was referring the Korean matter to the United Nations; Moscow immediately responded by proposing the joint withdrawal of occupation forces.

The State Department, meanwhile, undertook a thorough reexamination of US interests in Korea in an effort to determine how much energy and resources should be devoted to maintaining a US commitment there. On 15 September, State asked the JCS to provide an assessment of the strategic value of the military occupation of South Korea. Forrestal subsequently forwarded the Joint Chiefs' judgment that the United States, for several reasons, had "little strategic interest in maintaining the present troops and bases in Korea." If war broke out in East Asia, the JCS stated, the US occupation force in Korea would actually be a "military liability." Its withdrawal to Japan or elsewhere in the region, on the other hand, would strengthen the US defensive posture where it was more appropriate to do so, while at the same time reducing unnecessary expenses. As far as the Joint Chiefs were concerned, the sooner the US military presence was removed from Korea the better, lest the deteriorating political and economic situation on the peninsula either trap US forces in undesirable circumstances or exaggerate the loss of US "military prestige" that a withdrawal was likely to entail.[99]

Even before State had received the Joint Chiefs' assessment, Kennan went on record with his own views on the subject. After reading a report from the State Department's political adviser in Seoul, Kennan sent a memorandum to Butterworth in which he intended to "make clear . . . the position of the Planning Staff with regard to policy in Korea"—even though Kennan acknowledged that the issue appeared to be largely an operational military one. The PPS director reported that the staff's own discussions with military representatives had already indicated that Korea was not deemed militarily essential. Accordingly, Kennan argued that "our policy should be to cut our losses and get out of there as gracefully but promptly as possible."[100]

Kennan's view was far from unique within the State Department. At a 29 September meeting that was chaired by Marshall and attended by Lovett, Butterworth, Kennan, Rusk, and Allison, it was quickly agreed that the US position in Korea was "untenable." The group's only concern was that it would be difficult to "scuttle and run" without damaging US prestige. It would at least be necessary to seek a way out that involved a "minimum of bad effects." Because the Soviet proposal for joint withdrawal might offer such a vehicle, it was decided that Washington should tentatively support the idea in the UN. Kennan concurred in this decision, adding only that Washington should not commit itself too firmly to any one course of action. The goal, he said, should be "to get the best bargain we can but not to tie our own hands unnecessarily."[101]

Kennan subsequently used numerous opportunities to reiterate his belief that Korea was strategically expendable. In PPS 13, "Resume of World Situation," which he prepared in November 1947, he declared that Korea was a lost cause: "There is no longer any real hope of a genuinely peaceful and free democratic development in that country. Its political life is bound to be dominated by political immaturity, intolerance, and violence. Where such conditions prevail, the communists are in their element. Therefore, we cannot count on native Korean forces to help us hold the line against Soviet expansion. Since the territory is not of decisive strategic importance to us, our main task is to extricate ourselves without too great a loss of prestige."[102] Similarly, Kennan told a conference hosted by the navy secretary in January 1948 that the United States should "get out of Korea as gracefully as possible unless we determined that the southern half is of sufficient strategic importance to retain," which he doubted. In effect, Kennan concluded—at least at the time—that Korea was not one of those areas where his doctrine of containment was applicable. Instead, he placed Korea—unlike Japan, which he judged to be of sufficient strategic value that the United States was required to take action to prevent it from falling into Soviet hands—in the same category he had placed China. Neither of these two mainland countries, he argued, merited the commitment of US resources that would have been required to defend them against Soviet domination.[103]

Kennan incorporated this idea, specifically with regard to Korea, into his "strategic concept" proposal to Marshall in March 1948. In recommending that Washington adopt a strategic posture in East Asia that relied exclusively on off-shore island bases centered on Okinawa, Kennan said the United States should "not regard any mainland areas as vital to us." Korea, accordingly, should be evacuated as soon as possible. The US presence there, he argued, was predicated on an international mandate that had proved "unrealistic" and was "soon to be swept away by the march of events in that area." As far as Korea's self-defense was concerned, Kennan was prepared to recommend that, in conjunction with the US withdrawal, the US military commander in Korea be allowed to "go as far as he likes" toward "raising, training, and equipping a Korean constabulary." Kennan, however, does not appear to have been particularly concerned about the inherent capability of any such constabulary. His primary goal was the withdrawal of US troops; if the training of a local military force was seen as a prerequisite, Kennan was willing to give lip service to the idea.[104]

On 2 April 1948, the NSC approved a new policy toward Korea that was essentially consistent with Kennan's views. NSC 8, which was approved by Truman on 8 April, advised that US forces be withdrawn from Korea as soon as possible, and set 31 December 1948 as the target date. In order to achieve the "minimum of bad effects," Washington would also expedite the establishment in South Korea of both an indigenous government and an indigenous army capable of protecting the country against anything short of "an overt act of aggression by north Korean or other forces." Ironically—given the ultimate fate of this policy—the NSC paper also advised that Washington "should not become so irrevocably involved in the Korean situation that any action by any faction in Korea or by any other power in Korea could be considered a *casus belli* for the U.S."[105]

Many of Kennan's colleagues within the State Department—particularly Butterworth and Allison—later began to reconsider the advisability of a precipitous US withdrawal from Korea. The political situation there, instead of stabilizing, had grown increasingly volatile and polarized. After conservative leader Syngman Rhee's supporters swept the legislative elections in the South, Rhee became president of the Republic of Korea in August 1948, but his government was tenuous from the start. In September, the regime in the North declared the establishment of the Democratic People's Republic of Korea. Some officials at State were also concerned that a US withdrawal from Korea would increase Japan's vulnerability to Communist advances. Butterworth responded to these developments by suggesting that Washington postpone its withdrawal while the NSC conducted a review of US policy toward Korea. Marshall eventually agreed, and in January

1949—just before Acheson succeeded him—the State Department formally asked Forrestal for an urgent reappraisal of the situation in Korea.[106]

In March the NSC produced a revised Korea policy, NSC 8/2, which essentially reaffirmed Washington's determination to withdraw US occupation forces from South Korea, but moved the deadline back to 30 June 1949. The NSC paper admitted that this would leave the South potentially vulnerable to a Soviet-inspired attack from the North, but argued that "this risk will [prevail] equally at any time in the foreseeable future" and would not be appreciably diminished by "the mere further temporary postponement of withdrawal." The best way for Washington to reduce that risk, the paper argued, would be to "make it unmistakably clear" that the US withdrawal "in no way constitutes a lessening of US support" for the South Korean regime. This would be accomplished through a well-publicized program of political, economic, and military assistance to the Rhee government.[107]

Acheson accepted this assessment, which was essentially that of the Joint Chiefs, and approved NSC 8/2. However, he added a statement for the record: "In approving this paper in its present form, I wish to emphasize the view, which is held by the Department of State, that the success of the policy set forth therein may well be dependent upon the adequacy of the transfer of military equipment and supplies provided for . . . in furnishing the Korean Government with effective security forces. . . . It is our understanding that this transfer is well on its way to completion and . . . will be adequate to meet the foregoing desideratum."[108]

Kennan shared this view—that success in Korea depended on the veracity of the Joint Chiefs' claim that the South Koreans could be defended without resident US ground troops. He would later blame US military officers for convincing him that this was true. A "very high Air Force officer," Kennan later wrote, had told him during his trip to Japan in early 1948 that the US Air Force could, through its strategic bombing capability based at Okinawa, control "anything that went on in the way of military operations on the Korean peninsula." Subsequently, Kennan said, he and his State colleagues were told by Pentagon officers that South Korea's troops were "so well armed and trained that they were clearly superior" to the North's. These "rosy assurances" from the US military, Kennan claimed, prevented him and his colleagues from recognizing Korea as a possible theater of action when, in the early summer of 1950, they received reports that the Soviet Union was planning a military adventure somewhere. "I have always reproached myself," Kennan insisted in hindsight, for accepting the Pentagon's assessment of the South Korean military, when in fact "the reason they fared so badly at the outset was that we had not trained or equipped them very well."[109]

In any case, US policy toward Korea remained substantially unchanged between NSC 8/2 of March 1949 and the outbreak of war in June 1950. The withdrawal of US forces was completed in 1949, and Washington's military and economic assistance to Seoul became institutionalized. Kennan gave lip service to this approach when he appeared, on Acheson's behalf, before a House committee reviewing the Korean aid program in June 1949.[110] Kennan personally supported the idea of "political and economic" aid to Korea merely as a means of placating those who had reservations about the withdrawal of US military forces. During this period, however, he did not substantially alter his judgment that South Korea was strategically expendable.

Much has been written about the implicit statement of policy toward Korea that was contained within Acheson's speech to the National Press Club in Washington on 12 January 1950, in which he outlined the US "defensive perimeter" in the Far East—echoing Kennan's formulation of almost two years earlier. This perimeter, Acheson explained, followed the chain of offshore islands running from the Aleutians to Japan, through the Ryukyus, and on to the Philippines. Then he added: "So far as the military security of other areas in the Pacific is concerned, it must be clear that no person can guarantee these areas against military attack. . . . Should such an attack occur—one hesitates to say where such an armed attack could come from—the initial reliance must be on the people attacked to resist it and then upon the commitments of the entire civilized world under the Charter of the United Nations which so far has not proved a weak reed to lean on by any people who are determined to protect their independence against outside aggression."[111]

After the outbreak of the Korean War, critics of the administration's foreign policy said Acheson's speech had "given the green light" to the North's invasion by not explicitly including South Korea in Washington's defensive sphere. Acheson dismissed this argument as "specious, for Australia and New Zealand were not included either, and the first of all our mutual defense agreements was made with Korea." He also insisted that his reference to the UN Charter was intended as a warning to potential aggressors, which was nonetheless disregarded.[112] Certainly the North Koreans or Russians or Chinese might have taken Acheson's speech as a sign that the United States would be disinclined to intervene militarily in the event of an invasion of South Korea. However, this line of argument assumes that the absence of a "green light" from the West was all that was holding back an invasion.

In any event, Acheson's speech contained nothing substantially new. As noted earlier, the defensive perimeter concept had become a de facto basis for US planning in the region even though it had never been explicitly endorsed as a policy. As for Korea, Kennan had specifically excluded it from the US defensive perimeter in his original proposal, and the withdrawal of US military forces in 1949 had already suggested that Washington was not particularly interested in providing a military guarantee of South Korea's security. Thus, Acheson's "defensive perimeter" was neither original to him nor did it depart significantly from existing policy.[113]

Kennan himself was wholly ambivalent about Acheson's speech, partly because the speech coincided with Kennan's growing alienation from Acheson's decision making within the State Department. When he received a draft of the speech for review, he "found it dull and sanctimonious" and generated a draft of his own that echoed several elements of his long-standing cynicism about US policy in East Asia and his insistence that Washington minimize its engagement there. Historically, Kennan wrote, the United States had paid little attention to the region, and rightfully so, because of its limited strategic importance, xenophobia, and despotic regimes. World War II and the virus of Communism had changed things, but not in ways that created US interests—or a rationale for US intervention— where they did not previously exist. In particular, the political changes that had occurred had not "altered military realities in our disfavor," and thus many of the changes to US policy in the region that were being advocated appeared "either to involve an unsound engagement of our military power or to rest on a false concept of the function and possibilities of US aid." Acheson ignored Kennan's input, which historian Bruce Cumings referred to as "a typically arcane collection of turn-of-the-century ideas" and which was indeed obsolete as a viable US policy statement in 1950.[114]

Regarding the final version of Acheson's speech, Kennan wrote a decade later that he was "always puzzled at the beating" Acheson took over it. The speech, he claimed, no doubt reflected views prevalent within the Pentagon. Kennan's explication of its contents, however, was ambiguous and confusing:

> The language [Acheson] used was based, of course, on a misunderstanding. It involved, above all, a failure to distinguish between areas which we might find ourselves obliged to attempt to defend in the event of all-out war, for purely military reasons, and areas which, while not falling into this latter category, were ones in which we nevertheless would not be able to permit a provocative communist military aggression. . . . The whole idea, implicit in the interpretation given to Acheson's statement, that there was a portion of the world which we must defend at once even at the cost of major war and that the remainder of the world was so unimportant to us there could be no occurrence in it that would cause us to resort to arms: this interpretation represented a primitivization of thinking on this subject which was hardly worthy of those who entertained it.[115]

The distinction Kennan makes in the first half of this excerpt is not altogether clear. It is difficult to see how the United States could disallow military aggression in an area without implicitly or necessarily assuming an obligation to defend that area. Indeed, the latter is precisely what Washington subsequently opted to do in Korea in June 1950—with Kennan's encouragement, as will be seen.

Moreover, Kennan had argued elsewhere that there were in fact areas in the world that were "so unimportant" to the United States that Washington should resist a "resort to arms" to defend those areas from Communist aggression. He had effectively said this about China a year earlier, when he insisted that advocates of full-scale support for Chiang Kai-shek bore the burden of proving that two conditions had been met: that "there is sufficiently powerful national interest to justify our departure" from a long-standing policy of noninterference in other countries' affairs, and that "we have the means to conduct such intervention successfully and can afford the cost in terms of the national effort it involves." In Kennan's view, these conditions were not then applicable in China. The Nationalist regime was simply not worth fighting for, and a Communist takeover of China, although unfortunate and undesirable, would not significantly damage vital US strategic interests.[116]

Kennan said essentially the same thing about South Korea during his tenure as PPS director. He had urged a withdrawal of US occupation forces on the grounds that the country was not strategically important and that the local population was probably incapable of resisting Soviet influence. He had rationalized this approach, moreover, by giving lip service to the development of an indigenous army, even though he doubted it could save the country from "political immaturity, intolerance, and violence."[117] Kennan does not appear to have significantly altered this view at any time during 1949 or the first half of 1950. Until the North invaded, he apparently was prepared to abandon South Korea to its fate.

NSC 48: Benchmark of Kennan's Impact on East Asia Policy

On 30 December 1949, Truman approved the NSC paper designated NSC 48/2—"The Position of the United States with Respect to Asia"—which outlined Washington's strategic objectives in East and South Asia and recommended various policies designed to support those objectives. The NSC 48 series was the brainchild of Defense Secretary Johnson, who had clashed with Acheson on Asia policy within months of taking office. In June 1949, Johnson had inserted himself in Acheson's Asia policy review by formally requesting that the NSC prepare a comprehensive paper on the subject—a long-range alternative to what Johnson viewed as the State Department's "day-to-day, country-by-country approach." The State Department predictably reacted defensively, and the interagency wrangling over the text of the paper dragged on for six months. In the end, State won a victory of sorts. It successfully watered down or rejected most of the Pentagon's suggested changes to Asia policy, especially a proposal for expanding the US military commitment to the Nationalist regime on Taiwan. The resulting paper, however, was largely a restatement of existing policies and, as such, hardly seemed worth the pain and effort to the State participants in the process, who had denied the need for such a paper in the first place. More importantly, NSC 48 had a shelf life of only six months before the North Korean invasion transformed the context and the objectives of Washington's East Asia policy.[118]

Kennan was not involved in the deliberations over NSC 48. Indeed, he made a point of specifically dissociating both himself and the PPS from the paper. After receiving the Defense Department–inspired NSC draft for coordination, Kennan in early November sent a note to Rusk saying that the PPS was "reluctant to select specific parts of the paper for comment as to do so might lead to the inference that it agrees with the remainder." He added only the general comment that he thought the NSC draft greatly overemphasized military factors.[119] One month later, while Butterworth and FE were still haggling with Defense over the paper, Davies informed his FE counterparts that "Kennan takes the position with respect to the NSC Asia policy paper that the Policy Planning Staff neither approves nor disapproves the document."[120] As a result, NSC 48 was prepared and approved without any direct involvement by Kennan or members of his staff.

Despite—and even because of—Kennan's lack of personal involvement with the paper, and regardless of its short lifespan, NSC 48 serves as an extremely useful benchmark by which to measure Kennan's cumulative impact on East Asia policy as PPS director. The paper was approved at precisely the end of his tenure in that position, and it essentially summarized, at that point in time, the existing policies toward the Far East—many of which Kennan had earlier played a role in developing. Thus, even though he did not participate in the interagency deliberations that produced it, many elements of NSC 48 can be traced to Kennan's and Davies's influence.

First and foremost, NSC 48 established that Washington's overall and "immediate objective" in East Asia was "to contain and where feasible to reduce the power and influence of the USSR in Asia."[121] That this was taken for granted merely underscores the degree to which Kennan's original doctrine of containment of Soviet power and influence was the guiding principle behind US policy in East Asia, as elsewhere in the world. And the absence of any reference to containing Communist China also reflected Kennan's view that his doctrine applied only to the Soviet Union.

The country-specific sections of NSC 48 also reveal Kennan's influence to a surprising degree. The paper's characterization of the challenge facing US policy in China is based heavily on the analysis that Kennan and Davies had provided a year earlier in their comprehensive China paper, PPS 39, which later became NSC 34. Both papers (NSC 34 and NSC 48) said the foreseeable future of China would depend on both the Soviet Union's ability to control the Chinese Communist regime, and the latter's ability to extend its own domestic control over China. NSC 48's primary recommendations with regard to China simply reiterated those in NSC 34 (indeed, NSC 48 cited the earlier paper as its source): Washington should continue to recognize the KMT "until the situation is further clarified" and should in the meantime "exploit . . . any rifts between the Chinese Communists and the USSR and between the Stalinists and other elements in China."[122] Kennan, as already seen, had played a key role in crafting the substance and the language of both of these policies.

NSC 48's China policy proposals differed from Kennan's thinking in two respects. Whereas Kennan and Davies had argued during the fall of 1949 in favor of recognizing the Communist Chinese regime, NSC 48 recommended that Washington avoid doing so "until it is clearly in the United States['] interest." Secondly, the NSC opted to continue the tenuous and ambiguous policy of "attempting to deny" Taiwan to the Chinese Communists through only "diplomatic and economic means"—disregarding Kennan's extraordinary proposal the previous July that the United States should assert unilateral control over the island. In neither case was the NSC prepared to support a course of action as risky and politically unpalatable as those Kennan had suggested. Instead, NSC 48's treatment of the recognition and Taiwan issues underscores the fact that Kennan's influence on China policy had reached its limits by mid-1949.[123]

His profound influence on Japan policy, however, had not yet reached its limits. NSC 48's enunciation of US goals in Japan was a concise restatement of those Kennan had outlined in PPS 28 (later NSC 13), the document on which the "reverse course" in Japan was based. According to NSC 48, the "basic United States non-military objectives in Japan" remained "the promotion of democratic forces and economic stability before and after the peace settlement. To further this objective the United States must seek to reduce to a minimum occupation or post-occupation interference in the processes of the Japanese Government while at the same time providing protection for the basic achievements of the occupation and the advice and assistance that will enable the Japanese themselves to perpetuate these achievements."[124]

Indeed, the NSC's approval of NSC 48 explicitly reaffirmed Kennan's earlier paper as the basis for US policy in Japan. Because the question of a Japanese peace treaty was then under active review, NSC 48 itself stated that policy toward Japan would have to be reassessed after the treaty question was resolved.[125] This language, however, was approved by the NSC subject to "an understanding that nothing in [the relevant paragraph] changes the present policy toward Japan as contained in NSC 13/3 [the final version of Kennan's Japan policy paper] or prejudges the question of a possible Japanese peace treaty."[126]

Kennan's "strategic concept" for Japan was also incorporated into NSC 48. In language almost identical to that he had been using for nearly three years to describe Japan's strategic importance, NSC 48 stated: "In the power potential of Asia, Japan plays the most important part by reason of its industrious, aggressive population, providing a large pool of trained manpower, its integrated internal communications system with a demonstrated potential for an efficient merchant marine, its already developed industrial base and its strategic position."[127] More importantly, the NSC adopted as the US strategic posture in East Asia the defensive perimeter idea that Kennan had been among the first in Washington to suggest. According to NSC 48:

> From the military point of view, the United States must maintain a minimum position in Asia if a successful defense is to be achieved against future Soviet aggression. This minimum position is considered to consist of at least our present military position in the Asian offshore island chain, and in the event of war its denial to the Communists. The chain represents our first line of defense and in addition, our first line of offense from which we may seek to reduce the area of Communist control, using whatever means we can develop, without, however, using sizable United States armed forces. This first line of defense should include Japan, the Ryukyus, and the Philippines. This minimum position will permit control of the main lines of communication necessary to United States strategic development of the important sections of the Asian area.[128]

Accordingly, the NSC recommended that Washington proceed as Kennan had suggested nearly two years earlier: "The United States should make every effort to strengthen the over-all US position with respect to the Philippines, the Ryukyus, and Japan . . . [and] proceed apace with implementation of the policy set forth in regard to the Ryukyus in paragraph 5 of NSC 13/3 [Kennan's Japan policy paper]."[129]

NSC 48's mention of Korea is brief and contains no particular hint of Kennan's influence—but this is because he was part of the broad consensus at the time that saw South Korea as strategically marginal and advocated a minimal approach to its security. The paper says only that Washington should continue to provide political, economic, and military support to the South Korean regime in order to bolster its resistance to Communism and hopefully to facilitate peaceful reunification of the peninsula.[130] As already seen, this was a policy to which Kennan gave

lip service because he believed Korea was simply not worth a substantial investment of US resources.

Kennan's influence is again strongly present in NSC 48's sections on Southeast Asia. Indeed, much of the paper's discussion of the central dilemma facing
US policy there, and the recommended course of action, is lifted verbatim from
PPS 51—the Southeast Asia paper that Davies had drafted and Kennan had god-
fathered. The conflict between colonialism and native nationalism, the potential
implications of Soviet domination of the region, and the growing anti-Western
sentiment among the local populations—all these issues cited by NSC 48 are borrowed directly from its PPS forerunner.[131] Similarly, the NSC's recommendation
that Washington "use its influence" with the European colonial powers "to satisfy the fundamental demands of the nationalist movement" merely echoed the
Kennan-Davies proposals of early to mid 1949.[132]

As with Korea, dramatic events in 1950 redirected US policy toward Southeast Asia in ways other than those envisioned by NSC 48 or advised by Kennan.
Ironically, however, it was in these two areas—Korea and Southeast Asia—that
the subsequent divergence of US policy from the courses Kennan had recommended ultimately led to disastrous consequences.

KOREA

"A Labyrinth of Ignorance and Error and Conjecture"

Almost a decade after the Korean War, Kennan offered his own assessment of his involvement in US policy early in the conflict: "I believe that my own influence was important in the original decision to oppose by force of American arms the North Korean attack. I know it was important in causing us to stick with the show after the disaster on the Yalu. Nevertheless, I was never able to establish within the government my own interpretation of the causes and significance of the communist action in Korea."[1] In his memoirs, Kennan carried the last point further. Had his "interpretation" and advice been followed in the summer of 1950, he claimed, there "would have been no advance by our forces to the Yalu, no Chinese intervention, but distinctly better prospects for an early termination of the conflict. Against these consequences there will have to be weighed whatever advantages can be construed to have flowed from the bloody encounters of the remainder of the Korean War."[2]

Kennan's role during the summer of 1950 was primarily that of advising the Truman administration on Soviet intentions and actions with regard to the Korean peninsula. This involved him directly in two crucial decisions: Washington's initial determination to intervene militarily to repel the North Korean attack, and the subsequent decision several months later to extend the conflict back across the 38th Parallel into North Korea.

Kennan's personal involvement in these two decisions illuminates both the strengths and the weaknesses of his approach to East Asia—his prescience and perspicacity but also the flaws and inconsistencies in his judgment. The first decision, which he emphatically supported, appeared to negate the "defensive perimeter" concept Kennan had played a key role in formulating. By appearing to reverse his prior assessment that South Korea was not strategically important to the United States, it highlighted a dilemma he was never able to resolve about the relative strategic importance of US credibility and prestige.

On the other hand, if ever a policymaker had an opportunity to say "I told you so," it was Kennan after the extension of the war deep into North Korea—which he had vehemently warned against—prompted Chinese military intervention that sent US forces into a humiliating retreat. Kennan subsequently played a central role in lobbying hard against the risk of defeatism and against negotiating with the Soviet Union from a position of weakness. Finally, in the spring of 1951, it was Kennan—by then in private life—who was called on to make the initial overtures to the Soviets that eventually opened the door for a negotiated settlement to the war.

The significance of Kennan's involvement at each of these junctures is perhaps easy to overstate. He certainly was not the only person in Washington who insisted in June 1950 that US intervention against the North Koreans was necessary and appropriate, in July and August that crossing the 38th Parallel would be potentially dangerous, or in December that withdrawal would have been ignominious. Nor was his personal diplomacy in May 1951 necessarily the only channel for soliciting Moscow's support for cease-fire talks in Korea.

At the same time, Kennan's contributions on each of these occasions were not negligible. Because of his expertise in Soviet affairs, he was called on at each juncture to assess US policy options in Korea in terms of their potential impact on the Cold War balance of power. This he did insightfully—despite the fact that his judgments were not always embraced by the administration. When they were, he substantially contributed to the political rationale for many of the military and diplomatic decisions made regarding Korea. When they were not, as in the case of the 38th Parallel, the administration later realized that it might have avoided a major disaster if it had grasped and heeded Kennan's advice.

Kennan's prescience with regard to Korea must be weighed against the flaws in his approach to the problem. As noted in the previous chapter, he was not completely free of blame for helping, in the years before 1950, to create the situation in Korea that ultimately led to the North's invasion of the South. And as this chapter will show, his recommendations in Korea—as elsewhere in East Asia—were not always politically or diplomatically viable, even when they made good sense. Moreover, his fear of Communist intervention in Korea was misguided to the extent that he was so preoccupied with the Soviet threat that he never paid full attention to the Chinese side of the equation.

After the Invasion: Assessing Moscow's Role

Kennan, who stepped down as director of the Policy Planning Staff (PPS) on 1 January 1950 and had been serving since as counselor to the department, was scheduled to leave State for a sabbatical at the Institute for Advanced Study in Princeton, New Jersey, at the end of June. He spent the weekend of 24–25 June at his farm in southern Pennsylvania, where he had no telephone; it was only upon his return to Washington on the afternoon of Sunday the 25th that he learned North Korean forces had that day invaded the South. Kennan later complained that no one at the State Department had sought to notify him, attributing this in part to the nature of his relationship with Acheson. "I could not help but reflect," he wrote, "that General Marshall would have seen that this was done." In any case, upon his arrival in Washington, Kennan temporarily became acting director of the PPS again, since Nitze—who had replaced him as director of the PPS—had also been on vacation when the war broke out and was unable to return for several days.[3]

"The next two months," according to Gaddis, "were an extraordinary moment in Kennan's career. At no other point did he operate nearer to the top levels of government in a major crisis, or with greater freedom to provide advice." Some important decisions on the US response to the invasion had been made in Kennan's absence. Acheson, after learning of the North Korean action the previous night (Washington is a half day behind Seoul time), had notified Truman—who was spending the weekend at his home in Independence, Missouri—and authorized the US mission to the United Nations to request a meeting of the Security Council the following day. The Security Council met on Sunday afternoon and immediately approved a resolution, introduced by the United States, that condemned the North Korean attack and demanded its immediate reversal.[4]

Kennan later wrote that he "never approved of the involvement of the UN in the Korean affair, or understood the rationale for it." The United States, he argued, had accepted the Japanese surrender in Korea as well as the responsibilities of military occupation in the South: "The fact that we had withdrawn our own combat forces did not mean, in the continued absence of a Japanese peace treaty, that these responsibilities were terminated. We had a perfect right to intervene, on the basis of our position as occupying power, to assure the preservation of order in this territory."[5] There was no question, Kennan insisted, that such intervention was required: "It was clear to me from the start that we would have to react with all necessary force to repel this attack and to expel the North Korean forces from the southern half of the peninsula. I took this position unequivocally on that first day and in all the discussions that followed over the ensuing days and weeks."[6]

Both of these assertions appear inconsistent with the attitude Kennan had adopted toward Korea prior to the invasion. On the subject of UN involvement, he certainly had raised no objections in September 1947, when the State Department first referred the Korean problem to the Security Council. Moreover, his subsequent push for Washington to withdraw from the country and his explicit judgment that it was not strategically important to the United States certainly implied a belief that US protective responsibilities in Korea should have been terminated. As a result, it was not immediately clear why Kennan felt that it was "necessary" to come to the South's defense.

We will return to that issue. In any case, Kennan appears to have played only an indirect—although arguably still substantive—role in the key decisions that were made during the first week of the war. He was initially excluded from the inner circle of decision making, apparently by accident. Truman returned to Washington from Independence early in the evening of Sunday the 25th, having sent instructions that Acheson, Johnson, and their senior aides were to meet him for dinner and a conference at Blair House. As Kennan later recalled it:

> The Secretary had left word, I was told, that he specifically wished me to be included in the group to meet the President; but when the moment came for us to leave for Blair House, his secretary told me that somehow or other, by a process she did not understand, my name had been omitted from the list sent to the White House, and since the number of guests was limited there would be no place for me. This dinner had the effect of defining—by social invitation, so to speak—the group that would be responsibly engaged in the handling of the department's end of the decisions in the ensuing days. I found myself thus automatically relegated to the sidelines: attending the respective meetings in the Secretary's office, but not those that took place at the White House level.[7]

Acheson nevertheless asked Kennan to postpone his departure for Princeton, primarily so Kennan could advise him and other senior officials on the crucial Soviet aspect of developments in Korea.[8]

Kennan's first assignment in this regard came directly from the president. At that first Blair House meeting—during which Truman authorized the sending of military supplies to the South Korean army and emphasized that all US actions would be taken under UN auspices—the president requested a "survey of possible next moves by the Soviet Union."[9] This task was immediately assigned to Kennan. The following day, Monday the 26th, Kennan prepared a short memorandum outlining his view that the Soviet leadership was unlikely at that time to be planning additional military initiatives in areas other than Korea. Moscow's next move, he argued, would depend on the course of events in Korea and Washington's response to it. If future developments in Korea were "seriously damaging to western prestige," Kennan observed, this probably would "advance the hopes and plans" of Soviet leaders for adventurism elsewhere. In this regard, Kennan observed, there was "no question but that the area most immediately and dangerously affected" by the Korean invasion was Taiwan. Assuming, as Kennan did, that Taiwan was on the top of the Communists' wish list, a rapid collapse in South Korea might encourage the Communists—Soviet or Chinese—to move toward realization of "their Formosa project." Washington, on the other hand, probably could discourage or at least delay this by taking resolute action to oppose the Communist invasion of South Korea.[10]

In a meeting in Acheson's office that same day (Monday), Kennan reinforced the latter point by taking a firm position on the need for immediate US military intervention: "I stated it as my deep conviction that the US had no choice but to accept this challenge and to make it its purpose to see to it that South Korea was restored to the rule of the Republic of Korea. The question of what we should commit to this purpose was simply a question of what was required for the completion of the task."[11] When the "Blair House group" (again excluding Kennan) met again that night, it reached essentially the same conclusion. At this meeting, Truman approved a recommendation from Acheson, which was supported by the Defense Department, that the president authorize US air and naval forces to "offer the fullest possible support to the South Korean forces," which were falling back rapidly. Truman added that there was to be no US military action taken north of the 38th Parallel—"not yet." The president also ordered that the US Seventh Fleet, stationed in the Philippines, sail into the Taiwan Strait to prevent an attack on the island. In an indication of Kennan's indirect influence on this decision, the minutes of the meeting show that Rusk "pointed out that it was Mr. Kennan's estimate that Formosa would be the next likely spot for a Communist move." Finally, Truman authorized the introduction of a second resolution in the UN Security Council calling on all UN members to provide military aid to South Korea.[12]

During the earlier meeting in Acheson's office, Kennan had raised the question of what Washington should do if the Soviets became directly engaged against US forces in Korea. Webb returned the question to Kennan, asking him to draft a second memorandum, this one containing his "personal views" on the implications of a possible Soviet military involvement on the peninsula. Kennan did so on Tuesday the 27th, producing another paper that was immediately forwarded to Army Secretary Frank Pace for the military's comments. In this paper, Kennan observed that direct contact between US and Soviet military forces in Korea, because it could lead to general US-Soviet hostilities "with the most tremendous world-wide repercussions," would naturally require a complete reexamination of the US position in Korea. This might involve newer and enhanced obligations by the UN, and Truman would want to seek congressional approval before making any decision to widen the conflict.[13]

For the time being, Kennan suggested, US forces should be instructed to resist any Soviet efforts to interfere with the evacuation or protection of US citizens in Korea, and to immediately break off and report any engagement with Soviet military personnel. If, on the other hand, the Soviet Union deployed forces south of the 38th Parallel, Washington should immediately take the matter to the UN, stating publicly that the Soviets had transformed the conflict, thereby "threatening the peace of the world." Under such circumstances, Kennan thought the president should declare a state of national emergency.[14]

Later on that Tuesday, with no other senior State official available to do so, Kennan was called on to brief the NATO (North Atlantic Treaty Organization) ambassadors in Washington on the unfolding crisis. He noted in his diary that he was forced to improvise his remarks, having received no specific instructions or talking points. He focused the briefing on his assessment of Soviet motives on the Korean peninsula, but added the following: "I then said that in deciding to employ our own forces there we were not acting under any strong convictions about the strategic importance of the territory but rather in light of our analysis of the damage to world confidence and morale which would have been produced had we not so acted. I analyzed the probable consequences of a failure on our part to act, in their relation to Japan, to Formosa, to the Philippines, to Indochina, and to Europe. I told them we had no intention to do more than to restore the status quo ante and no intention to proceed to the conquest of northern Korea."[15] This is perhaps the most explicit revelation of the distinction in Kennan's thinking that allowed him to support US military intervention in Korea without compromising—in his mind—his adherence to the defensive perimeter concept. But his assurance to the NATO ambassadors that Washington did not seek more than the status quo ante would come back to haunt him.

Acheson told the president about Kennan's two memos—the Monday memo on "possible further danger points" and the Tuesday memo on the implications of Soviet military involvement in Korea—at a meeting of the National Security Council (NSC) on Wednesday the 28th. State and Defense, Acheson said, were working together on an assessment of possible Soviet moves, and he had given Defense a paper addressing "the care which would be taken to avoid action in Korea involving Soviet forces." Johnson responded that he had "no quarrel" with the latter paper but suggested that the department "change the phraseology" somewhat. Pace recommended that "the Top Secret character of the paper in question should be carefully guarded."[16]

Johnson's and Pace's comments reflected the friction that was beginning to emerge between the State Department and the Defense Department, and that would soon be a source of frustration to Kennan in particular. Johnson appears to have felt that Acheson and his State colleagues were making recommendations to the president regarding military actions in Korea without fully coordinating their suggestions with the Defense establishment. Johnson, in fact, telephoned Acheson on 29 June to request that Rusk and the other State Department officials who were working on the Korea problem be instructed to coordinate their decisions with General James Burns, Johnson's liaison officer with State.[17]

The Defense Department's mistrust of State soon began to hamper Kennan's contributions to the decision-making process. The two memos he had drafted on 26 and 27 June had rankled the Pentagon because they addressed issues of direct concern to the Defense Department but had been prepared overnight within the State Department and had become talking points for Acheson at the White House before the military had time to assess their contents. Kennan and his colleagues, however, were merely trying to respond quickly to the president's requirements. When the NSC consultants met on 29 June to "allocate overall responsibility for preparation of a paper" in response to Truman's request for a survey of possible next steps by the Soviets, Kennan voiced his understanding that the White House had wanted a "simple, informal review" of the situation. His "danger points" memo of 26 June had been such a paper, but a new version was required to account for developments since then and to incorporate views from the Defense Department. Kennan suggested that the new paper address two alternative scenarios: (1) that the Soviet Union had decided on a general war, or (2) that Moscow at present had no plans to provoke war. The NSC consultants subsequently agreed to have Kennan take the lead in drafting the paper, which would effectively supersede his two previous memos.[18]

Davies was one of the drafters of input to the new memo, and apparently the first to examine the potential Chinese Communist role in what was happening in Korea. Prompted by statements from Beijing that condemned the US decision to intervene and especially to deploy forces to the Taiwan Strait, Davies presumed that the Chinese statements were part of a Moscow-directed effort to "inflame the Asiatics" against the West, and that Beijing would "carry the torch for the rest of the Communist world in the Far East." Subsequent events and evidence would later show that Davies was misreading the situation, in terms of both the Soviet role and potential Chinese actions. He assessed that the Chinese Communist regime was "undoubtedly deterred from impetuous action" by its domestic preoccupations and presumably limited offensive capabilities. Korea, moreover, "being outside their sphere is in any event of slight interest to them." On the other hand, he allowed that China's next moves were hard to ascertain: "They may, although one can only guess at this stage, ally themselves militarily with the North Koreans in hostilities on the peninsula"; try to attack Taiwan, Hong Kong, or Burma; or even "join forces with the Vietminh."[19]

Although providing evidence that Chinese intervention in Korea was recognized as a possibility, Davies's memo shows that Washington was slow to focus on China because of its preoccupation with Moscow as the key player. Kennan momentarily picked up on the idea that the crisis in Korea might be generating "a great strain on Soviet satellite relationships" that Washington could exploit: on 30 June he suggested to Acheson a propaganda campaign aimed at characterizing the Chinese as Soviet puppets that were at risk of "sacrificing the blood and treasure of China for purposes which have nothing whatsoever to do with Chinese interests." Both Kennan and Davies, however, were constrained in their thinking by their belief that Beijing remained little more than a Soviet satellite, and that it had little strategic interest of its own in Korea.[20]

On Friday the 30th, Kennan completed an enlarged and revised memorandum entitled "Possible Further Danger Points" which, on 1 July, was submitted to the NSC and designated NSC 73.[21] Kennan argued in this paper that Moscow had launched the Korean invasion—which everyone in Washington assumed was the case—not in an attempt to start a general war or to force a showdown with the United States. Instead, the Soviets' purpose was strictly to gain strategic control over the Korean peninsula, probably for what Moscow considered defensive purposes. The Soviets, furthermore, expected their action to leave Washington two choices: either to commit US forces to a war of attrition on the Asian mainland or to acquiesce to Soviet control of Korea and accept the consequent loss of US prestige. Moscow, Kennan believed, was probably surprised that Washington had chosen the former, but had not changed its calculations as a result.[22] For the time being, he argued, the Soviet Union was unlikely to commit its forces directly in Korea, or to risk a general war by attacking anyplace else. Moscow, however, would probably encourage the Chinese and other Communist countries to take steps aimed at embarrassing the United States. Drawing on Davies's input, he cited Taiwan, Tibet, Hong Kong, and Indochina as potential Chinese targets, with Taiwan the most likely target. If Chinese troops entered the war in Korea, Kennan stated, "it is our assumption that we would not hesitate to oppose" them and that the United States would then have "adequate grounds" for direct attacks on Chinese territory—although such a development would also require a reassessment of US options. Regardless of where any Soviet surrogates (and he included China in this category) took action, Kennan concluded, "the testing of our firmness . . . may take every form known to Communist ingenuity."[23]

This view—that the Soviets were probably not plotting a general offensive—was received with skepticism throughout the administration. Kennan, however, was not alone in advocating it. His close friend and fellow Russia expert Charles Bohlen, who was at that time assigned to Paris but had temporarily returned to Washington at Acheson's request in the wake of the Korean invasion, shared Kennan's judgment that Moscow was not likely either to engage its own troops in Korea or to launch attacks elsewhere. According to Bohlen, however, Acheson and "most others in the State Department," along with the military establishment, interpreted the Korean invasion as "ushering in a new phase of Soviet foreign policy" aimed at expanding the Communist bloc. As Bohlen later wrote, "Kennan and I argued in vain against this thesis," which Truman accepted. Kennan attributed his and Bohlen's failure to carry the day to the "militarization of thinking" about the Cold War in official circles, which created an atmosphere in which "any discriminate estimate of Soviet intentions was unwelcome and unacceptable."[24]

The Defense Department appeared to have been particularly unwilling to accept NSC 73. Kennan later claimed this was because the military commanders were "so frightened by their failure to predict the initial invasion that they did not want to sign onto the prediction that no other attack was forthcoming elsewhere."[25] Whatever the reason, the Defense establishment proceeded to obstruct interagency coordination of NSC 73. On 11 July, Nitze (who was then again managing the PPS) and Jessup reported to Acheson that "the staff level" at the Defense Department had rewritten Kennan's paper, after which the Joint Chiefs of Staff (JCS) had rewritten it again without consulting State, which naturally had several problems with the military's version.[26] The same day, Kennan complained about this to Acheson. According to the minutes of the secretary's morning meeting: "Mr. Kennan said that [the JCS comments on his paper] did not address themselves to the substance of NSC 73 but rather just put in a lot of qualifying language which makes the paper seem asinine. He expressed himself as being very bitter over what the JCS had done to 'his' paper."[27] Acheson approved a suggestion by Kennan that Nitze inform his Defense Department counterparts that State was willing to discuss NSC 73 with Defense only if the military representatives were prepared to talk substance, rather than to "haggle over language."[28]

This approach apparently made for little progress. Two days later, Bohlen suggested that State stop "fooling around" with Defense on NSC 73, adding that "the JCS paper was meaningless and that we would just waste time trying to get an agreed position." Bohlen was eventually proved correct. Over the next six weeks, NSC 73 was repeatedly revised and reconsidered, and no interagency consensus was ever reached. At an NSC meeting on 24 August—the day before Kennan finally left the State Department for Princeton—the paper, now known as NSC 73/3, was effectively shelved. By that time, no one claimed sponsorship for it. Acheson described it to the council as "not good enough as a basis for firm decisions at this time," and Johnson "agreed that this was a hastily drawn paper." In the end, Kennan's paper was adopted, subject to a final group of JCS amendments, only for "continuing study"; it was to be used as a "working guide, with the understanding that final recommendations to the President regarding US actions in the event of any of the contingencies envisaged therein would be deferred until it is established that the event is certain to occur."[29] NSC 73 was never revived.

Kennan, having given up on NSC 73 weeks earlier, had persisted through other channels in pushing his assessment of Soviet actions and motives in Korea. On 8 August, he forwarded directly to Acheson a lengthy personal memo containing "a round-up of Communist intentions," based on the evidence to date—but still focused on Moscow as the central actor, and thus largely inattentive to the potential fault lines between Moscow, Pyongyang, and Beijing. Kennan began by reiterating the central judgment of NSC 73: that Moscow launched the Korean operation not to provoke a general war but simply to gain control of South Korea, and probably had not expected the United States to respond as it did. Subsequently, the Soviets had "no doubt been surprised and impressed" with the success of the North Korean forces, and probably looked forward to the possibility of a US/UN evacuation from the peninsula. This, Kennan believed, probably accounted for Moscow's resumption on 1 August of its seat on the UN Security Council, which the Soviets had been boycotting since January 1950 (after the UN refused to give Nationalist China's seat to the Communist regime on the mainland). Now, in early August, Moscow probably anticipated the opportunity to strike a UN settlement in Korea on the basis of a Communist victory.[30]

At the same time, Kennan observed, Soviet leaders were probably worried about the alternative possibility that US and UN forces would survive and launch a counteroffensive. Moscow was bound to be especially uncomfortable with the chance that the conflict on the peninsula might expand toward the Soviet border. As a result, Kennan speculated, the Soviets were probably preparing to commit "puppet Chinese forces from Manchuria" or even their own military units "to forestall any US advance beyond the 38th Parallel." In any case, Kennan emphasized, "when the tide of battle begins to change, the Kremlin will not wait for us to reach the 38th Parallel before taking action. When we begin to have military successes, that will be the time to watch out. Anything may then happen— entry of Soviet forces, entry of Chinese Communist forces, [a] new strike for UN settlement, or all three together."[31]

Kennan sounded the alarm in a second memo to Acheson a week later, after learning from a press release from the supreme commander of Allied powers (SCAP) that US planes on 12 August had bombed the North Korean port of Rashin, which was less than 20 miles from the Russian border. Kennan had simultaneously seen a newspaper report suggesting that Rashin was actually a Soviet submarine base and that the "official" reason for the bombing raid was to interdict Soviet supplies to North Korea even though there reportedly had been no such transfers through Rashin since the beginning of the war. In Kennan's view, these circumstances and MacArthur's subsequent imposition of press censorship on US military activities made it "entirely plain that the relationship of Rashin to the hostilities in South Korea was only a pretext for our bombing and that the real reason for it was the desire to injure the Soviet strategic position in the Far East."[32]

Given that Soviet leaders were "pathologically sensitive" to any foreign military activity in the area, Kennan warned that the bombing of Rashin "drastically heightens the importance and actuality" of his admonition to Acheson a week earlier about Moscow's probable response to any spread of the Korean conflict toward the Soviet border. Accordingly,

> [W]e must be prepared at any time for extreme Soviet reactions going considerably beyond, and therefore not fully in accordance with, the analysis I gave on August 8. In the light of this situation, it is entirely possible that a Soviet military re-entry into North Korea might occur at any time. . . . We also cannot exclude the possibility that this evidence, as it must appear to them, of a United States intent to damage their strategic interests under cover of the Korean war . . . will naturally affect their estimate of the possibility of avoiding major hostilities, and of the relative advantages of a Soviet initiation of such hostilities as opposed to a waiting policy based on the continued hope of avoiding them altogether.[33]

Webb brought Kennan's 8 and 14 August memos directly to Truman's attention on 17 August. The president's response was that "we would have to take whatever risks were necessary to destroy the points from which supplies were flowing." Kennan, disturbed that Truman had missed his point, subsequently asked Webb to inform the president, if the opportunity arose, that there was no firm evidence that supplies were flowing through Rashin.[34]

Subsequent events, of course, demonstrated that Kennan's fears about the bombing of Rashin were greatly exaggerated. The Soviets did not respond with their own forces to expand hostilities, in either Korea or anyplace else. Kennan subsequently blamed his miscall in part on the military, and on MacArthur in particular. The State Department, Kennan complained, was never able to get from the Defense Department or its intelligence units any conclusive information with regard to Rashin or on US military reconnaissance activities. "For anyone thus kept in the dark" about US actions that directly touched on Russian military sensitivities, Kennan complained, "it was obviously impossible to make any adequate assessment of Soviet intentions."[35]

Indeed, Kennan was by this time extremely frustrated with the decision-making process in Washington. Not surprisingly, he was especially upset that his voice was not being heard. Unable to acknowledge that much of his advice was misdirected, he naturally blamed the mind-set of his colleagues and superiors. From Kennan's perspective, his and Bohlen's expertise in Soviet affairs was being dismissed as too arcane and subjective and thus too risky to serve as the basis for crucial policy decisions. As he wrote in his diary in mid-July:

> Plainly, the government has moved into an area where there is a reluctance to recognize the finer distinctions of the psychology of our [Soviet] adversaries, for the reason that movement in this sphere of speculation is all too undependable, too relative, and too subtle to be comfortable or tolerable to people who feel themselves confronted with the grim responsibility of recommending decisions which may mean war or peace. In such times, it is safer and easier to cease the attempt to analyze the probabilities involved in your enemy's mental processes or calculate his weaknesses. It seems safer to give him the benefit of every doubt in matters of strength and to credit him indiscriminately with all aggressive designs, even when some of them are mutually contradictory. In these circumstances, I was inclined to wonder, and I think Chip was too, whether the day had not passed when the Government had use for the qualities of persons like ourselves.[36]

It was in this frame of mind that Kennan, before leaving the State Department at the end of August, composed a long memorandum for Acheson in which he outlined his concerns about East Asia policy and made several recommendations that he acknowledged were probably "too remote from general thinking in the Government to be of much practical use." In this memo Kennan appeared to revert to his prewar position on the strategic importance of Korea. Having insisted in late June on the need to expel the Communists from the South, he now judged that it was "beyond our capabilities to keep Korea permanently out of the Soviet orbit." Indeed, Kennan suggested, it was not essential to the United States that this be done: "We could even eventually tolerate for a certain period of time a Korea nominally independent but actually amenable to Soviet influence, provided this state of affairs were to be brought about gradually and not too conspicuously. . . . A period of Russian domination, while undesirable, is preferable to continued US involvement in that unhappy area, as long as the means chosen to assert Soviet influence are not, as was the case with those resorted to in June of this year, ones calculated to throw panic and terror into other Asian peoples and thus to achieve for the Kremlin important successes going far beyond the Korean area. But it is important that the nominal independence of Korea be preserved."[37] It seems highly unlikely that such an arrangement could ever have been realized "gradually and not too conspicuously"; that there could have been any Western control over the "means chosen to assert Soviet influence"; and thus that it would ever have been possible under such a scenario to guarantee the preservation of Korea's "nominal independence." Kennan nonetheless proposed a formula: Washington's concession of Korea to Moscow would be contingent on the creation of a "stable and secure situation in Japan." This could be accomplished through the negotiation of an agreement under which the United States would consent to the neutralization and demilitarization of Japan, while the Soviet Union would consent to a cease-fire in Korea and the joint withdrawal of US and North Korean forces, followed by effective UN control of the peninsula "for at least a year or two." Presumably the Soviets would then be allowed to "gradually and inconspicuously" reassert their influence over a reunited Korea. As a safeguard, Kennan allowed that if there were any "further Russian tactlessness" in Korea, US military forces could be reintroduced into Japan.[38]

Kennan admitted that his scheme was probably politically impossible to achieve. Neither the public nor the Congress, he acknowledged, would be able to view such a settlement as anything less than an appeasement of the Communists, and for that reason alone the administration, unwilling to provide fuel for its critics, was not likely to embrace Kennan's proposal. Why, then, did he offer it?

Kennan's recommendation may have been less a genuine proposal than a product of his frustration and resentment at having lost his voice in policymaking. His reaction, as already seen, was to criticize the folly of those who had excluded and ignored him. "Utter confusion" reigned in the direction of US foreign policy, he wrote in his diary a week before drafting his memo to Acheson: "The President doesn't understand it; Congress doesn't understand it; nor does the public, nor does the press. They all wander around in a labyrinth of ignorance and error and conjecture, in which truth is intermingled with fiction at a hundred points, in which unjustified assumptions have attained the validity of premises, and in which there is no recognized and authoritative theory to hold on to."[39] Kennan later observed that "nothing seemed more futile" during the late summer of 1950 "than the attempt to infuse mutual understanding of concept, consistency of concept, and above all sophistication of concept into this turmoil of willful personalities and poorly schooled minds."[40] Under such circumstances, Kennan probably drafted his 21 August memo as a means of going on record against what he considered the short-sightedness and imprudence of prevailing US policy toward Asia in general, and Korea in particular. He may have found it easy to include a proposal that he knew would never be accepted but that might nonetheless be an "authoritative theory to hold on to."

Kennan, however, overlooked the degree to which his own concept for a settlement in Korea lacked the "consistency" and "sophistication" he claimed were necessary. Acheson was astounded at Kennan's suggestion. "Ideas such as these," the secretary later wrote in his memoirs, "could only be kept in mind as warnings not to be drawn into quicksands." He described Kennan's memorandum as "typical of its gifted author, beautifully expressed, sometimes contradictory, in which were mingled flashes of prophetic insight and suggestions, as the document itself conceded, of total impracticability." Acheson also instructed that the memo not be circulated within the department.[41] Kennan ultimately opted not to mention it in his memoirs. His plan clearly was not feasible, and he recognized it as such.

Kennan's proposal, moreover, reflected his inconsistency and apparent equivocation on the Korea issue. If the United States could tolerate a Soviet-dominated Korean peninsula, then why had Kennan so firmly advocated the commitment of US forces to repel the invasion, especially when he had earlier declared that the Korean peninsula was strategically expendable? Here is the answer Kennan offered to this question in his 21 August memo to Acheson: "It was not tolerable to us that communist control should be extended to South Korea in the way in which this was attempted on June 24, since the psychological radiations from an acquiescence in this development on our part would have been wholly disruptive of our prestige in Asia."[42] He offered the same explanation in his briefing to NATO ambassadors on 27 June, when he said the US military intervention was based not on "any strong convictions about the strategic importance of [Korea] but rather in light of our analysis of the damage to world confidence and morale which would have been produced had we not so acted." Kennan told Acheson he saw a "wholly valid and vital distinction" between acquiescing to the invasion, on the one hand, and allowing a "gradual and inconspicuous" extension of Soviet control over Korea, on the other.[43]

It is not clear what makes this distinction either valid or vital, because it is difficult to see how either scenario could have unfolded without a loss of US prestige in Asia. Kennan's argument can be interpreted as indicating that he considered such a loss tolerable only if it were subtle and phased over time; it was only a sudden and dramatic loss of US prestige that was unacceptable. The point is arguable. But even if Kennan's logic had not been flawed, it remains unclear why he considered US prestige to be a factor worthy of more consideration in Korea than he had been willing to give it in China. He had argued for US withdrawal from the Chinese civil war on the grounds that it could have been won only if US forces had taken over from the Koumintang (KMT) the primary burden of fighting, and that this had not been worth the effort because China was not strategically important to the United States. He had even specified that the extension of Soviet control over China would be unfortunate but tolerable. The situation in Korea would appear to have been identical. Kennan himself had said as much before the invasion, when he had deemed the peninsula strategically unimportant and consigned it to the Communists—which in August 1950 he was again prepared to do.

As Gaddis has noted, this episode exposed the impracticality of Kennan's defensive perimeter concept (although it was not his alone). It also exposed the latent inconsistency between the geostrategic calculus inherent in that concept and Kennan's simultaneous belief that US credibility and prestige were strategically important in their own right—"that psychology was as important as industrial-military capability in shaping world politics."[44] Unfortunately, these two strategic considerations were sometimes at odds, and on such occasions an emphasis on upholding US prestige and credibility could lead to actions by the United States that previously were—or might otherwise have been deemed—inadvisable, risky, or simply bad ideas. This can especially be the case when domestic political considerations rather than geostrategic considerations drive foreign policy decisions—something Kennan routinely warned against. In this case, he fell victim to the same problem, although he would have asserted that it was the international prestige and credibility of the United States that was at stake, rather than the domestic political credibility of US leaders. Kennan later chalked this up to what he called "an ultimate reality of world leadership—the one we see in Korea, and many of our people don't like; and that is that there are situations in this world where not even worthy and necessary ends can be achieved without the application of force—and not just force applied in great blind occasional surges, to the blare of trumpets, but rather taking the form of wearisome, endless, unpleasant vigilance in extremely unpleasant places."[45] In Korea, Kennan calculated that the goal of maintaining US prestige was "worthy and necessary" even if Korea itself was strategically expendable.[46]

Kennan's thinking in this regard was not unique. Truman, Acheson, and the rest of the administration had all immediately embraced the need to intervene on South Korea's behalf because they perceived that it had essentially become "a symbol of American reliability worldwide" and that allowing Soviet domination of the Korean peninsula might invite Communist aggression elsewhere.[47] But having made that commitment, the administration faced crucial follow-on decisions on how far to go in implementing it. As Kennan was trying to assess Communist intentions in Korea, neither he nor his superiors and colleagues in Washington were entirely clear on what the intentions and plans of the United States itself were. This became a pivotal question after US forces started to push their way back toward the 38th Parallel.

The 38th Parallel Debate

According to Kennan, during the initial period after the North Korean invasion in June, he and everyone else in Washington operated under the assumption—which was clearly stated in the original Security Council resolution—that the US/UN goal was only to push the North Korean invaders back over the 38th Parallel. Kennan said as much during his briefing for NATO ambassadors on Tuesday, 27 June—only two days after the attack. "I confidently and innocently assured them," he later wrote, "that we had no intention of doing more than to restore the status quo ante."[48]

Privately, Kennan was not sure precisely what this meant with regard to the 38th Parallel itself. The next day he expressed alarm after Webb, during a meeting with Acheson, said the Pentagon considered MacArthur's standing orders sufficient to address any changes in the military situation. Kennan, perhaps because of his familiarity with MacArthur's tendency to act on his own authority, had no such confidence: "I said that never had I ever spoken about anything at that table in the Secretary's office about which I felt more strongly than I did about this, that we were dealing here with a matter of the utmost seriousness and it was of the greatest importance that we know at all times exactly what it is that we were doing and not let ourselves get carried away into anything by accident."[49] He amplified this point directly with military officials later that same day, just as the air force was requesting authorization to operate above the 38th Parallel: "I . . . emphasized that what I was interested in was getting everyone in our Government, including General MacArthur's headquarters and the men on the planes and the ships, to realize that if they encounter Soviet forces this would constitute a new situation requiring new decisions. . . . I pointed out that if we did not make this distinction clear, and went on the basis that our existing orders would be followed out, come what may, and required no amplification, then we would be assigning to the Russians or to chance the decision as to whether there would be a new world war."[50] Based in part on these discussions, a draft statement was generated for interagency consideration. Kennan suggested to Acheson that Washington "continue to state it as our purpose not to reoccupy any territory north of the parallel" but to allow US forces to "operate anywhere in Korea where their operations might promote the achievement of [their] mission." This emerged as the consensus view. Kennan claimed no credit for originating it, because "other people had been thinking along the same lines," but he thought he was instrumental in establishing it as State's position.[51]

At a meeting of the NSC consultants the following day, Kennan said explicitly that "it might be that we would have to permit air operations" north of the 38th Parallel "in order to dislodge the communist forces from South Korea." When NSC Executive Secretary James Lay suggested that US forces might be justified in crossing the line if Chinese forces intervened in the conflict, "Mr. Kennan agreed. He said that if we caught Chinese Communists in South Korea we could go north of the 38th Parallel and even bomb in Manchuria."[52] These excerpts reveal an early ambiguity in Kennan's position regarding the 38th Parallel, and—if his comments at the meeting were accurately quoted—a willingness to take the air war into China if the Chinese intervened south of the 38th Parallel. Although he later claimed that he never condoned crossing the line, the record shows that he had been willing to make tactical or conditional exceptions. At the same time, Kennan appears to have been relatively consistent, and even emphatic, in his reservations about the use of US ground—as opposed to air—forces north of the 38th Parallel. Such a deployment, he believed, would clearly go beyond the status quo ante.

It was Washington's commitment to merely restoring the status quo ante that Kennan saw eroding over the course of the summer. He detected this first on 10 July, after the administration received word that India had approached both Moscow and Beijing with a proposal to end the Korean conflict on the basis of both UN-supervised restoration of the status quo ante in Korea and Chinese Communist admission to the UN. Acheson and his advisers immediately rejected both conditions—the first on the grounds that it would leave South Korea indefensible and vulnerable to a renewed attack from the North, and the second on the grounds that it would "reward an aggressor." On 13 July, President Rhee told the press that South Korean forces, for their part, would not stop at the 38th Parallel if and when they regained the offensive.[53]

The following day, the PPS—disturbed at the vagueness of the US position—seized on the issue, largely under the influence of Kennan and Bohlen, both of whom were then working out of the PPS. Bohlen later wrote that he and Kennan were "particularly opposed to plans for a counter-invasion of North Korea. We warned that Communist countries would react strongly if hostile forces approached their borders. . . . It was folly, Kennan and I argued, to take the chance of prodding China and/or the Soviet Union into a war. Sufficient military force should be used to throw back the invaders, we agreed, but large-scale retaliation was not necessary because the attack on Korea was not a prelude to [Soviet-backed] invasions elsewhere."[54] In support of this view, PPS officer Herbert Feis on 14 July sent a memo to Acheson strongly recommending that Washington disassociate itself from Rhee's statement lest it be interpreted by other governments as a reflection of US policy and intentions. Such a misunderstanding, Feis argued, might upset other members of the UN and increase the chances of Soviet or Chinese Communist intervention in Korea. Separately, Bohlen told Acheson that the PPS would immediately start drafting a paper assessing what Washington should do if the North's offensive was turned back and US/UN forces returned to the 38th Parallel.[55]

The PPS's efforts to secure an affirmation of Washington's commitment to the status quo ante soon encountered strong resistance. John Foster Dulles, who had joined the State Department only a few months earlier as Acheson's special negotiator on the Japanese peace treaty issue, was drawn into the secretary's inner circle of advisers on Korea early in July. A staunch anti-Communist, Dulles was adamantly opposed to any appeasement of the North Koreans. On 14 July, the same day Feis and Bohlen raised the matter with Acheson, Dulles sent a memo to Nitze expressing his dismay with the idea circulating in the PPS that Washington should state publicly that the North Koreans would be allowed to simply retreat back across the 38th Parallel. In Dulles's view,

> the 38th Parallel was never intended to be, and never ought to be, a political line. . . . If we have the opportunity to obliterate the line as a political division, certainly we should do so in the interest of "peace and security in the area" [as stated in the UN Resolution of 27 June]. . . . It would be folly to allow the North Korean army to retire in good order with its armor and equipment and re-form behind the 38th parallel from whence it could attack again. . . . [It] should be destroyed, if we have the power to destroy it, even if this requires pursuit beyond the 38th parallel. . . . I believe strongly that we should not now tie our hands by a public statement precluding the possibility of our forces, if victorious, being used to forge a new Korea which would include at least most of the area north of the 38th parallel.[56]

The next day Allison, then assigned as Dulles's special assistant, seconded the motion. In a memo to Rusk, Allison expressed his "most emphatic disagreement" with the PPS's suggestion for a public statement renouncing any plans to cross the line. "It would be utterly unrealistic," he argued, "to expect to return to the status quo ante bellum." Washington was obliged "at the very least" to destroy the North Korean Army, either by the use of force or through a UN-imposed disarmament.[57]

Kennan was greatly alarmed by this line of thinking. A few days later, after two PPS members reiterated to him their concern about the lack of a clear indication of Washington's intentions with regard to the 38th Parallel, he raised the issue at

Acheson's morning meeting. Kennan recorded his comments in his diary: "We must remember, I said, that what we were doing in Korea was, although for good political reason, nevertheless an unsound thing, and that the further we were to advance up the peninsula the more unsound it would become from the military standpoint. If we were actually to advance beyond the neck of the peninsula, we would be getting into an area where mass could be used against us and where we would be distinctly at a disadvantage. This, I thought, increased the importance of our being able to terminate our action at the proper point; and it was desirable that we should make sure we did not frighten the Russians into action which would interfere with this."[58] At this stage, little attention had been given to the possibility of Chinese intervention.

The debate over the 38th Parallel moved to the front burner on 17 July, when Lay notified the State Department and other agencies of a request from Truman for a paper on "future United States policy with respect to Korea," focusing specifically on what Washington should do if and when North Korean forces were pushed back to the Parallel. Rusk, who was then assistant secretary for Far Eastern Affairs, instructed the PPS, FE, and the other divisions at State that had been studying the problem to prepare a single departmental position paper. He assigned Allison the responsibility for overseeing the process.[59]

The PPS completed a draft paper on the 38th Parallel on 22 July. In it, the staff tried to emphasize the distinction between the long-term goal of reunifying and granting independence to Korea and the immediate goal of turning back the North's invasion. The US/UN forces that were then in Korea were there under recent and specific Security Council resolutions, strictly to pursue the second goal. Any action by those forces beyond that—particularly anything aimed at fulfilling the first goal—would require additional Security Council authorization. According to the PPS, it was unlikely that the UN, under the prevailing circumstances, would approve the use of military force north of the 38th Parallel for the purpose of imposing a reunification settlement. In any case, the political advantages of any such attempt to reach a "final" settlement were outweighed by the "risks of bringing on a major conflict with the USSR or Communist China." In conclusion, the PPS recommended that Washington reaffirm its immediate commitment to restoring the status quo ante and defer any change in that policy until subsequent developments required it.[60]

On 24 July, Allison fired back with another "emphatic dissent" from the "philosophy and conclusions" of the PPS paper, charging that its implication that North Korea was a separate country had "no foundation in fact or morality." He completely dismissed the PPS's distinction between long-term and short-term goals, claiming that the two were inseparable. The South Koreans, Allison insisted, made no such distinction, and they themselves were urging that the present opportunity be seized on to effect the reunification of the peninsula. If Washington failed to do so, the South Koreans would lose faith in the United States.[61]

Allison said the PPS had correctly identified "the nub of the problem": whether the advantages of an attempt to reunify the peninsula were worth the risk of war with either Moscow or Beijing. He simply disagreed with the PPS's answer to the question: "That this may mean war on a global scale is true—the American people should be told and told why and what it will mean to them. When all legal and moral right is on our side why should we hesitate?"[62] The PPS paper, Allison charged, was recommending nothing less than appeasement—"a timid, half-hearted policy designed not to provoke the Soviets to war." On the contrary, he insisted, Washington should "determine now that we will accept in Korea no solution" that did not eliminate the North Korean Army, reunify the peninsula, and admit Korea into the UN as an independent country. The United States should declare this agenda before the world; any UN member that did not support it could do so only out of fear.[63]

The PPS, under Nitze's management, backpedaled considerably in response to Allison's objections. Nitze later acknowledged that he had "judged it impossible to reach definite conclusions" on the issue and opted to recommend to Acheson that a decision on the 38th Parallel be deferred pending the results of the counterattack MacArthur was planning.[64] As a result, the PPS's next draft—dated 25 July—was greatly watered down. It eliminated the judgment that majority support in the UN for military action across the 38th Parallel was unlikely, emphasizing instead that other UN members would simply want to exhaust all other possibilities before considering such action. The PPS also incorporated Allison's observation that the South Koreans themselves were eager to see reunification of the peninsula. Most importantly, the PPS retracted its judgment that the potential risks of an attempt to reunify Korea outweighed the possible advantages; the paper merely concluded that any decision on the subject was premature. For the time being, Washington was not committed to using force to reunify Korea, and should keep it that way "by maintaining the greatest possible degree of flexibility and freedom of action." The staff thus recommended: "Decisions regarding our course of action when the UN forces approach the 38th parallel should be deferred until military and political developments provide the additional information necessary to enable us: (a) to base our decisions on the situation in Korea and in other parts of the world at the time; (b) to consult with other UN members . . . and (c) to keep our military capabilities and commitments in safe balance."[65] Nitze presumably hoped that, under such conditions, it would never be necessary to cross the line.

This time Allison found the PPS's draft palatable. He advised Rusk that the paper could be "supported by FE with only minor changes" because its conclusions, although falling short of what he himself would have preferred, probably went "as far as we can reasonably expect at the present time." At the same time, he advised Rusk to point out to Webb that FE thought "continued studies should be made of the whole question." This approach was essentially consistent by that time with the PPS's position, which Nitze described to Webb on 28 July as being that Washington should wait until US/UN forces approached the 38th Parallel before deciding what to do next.[66] Dulles concurred, saying the key was to remain flexible, although he later recorded in a note to Nitze his reservations about much of the body—as opposed to the conclusions—of the PPS paper. Dulles wrote on 1 August: "In my opinion, there is every reason to go beyond the 38th Parallel except possibly one, and that is our own incapacity to do so and the fact that the attempt might involve us much more deeply in a struggle on the Asiatic mainland with Soviet and Chinese Communist manpower."[67]

This last caveat, of course, was precisely the danger that Kennan had focused on from the beginning of the debate. His warning, however, had been pushed to the margins by the consensus that emerged among Acheson, Rusk, Dulles, and Allison—all of whom played down the threat in favor of other political considerations—and by Nitze's willingness to compromise on the PPS's position. Thus, from the end of July onward, as historian William Stueck has observed, Kennan was the only high-level State Department official who consistently opposed crossing the 38th Parallel. His isolation in this regard was perhaps most evident when he learned thirdhand from a PPS colleague that Dulles had told a journalist that "while he used to think highly of George Kennan, he had now concluded that he was a very dangerous man" because of Kennan's opposition to UN military action north of the 38th Parallel and his readiness to allow Communist China's membership in the United Nations.[68]

In the final weeks before he left the State Department at the end of August, Kennan nevertheless continued his efforts to alert Acheson to the risks of crossing the line. As already seen, he wrote memos to the secretary on 8 and 14 August analyzing the concerns Moscow was certain to have about the possibility of the Korean conflict moving toward the Soviet border.[69] Kennan's final appeal on the 38th Parallel was contained in his 21 August memo to Acheson, also cited above, in which he proposed the neutralization of Korea and Japan. On this occasion, Kennan pleaded with the secretary to recognize the risks that were being run: "We have not achieved a clear and realistic and generally accepted view of our objectives in Korea. . . . [Moreover, by] permitting General MacArthur to retain the wide and relatively uncontrolled latitude he has enjoyed in determining our policy in the [region], we are tolerating a state of affairs in which we do not really have full control over the statements that are being made—and the actions taken—in our name."[70] These warnings—at least at the time—were lost on Acheson, who, as already seen, dismissed Kennan's memo on the basis of the impractical and politically unacceptable recommendations it contained.

Kennan used one additional channel to deliver his warning. The day after he wrote his memo to Acheson, Kennan held an off-the-record press conference at the State Department for several journalists. During the meeting, he voiced his personal view that the risks of crossing the 38th Parallel would be "very, very great, and probably exorbitant" because of the potential Soviet reaction. Not only might Moscow deploy its own military forces in Korea, it might "nominally" introduce Chinese troops—"goodness knows who would be really controlling them," Kennan added. However, to avoid creating the impression of differences within the administration, Kennan made it clear that these were his personal views and were to remain off the record.[71]

Kennan's foreboding and his concerns about the administration's lack of a clear position on the 38th Parallel were well justified. On 24 August, Lay told State's representative on the NSC staff that he was surprised at the ambiguity of the department's papers on Korea, particularly the final PPS draft on the 38th Parallel question: "He pointed out that the President had asked for policy recommendations on what we do when we reach the 38th Parallel. [Lay] said that he could hardly understand how, in the light of the President's specific request, we could reply to the President merely stating that we have no policy recommendation at this time."[72] Perhaps in response to Lay's remark, by 31 August the department had prepared NSC 81, "US Courses of Action in Korea," combining the many separate papers on the topic—including the PPS paper on the 38th Parallel, which had been the subject of deliberations over the previous month.[73]

NSC 81, however, remained equivocal and noncommittal on the subject of the 38th Parallel. At an NSC meeting on 7 September, Johnson reported the Joint Chiefs' concern that NSC 81 "envisaged stabilization of a front on the 38th Parallel." The paper was amended in response to his comments, but the final version—NSC 81/1—still essentially deferred a decision on what to do when US/UN forces reached the line. US forces were given legal authorization to operate above the Parallel "to compel the withdrawal of the North Korean forces behind this line or to defeat these forces," but a decision on how far to advance would depend on the Soviet and Chinese reactions.[74]

On 15 September, four days after Truman approved NSC 81/1, UN forces under MacArthur's command landed at Inchon, launching the massive counteroffensive that within a matter of weeks pushed the North Koreans back to the 38th Parallel. On 30 September, the British representative to the UN introduced in the General Assembly a new resolution—which the State Department had helped to draft—restating the goal of a reunified Korea and implicitly condoning military operations north of the Parallel. Because the vote was in the General

Assembly rather than the Security Council, the resolution was approved on 7 October despite Soviet opposition. Interpreting it as he saw fit, MacArthur sent UN forces across the 38th Parallel two days later.[75]

This combination of developments proved fateful, as Acheson himself later wrote in an explicit acknowledgment of the prescience of Kennan's warning: "The trouble inherent in the [UN] resolution itself and the encouragement it gave to General MacArthur's adventurism lay in the fact that it was not thought through and it masked in ambivalent language the difficulties and dangers against which Kennan had warned in [his 21 August] memorandum."[76] Indeed, on 24 October MacArthur unilaterally lifted all restrictions on his forces and ordered them north toward the Yalu River, North Korea's border with China. Suddenly, South Korean advance forces met with resistance from Chinese "volunteer" units; UN forces pulled back, and after a few days the Chinese seemingly disappeared. On 24 November, MacArthur launched a final "win the war" offensive. The next day, Chinese armies launched a massive counterattack that sent US and UN forces fleeing back down the peninsula in retreat.[77]

Kennan had essentially been proved correct in his warnings. Certainly he was off target in some respects. He had paid too little attention to the possibility of Chinese, as opposed to Soviet, military intervention in Korea.[78] In addition, it was not the crossing of the 38th Parallel itself but MacArthur's subsequent drive to the Yalu that led to the realization of Kennan's worst-case scenario. On the other hand, only many years later was evidence available in the West to reveal the roles that Beijing and Moscow played in the early stages of the Korean War; to a large extent Kennan, like the rest of Washington, was simply in the dark. In any event, Kennan had specifically warned about the dangers of MacArthur's tendency to follow his own lead. And he was correct in recognizing the fundamental danger that was inherent in the ambiguity and uncertainty of US policy in Korea. This is what Acheson later credited Kennan with having forewarned in his 21 August memo.

Disaster at the Yalu

"It was with something more than a lack of confidence or enthusiasm," Kennan wrote in his memoirs, "that I watched, after removal to Princeton in early September, the further course of the Korean War."[79] In a letter he drafted on 15 November 1950, he lamented what he considered the entirely predictable consequences of the success of the Inchon landings and the rapid movement north of US forces. Both the Soviets and the Chinese, having been taken by surprise, were probably drawn into "the most anxious and alarmed consultations"—perhaps their first such consultations on the subject of Korea, he speculated. In any case,

Kennan argued, the United States "had no right to expect our own conduct in the Korean matter to produce results much different than those we have seen. When . . . we withdrew our forces from Korea, failed to give adequate armaments to the South Korean forces, and permitted statements to appear here which could easily be interpreted as expressions of military disinterestedness, we ourselves established, it seems to me, the pre-conditions for action by the Korean Communists."[80] Although Kennan here was overlooking his own role during 1948 and 1949 in creating the impression of "military disinterestedness," he judged that the Chinese intervention was a predictable result of the UN forces' push to the Yalu.

On Friday, 1 December, after the scale of the military debacle in North Korea had become apparent, Bohlen, who had since returned to Paris, telephoned Kennan at Princeton and urged him to go to Washington. Bohlen was deeply concerned that, under the circumstances, there was no one advising the administration who was knowledgeable about and experienced in Soviet affairs. He advised Kennan to make himself available to Marshall, who in September had returned to the government as secretary of defense (replacing Johnson), and to Acheson. Kennan subsequently telephoned some friends at the State Department to offer his services, and the following day he was notified—on Nitze's authority—that Acheson wanted him to come to Washington. He "took the next train" from Princeton and reported to the State Department on Sunday morning, 3 December.[81]

Kennan found the administration in "disarray."[82] Webb, in Acheson's absence, briefed Kennan on the situation:

> [Webb said] the military leaders felt that a complete withdrawal from Korea was the only alternative to the loss of what was practically our entire ground establishment. They thought that we had perhaps 36 hours for a decision as to an orderly withdrawal. If that decision was not made, the result might be complete disaster and effective loss of the entire force. He said discussions were in progress concerning the attitude we should adopt in the United Nations and in the conversations with [British Prime Minister] Attlee, who was expected to arrive [in Washington] the following morning. . . . One of the variants that would be discussed with the British would be a direct approach to the Russians with a view to bringing about a cease-fire in Korea. What they wanted from me, he said, was a view as to the prospects of negotiation with the Russians on this problem at this time.[83]

Later in the afternoon, Acheson returned from a meeting at the White House with Truman, Marshall, and Bradley. The secretary confirmed that the mood and outlook were bleak and that the White House discussion had focused on how best to evacuate US forces and negotiate a cease-fire. Acheson also confirmed Webb's instructions to Kennan to draft a memo on prospects for negotiations with Moscow.[84]

That afternoon, Kennan—with the help of Davies and G. Frederick Reinhardt, another Russia expert—prepared what he later referred to as four pages of "the bleakest and most uncomforting prose that the Department's files can ever have accommodated." According to Kennan, "we could do no other."[85] Any approach to the Russians requesting a cease-fire, the paper stated, would be interpreted by Moscow as "a bid for peace by us on whatever terms we can get." Soviet leaders, accordingly, would ruthlessly try to exploit the weakness of the US position and maximize the damage to US prestige that could be derived out of any settlement. Under the circumstances, Kennan wrote, Moscow's response to any US approach was certain to be "an arrogant and offensive one." In short, Kennan concluded that the "present moment is probably the poorest one we have known at any time in the history of our relations with the Soviet Union for any negotiations with its leaders. If there is any soundness at all to the principle of negotiation from strength, then this is the worst time for us to attempt negotiation. . . . I see not the faintest reason why the Russians should wish to aid us in our predicament, and therefore no reason to believe that we could improve our position by an approach to them."[86]

Kennan carried this dismal message to Acheson's office that Sunday evening, but the secretary was on his way out. According to his memoirs, Kennan held on to the paper and instead accompanied Acheson home for dinner and an earnest discussion of the crisis the country was facing. The next morning—Monday, 4 December—Kennan delivered to Acheson both his memo on the Soviets and the following handwritten note:

Dear Mr. Secretary:

On the official level I have been asked to give advice only on the particular problem of Soviet reaction to various possible approaches.

But there is one thing I should like to say in continuation of our discussion of yesterday evening.

In international, as in private, life what counts most is not really what happens to someone but how he bears what happens to him. For this reason almost everything depends from here on out on the manner in which we Americans bear what is unquestionably a major failure and disaster to our national fortunes. If we accept it with candor, with dignity, with a resolve to absorb its lessons and to make it good by redoubled and determined effort—starting all over again, if necessary, along the pattern of Pearl Harbor—we need lose neither our self-confidence nor our allies nor our power for bargaining, eventually, with the Russians. But if we try to conceal from our own people or from our allies the full measure of our misfortune, or permit ourselves to seek relief in any reactions of bluster or petulance or hysteria, we can easily find this crisis resolving itself into an irreparable deterioration of our world position—and of our confidence in ourselves.[87]

Acheson "agreed enthusiastically" with Kennan's sentiments and read this note at a meeting in his office that morning that included Webb, Jessup, Rusk, Nitze, and Kennan himself. The meeting, at which Kennan also briefed the group on his thinking about the futility of an approach to Moscow, focused on how best to fulfill the requirements of Kennan's admonition to bear the crisis and stand firm. Both Rusk and Kennan observed that defeatism at the Pentagon was the most ominous threat. The military was prepared to withdraw completely from Korea; although this might make perfect sense militarily, it was bound to be politically devastating. Rusk and Kennan argued that it would be preferable—assuming it were possible—to establish "some sort of a beachhead" in Korea from which US forces could salvage their position and maintain a credible presence on the peninsula.[88]

After this meeting concluded, Acheson telephoned Marshall at the Pentagon to float the idea. Borrowing the language used earlier by Rusk and Kennan—including a comparison between the US predicament in Korea and that which faced Great Britain during the two World Wars—the secretary of state respectfully asked the general whether a "calm military analysis" might support the idea of a "holding operation" in Korea. Marshall thought the idea a good one, although it was at that moment too early to gauge what was happening on the battlefront, and he cautioned against getting into "an irretrievable hole." Acheson fully agreed, but Marshall accepted his invitation to send Rusk and Kennan over to the Pentagon to discuss the matter.[89]

Kennan, Rusk, and deputy undersecretary of state H. Freeman Matthews immediately left to meet with Marshall. After Rusk outlined State's suggestion for the general, Kennan reinforced it by observing that "our complete withdrawal from the peninsula would be mercilessly exploited by [Moscow] to our disadvantage." Marshall repeated his agreement in principle, but also his statement to Acheson that the situation was, for the moment, "obscured by the fog of battle." Not convinced that he had sufficiently made State's point to Marshall, "Kennan pushed him," in Acheson's words. The State Department, Kennan said, was not trying to make military policy, and was prepared to accept a judgment that securing a beachhead would entail prohibitive losses. State wished only to impress upon Marshall the "political implications of this decision." At this point, Lovett—then Marshall's undersecretary of defense—joined the meeting from a briefing on Capitol Hill, bringing the news that sentiment there was defeatist and supported an immediate withdrawal from Korea. Kennan lamented that this only made the administration's decision more problematic.[90]

Ultimately, as Kennan himself observed, it was Truman who decided that the United States would not abandon its mission in Korea. Kennan, however, later said he believed that his warnings against defeatism and his goading of Acheson and Marshall had helped to boost morale and thus preempt a decision to pull out of Korea. Kennan said he had the "feeling that my own presence . . . was important in continuing the Korean War" after the Chinese intervention. By "pleading all day with these people," Kennan thought, he had played "a small but not negligible part in steadying down the military" when it was inclined to give up the fight.[91]

Kennan probably gave himself too much credit for his role in boosting morale in Washington during early December 1950. He was there for only three days, and the decision to fight on in Korea probably would have been made without him, given Truman's determination not to withdraw. Rusk later said that Kennan was only one among many who thought Washington should "hunker down" after the disaster on the Yalu, and that Kennan had not significantly affected morale one way or the other.[92]

Kennan, however, probably played a decisive role during this period in preempting any serious consideration of approaching the Soviet Union with a proposal for a negotiated settlement. Acheson, in his meeting with Attlee on 5 December, quoted Kennan's memo of the day before in saying that it was the worst time ever for negotiating with the Russians: "They saw themselves holding the cards and would concede nothing."[93] In this respect, Kennan had served precisely the purpose that Bohlen had in mind when he urged Kennan on 1 December to go to Washington: to provide the expertise required to assess the Soviet outlook toward the crisis and how Washington should deal with it. The irony, of course, is that Kennan was called on to help the administration deal with a crisis that was, at least in part, the result of his colleagues' failure to heed his explicit advice on the same subject four months earlier.

Prelude to an Armistice: The Kennan-Malik Talks

Kennan returned to Princeton on 5 December 1950. Before doing so, however, he took the opportunity to try to dissuade the State Department's "senior UN enthusiasts" from introducing a new Security Council resolution that would have condemned the Chinese Communists as aggressors in Korea. Such a step,

Kennan warned, could only aggravate the differences between Washington and London, among other allies, on the subject of China. As Kennan wrote to Bohlen, the desire to use the UN as a means of highlighting the supposed unity of the allies on the Korean problem was "really disturbing and dangerous." Kennan believed this could easily backfire, and he suggested that Washington do just the opposite: "Our only possible course at this moment was to get the UN out of the Korean business as rapidly and painlessly as possible and to avoid everything that might accentuate the public effect of what was bound to be the difference in attitude between ourselves and our allies."[94] Kennan repeated this view in a letter to Nitze in early January 1951, apparently after learning that a UN resolution condemning China was still under consideration. It would be a "terrible mistake," he argued, to keep trying to use the UN as a vehicle for US policy in Korea.[95]

In his letter to Nitze—which was written after the immediate crisis of the Chinese intervention had passed—Kennan speculated that Washington at that stage had two alternatives in Korea: either to stabilize the battlefront and negotiate a settlement or to voluntarily leave, declaring that it no longer served any useful purpose to attempt to reestablish the Republic of Korea.[96] Kennan's mention of the second option as a viable one reflects a striking reversal of his position of only one month earlier. Indeed, Kennan appears to have again reverted back to the view he had recorded well before the initial North Korean invasion, and again to Acheson in August 1950—that the United States could afford to surrender the peninsula to its fate. In retrospect, this might be characterized as his "fair-weather" assessment of Korea's strategic importance. In June 1950 and again in December, he had insisted that US prestige required a firm commitment not only to remain in Korea but to fight there. On each occasion, however, he shortly returned to a narrower view: in August, he had proposed a plan that would have ceded South Korea to the Soviets, and in January 1951 he once again saw US withdrawal as an acceptable option.

In any case, he did not actively pursue that option in early 1951. Instead, he became involved in a diplomatic initiative that ultimately set the stage for the other option—that of negotiating a settlement after the battlefield had stabilized. On 17 March 1951, Kennan forwarded to Acheson a letter expressing his view that the time was ripe to consider dealing with the Russians on the question of Korea. The "worst time" for doing so had passed, and Washington would no longer have to negotiate from a position of total weakness. Moscow, Kennan insisted, would sooner or later have to be consulted if a Korean settlement was to be reached, and the military stalemate that had developed on the peninsula by that time was as unsatisfactory to Soviet leaders as it was to Washington. Although Kennan was prepared to acknowledge that any final settlement would have to be nominally worked out under UN auspices, he thought it crucial to start the process by dealing primarily with Moscow, and to do so "through informal channels and with the obligation of complete secrecy."[97]

Just such an opportunity—including a pivotal role for Kennan himself—arose a few weeks later. On 2 May, Frank Corrigan and Thomas Cory, two members of the US delegation to the United Nations, were invited to share a limousine ride in New York with Jacob Malik, the Soviet ambassador to the UN, and Malik's deputy, Semyon Tsarapkin. At one point during the conversation, Malik observed that many unresolved international issues, including the conflict in Korea, "could and should be settled" by discussion between the United States and the Soviet Union. Separately, Malik asked what had become of Kennan, whom he said had had "a great and unfortunate influence" on US policy toward Russia; Malik said he had "no doubts that Kennan's voice is still heard" in Washington.[98]

After hearing of this conversation, Davies, then in his final months at the PPS, saw in it a possible opening for a dialogue with the Russians on the subject of a cease-fire in Korea. Davies had written a short memo in late March suggesting that Moscow might be interested in a settlement.[99] On 8 May, he wrote to Nitze suggesting that Washington quietly follow up on the apparent overture from Malik, and recommending specifically how to do so: "I think that the risks of a disclosure of the conversations for propaganda purposes can be avoided if our representative is someone whom the Kremlin feels (a) will not seek a personal, political advantage through publicizing his role, and (b) although not a high American official, is in a position to speak with authority and in confidence for the Government. That person is Kennan. Kennan should be asked to do the job, be briefed and meet with Malik at a three-some dinner with Cory."[100] Acheson thought Davies's idea a good one. Ten days later Matthews called Kennan to Washington to meet with the secretary to discuss this delicate mission.[101]

Working through Cory and Tsarapkin, Kennan arranged a meeting with Malik that took place at the latter's home on Long Island on 31 May. The conversation, though two and one-half hours long, produced little of substance. Indeed, it got off to a bad start when Malik spilled a tray of food on himself. The Soviet ambassador subsequently evaded the question of Moscow's interest in a cease-fire, instead repeatedly asking Kennan about Washington's attitude toward the Chinese Communists. Kennan interpreted Malik's focus on China as evidence of some discomfort in Sino-Soviet relations that might be constraining Moscow's pursuit of a cease-fire. The two men nonetheless agreed to meet again. At their second meeting, on 5 June, Malik—clearly having received instructions from Moscow in the interim—stated that the Soviets "wanted a peaceful solution of the Korean question—and at the earliest possible moment." The Soviet Union, however, could not participate in any cease-fire discussions because its forces were not involved in the conflict. Adding his "personal advice," Malik suggested that Washington contact the North Koreans or the Chinese on the matter.[102]

Kennan interpreted Malik's remarks at their second meeting as a "major policy statement" from the Soviets—"more significant, rather than less, by virtue of the fact that it was intended for communication in a non-public channel." He advised Acheson to seize on any opportunity to move toward a cease-fire in Korea. Two weeks later, Kennan repeated this plea in a letter to Acheson in which he argued that Moscow's behavior over the previous year had "at every turn" confirmed his belief that Soviet leaders (a) did not want the Korean conflict to develop into a war between the United States and the Soviet Union, and (b) were "congenitally suspicious" of US motives and "pathologically sensitive" to the presence of US military forces near the Soviet or Chinese borders. For this reason, Kennan argued, "the presence of our forces in that vicinity for nearly a year has been for them a nerve-wracking and excruciating experience, straining to the limit their self-control and patience. . . . If we continue to advance into North Korea without making vigorous efforts to achieve a cease-fire, I fear they will see no alternative but to intervene themselves."[103]

On 23 June, three days after Kennan wrote this letter, Malik delivered a speech over the UN radio network that contained a public affirmation of his earlier, secret message to Kennan—that Moscow thought the war in Korea could and should be settled. As a first step, Malik said, "discussions should be started between the belligerents for a cease-fire and armistice providing for the mutual withdrawal of forces from the 38th Parallel." Acheson, after confirming the authoritativeness of Malik's statement through the US ambassador in Moscow, authorized the broadcast of a message from General Matthew Ridgway, commander of UN forces in Korea, saying the United States was prepared to enter into negotiations. This message was sent on 30 June and received a positive response from the North Korean and Chinese commands two days later. The first round of cease-fire talks opened on 10 July.[104]

The negotiations that followed, as Kennan himself later observed, were "long, wearisome, and—from the American and United Nations standpoint—exasperating almost beyond belief." Had the negotiators on the US/UN side known of Kennan's involvement in making the talks possible, he mused, some of them "would have cursed me for the effort, and I could scarcely have blamed them."[105] Nevertheless, inasmuch as the negotiations ultimately were the vehicle for the armistice that suspended the conflict two years later, Kennan must be credited for his role in helping to make them possible. How crucial that role was is certainly debatable. The speech Malik delivered on 23 June, or another Soviet initiative with the same effect, might have come eventually even if Kennan had never met with Malik. Alternatively, Acheson might have used another avenue or opportunity for floating the proposal for cease-fire talks.

It is probable, however, that Kennan's meetings with Malik at least opened the door to negotiations earlier than they might otherwise have occurred. Indeed, given the delicacy of the operation and the uniqueness of Kennan's qualifications for conducting it, the peace talks might not have begun until significantly later if Kennan had not been involved when he was—and he may have been correct about the increased risk of Soviet intervention in the Korean War during the interim. In that respect, the Kennan-Malik talks may have helped avert yet another crisis on the battlefield that neither side would have wanted. For his part, Kennan considered the success of his meetings with Malik to be, at the very least, a clear indication of the "great and sometimes crucial value" of informal, secret diplomacy.[106]

In a paper he drafted in September 1951, Kennan stated that he had generally agreed with US policy toward Korea—except for the involvement of the UN and MacArthur's "unfortunate advance" to the Yalu—but that he considered the long-term problem of Korea soluble only in the context of a deal with Moscow that would involve Washington's willingness to neutralize Japan. This was the arrangement he had recommended to Acheson in August 1950. Kennan believed that Soviet leaders had been encouraged to launch the invasion of South Korea in part by the indications they had received of US plans to establish a permanent military presence in Japan.[107]

One of the flaws in this argument—and in Kennan's entire approach to the Korean problem at the time—was the assumption that the North Korean invasion was basically a Soviet operation. Kennan failed to fully recognize the fault lines between the Soviet, Chinese, and North Korean Communists. But he was not alone in this respect. Practically everyone in Washington took for granted at the time that Pyongyang was acting under instructions from Moscow, and that Beijing—when it became involved—was similarly acting in concert with the Soviet Union. As noted earlier, it was not until several years later that historians were able to dissect the relevant decision-making processes in the three Communist capitals and the ties among them. The evidence available to those historians was simply not available to Kennan and other policymakers in 1950. If it had been, Kennan might have had a more balanced view of the threat of Soviet intervention, which he consistently exaggerated. He might also have recognized that the Korean War was "nerve-wracking and excruciating" to Moscow—which he correctly ascertained—not only because it brought US forces into the Soviet Union's backyard but also because Moscow did not have the level of control it wanted over either the North Korean or Chinese Communist regimes. Finally, Kennan might have been less surprised than he was at the nature and extent of Chinese Communist intervention in the war.[108]

AFTERMATH OF KOREA
The End of a Strategic Vision for East Asia

In his 21 August 1950 departure memo to Acheson on East Asia policy, Kennan warned that "the course upon which we are today moving is one, as I see it, so little promising and so fraught with danger that I could not honestly urge you to continue to take responsibility for it."[1] Most of Kennan's fears in this regard were subsequently realized. The consequences of the outbreak of the Korean War effectively extinguished his "strategic concept" for the region by negating the defensive perimeter idea, sweeping away his notion of a neutralized Japan, over-ruling his advice against supporting the Nationalist regime on Taiwan, and committing the United States to deeper intervention in Southeast Asia, which Kennan had similarly warned against. The result was an American policy of containment in East Asia that was more extensive and more militarized than Kennan had envisaged or supported. This marked his final retreat and disillusioned withdrawal from official involvement in US policy in the Far East.

The Myth of Japanese Neutrality

Kennan had faded from involvement in Japan policy in late 1949 and the first half of 1950, and had become increasingly cynical about Washington's inability to re-solve the dilemma it faced there. He told a group of Central Intelligence Agency (CIA) officers in October 1949 that he found it "awfully hard, really, to find any conceivably optimistic picture of what can happen with regard to the Japanese from here on." The occupation, he reiterated, had outlived its usefulness but had not left Japan well prepared for its future. Whatever that future held, Kennan said frankly, "I don't think it will be a very good one from our standpoint. The Japanese will not conform to our ideas as to what constitutes nice people."[2]

After the Korean War broke out and Kennan was recalled from Princeton to help Acheson deal with the crisis, he was drawn back into Japan policy. Dulles, it will be recalled, had been given responsibility for expediting a peace treaty with Tokyo that—contrary to Kennan's "strategic concept"—would presumably include US military basing arrangements. By mid-July, Dulles and Allison, who had been assigned as Dulles's assistant, were already well advanced in their drafting of a treaty. Kennan, however, was troubled by several elements of their approach, which in many ways reflected Dulles's ideological outlook. Dulles, for example, wanted the treaty to require the Japanese to preserve the substance of the political and social reforms instituted under the occupation. Kennan viewed this as inconsistent with the idea that the US "regime of control" would eventually be lifted and the Japanese again given control over their internal affairs.[3] Moreover, as he wrote Dulles in a memorandum on 20 July, Kennan considered the reform program to have been of "dubious wisdom," and he saw no reason "to perpetuate the memory of something which has been at least partially a mistake." The peace treaty should instead be as brief and succinct as possible; its primary purpose should simply be that of terminating the state of war. From Kennan's perspective, "anything more than that, and particularly anything reflecting a continuation of the school-masterish and smug attitude which has detracted so much from the excellent achievements of our occupation, can only be unhelpful."[4]

Most importantly, Kennan took exception to what he perceived as Dulles's support for full-scale Japanese rearmament. In response to a paper Allison had prepared on the threat of Communist infiltration in Japan, Kennan on 18 July sent a memorandum to Rusk that attributed the problem to Washington's persistent failure to strengthen Japan's internal defenses, as NSC 13 (Kennan's "reverse course" Japan policy paper) had recommended two years earlier. Citing MacArthur's willingness to enhance the existing Japanese police force, Kennan again advised that State urge Defense to establish "a strong, mobile central police force, capable of acting anywhere in Japan," including a "small but excellently equipped naval unit capable of contributing significantly" to any amphibious threat to the country. He later claimed that he wrote this memo to counter Dulles's plans for a more substantial rearming of Japan. A week later, moreover, Nitze forwarded to Acheson a Policy Planning Staff (PPS) memorandum, almost certainly inspired by Kennan, urging that immediate steps be taken to enhance Japan's internal security apparatus and increase its responsibility for its own defense. The PPS recommended that this be done in ways other than that suggested by Dulles, which evidently was to establish regular Japanese military units.[5]

By early August, Dulles had prepared a "short version" of a draft peace treaty, which he sent to Kennan, among others, for coordination.[6] By this time Kennan recognized that the process was moving forward irrespective of his personal recommendations. Moreover, he was only days away from his final departure for his sabbatical, and he wished to avoid the appearance of leaving the department as a result of policy differences with Acheson, Truman, Dulles, or anyone else.[7] Under the circumstances, Kennan chose the path of least resistance. He withdrew from the debate, but not before recording his reservations for Dulles: "If . . . it is regarded as accepted that we must have a treaty with Japan allowing for the continued presence in that country of American armed forces, coupled with their freedom to move anywhere in Japan and to make use of Japanese facilities at the will of the United States Commander, and that these obligations must be anchored in the peace treaty itself, then, while I have misgivings about the success of such a general policy, I think that the draft of the key provisions, namely those dealing with the stationing of forces in Japan, is as good as any I could devise, and I have no suggestions for improvement."[8] Kennan probably judged it especially futile to offer any further comment or guidance to Dulles after learning that Dulles had privately denigrated him. This was the occasion cited earlier in which Kennan found out through a PPS colleague that Dulles had described him to a journalist as "a very dangerous man."[9]

Kennan nonetheless felt strongly that the administration was making a mistake, and that the peace treaty discussions were headed in the wrong direction. Consequently, immediately after drafting his response to Dulles, he wrote the 21 August memo to Acheson that renewed his call for the neutralization of Japan. The decision to leave US forces in Japan, and especially as part of the peace settlement itself, Kennan argued, risked undermining the future of US-Japan relations and confusing the Japanese as to their own national interest:

> We cannot, in the long run, continue successfully to keep Japan resistant to Soviet pressures by using our own strength as the main instrument in this effort. . . . If we insist on keeping troops in Japan, their presence there will inevitably be a bone of political contention. . . . We will not be able to establish a healthy diplomatic relationship to the Japanese, which could develop and enlist their sense of self-interest. . . . Finally, if the Japanese agreement to the presence of such forces is anchored in a treaty of peace . . . it will never have full legitimacy in Japanese eyes. This element of duress will always rise to plague us in all our future relations to the Japanese, and to divert Japanese attention to the problem of "how to get United States troops out" rather than "how to meet Soviet pressures against Japan."[10]

Kennan's solution was to revive the idea he had supported two years earlier but had seemingly abandoned in the interim. "Our best bet," Kennan recommended, was that of negotiating with the Soviet Union the neutralization and demilitarization ("except for strong internal police forces") of Japan. Kennan speculated that this might be possible as part of a deal in which the Soviets would agree to a withdrawal of both North Korean and US forces from South Korea.[11]

This was the memo about which Kennan admitted that his ideas were probably "too remote from general thinking in the Government to be of much practical use" and would probably also be met with "violent and outraged opposition" both within the administration and in Congress. This was also the memo that Acheson dismissed as "typical of its gifted author" but containing suggestions of "total impracticability."[12] Needless to say, Kennan's advice was ignored. Two weeks later, the State and Defense Departments agreed, in a joint memorandum later approved by Truman, to begin negotiations leading to conclusion of a peace treaty with Japan.[13] The retention of US military bases in Japan was not, as Kennan had feared, incorporated into the actual multilateral peace treaty (which was ultimately signed in September 1951 and came into force in April 1952), but it was ensured under the terms of a bilateral security treaty between the United States and Japan that was signed simultaneously.[14] The effect, from Kennan's perspective, was the same. Japan was not only rearmed but remilitarized, and any plans to neutralize it as part of a US "defensive perimeter" strategy—while retaining US forces only on Okinawa, as Kennan and at one point MacArthur had recommended—were lost.

Kennan later argued that Washington's failure or refusal to pursue the neutralization of Japan and to proceed with a separate peace treaty, and especially to accompany the peace settlement with the indefinite retention of US bases in Japan, probably encouraged Stalin to approve the attack in Korea in 1950. This idea, Kennan observed, appears never to have "entered the mind of anyone in Washington except myself" at the time. Acheson, in his memoirs, concurred in Kennan's observation, but only to make the point that it never occurred to Acheson and his colleagues that "unilateral concessions—to avoid pejorative terms—would change, by ameliorating, Soviet policy." In any case, Acheson argued, the decision to proceed with a separate treaty and a bilateral security agreement with Japan was not made until several months after the Korean invasion.[15]

Kennan delivered a lengthy response to Acheson in the second volume of his memoirs. The proposal contained in his 21 August 1950 memorandum did not, Kennan insisted, involve "unilateral concessions." It would have required a Soviet withdrawal from Korea in exchange for the US withdrawal from Japan. More emphatically, Kennan argued, the Soviet Union did not have to wait until September 1950, when the Truman administration formally decided to pursue a separate peace treaty and a long-term basing agreement with Japan, to ascertain "what was cooking in Washington." According to Kennan, press reports in the United States, Japan, and Russia were sufficient to show that "by the middle of February 1950, at the latest . . . it was clear to all responsible people in Moscow (1) that the treaty for which the State Department was angling was to be a separate one . . . ; (2) that this treaty was to mark, or be accompanied by, an arrangement that would turn Japan into a permanent military ally of the United States; (3) that the arrangement would provide for the continued use of the Japanese archipelago by the American armed forces for an indefinite period to come; and (4) that the remaining differences of opinion within the official American establishment in this matter were ones that might at best delay, but would not prevent, the ultimate realization of such a program."[16] Kennan made this argument on several occasions after he left the State Department in 1950.[17]

The Korean War was not the only misfortune Kennan attributed in part to Washington's decision to pursue a separate peace treaty and long-term basing arrangements with Japan. That decision, he wrote in 1959, had by then had a decade to show its effects: "It has produced the Korean War and brought the Chinese into Korea. It is producing a growing friction with the Japanese. It has left the Russians no choice whatsoever but to stake everything on the Chinese card. It has deprived us of all bargaining latitude with respect to the waning asset of Formosa. Perhaps this is realism and consistency. I fail to see it."[18]

Several of these linkages were undoubtedly overstated; at least one was proved wrong by the emergence soon thereafter of the Sino-Soviet split. Nonetheless, Kennan was correct in observing that the US decision to seek a separate peace treaty and a security treaty with Japan could hardly have been viewed by the Soviet Union as a desirable development. On the contrary, Moscow certainly viewed it as a decisive shift—to its disadvantage—in the balance of power in the region. If Washington's decision, or the early indications of it, was not a factor in the Soviets' decision to support the North Korean invasion of the South, it served at the very least to fuel the mutual mistrust and suspicion between the United States and the Soviet Union that characterized the early stages of the Cold War.

If Kennan was correct in this respect, however, he could not also have been correct about the viability of any plan to successfully demilitarize and neutralize Japan. Acheson himself observed "an element of inconsistency" between Kennan's dual claims that the US peace settlement provoked the Soviets in Korea and that Japan could have been neutralized through an understanding with Moscow. Even MacArthur had acknowledged by September 1949 that no guarantee from the Soviet Union in that regard could be fully relied on.[19]

Most importantly, the contemporary evidence shows that Kennan himself was never as committed to the idea of a neutralized Japan during the years 1948–50, when the issue was actually being confronted, as he was years later, when he had the luxury of writing with hindsight. In March 1948, when he wrote his "strategic concept" memo for Marshall and the first draft of his Japan policy paper (PPS 28), Kennan identified the demilitarization and neutralization of Japan as the ideal final solution to the problem of Japanese security. He retreated from this view, however, in the face of opposition from the military establishment in Washington, and placed it on a back burner when the peace treaty and security issues were deferred during the deliberations that produced NSC 13/2 and NSC 13/3. When Acheson subsequently revived and pressed the long-term security issue in 1949, Kennan does not appear to have aggressively renewed his call for a neutralized Japan. Indeed, the idea was not mentioned in NSC 49/1—Kennan's September 1949 response to the Joint Chiefs' assessment of US security requirements in Japan—or in the survey of US foreign policy goals that Kennan prepared in January 1950 for an appearance by Acheson before the Senate Foreign Relations Committee. Moreover, Kennan actually concurred in the peace treaty drafts of mid-1950 that clearly indicated Washington's plans to retain military facilities in Japan indefinitely. It was not until his 21 August 1950 memo to Acheson that Kennan again went on record as favoring the idea of negotiating with the Soviet Union for the neutralization of Japan.[20]

It is also difficult to reconcile the idea of a neutral Japan, guaranteed in part by the Soviet Union, with Kennan's fundamental belief that the greatest threat to Japanese political stability was that of Communist subversion. This belief was the basis for his consistent argument that Japan should be allowed to strengthen and expand its self-defense forces, an idea that ran the risk of being perceived by the Soviets as inconsistent with the country's demilitarization. Kennan certainly acknowledged that plans to rearm Japan in any degree were perceived this way by the other, friendlier Allies. He appears never to have considered that his own plans for strengthening Japan's internal security apparatus would arguably fall within the realm of "rearmament." Kennan, in short, was never able to devise a plan that achieved a balance between ensuring Japan's own security and ensuring US strategic interests in the region, without implicitly antagonizing the Soviet Union. He was not alone in this respect, however. This was precisely the problem that delayed the consensus within the Truman administration over the timing and terms of a peace settlement with Japan, and Kennan was correct in observing that the arrangement that was ultimately worked out, after the outbreak of the Korean War, essentially failed to achieve that balance. In the end, Japan became a military ally of the United States, and the host to American bases, thus negating his version of the "defensive perimeter" idea and ending any hope of agreement with the Soviet Union on the neutralization of Japan.[21]

Containment Comes to Southeast Asia

As with Japan, the Korean War pulled US policy in Southeast Asia decisively away from Kennan's strategic concept and his policy recommendations. But it had already started moving in that direction, partly because of concerns about the implications of the Communist victory in China and political pressure to do something to contain it. As already seen, PPS 51—the Southeast Asia paper that Davies had drafted in 1949—characterized the region as "a vital segment on the line of containment" of Soviet influence but offered little in terms of operational policy recommendations to deal with the implications of this assessment.[22] However, the paper subsequently was used in part to provide the rationale for reinforcement of the US military role and presence in Southeast Asia. In particular, historians Robert Blum and Andrew Rotter have chronicled how the Military Assistance Program (MAP), established under the Mutual Defense Assistance Act (MDAA) of 6 October 1949, came to include a congressional allocation of $75 million in MAP funds for the "general area of China." According to Rotter, this was "widely understood to mean Southeast Asia." When Truman later approved NSC 48/2 ("US Policy toward Asia") on 29 December 1949, the document specified that this $75 million "should be programmed as a matter of urgency." By early 1950, even before the outbreak of the Korean War, some of the funds had already been allocated to Indochina and other Southeast Asian countries.[23]

This diversion of military assistance to Southeast Asia was a partial response to congressional and public criticism of the US retreat from China. "The American containment policy in Southeast Asia," in Blum's words, thus "arose from the ashes of its failed China policy." To respond to and compensate for the Communist victory in China, the Truman administration "transformed an area that most Americans barely knew into one deemed so vital that its defense justified a major effort to keep it from falling into the Soviet orbit."[24]

This was not what Kennan had intended. He was at best ambivalent about the strategic importance of Southeast Asia, and about a military approach to containment. In any event, he had excluded the region from consideration for inclusion in such an approach. Moreover, he rejected the idea that the US withdrawal from mainland China—which he had played a key role in justifying—should necessitate tenuous military commitments to the south. But Kennan's influence over such decisions had eroded, and his notion of containment, particularly in Southeast Asia, was being overtaken by events and politics. The outbreak of the Korean War eclipsed it altogether.

Immediately after the North Korean invasion, delivery of some of the MAP funding to Indochina was expedited. In August 1950, both Kennan and Davies issued their final pleas against a US military commitment there. On 16 August, Davies, in response to dire reports about the military situation of French troops in Indochina, drafted a memorandum questioning the realism of US policy there. The French position was "imperiled," and reports from Indochina made it questionable whether US military intervention could make any difference: "We would be deceiving the French government were we to offer encouragement of decisive military support. Furthermore, we would be undertaking a responsibility for the course of military events in Indochina which could be flung back in our face with recriminations should the military effort fail. The conclusion, therefore, is that if the French—and we—are to be spared a humiliating debacle in Indochina, some means other than reliance on military force must be found."[25]

Davies argued that a solution to the problem could come only in the form of concessions from France. As Kennan and others had repeatedly acknowledged, pressuring Paris could easily be counterproductive. Nevertheless, Davies insisted, "we would be less than frank with the French if we did not expose to them our views" on the situation in Indochina. To that end, Davies suggested that Washington at the very least tell Paris that, from the US perspective, the "genuine nationalism in Indochina would not . . . be satisfied with anything less" than independence. The French government could respond however it wished. But if Paris did not adopt a "bolder political approach" toward Indochina, Davies argued, the United States should be prepared to reassess its own policy toward the colony.[26] Presumably Davies hoped that such a reassessment would result in a decision to disengage from any involvement in the Indochina conflict.

Kennan himself weighed in for the last time in his 21 August 1950 departure memo to Acheson on East Asia policy.[27] In Indochina, he observed, "we are getting ourselves into the position of guaranteeing the French in an undertaking which neither they nor we, nor both of us together, can win." Echoing the policy direction he had advocated since early 1948, Kennan recommended that Washington instead withdraw from Indochina as part of a concerted effort to "terminate our involvements on the mainland of Asia as rapidly as possible and on the best terms we can get." Specifically with regard to Indochina, Kennan recommended that Washington should tell Paris

> that the closer view we have had of the problems of this area, in the course of our efforts of the past few months to support the French position there, has convinced us that that position is basically hopeless. Stressing that this has been, and continues to be, their own responsibility, we should say that we will do everything in our power to avoid embarrassing the French in their problems and to support them in any reasonable course they would like to adopt looking to its liquidation; but that we

cannot honestly agree with them that there is any real hope of remaining successful in Indochina, and we feel that rather than have their weakness demonstrated by a continued costly and unsuccessful effort to assert their will by force of arms, it would be preferable to permit the turbulent political currents of that country to find their own level, unimpeded by foreign troops or pressures, even at the probable cost of an eventual deal between Vietnam and Viet-Minh, and the spreading over the whole country of Viet-Minh authority.[28]

This advice, of course, was out of step with the direction US policy was headed, and it was overruled. As already seen, Acheson did not consider Kennan's approach to be politically or diplomatically viable. Moreover, Kennan had lost his voice at the State Department, and Davies was soon to lose his. And so, as Davies characterized it later, "Washington, ignoring the alternatives of realpolitik and neutrality . . . drifted and lurched toward miasmal involvement of the American people in Indochina."[29]

Stirring the Ashes of China Policy

The outbreak of war in Korea also hardened the direction of American policy toward China, reinforcing antagonism and suspicion toward the Communist regime on the mainland, and prompting an affirmation of US support for the Nationalist government on Taiwan. Truman immediately chose to commit Washington to the defense of the island, and deployed US naval forces to the Taiwan Strait to deter any further Communist adventurism. This partially vindicated Kennan's insistence a year earlier that Taiwan was strategically important enough to merit deployment of US forces to keep it out of Chinese Communist hands. Kennan himself revived his suggestion for military steps to that end. In mid-July 1950, according to his diary, he was alarmed by an intelligence assessment of the situation on Taiwan, which he thought was not being taken seriously enough, and he was concerned that the United States was relying too much on Koumintang (KMT) forces on the island to defend it against a possible Communist invasion. He drafted a memo urging Acheson to make sure the Pentagon was fully attentive to the seriousness of the situation and recognized that Washington had "the capability of influencing the course of events directly. Here it seems to me that the important thing for all of us to bear in mind, including the Defense Establishment, is that we can rely on no one but ourselves. The Nationalist forces on the island must, in view of their national temperament, their past experiences and their unfortunate leadership, be regarded as wholly unreliable.

This is not to say that they will not fight; it is only to say that they cannot be depended upon to fight."[30] Kennan was supported in this view by Bohlen, who suggested to Rusk that something be done to "help improve the military position on the island," given the threat of a Communist attack and the weaknesses of KMT forces. Bohlen also suggested to Acheson that "we should get word to the Chinese Communists what they might have in store for them if they attack Formosa."[31]

Fortunately, a Communist attack on Taiwan never came. Truman's decision to deploy the US Navy appears to have been enough to dissuade the Chinese Communists from any plans they had to attack the island. But it was repugnant to Kennan that Chiang Kai-shek should be the beneficiary of this decision. He blamed this in part on Washington's inability to dissociate itself from Chiang earlier, and on the Pentagon's ambivalence in 1949 about Taiwan's strategic value. It was this combination that left the United States, when the Korean War broke out, with no alternative but to guarantee the security of what Kennan deemed a distasteful regime on Taiwan. This attitude characterized his feelings toward the KMT for years thereafter; and he clung to the idea that Washington had missed an opportunity in 1949 to preempt KMT control of the island by seizing it "the way Theodore Roosevelt might have done it." During the Taiwan Strait crises of the mid to late 1950s, Kennan again told his diary: "Alone among senior officials in Washington I urged . . . that Formosa be put directly under MacArthur's control, [with] no nonsense about returning it to China."[32]

Kennan was drawn into one more issue regarding China that arose in the wake of the Korean invasion. In July 1950, just weeks after the North Korean attack, Washington received word that the Indian government had approached Moscow and Beijing with a proposal for settling the Korean conflict that would have involved restoring the status quo ante and admitting Communist China into the United Nations. In a series of meetings with Acheson, Rusk, and others, Kennan suggested that it might be to Washington's advantage to avoid blocking any international effort to seat Beijing in the UN. He saw this as a wholly separate issue from that of US bilateral diplomatic recognition. In Kennan's view, it made "not the slightest difference" to US interests whether Communist China was admitted to the UN, and doing so would impose no obligation on Washington to grant it diplomatic recognition.[33]

More fundamentally, Kennan argued that any attempt by Washington to keep Communist China out of the UN might be interpreted by other countries as "governed by ulterior and imperialistic motives." He explained this in his diary, with shades of MacMurray's emphasis on the need to base the US approach to China on strategic calculation rather than sentimentality. Kennan said he "shuddered over the implications" of the administration's resistance to accepting Beijing's membership in the UN if it was driven by "an emotional state . . . rather than a cool and unemotional appraisal of our national interest."

> The position we were taking . . . seemed to imply that the basis of our policy would be an emotional anti-communism which would ignore the value to ourselves of a possible balance between the existing forces on the Asiatic continent, would force everyone to declare himself either for us . . . or against us, that this would break the unity not only of the non-communist countries in Asia but also of the non-communist community in general, and would be beyond our military capacity to support. It rested . . . on the encouragement in the minds of our people of a false belief that we were a strong power in Asia, whereas we were in reality a weak one. Only the very strong can take high and mighty moral positions and ignore the possibilities of balance among the opposing forces. The weak must accept realities and exploit those realities to their advantage as best they can.[34]

Kennan had not previously characterized the US position in East Asia as "weak," but this reflected his assessment of the limits on Washington's ability to control trends and events in the region—and the need for the United States to calibrate its ambitions based on an accurate understanding of the balance of power. Here was an early reflection of the stark realist perspective that would long distinguish his mind-set.

In his diary, Kennan went on to lament the "moral indignation about the Chinese Communists" that he saw infecting policy discussions, and warned that Washington was grappling with the same problem that had afflicted "we old Russia hands" twenty years earlier:

> We were not unaware then, and we are not unaware now, of the fundamental ethical conflict between their ideals and ours. But we view the handling of our end, in this conflict, as a practical matter similar to many other matters with which diplomacy has had to deal through the course of the centuries. . . . In our own consciences, in our own concept, that is, of our obligations to ourselves, we Americans may be profoundly aware that we are "right." In our participation on the international scene, we are only one of the contenders for the privilege of leading a national existence on a portion of the territory of this world, on reasonably favorable terms. Other people are our enemies, and we must deal with them accordingly. But let us recognize the legitimacy of differences of interest and philosophy between groups of men and not pretend that they can be made to disappear behind some common philosophical concept.[35]

As will be seen, elements of this analytical perspective characterized Kennan's attitude toward the Chinese Communist regime for the rest of his life.

In any event, based on these views Kennan advised in July 1950 that the United States abstain from any UN Security Council consideration of Communist Chinese membership. This approach, he believed, would dispel any confusion about the "integrity of our position" while at the same time improving the prospects for a settlement in Korea. According to Kennan, he was "shouted down" on this idea by Dulles, who insisted that even US acquiescence to Chinese Communist membership in the UN would look like appeasement, and probably would not produce the desired effect of Soviet concessions on Korea. Unfortunately for Kennan, both Acheson and Bohlen agreed with Dulles. Kennan "recognized the force" of their argument and surrendered to it, but not without privately lamenting what he assessed as its implications. He wrote in his diary that he hoped "some day history will record this as an instance of the damage done to the conduct of our foreign policy by the irresponsible and bigoted interference of the Chinese lobby and its friends in Congress."[36]

Kennan was soon to experience at a more personal level the damage that could be done by the China Lobby and its friends in Congress.

The Case of John Paton Davies

Another casualty of the outbreak of the Korean War was any expectation that Washington could in the near term exploit potential fault lines in the relationship between Beijing and Moscow. Efforts to do so were not wholly withdrawn or abandoned, but they were hindered and delayed by the appearance of close Sino-Soviet relations in the wake of the North Korean invasion.[37]

Davies had been involved in pursuing such efforts. In the fall of 1949, he had developed an idea for circulating unspecified "black propaganda" in China that would appear to come from Soviet sources and would plant the seeds of dissension within the Chinese Communist Party (CCP) and between Beijing and Moscow. According to Davies, his was the only active policy devised within the government to promote Chinese Titoism. Kennan supported the idea and forwarded some of Davies's ideas to Rusk, for consideration by the State Department's Office of Far Eastern Affairs (FE).[38]

On 16 November 1949, Davies—to whom Kennan had delegated full responsibility for carrying the plan forward—met with representatives of the CIA to discuss operational planning for his scheme. Davies's plan apparently involved having the CIA contract indirectly and covertly with several prominent experts on China—including John King Fairbank, Edgar Snow, Agnes Smedley, and Anna

Louise Strong—to produce propaganda documents for circulation in China. The plan was never realized. According to Davies, the project simply proved itself to be a better idea in theory than in practice; it was too complex and "too highly specialized" for the CIA's limited capabilities and personnel at the time.[39]

Davies's attendance at the 16 November meeting, however, would come back to haunt him. Within months a series of developments would launch the "who lost China" debate and resurrect Hurley's December 1945 accusations against Davies and other State Department China hands for alleged Communist sympathies and disloyalty to US policy. After the publication in early 1950 of several newspaper and magazine articles that were inspired by the China Lobby and focused on the wartime and postwar activities of the China hands, Wisconsin senator Joseph McCarthy delivered his infamous speech in Wheeling, West Virginia, on 9 February in which he alleged that the State Department was infested with Communists. These events spurred a series of congressional hearings and internal investigations by the State Department Loyalty Board that pulled in Davies as a witness and eventually as a target and defendant. On 27 June 1951, he was suspended from duty pending completion of the latest of what would become nine Loyalty Board investigations of him. On that date he received a letter from the board chairman outlining the charges against him, which included being "anti-Chiang Kai-shek" and "pro-Chinese Communist" during the war in ways inconsistent with and aimed at thwarting US policy; and aiding, abetting, and closely associating with Chinese Communist sympathizers—including recommending them as US policy consultants (the latter charge referring in part to his proposal to the CIA in November 1949).[40]

One month later Davies was cleared and reinstated by State's Loyalty Board, but in August 1951 he was called to testify before the McCarran Committee—the Internal Security Subcommittee of the Senate Judiciary Committee—which was investigating McCarthy's charges against various government personnel. The McCarran Committee had acquired documents prepared by one of the two CIA participants in the November 1949 meeting at which Davies had outlined his plan for "black propaganda" in China. Both CIA officials eventually testified before the committee on the details of Davies's plan, focusing on its intention to employ the services of individuals who were themselves avowed or suspected Communists. The two witnesses ("scoundrels—the only adequate word to describe them," Davies later said) essentially accused him of trying to infiltrate the CIA with Communist spies.[41]

As the case against Davies got deeper, Kennan (who by this time was on sabbatical at the Institute for Advanced Study in Princeton) came strongly to his defense, first internally and eventually—as the need arose—in public. In a letter to the chairman of the Loyalty Board, Kennan summarized the history of his professional relationship with Davies, which he characterized as "one of the ut-most intellectual intimacy." Based on that experience, Kennan wrote, "I can say without hesitation that I have never observed the slightest trace of disloyalty in thought, word, or action on Davies' part. On the contrary, he has applied himself to his responsibilities in Government with a devotion which I think can have been surpassed by very few people and with an intellectual honesty which has left nothing to be desired. . . . Davies has one of the very few really superior and original political minds in our Government."[42] Kennan was drawn further into the case after Davies was reassigned in late 1951 from the PPS to the US High Commission in Germany, but even there was unable to escape the witch hunt because the investigations—and especially the CIA-related allegations—continued to swirl. Kennan felt compelled to personally respond to those allegations because they involved activities Davies had engaged in under his supervision at the PPS. After those activities became public, Kennan was frustrated by the challenge of responding on an issue that involved classified information.[43]

Kennan's disgust with both McCarthy's assault on Davies and the other China hands and what he considered the administration's pusillanimous response to it intensified as the episode unfolded. He wrote to Davies in Germany in January 1952: "The whole phenomenon of McCarthy-ism has become so painful to me that I can hardly react normally to any of its manifestations. . . . It leaves me with a sense of deep frustration and depression, and I am aware at all times that we are operating against the background of an ugly situation, marked by an absolutely terrifying lack of appreciation, on the part of practically everyone in authority in official Washington, of the fitness of things and of the requirements for dignity and effectiveness in public service."[44] Kennan told another correspondent that Davies was "the victim of as cruel and terrifying an injustice as I have ever seen befall a civil servant," and he told Acheson privately that he would consider resigning from the Foreign Service if the department failed to stand behind Davies—even though Kennan in early 1952 was selected to be the US ambassador to Russia.[45]

Davies was called back to Washington from Germany in November 1952 for another Loyalty Board hearing. Kennan testified on Davies's behalf before the McCarran Committee—which he later described as "as sinister a group of people as I can recall ever having to appear before."[46] Later that month, Kennan tried in a letter to offer Davies what advice and consolation he could:

> I have never ceased to have complete confidence in your loyalty and integrity as well as admiration for the many exceptional qualities you have brought to your work in government; but I cannot encourage you to hope that either my confidence in you or my testimony . . .

will appreciably mitigate the difficulties that lie ahead. . . . I am afraid that against this type of damage to your reputation and your interests . . . you are substantially without recourse. . . . If you are to adjust to this situation without bitterness and without damage to your own balance of judgment, you will have to reach down into the depth of your own feelings as an American and summon from them a degree of understanding and faith in our national destiny far more profound than most citizens are ever called upon to muster. If you do this, you will have done something very great, and under terrible odds; for there is no greater burden and no greater trial than to have been unjustly rejected and denied confidence by the elected representatives of your own people. If you do it, I can give you no assurance that you will see any great public appreciation for it within your own lifetime. I can say, however, that seldom have men proved capable of this sort of an act of faith and self-mastery without leaving a deep impression at some point on the minds and the hopes and the resolution of other men, either in their own generation or in succeeding ones. I can conceive that in the knowledge that one had met and faced successfully a trial as bitter as this there might be satisfaction deep enough to over-balance some of the immediate bewilderment and suffering I know it must have brought to you.[47]

By May 1953, Davies had again been reassigned—this time essentially exiled—to the US embassy in Peru. During this period, Kennan advised Davies to refrain from fighting back publicly, which Kennan thought would be counterproductive. Kennan himself had refrained from addressing the issue in public, partly for bureaucratic reasons and partly because of the classified nature of the charges against Davies.[48] But when McCarthy in November 1953 gave another public speech that singled out Davies and charged him with trying to infiltrate the CIA with Communist agents, Kennan could resist no longer—observing that Davies was being "helplessly pilloried before public opinion, and could do nothing further in his own defense." Kennan sent a telegram to Davies in Peru saying that because of the McCarthy statement he had "decided [to] throw myself publicly into your case." He followed this up with a letter to the *New York Times* in which he defended Davies's record, loyalty, and involvement in the November 1949 meeting with the CIA. By that time, Kennan calculated that McCarthy had overplayed his hand and public sentiment was shifting in Davies's favor.[49]

In January 1954, Kennan again advised Davies to refrain from publicly responding to McCarthy: "The longer you can hold to a quiet and dignified posture, continuing to suffer in silence and to render effective service to the Government, while the professional reputation-hunters are permitted to work out on you, the harder you may make it for the Executive Branch of the Government to wash their hands of you. Any rash or extreme action on your part will immediately be seized upon in Washington as an excuse for saying that you have now ruined your own case and the Government would have liked to have stood up for you but . . . I realize the preposterousness of this as well as you do."[50] In the end, this strategy and Kennan's intervention were not enough to save Davies. On 5 November 1954, even though a final Loyalty Board appointed by then Secretary of State Dulles had failed to find Davies guilty of any disloyalty, Dulles dismissed him from the Foreign Service for "lack of judgment, discretion, and reliability." Rather than prolong the ordeal, Davies accepted this "melancholy outcome . . . confident that when the aberrations then seizing the country had passed, I would be vindicated." But he obliged Dulles to fire him, rather than agreeing to resign: "Resignation would have meant less public and categoric disgrace, and less dismal prospects of getting a job. But I decided against resigning. The issues should not be fuzzed and evaded. If Dulles and company wanted to be rid of me, it was for them to act and give their reasons. I should not, in a vain and desperate effort to escape disgrace, flee through the back door of resignation, thus giving Dulles what he wanted—riddance of me—without having to take responsibility for my departure."[51] Disgusted with Washington and with the department's failure to protect him, Davies retired to private life in Peru, where he would remain for ten years.[52]

For his part, Kennan later acknowledged that the Davies case "weighed on my conscience and my thoughts for years," and that he himself probably would have resigned in protest over the State Department's treatment of Davies had he not separately left when he did in 1953.[53] In any event, beyond this deep personal impact on Kennan, the Davies episode crystallized his cynical and negative attitudes toward the political drivers of US policy in East Asia, especially China.

VIETNAM

"My Piece Has Been Spoken"

Once the original decision was made in 1950 to assist the French in Indochina—overruling Kennan's advice and warnings—US involvement there escalated as a matter of course. The Truman administration gradually increased military aid to the French, and the US commitment was subsequently deepened by Eisenhower and Dulles. In the wake of the French defeat at Dien Bien Phu in 1954 and the subsequent partition of Vietnam, the United States gradually supplanted France as the foreign patron of Indochina's anti-Communists. Bao Dai was eventually replaced as head of government in South Vietnam by Ngo Dinh Diem, whose administration came to depend on American sponsorship.

Kennan, by then fully ensconced at Princeton, watched these developments with a deep sense of foreboding. He told an audience at Haverford College in April 1955 that the situation in Southeast Asia could hardly be worse than it was. The United States had little control over what was happening there, and the future looked bleak for Western interests in the region. As for Indochina in particular, Kennan said, "I would share the blackest apprehensions of our most distinguished prophets of doom."[1]

Another decade later, in a sequel to his involvement in Southeast Asia policy during 1948–50, Kennan gradually entered the public debate over US policy in Vietnam. His response to the Vietnam War reflected both the prescience of his views toward Indochina nearly two decades earlier and one of the flaws of his approach at that time. In Indochina as in Korea, Kennan was never able to enunciate a policy that would have reconciled his desire to eliminate US commitments on the mainland of Asia with his belief that US credibility and prestige should not be compromised there. As a result, his approach to the Vietnam War was somewhat equivocal—until the sacrifice of US prestige became a fait accompli.

Fifteen Years Later: Kennan and the Vietnam War

Kennan's "blackest apprehensions" about Vietnam played out much as he had feared a decade earlier. Because he viewed Diem much the same way he had viewed Chiang Kai-shek, Kennan considered US support for Diem an ill-advised and counterproductive entanglement. It is ironic, then, that in one of his first public statements regarding the US presence in Vietnam—made while Kennan was US ambassador in Yugoslavia (1961–63)—he took it upon himself to defend Washington's ties to Diem. In February 1962, in response to an editorial in the Belgrade newspaper *Borba* that criticized "Diem's foreign allies," Kennan sent a letter clarifying the US attitude toward Vietnam: "It has never been our position that the Diem regime has been without fault or that its measures and policies have invariably met with full approval in all parts of the [Vietnamese] population. But we hold it to have at least as much popular support as a number of regimes in other Asian countries with regard to whose popularity *Borba* has never, to my knowledge, raised questions."[2] The Viet Minh themselves, Kennan went on, had a dubious claim on popular support in South Vietnam—where at least relatively free and fair elections had been held, unlike in the Communist-controlled North. Kennan was more ambiguous, however, in addressing *Borba*'s criticism of the overall rationale behind Washington's involvement in Vietnam. The United States was committed, Kennan said, to resisting the obvious efforts of the Communist bloc to expand its power at the expense of the United States: "We are serious in our determination that these efforts should not succeed for lack of anything we can do, within our means, to prevent this. . . . We would like it to be clear that this conflict is not going to be resolved, in Vietnam or anywhere else, on the basis of simple capitulation, on our part, to forces of terror and concealed foreign domination."[3] Kennan thus characterized Vietnam itself as incidental to the Cold War; he made no attempt to particularly defend the US presence there.

This letter, of course, was an obligatory diplomatic response by a US ambassador to public criticism of US policy in his host country. As such, it was not necessary that the letter reflect Kennan's personal views. It is nonetheless interesting to note the extent to which the carefully chosen language of the letter reflected his private misgivings about Diem—and the implication, consistent with Kennan's personal views, that the containment of Soviet Communism was more important than the specific case of Vietnam, which Kennan had years earlier deemed strategically unimportant to the United States.

After his return to the United States from Yugoslavia, Kennan apparently felt obliged to withhold judgment on the Vietnam question and to offer his nominal support to the actions there of President Lyndon Johnson's administration. Indeed, in an article published in November 1964, he suggested that the US public should offer its "good wishes and support" to the "unpleasant and unaccustomed task" the administration faced in Southeast Asia. The delicacy of US policy toward the region was such that it "cannot stand much jogging of the elbow." Moreover, Kennan said, the government "will not be helped by demands that it abandon the effort altogether, in what would necessarily be a panicky and ignominious withdrawal that could only present our adversaries with a gratuitous bonanza. On the other hand, it will also not be helped by demands that it lose all sense of measure and restraint and try to solve the limited problems of the moment by opening up new ones without limit."[4]

A. J. Muste, the editor of the leftist journal *Liberation*, took Kennan to task for his implicit support in this article for the US military presence in Vietnam. In an exchange of letters that Muste later published, Kennan responded to Muste's argument that US policy toward East Asia had been counterproductive and that Washington should withdraw completely from Vietnam. Kennan's reply revealed his ambivalence and even his uncertainty at that stage about the best course of action for the United States in Vietnam: "You are right, I fear, that we have done little good anywhere . . . with our activities in Asia to date. Whether the alternatives would have been better, also seems doubtful. I accept your view as an argument for complete withdrawal and isolation . . . and I can only say that this is a view I can respect as much as any other. There is much to be said for it, even if it does imply an admission of complete failure and helplessness on our part."[5] Despite this seeming pessimism, Kennan appeared at this stage to believe that some effort might still be made to prevent Vietnam from falling "behind an iron curtain" where it would be dominated by the Chinese or Soviet Communists. In a letter to another correspondent in December 1964, he expressed his hope that the United States avoid a settlement in Southeast Asia that allowed the region to "recede successively from contact with ourselves and the western world."[6]

These ideas would appear to be inconsistent with Kennan's suggestion fifteen years earlier that Washington could afford to ignore Southeast Asia. Like his attitude toward South Korea earlier, Kennan's approach toward Vietnam in the early 1960s reflected his tendency to support—or at least acknowledge the rationale for—US involvement, under hostile conditions where US credibility and prestige were at stake, in an area where he had previously judged such intervention to be inadvisable. In both cases, the difference seemed to lay in the weight of the prestige factor.[7]

In any case, Johnson's decision in February 1965 to begin the aerial bombing of North Vietnam led Kennan to redefine his position and retreat from the equivocal views he had espoused up to that point. Kennan viewed the bombing as a drastic step in the wrong direction—analogous to the crossing of the 38th Parallel in Korea. He characterized it in his diary as "a sort of petulant escapism [that] will, I fear, lead to no good result." It risked expanding the war beyond the original rationale for US involvement—and beyond the capacity of the United States to win—and it could easily be counterproductive both politically and diplomatically. Shortly after Johnson issued the bombing order, Kennan told an audience at Ripon College that the administration needed to clarify its objectives in Vietnam and take note of the limitations on its capabilities there. The bombings, he said, could be useful only if their purpose was to gain leverage with which to negotiate a US withdrawal. Even then, he found them extremely "distasteful."[8]

As the bombings continued, Kennan quickly fell into the same disillusionment and despair that characterized his attitude toward US policy in Korea in the autumn of 1950. The administration, he wrote in a letter in late August 1965, had "involved itself in Vietnam in such a way as to lose almost all flexibility of choice not only in that particular area but in our approach to the communist world generally." Frustrated and cynical about the administration's neglect of his advice, Kennan resigned himself to watching from the sidelines as the consequences unfolded: "I feel, in general, that I have had my day in court. My views are known. They have never commended themselves to our governmental leaders nor to our opinion-forming establishment in general. I could do no less than to state them, when and as the occasion indicated; now that they have been stated, and overwhelmingly rejected by influential American opinion, I can do no more, it seems to me, than to fall silent."[9]

Kennan, however, was unable to remain silent for long. On 12 December 1965, he offered his assessment of the situation in Vietnam in an article in the *New York Times*. He granted that the Communists in Vietnam were a ruthless and nefarious enemy, but he questioned whether the United States should bear the responsibility of defeating them. On a more tactical level, he questioned whether "such Vietnamese as we might find to install in power in the unlikely event of a sweeping military success" would govern the country any more effectively. He also doubted that the Vietnamese Communists, if they succeeded, would allow themselves to be puppets for either Beijing or Moscow.[10]

Kennan's primary complaint was that Washington's policies in Vietnam were both distracting it from other international responsibilities and making those responsibilities more difficult to meet. This, he speculated, was shortsighted and foolish: "If we can now find nothing better to do than to embark upon a further open-ended increase in the level of our commitment simply because the alternatives seem humiliating and frustrating, one will have to ask whether we have not become enslaved to the dynamics of a single unmanageable situation—to the point where we have lost much of the power of initiative and control over our own policy, not just locally but on a world scale."[11] He acknowledged that Washington's choices in Vietnam had never been easy or obvious, and that a "precipitate withdrawal . . . would be one of the worst of the alternatives before us." At the same time, it was not clear, Kennan observed, why the United States had assumed an obligation in Vietnam in the first place.

In Kennan's view, the war itself needed to "simmer down" before any constructive attempt could be made to resolve this dilemma. Only then would the two sides be able to reassess their positions and, hopefully, take steps leading toward some kind of settlement. He had no specific guidance to offer in this regard, and he frankly admitted that his approach offered no guarantees. Clearly, however, Kennan had one immediate goal in mind—the end of the bombing of the North. "One does not control what one bombs," he wrote; "And it seems to me the most unlikely of contingencies that anyone should come to us on his knees and inquire our terms, whatever the escalation of our effort."[12]

Kennan carried the message of his 12 December article to a wider audience in February 1966, when Senate Foreign Relations Committee Chairman William Fulbright summoned him to testify in hearings on the subject of Vietnam. Kennan's appearance before the committee was televised live and generated front-page news stories.[13] In his testimony, he reiterated his view that the US involvement in Vietnam was distracting Washington from other international priorities, and his belief that escalation of the conflict—particularly the bombing of North Vietnam—was unlikely to facilitate anything approximating "victory." But he also repeated his acknowledgment that a "precipitate and disorderly withdrawal could represent in present circumstances a disservice to our own interests."[14]

Kennan instead supported a middle course between escalation and withdrawal: that of adopting a defensive military strategy that focused on securing "enclaves" where US and South Vietnamese forces could maintain their position on the battlefield while the conflict as a whole was allowed to simmer down. This idea was not original to Kennan; it had been proposed a few weeks earlier by retired US Army General James Gavin, who subsequently also testified before the Senate Foreign Relations Committee.[15] Echoing Gavin's thinking, Kennan argued that the enclave approach offered the best opportunity for facilitating a settlement: "I would recommend . . . that we try to limit the conflict rather than to expand it, that we adopt in general a defensive strategy and put ourselves in a position where we cannot be hurried, where we cannot be panicked, where we can afford to wait, and let the logic of this situation then gradually sink in on our opponents, and I think then there is a possibility that with a little greater patience than we have shown thus far, possibilities for an acceptable resolution of the conflict may open up."[16] Kennan hastened to add, however, that an "acceptable resolution" would not necessarily be one that held "any triumphs or indeed any great satisfaction from our standpoint."[17] In his view, Washington needed to extract itself from Vietnam, regardless of whether it could do so triumphantly.

This was simply because he believed that Vietnam was not worth the effort, and that the United States had no compelling reason to be fighting there. Here Kennan reaffirmed the view of Indochina he had formulated fifteen years earlier— that it was not strategically valuable enough to justify an open-ended US commitment. As he told the Senate:

> If we were not already involved as we are today in Vietnam, I would know of no reason why we should wish to become so involved, and I could think of several reasons why we should wish not to. Vietnam is not a region of major military, industrial importance. It is difficult to believe that any decisive developments of the world situation would be determined in normal circumstances by what happens on that territory. If it were not for the considerations of prestige that arise precisely out of our present involvement, even a situation in which South Vietnam were controlled exclusively by the Viet Cong, while regrettable, and no doubt morally unwarranted, would not, in my opinion, present dangers great enough to justify our direct military intervention.[18]

Kennan argued that the logic that had originally drawn the United States into Vietnam was no longer valid. The "so-called domino effect," he said, appeared less menacing than it had previously, and the Sino-Soviet rift had increased the likelihood that a Communist South Vietnam would "follow a fairly independent course."

In any case, Kennan insisted, Washington should never have allowed itself to assume from the South Vietnamese people themselves the primary burden of defending the country. "This is not only not our business," he said, "but I don't think we can do it successfully." When a senator questioned Kennan's implication that the South Vietnamese military should be abandoned to its fate, he responded bluntly: "Senator, if their morale is so shaky that without an offensive strategy on their part they are simply going to give up the fight, I do not think they are worth helping anyway. And, as for the question of our having a moral obligation to them, they have had enormous help from us to date. I mean, goodness, they have had help in billions and billions of dollars. How many countries are you going to give such a claim on our resources and our help? If they cannot really do the trick with this, I feel strongly that the trouble lies somewhere with them and not with us."[19]

Kennan's testimony before the Senate drew a flood of media attention that the Johnson administration could not ignore. Indeed, an anti-war group within the New Jersey Democratic Party subsequently tried to draft Kennan as a Senate candidate.[20] The day after Kennan's appearance, the president was asked about it during a press conference. Johnson responded that there was "not a great deal of difference between what [Gavin] and Kennan are saying and what the Government is doing."[21] Kennan's old colleague Dean Rusk, who as Johnson's secretary of state was himself grilled during the Senate hearings, called Kennan shortly thereafter to complain about his implicit criticism of the administration's policy in Vietnam. In a follow-up letter to one of Rusk's assistants, Kennan tried to correct what he viewed as Rusk's misunderstanding of his statements, and to emphasize that he had not volunteered to testify. He also tried to clarify, for Rusk's benefit, precisely where he differed with the administration. Kennan suggested that mistakes had been made in three areas: (1) in Washington's association with the "parochial ambitions" of the South Vietnamese regime, (2) in the "usefulness and wisdom" of the bombings in the North, and (3) in the "style of our entire operation," which he saw as haphazard and poorly coordinated.[22]

The bottom line of Kennan's testimony, however, was essentially the idea that containment was not applicable to Vietnam. Indeed, this was specifically raised during the hearing when a senator asked Kennan, "How can we contain in Vietnam?" Rather than state flatly that he saw no need to do so, he answered the question obliquely. Washington "would do better," he said, "if we really would show ourselves a little more relaxed and less terrified of what happens in . . . the smaller countries of Asia . . . and not jump around like an elephant frightened by a mouse every time these things occur. It is my feeling that no one is going to be able to draw blood from a stone, and no one is going to make much more out of these territories than what is in them, and I do not think that even the Communists in most instances are going to do anything with these territories that is necessarily going to be as tragic as we think."[23] The United States, Kennan concluded, was "a very great power" that "could absorb probably more of this sort of thing than one thinks."[24] In effect, he was suggesting that Washington simply recognize and acknowledge that Vietnam was expendable.

Kennan had explicitly made this point—that he deemed Vietnam outside the line of containment—in a lecture at Denison University on 9 February, just one day before his Senate testimony. Vietnam, he stated, was "vital neither to our interests nor to the peace of the world." This judgment was reinforced, in his view, by the Sino-Soviet rift, which he saw as the ideal vehicle of containment.

Southeast Asian Communists, Kennan argued, were more likely to play Beijing and Moscow off each other than to align themselves decisively with either. As a result, monolithic Soviet-led Communism—the original target of containment—was not a serious threat in Vietnam.[25]

As quickly as he rendered this judgment, however, Kennan raised the prestige factor, which tended to contradict, if not undermine, his own argument for disengagement. Although the basic theory of containment would not have justified the US presence in Vietnam, Kennan said, the theory nonetheless dictated that the United States—given the situation as it existed in early 1966—was obliged to stay there long enough to seek a settlement that did not significantly enhance Beijing's or Moscow's prestige at Washington's expense. Unfortunately, Kennan argued, the administration was frustrating this goal through its escalation of the war and its efforts to achieve a "nice democratic Vietnam," which he believed was impossible. For that reason, he concluded, "I am obliged to say that what we are trying to do in Vietnam today, in the military sense, goes beyond anything the original containment theory was meant to justify, and beyond anything which the application of that theory to the conditions of today in Southeast Asia would warrant."[26] Nonetheless, as long as US prestige was at stake, Kennan did not yet advocate a complete US withdrawal from Vietnam.

Perhaps not surprisingly, Kennan's highly publicized statements of February 1966 were not heeded by Johnson and Rusk, and he became even more pessimistic about the course of events in Vietnam and the way the administration was handling them. His mood was captured in a letter he wrote in late May 1966:

> I have a feeling of miserable unhappiness and helplessness about this whole situation. I see a series of catastrophic possibilities, and no favorable ones, at the end of the path on which we are now advancing. And it is particularly shocking to see the President and the Secretary of State doing all in their power to stimulate and to enlist behind this hopeless effort the most violent sort of American patriotic emotionalism—conveying the impression that what we are now involved in is a great national cause, that we have passed the point where any useful purpose could be served by discussion about the desirability of our action, that we must now all stand together behind the boys on the battlefield, that we are full of "determination," etc. I wish I could do something more, myself, but I have the feeling that my piece has been spoken, and that further remonstrances would do no good.[27]

But as the war intensified and the commitment of US troops increased, Kennan soon felt the need to break his silence again. On 25 September, he wrote another letter to the *New York Times*, this time to address the "strong possibility that we may be approaching the point of no return in the drift toward major war." Kennan renewed his plea for "a wide measure of moderation and restraint," and particularly for the end of the bombing of North Vietnam. The bombing campaign, Kennan believed, not only was not improving chances for a peaceful settlement; it was also having a negative effect on world opinion.[28]

By November 1966, Kennan was ready to compromise on the prestige factor. He told an audience at the Woodrow Wilson School in Washington, DC, that the United States should extract itself from Vietnam "as soon as this can be done on anything less than humiliating terms." He now viewed the US involvement there as "unnecessary, unprofitable, [and] unpromising" and saw "no conceivably favorable outcome" to continued US military engagement. The only viable solution, he suggested, would be an international agreement to neutralize Vietnam. Under such a scheme, Kennan argued, it would make no difference whether the country was Communist or not. Nor did it matter, he said bluntly, what happened to the South Vietnamese regime; it would in any event be guided by self-interest, and so should Washington. Kennan was asked whether he expected the Johnson administration to follow this advice. "Not in the slightest," he said.[29]

By the end of 1966, Kennan had largely given up the fight and was finally inclined to withdraw into silence. For the most part he did so, although he was again called before the Senate Foreign Relations Committee in late January 1967. In this appearance, Kennan addressed the subject of Vietnam only to repeat his opposition to the bombing in the North and his continued support for Gavin's "enclave" strategy. After that, he made little public comment on Vietnam throughout 1967—"in reluctant deference," he wrote late in the year, "to the numerous intimations from [Johnson and Rusk] that criticisms of their policy played into the hands of the enemy."[30]

In private, however, Kennan remained staunchly opposed to the war and was often consulted for his views by other public figures and scholars. One of these was Columbia University professor Arthur Schlesinger Jr., who had been a special adviser to Kennedy. In a lengthy 17 October 1967 letter to Schlesinger, Kennan outlined what he saw as "the crucial weaknesses" of Johnson's policy in Vietnam, which in his view resulted from "confusion in the analysis of the problem and in the shaping of our own response."[31]

The primary element of confusion, which Kennan associated in particular with Rusk, was the failure to acknowledge that the Vietnamese conflict was essentially a civil war rather than an international one. Closely linked to this was the administration's misrepresentation of the war as one in which the Chinese Communists were intimately involved as the ultimate enemy. Here Kennan expressed his belief that "the Chinese have not taken any active part in this war," and that a successful Vietnamese Communist regime was more likely to be independent than a puppet for Beijing.[32]

Kennan then focused on his complaints about the US response to the Vietnam problem. "Of these," he stated, "the most central, most fateful, and least excusable" was the administration's failure to acknowledge that it could never do more for the South Vietnamese than what they were willing and able to do for themselves: "A correct approach to this problem would have begun with the recognition that . . . the possibilities for our success were limited by the qualities of determination, strength, morale, leadership, etc., that were present in the Saigon regime. If the non-Communist South Vietnamese, as seems to have been the case all along, were incapable of producing out of their midst a political vitality commensurate with that of the Vietcong, then we should have recognized at the start that this patient was beyond saving, either by us or by any other outside party, and our concern should have been to soften the impact of his demise, not to try to keep him alive by crawling into his skin."[33] This language, and especially that which followed, was strongly reminiscent of Kennan's attitude toward Chiang Kai-shek's Nationalist Chinese regime during 1948–49:

> Surely a South Vietnamese body politic which, even with the help of fifty to a hundred billion dollars worth of aid from us, and with the support of an American army of a half a million men, has shown itself unable to cope with the problem of Communist infiltration and intimidation in its own villages, is not likely to be able to look after its own interests very well in the wake of an eventual American withdrawal. Against this background of political torpor and frailty on the part of those we are trying to help, the best we could hope to achieve by further military successes in this encounter would be to saddle ourselves with a longterm occupational commitment—a commitment which would itself be apt further to weaken, rather than to strengthen, the political vitality of the South Vietnamese.[34]

Kennan saw equally egregious miscalculation in the administration's apparent belief that Ho Chi Minh and the Viet Cong would eventually call off the struggle and sue for peace if and when they were persuaded of Washington's determination to "stay the course." This, Kennan said bluntly, was a "chimerical hope" because surrender was not in the Communist tradition. On the contrary, "they might prefer to go down fighting."[35]

In his final comments for Schlesinger, Kennan addressed what he considered the faint hope, under the prevailing circumstances, of a negotiated settlement. Again repeating his plea of nearly two years earlier, he insisted that de-escalation of the conflict was a prerequisite to any settlement, negotiated or otherwise. This, moreover, meant above all an end to the bombing of North Vietnam: "The bomb-ings should stop because they obviously represent an extravagant and profoundly misconceived undertaking, in which the relationship of military result to the re-sources committed is absurdly uneconomical, and which suffers further from the fact that it flies in the face both of the sensibilities of the world public and of the moral conscience of our own. They should stop for these reasons, whether their termination leads to negotiations or not. If their cessation does lead to negotiations, so much the better . . . but the public should not be given the impression that the cessation is not desirable *unless* this were the result."[36]

This letter to Schlesinger was essentially an academic treatise. Needless to say, it had no impact on administration policy, nor was it necessarily intended to. Ken-nan by this time was merely one voice in a chorus of critics of Johnson's Vietnam policy. But his was an eloquent voice, and he again took it public in 1968. In what was probably the most politically partisan act of his career, Kennan endorsed Sen-ator Eugene McCarthy's presidential candidacy almost exclusively on the basis of McCarthy's opposition to the Vietnam War. Indeed, some of Kennan's most em-phatic public criticism of the war, and of Johnson's handling of it, was contained within a speech he gave introducing McCarthy to an audience in Newark, New Jersey in February 1968. On that occasion, he characterized the US involvement in Vietnam as "devoid of a plausible, coherent, and realistic object." The John-son administration, despite "a long series of pleas and warnings from wise and experienced people," had committed what could only be viewed as "a massive miscalculation and error of policy, an error for which it is hard to find many par-allels in our history, an error rendered doubly serious and difficult to excuse by the number and quality of the warning voices that have been raised against it." It was fortunate, Kennan said, that an election year had arrived to give the nation an opportunity to remedy the situation by summoning new leadership.[37]

In another public speech on 1 June 1968, Kennan expressed his hope that "fur-ther escalation" of the Vietnam War had at last become "politically unthink-able." He was not optimistic, however, about the peace negotiations which by that time had begun. He observed only that "successful liquidation" of the US com-mitment in Vietnam was "a prerequisite to any successful national policy over the coming four years, whether at home or abroad."[38]

Kennan maintained this position after Richard Nixon was elected president in November 1968. A year later, after perceiving that the Nixon administration was temporizing, Kennan finally issued a call for the speedy withdrawal of US forces from Vietnam. It was no longer worthwhile, he argued, to continue "hold-ing the South Vietnamese regime up by the scruff of the neck like a limp puppet." It was "not up to us" to mediate the civil war in Vietnam: "What we should have is military withdrawal and more quickly than the President seems to envisage—but combined, of course, with every effort to mitigate [its] unfavorable effects. Let us do all we can to prepare the South Vietnamese regime for its additional burdens, giving it whatever it needs in the way of military equipment and training to meet the political competition it has to face. But then let us really withdraw. What remains is their task, not ours."[39] This statement in one respect is reminiscent of Kennan's attitude toward the South Koreans in 1948–49. At that time, he gave lip service to the idea of bolstering the South Koreans' capacity for self-defense, when in reality he was willing to surrender South Korea to its fate—which he fully expected to be Communist domination.

The statement, however, again reflects the fundamental inconsistency that was common to Kennan's thinking about both Vietnam and Korea. As he had with Korea, Kennan had declared Vietnam to be strategically unimportant to the United States while at the same time declaring that American prestige should not be abandoned there. In Korea these two ideas had proved irreconcilable: in June 1950, after the withdrawal he advocated had facilitated the Communist invasion from the North, Kennan led the charge for US military intervention to defend US prestige on the Korean peninsula. Now, in 1969, he was advocating the withdrawal of US forces from Vietnam without suggesting how American prestige was to be upheld in the process. Surely if there was a way to "mitigate the unfavorable effects" of a US withdrawal, the Johnson administration would have seized on it much earlier, and many of the dilemmas of the US presence in Vietnam could have been avoided.

Historian Walter Hixson has characterized Kennan's call for a US withdrawal from Vietnam in late 1969 as a "belated abandonment" of containment there.[40] Kennan, however, had in fact abandoned containment in Vietnam more than 20 years earlier. Nor was Kennan, as Hixson has suggested, particularly concerned about the "domino effect" in Southeast Asia. What Kennan had failed to do was reconcile his original decision that Indochina was expendable with his instinctive defense of US prestige when it was challenged by Communist forces. He ultimately resolved this dilemma only when he concluded that even US prestige could not be salvaged in Vietnam.[41]

In February 1970, Kennan returned to Denison University to give another speech—this one entitled "Beyond Vietnam"—on the fourth anniversary of the 1966 speech at Denison in which he had declared that Vietnam was "vital neither to our interests nor to the peace of the world" and thus outside the scope of containment. On this occasion he reiterated his desire for a US withdrawal from Vietnam—as "a matter of necessity," no longer of choice—but he emphasized two additional themes. First, Kennan asserted that the prolonged US intervention in Vietnam was fueling international "cynicism about our motives and methods" that was a growing liability for Washington regardless of how "overdrawn and unjust" the criticism of the United States might be. Second, Kennan made a point of distancing himself from and even condemning the radical ideological opponents of the war: "I do not share the view that we have gone into Vietnam for evil purposes. I don't believe we have knowingly done monstrous things to the Vietnamese people. I feel no part of that admiration and sympathy for our communist opponents that many critics of the Vietnam War have professed to feel. I see those opponents as brutal, bigoted fanatics. Finally, I do not like, any more than thousands of other people do, some of the methods by which opposition to the Vietnam war has been manifested here at home in these last years."[42] Kennan nonetheless reaffirmed that the US involvement "has got to stop, and the sooner the better."

US military involvement in Vietnam, however, dragged on for another three years. In the spring of 1972, after a major North Vietnamese offensive into the South, Nixon renewed his pursuit of a negotiated peace but made no progress. In a national address on 8 May 1972, he attributed this lack of progress to North Vietnam's rejection of a cease-fire proposal and intransigence at the negotiating table. Nixon announced that Washington's only viable option was imposing a blockade and mining North Vietnam's ports—in order to undermine its offensive capabilities—and continuing air and naval strikes. According to Kennan's diary, he was contacted by a White House official—at Nixon's personal instruction—to solicit his views on the president's policy statement: "I said I was afraid I could give the President small comfort here. There were important points on which I simply could not go along with him. One was the bombings. I had never seen evidence that strategic bombing was very effective when it came to interdicting the flow of supplies to the battlefield. . . . Secondly, I thought it likely that the . . . people of South Vietnam were probably most concerned that the war should stop, and would be willing to pay the price of having a North Vietnamese Communist regime pinned on them, if that would only lead to the cessation of hostilities. . . . [As] far as the future was concerned, we ought to go ahead and get the troops out of there as fast as possible." In an effort to soften the blow, Kennan emphasized to the Nixon aide that he had avoided associating himself with any of the president's public critics "partly because I had sympathy with him in the problems he faced" but also because Kennan's views diverged in some respects from many of the public critics and he "did not want to invite any confusion as to my own position."[43]

By then, Kennan had indeed finally withdrawn from the public debate over Vietnam, no doubt recognizing that nothing more could come of his engagement with it. The direct US military role in the war finally ended a year later, after the signing of the Paris Peace Accords in January 1973. Kennan had been largely correct in his warnings in 1949–50 about the dangers of US involvement in Indochina, and in his analysis in the 1960s about the mistakes Washington had made in Vietnam—particularly in the assessment he wrote for Schlesinger in October 1967. "The lessons of Vietnam are few and plain," he wrote in 1975: "not to be hypnotized by the word 'communism' and not to mess in other people's civil wars where there is no substantial American interest at stake." Two years later, he reiterated the need to absorb those lessons: "No one believed more strongly than I did . . . in the folly of the undertaking. We miscalculated in a number of respects. We found that the venture could not be carried to completion as we had conceived it. Very well. We took cognizance of our failure, pocketed our losses, and retired. It is for us now to come to terms, quietly, in our own minds and hearts, with the experience."[44]

Conclusion

LEGACIES OF ENGAGEMENT WITH EAST ASIA

Kennan's professional experience with East Asia policy began with profound impact and ended with deep frustration. Despite his early and dramatic success as director of the Policy Planning Staff (PPS) in guiding postwar US policy toward China and Japan in strategically pragmatic directions, his subsequent efforts to influence policy toward Korea and Southeast Asia were much less successful. Moreover, his vision for the US approach to both China and Japan was short-lived, given Washington's decisions after the outbreak of the Korean War to embrace the Nationalist government on Taiwan (which Kennan despised) and establish long-term military bases in Japan (which he opposed). Thus, even where his impact on American policy in East Asia was profound, it was in many respects ephemeral.

Kennan attributed this to misguided and politically driven mind-sets in Washington, and the difficulty of trying to understand the mind-sets of East Asian countries themselves. He wrote in 1960: "The entire vocabulary of Western politics and historiography is inadequate as a means of understanding and describing the political realities of the Orient. . . . The fact is, quite simply, that we are dealing here with a wholly different world not only geographically but also in thought and feeling, perhaps even in the nature of political reality."[1] Here again Kennan adopted the perennial stereotype of the "inscrutable" Asians, which clouded some of his judgments and which he may have used to rationalize some of his failures. But over time he found the US approach to East Asia equally inscrutable, or at least frustrating and ill fated.

Kennan echoed most of these sentiments in his engagement with East Asian issues for the rest of his life, as already seen in the case of the Vietnam War. After retiring from government in 1953, he spent the next half century at the Institute for Advanced Study in Princeton, New Jersey (with the exception of his 1961–63 tenure as ambassador in Yugoslavia). During that period he was occasionally prompted by events or by invitation to express his views or offer policy recommendations on Far Eastern affairs. Both the consistency and the evolution of Kennan's views on these occasions reflect ideas about the region that he had inherited or embraced during his time as PPS director.

Containment and East Asia

Perhaps most surprising about Kennan's approach to East Asia from the beginning was how narrowly he applied his doctrine of containment there. As has been shown, his focus was almost exclusively on Japan, because only there—in Kennan's view—did the following combination exist: (a) a strategically consequential area that was of vital interest to the United States and (b) a real or potential threat of Soviet domination. This was the reason he made Japan the centerpiece of his "strategic concept" for US policy in the region and undertook pursuit of the "reverse course." And although his ideas for the requisite US force posture in Japan were overridden (as Washington came to pursue globally a more militarized version of containment than he later claimed to advocate), Kennan never retreated from his belief that Japan was the forward line of US resistance against Soviet influence in East Asia.

As has also been shown, Kennan early on had excluded Korea and Southeast Asia from the applicability of his containment doctrine. Neither of them, in his view, was strategically important enough to the United States that Soviet domination of either would represent a grave threat or intolerable loss to US interests. In both places, however, he was inconsistent in his application of this principle. After the outbreak of the Korean War, he invoked the need to uphold US credibility and prestige in supporting US military intervention aimed at pushing back against an extension of Soviet influence. And during the Vietnam War, Kennan delayed advocating a US military withdrawal until a loss of US prestige was unavoidable. But in both places he ultimately was prepared to accept Soviet domination—if it came—as something that was unfortunate but tolerable.

This was essentially Kennan's view with regard to China. Although his dismissal of China's strategic importance effectively surrendered it to the Communists, he did not view this as betrayal or abandonment of containment. He simply denied that the doctrine was applicable to mainland China, because it was targeted specifically and exclusively at Soviet Communism. It was designed, moreover, to prevent the spread of Moscow's influence into areas that were strategically important to the United States—and Kennan never considered mainland China to be such an area. As early as April 1948, in a draft letter to journalist Walter Lippman, he rejected Lippman's suggestion that containment was destined to fail as a strategic doctrine on the grounds that the United States could not apply equal pressure against Soviet influence everywhere it appeared. Containment, Kennan said, was never intended to be applied everywhere—particularly not in China. The United States, he argued, had in fact recognized and accepted Soviet influence in much of northern China as part of the Yalta accord in 1945. At that time, moreover, it was seen as likely that Russia would extend its influence further into China: "What of it? I never said we would—or should—be able to hold equally everywhere. But I felt there was a good sporting chance that we would be able to hold in enough places, and in sufficiently strategic places, to accomplish our general purpose. I know now that there was."[2] Kennan thus dismissed China from any discussion of containment.

Years later, however, his perspective would evolve. In 1960, after a decade of Chinese hostility toward the United States in the wake of the Korean War, Kennan asserted that it was a vital US interest to erect "firm barriers" to what he characterized as "contemporary Chinese imperialism," and specifically to "see to it that the major archipelagos and islands lying off the coast of East Asia do not become susceptible of exploitation by mainland forces hostile to the peace and freedom of the Pacific community." This clearly implied a desire to prevent the spread of Chinese influence within the region, and his approach seemed wholly consistent with his original characterization—in the 1947 "X" article—of the means of containing Soviet Russia: through the "adroit and vigilant application of counterforce at a series of constantly shifting geographical and political points." But Kennan did not conceptualize or talk about China in terms of "containment," and he continued to characterize China as internally preoccupied, diplomatically isolated, and incapable of posing an offensive threat to the United States.[3]

In a speech four years later, however, Kennan shifted at least rhetorically, using "containment" to describe US policy toward China. Beijing's Communist leaders, he said, hated the United States because of its "temerity to stand in their path and to obstruct the expansion of their power." Kennan said the United States had "no choice but to place ourselves in that path" in order to preserve the post–World War II regional balance of power and to prevent the emergence of "an Asia dominated by people so prejudiced against us, ideologically, as the Chinese Communists." He then nominally invoked his doctrine: "And as part of this effort of containment (*for that is really what it is* [emphasis added]), we have tried to see to it that Communist China was denied recognition, denied admission to the UN, denied the advantages of normal participation in the life of the international community until such time as its leaders would moderate their ambitions, desist from their expansionist efforts, and accommodate themselves to the continued existence of independent governments elsewhere on the Asiatic continent. . . . This effort at containment I have been talking about has been going on now, in one way or another, for a decade and a half."[4] On this occasion, Kennan insisted that the United States was seeking only to prevent the extension of Chinese Communist power to "those insular and peninsular appendages of the Asiatic continent"—this time including both South Korea and the offshore island countries. He emphasized that the US approach was wholly defensive, not "purely, or even primarily, a military" strategy, and not aimed at overthrowing the Chinese Communist regime. Kennan may have been using "containment" as a way of disparaging what he perceived as an overly antagonistic approach to Beijing by Washington. But whatever definition of "containment" he had in mind, it is hard to distinguish what he was advocating from his own approach to the Soviet Union.

In any event, Kennan also introduced the thought that the Sino-Soviet split, which by then was fully apparent, was profoundly relevant to the issue of containing Communism, if not to containing China: "The basic fact that world communism is becoming pluralistic rather than a monolithic phenomenon represents, unquestionably, the most hopeful thing that has come over the world situation in the past twenty years." By 1967, when Kennan published the first volume of his memoirs, he was crediting the Chinese Communists with the crowning achievement of containment in its strictest sense. By asserting its independence from the Kremlin, Beijing had challenged Moscow's claim to leadership of the Communist world, making it a bipolar one. The Sino-Soviet split was thus "the greatest single measure of containment that could be conceived. It not only invalidated the original concept of containment, it disposed in large measure of the very problem to which it was addressed"—that of counterbalancing the international control of Soviet Communism.[5]

By then Kennan had firmly settled on a definition of containment that excluded China as a target. His explication came in a 1966 speech entitled "Containment: Russia and China," which was prompted by the fear of Chinese Communist influence in Vietnam. Having emerged by then as a public critic of US intervention in Vietnam, Kennan probably sought to refute the notion that it was necessary to contain China there. He started by admitting that his theory of containment—as initially presented in the "X" article—had been ill defined. Among the omissions he acknowledged was his failure to specify that all areas of the globe were not equally important. He recalled, however, that he had originally identified five strategic power centers in the world: the United States, Britain, continental Europe, Russia, and Japan. "Please note," Kennan observed, "that China did not enter into this category. I personally do not consider that it enters into it today." The containment doctrine was about keeping the other power centers outside Soviet control. China was beyond that scope, even though it was under Communist control, because it was not, in Kennan's view, a strategic power center and, in any event, was not under *Soviet* Communist control. With regard to "containing" Communist China, the only relevant factor was Washington's post–World War II commitments to Japan, Taiwan, and South Korea, which would have been undermined by Communist control of those countries. But Kennan appeared confident that China either did not intend or did not have the capability to assert control over those areas. Consequently, although Communist control of China was undesirable, regrettable, and disturbing, it was "not an intolerable threat, in itself, to world peace, and does not represent anything we cannot live with for a good long time." Kennan acknowledged the implicit threat of Chinese Communist expansion elsewhere in Asia, but he concluded that it appeared to be possible only in areas that were not strategically important to the United States—here he included Vietnam—or would not be capable of posing a substantial military threat if they were under Chinese Communist control. These circumstances, in Kennan's judgment, further negated the applicability of the containment doctrine to Chinese Communism.[6]

Kennan reaffirmed this view in 1973 when again asked whether containment applied to China. He responded that the strategy did not have "any great relevance" there because China was not a "highly expansive power" except with regard to its prior territorial claims, especially Taiwan. Beyond that, Kennan assessed, the Chinese aspired "to know how to make friends and influence people" within East Asia, but they did not appear to be trying to impose "direct Chinese domination" over neighboring countries—as the Soviet Union did.[7]

On balance, and especially in retrospect, Kennan was ambivalent and inconsistent on the applicability of containment to Communist China. It was perhaps his prerogative to exclude China from his own doctrine by narrowly defining the doctrine as targeted exclusively at the Soviet Union. But his insistence on erecting "firm barriers" to an expansion of Chinese power, his justification for standing in its path, and his explanation of what policies this would require amounted to essentially the same strategy and tactics he advocated against the Soviet Union.

Moreover, Kennan's insistence that containment did not apply to China because it was not strategically relevant to the United States was remarkably inattentive to China's strategic potential and thus lacking in prescience. It was also inconsistent with his own judgment about the implications of the Sino-Soviet split, which greatly enhanced China's strategic value to the United States in ways he recognized and admitted. Indeed, the rift between Beijing and Moscow was a primary catalyst for the US opening to China in the 1970s.

Ironically, although Kennan denied the applicability of his containment doctrine to China, his support for the goal of limiting China's influence within East Asia relative to the United States validated the perception of the Chinese themselves, who came to refer to that US goal—Washington's determination "to stand in their path and to obstruct the expansion of their power," as Kennan had described it[8]—as a policy of "containment." Thus, a version of his doctrine became operative in the region even though it had renounced its name.

The Legacy of Kennan's China Experience

When Kennan left the State Department, he carried with him several firmly established ideas about China and how to deal with it that long resonated in his commentary on Chinese affairs and China policy. "As for China," he wrote in 1951, "I have no use for either of the two regimes." Channeling both MacMurray and Davies, Kennan was contemptuous of Chiang Kai-shek's Nationalist government on Taiwan. He never accepted any rationale for a continued US commitment to Chiang after the generalissimo fled to the island; on the contrary, he considered it "both fateful and discreditable." During the Quemoy crisis of 1958, he expressed his hope that the episode would provide an opportunity for Washington to "free ourselves from excessive commitment to the personal fortunes of Chiang as a figure on the Chinese scene." As late as 1984 he observed that the Communist takeover of China was primarily attributable to "the weakness and corruption of the Chiang Kai-shek regime, and the tendency of that regime to lean on us instead of pulling up its own socks."[9]

Kennan came to exhibit no less contempt for the Chinese Communists after they had attacked US forces in Korea and embraced xenophobia and authoritarianism. He castigated the leaders in Beijing as a group of "embittered fanatics" who had chosen to become rabid enemies of the United States: "I have never seen anything that would suggest to me that these men have the faintest concern for Western values of any sort. I have the impression that there is no catastrophe that could befall Western civilization, however appalling the destruction of historic values and however tragic the suffering, which they would not witness with satisfaction and enjoyment."[10] This view was only reinforced over time. In 1960, Kennan observed that China's Communist regime was engaged in a campaign of anti-Americanism "more vicious, more violent, more impregnated with hatred and falsehood, than any propaganda effort any government has ever conducted." Even Stalin at his worst, he wrote in 1964, was less emotional and more pragmatic than the leaders in Beijing, with "their extraordinary belief that the sort of gray, joyless hell they have drawn over the Chinese people has something to do with human progress."[11]

Kennan had also reached several firm conclusions about the Chinese nation as a whole—judgments also based in part on ideas he had absorbed from Mac-Murray and Davies. On the one hand, he acknowledged China as "the seat of a great culture which deserves our highest respect" and he credited the Chinese with being "an extremely mature, intelligent, industrious and resourceful people" and indeed "the most intelligent, man for man, of the world's peoples."[12] On the other hand, they had shown themselves to be "intensely xenophobic and arrogant" and "capable of great ruthlessness when they considered themselves to be crossed." The Chinese were "heirs to a political philosophy and a tradition of statesmanship that has never really adjusted itself to a relationship of equality between China and the outside world." China was, in short, "a nation animated by a rather outrageous superiority complex toward the rest of mankind and led congenitally by governments that pursue their own interests, with a cynicism and ruthlessness and finesse second to none in the annals of the behavior of modern great states."[13]

Kennan retained this cultural perspective on the Chinese for decades thereafter. As late as 1999 he told an interviewer: "The Chinese, to my opinion, are the French of Asia. . . . They are both proud people. Both are conscious of being the bearers of a great cultural tradition. They don't really, in either case, like foreigners; or at least they don't particularly appreciate the presence of foreigners in their midst. They like to be left alone."[14] Kennan claimed it was through this combination of arrogance, diplomatic skill, and xenophobia that the Chinese had "succeeded in corrupting a large proportion of the Americans who had anything to do with them." In his view, Americans who believed themselves to be building a bilateral friendship with China had been repeatedly duped. "How many more lessons do we have to have," he wrote in 1958, "before we learn that the Chinese have thought us fools for our generous impulses and have hated us all the more for the necessity that compelled them to accept the benefits?"[15]

It was for those Americans enamored of China that Kennan reserved perhaps his most visceral criticism, again reminiscent of MacMurray: "We, in our sentimentalities, our bumbling goodwill, our thirst for trade or converts, our political naiveté, and the ease with which we could be both flattered and misled by the obsequiousness of talented servants who hated our guts behind their serving-screens, were simply not up to them."[16] Kennan condemned in particular the China Lobby, whose efforts had for so long frustrated his own efforts to help devise a pragmatic and realistic China policy—and whose partisan recriminations had destroyed Davies's career and filled the public mind with "myths" assigning blame for the "loss of China." On the latter point, Kennan said the United States "had never *had* China" and thus "could scarcely have lost it." The China Lobby, he believed, had fostered political divisions in the United States "to the vast detriment of our society and to the amused enjoyment of our most bitter enemies." Kennan's contempt was so intense that he wrote in 1956 that he would prefer a relationship with China "founded on total hostility and suspicion" to one driven by the constituencies and motivations of the China Lobby.[17] His verdict on the impact of this mind-set on US policy toward China was damning: "We paid . . . a heavy price for our emotional commitment to China . . . [and] we received in return precisely nothing. Never has any policy of this government suffered such a disastrous failure as that policy which over fifty years staked our interests in East Asia on the prospective gratitude and favor of the Chinese people."[18]

This appears to have been the foundation for Kennan's long-standing belief that the United States should and could simply divest itself from engagement with China. In 1950 he actually took consolation in the fact that the collapse of Nationalist forces and the victory of the Chinese Communists had effectively "spelled the elimination of United States influence from the mainland of Asia." Kennan was content to leave it that way. "The less we have to do with China the better," he wrote in 1951; "We need neither covet the favor, nor fear the enmity, of any Chinese regime." Kennan considered the withdrawal of the United States from mainland China to be a positive step in the sense that it broke the spell and gave Washington its first opportunity in fifty years to reassess its relationship with China. Moreover, he hoped that the period of US isolation from China would endure for a long time so that "our people might be cured both of their silly dreams of intimacy with the Chinese and of their equally silly excesses of moral indignation over the behavior of Chinese governments." Until that time arrived, Kennan recommended that Americans "had better be kept away from the Chinese; they are now like moths before the flame, whenever they come near them."[19] Kennan reaffirmed this judgment as late as 1970: "I remain incorrigible and unrepentant in my wish that the American public and its political establishment could get over its infatuation with the mainland of Asia and could recognize that we have very little to contribute to that part of the world and even less to expect from it. We should be content to leave it alone, and to be left alone by it."[20]

Through the 1960s Kennan retained his ambivalence on whether the United States should recognize the Chinese Communist regime or support its admission to the UN. Regardless of the benefits either step might yield, neither was likely to change the regime's "loathing for us or their determination to see our influence and activity removed, lock, stock, and barrel, from Asia and the Far East generally."[21] In the long run, Kennan believed, the Chinese Communists would ultimately come around and seek engagement with the United States out of necessity:

"When the discipline of adversity has done its work, when it has driven home the lessons which it alone is capable of bringing to arrogant and excited people, and when anti-American and other illusions which now distort Chinese policy have been shattered as completely as those which for so many years guided American policies toward China, then, perhaps, an era will open when the tremendous possibilities of a Chinese-American relationship devoid of patronization on the one side, of arrogance and hatred on the other, can be realized."[22] Kennan acknowledged in 1965 that the absence of any relations with China was "wholly unnatural." He believed, however, that any normalization process would take a long time and would eventually require bargaining and compromise—"like any great adjustment of international relations." In the meantime, Kennan advised in 1970 that the United States should not hope for or expect too much from the Chinese Communists: "They are not likely to harm us. They are also not likely to help us. What we have to do is learn, at long last, to leave them alone: to go our way and let them go theirs."[23]

When President Nixon neglected this advice and launched his "opening" to China in 1972, Kennan was initially critical, probably in part because of his Democratic Party sympathies. He wrote that Nixon's visit to Beijing "cannot fail to raise hopes and anticipations at home which no one could seriously expect to satisfy." It would also be a blow to US allies in East Asia: marking "in one way or another, the end of the Chiang regime on Taiwan," a severe shock to South Korea, and "a grievous loss of face" to the Japanese that "they will not soon forget." While Kennan acknowledged that the visit might have some positive consequences, on balance it "cannot have enhanced America's reputation for steadiness and reliability." As a professional diplomat, he also faulted Nixon and National Security Advisor Henry Kissinger for front-loading summitry when so many bilateral political issues were unresolved. Kennan bluntly accused Nixon of pursuing the visit primarily for domestic political reasons, and lamented what he anticipated as the revival of the "sentimental enthusiasm for China." In any case, he predicted that "the importance of the Nixon visit will be largely exhausted, like the President himself, by the time he sets foot in the United States" because it will have been more symbolic than substantive, and would not have achieved "any greater understanding between the two peoples than has existed in the past."[24]

Kennan's assessment of the Nixon trip mellowed over time, but only marginally. One year later he told an interviewer that Nixon had essentially "turned over half of the US influence . . . in the Far East to the Chinese Communists," but Kennan—maintaining his isolationist perspective—said this was not necessarily bad because US efforts to play a leading role there were "unnatural" and there was "no great future in American intimacy with China." By 1977, however, he allowed that the Nixon-Kissinger breakthrough had been "constructive" but would have been more so if it had been conducted "in a normal and businesslike manner and without the histrionics of the Nixon visit to Peking."[25]

In any event, the strategic shift represented by Nixon's opening to China ultimately did not alter Kennan's long-standing view that the United States should keep its distance from China and deal with it only as warranted by diplomatic requirements. In 1973 he recommended that Washington only "have outwardly polite and respectful relations" with Beijing and pursue "minimal facilities" for cultural and intellectual exchanges. In 1977, commenting on those who aspired to US friendship and partnership with China, he was "unable to see the foundation for such a view." Chinese and US national interests, he asserted, did not coincide and we should not pretend otherwise. The two countries should "collaborate where we can, agree to differ where we cannot, and see whether we cannot contrive to live reasonably peaceably together for the time being, despite our differences, not asking too much of each other—or too little."[26]

At the same time, Kennan recognized that diplomatic normalization with Beijing was inevitable. To that end, he supported and even advocated the downgrading of US relations with Taiwan, including abrogation of the US-Taiwan mutual defense treaty that had been signed in 1955. But he acknowledged that this needed to be done in a way that ensured both Taiwan's security and the security of US interests in the region. Kennan's bottom line on Taiwan had long been that it simply needed to be kept out of hands that were hostile to or problematic for the United States; only in this respect was the island important to US security. He did not want to see it under Beijing's control, but—given his unhappy experience with Chiang—he did not trust the Nationalist government on the island to govern it wisely or securely. Instead, Kennan asserted, Taiwan's long-term status should be held open until the regimes on the mainland and the island reached an arrangement that was mutually acceptable to them—and to the people on Taiwan. In the meantime, the United States could maintain pragmatic relations with both sides, while still keeping Beijing at a distance.[27]

Even China's "reform and opening up" under Deng Xiaoping in the 1980s and 1990s did not alter Kennan's desire to avoid more than superficial US relations with Beijing. In his diary in 1996, he reaffirmed his mind-set in terms that were strikingly inattentive to China's growing strategic importance: "I cannot see that we have anything to gain from a closer government-to-government relationship with that country. I would like to see us treat them on the diplomatic level with the most impeccable courtesy (which they would understand) but to have, beyond that as little as possible to do with them, and, in the areas where we have to deal with them, to treat them with no smaller a firmness than they are accustomed to putting forward in their relations with us. This would apply in no less measure in problems of trade than anywhere else."[28] On this occasion Kennan was especially dismissive of engaging Beijing on matters of trade or—in the wake of the Tiananmen Square crackdown of 1989—human rights. He advised that "we should guard against allowing our business world to develop any extensive dependence on China in commercial matters" and that we should "desist, finally and completely, from any and every effort to press the Chinese government, now or in [the] future, on matters of human rights"—because the latter "is their concern, not ours."[29] Commenting on China's domestic governance in 1997, Kennan included it among major countries that face more internal problems than they pose externally. Such countries, he wrote, are "dangers both to themselves and to others—not because they necessarily have evil intentions, but because the effort to exert political control over such vast and varied numbers of human beings is too much—too much for democratic processes, too much even for effective despotic authority."[30]

Finally, in what was probably Kennan's last written commentary on China, he wrote in 2001—when he was 97: "I simply fail to understand the long-standing infatuation of our press and public for that country. . . . Whatever we do, they are not going to love us. Where interests conflict, we should look first to the traditional institutions of diplomatic intercourse for the necessary composing of differences. Such problems are normal in the relations among great states. If the problems prove difficult of solution at any given time, this is no reason for seeing China as a dangerous enemy. If, on the other hand, they yield to amicable negotiation, there is no reason for regarding China as a major ally. In either case, I see no reason for over-dramatization of the relationship."[31] Kennan thus never retreated from his inclination—and his recommendation—to pay China no more attention than dictated by necessity.

In retrospect, this appears to reflect Kennan's embrace of MacMurray's assessment that China ultimately was not—and was unlikely to ever become—strategically important or even relevant to the United States. He internalized this early on, and his frustrations in dealing with Nationalist China during the late 1940s and with Communist China thereafter reinforced it—as did his desire to avoid any US engagement with the Chinese that would give the China Lobby, and other constituencies with sentimental attachments to China, renewed opportunities to drive American policy in unrealistic or counterproductive directions. To undergird his argument that China *should* be left alone, Kennan convinced himself that it *could* be left alone, because it was not important—especially compared with Japan—and lacked the capacity to either threaten the United States or command its attention.

This judgment was consistently reflected in his writings. He expressed alarm when a British diplomat calculated in 1950 that China over the long term would be more important than Japan and thus deserved priority in Allied thinking and planning. Kennan responded that China would "never be dependable from the standpoint of Western interests" because, as he expressed on several occasions through the 1960s, China was "not the great power of the Orient." It had neither the military nor the economic and industrial capacity to project power or to pose "any insuperable military threat or problem to us." Indeed, he judged that China's weakness was a fundamental source of many of the problematic trends in East Asia and Washington's difficulties in dealing with it.[32]

Interestingly, this is one of the few issues on which there was a discernible difference in views between Kennan and Davies, who appears to have been more realistic about China's potential strategic weight and importance. In a 1953 letter to Kennan from his "exile" in Peru, Davies enclosed a draft essay entitled "Foreign Policy in the Long View," in which he anticipated the challenges the United States would face if it tried to retain its postwar predominance by keeping down "virile, ambitious people occupying natural power bases." He referred specifically to China, which "notwithstanding certain serious industrial deficiencies . . . is likely to be a considerable power, provided that it has Manchuria." Moreover, Davies—in contrast to Kennan—ranked China above Japan, which he assessed "could not be a significant center of power" unless it had influence in or control over other areas that could help meet its need for natural resources. Kennan, in his response to Davies, did not address this divergence of views; he focused instead on questioning Davies's underlying premise about the viability of US predominance.[33]

Given Kennan's frustrating personal experience with China policy, it is perhaps understandable that when he left government he was eager for Washington to wash its hands of China, and to rationalize that desire by dismissing China's importance. Over the long term, of course, it was not possible for the United States to simply ignore China; and Kennan was uncharacteristically shortsighted and unrealistic when he assessed well into the 1970s and beyond that China would never become a force to be reckoned with.[34] It is surprising and unfortunate that Kennan's personal disgust with the Chinese leadership—both Nationalist and Communist—and for Chinese diplomacy allowed him to deny and overlook the importance of China as long as he did. Late in life he hinted at an explanation. In a 1998 letter to Davies, when Kennan was almost 94, he explained why his extensive writings included little about China: "The reason for this is obvious. I knew, and still know, very little about it."[35] Of course, Kennan had learned quite a lot about China earlier in his career. But he appears never to have overcome his distaste for dealing with it.

Kennan and the US-Japan Alliance

Having set in motion the "reverse course" in Japan, Kennan was immensely grat-ified by its long-term impact. But he failed to realize his tandem goal of neutral-izing Japan militarily, or to persuade anyone of the viability of that goal. In later years he instead came to focus on the presence of the US bases there and the "grow-ing friction with the Japanese" that resulted from them. He had identified this as a potential problem in his 21 August 1950 memo to Acheson, when he warned that a long-term US military presence in Japan "would inevitably be a bone of political contention."[36] In 1956, Kennan said such a presence was bound to be an unnatural and unnecessary burden on Japanese-American relations unless and until it was replaced with arrangements that were more respectful of Japanese sov-ereignty and more acceptable internationally. Echoing the observations he had made in 1948 about the impact on Japan of the US presence there, Kennan de-scribed the US military facilities as a "handicap rather than an aid" in presenting a positive image of Americans to the Japanese.[37] He no doubt felt vindicated in this view when the renegotiation of the 1951 bilateral security treaty in 1960 prompted violent public protests in Japan against the treaty's perceived infringe-ment on Japanese sovereignty. He told an audience in Seattle several months later that the United States should not expect or oblige Tokyo to wholly align its poli-cies with Washington, and should "be careful not to apply to [the Japanese] that self-indulgent patronizing favor that misled us so grievously in the case of China."[38]

In 1964, Kennan visited Japan for the first time since 1948 and subsequently published a retrospective assessment in *Foreign Affairs* entitled "Japanese Secu-rity and American Policy," in which he expressed his disillusionment with Wash-ington's tendency to ignore the negative impact of the US military presence in Japan and to take the security relationship with Tokyo for granted. The Japa-nese, he said, must ultimately resume responsibility for their own defense and, more importantly, reclaim their role as an independent player in world affairs: "There is—and Americans may as well face it—a perfectly natural desire among the Japanese to escape at least partially from the cloying exclusiveness of the American tie, from the helpless passivity it seems to imply . . . and to throw open a sector of the international horizon where Japan could have a set of relation-ships and an importance of her own, not dependent on American tutelage, perhaps—who knows?—even helpful, ultimately, to the United States in an area where we seem to have difficulty helping ourselves."[39] Kennan also criticized what he saw as Washington's inclination to view Japan largely as a "passive instrument in an all-out cold war" because this constrained Tokyo's ability to forge construc-tive relations with its mainland neighbors—something that would be impor-tant to Japan's long-term security. He reiterated this concern in a letter a month later, after attending a conference in New York that discussed the stationing of US nuclear submarines in Japan: "I came away shaken by the apparent inability of the members of the group, including outstandingly those who came from Washington, to look at the Japanese situation in terms other than those of our military competition with Russia and China, and to believe that Japanese-American relations could contain any other values of importance. . . . I have dismal misgivings about such an outlook; for in the long run it can only place us in conflict with the Japanese, who are interested in a more hopeful world than the one we seem [to] envisage."[40] Accordingly, Kennan in his *Foreign Affairs* article recommended that Washington invite Tokyo into consultations "on the suitability of the various arrangements" and the term of the security treaty, and also consider renewing conversations with Moscow about a possible "joint guarantee of Japanese security" that might realize "at long last, General MacArthur's far-sighted concept" of Japanese neutrality. As in 1950, however, these recommendations—especially the idea of engaging the Soviets on Japan—were deemed impracticable and ignored in Washington, regardless of the validity of Kennan's underlying concerns about the long-term impact of the US military presence on US-Japan relations.[41]

By the 1970s, Kennan conceded that his earlier warnings about the psychological impact of the US bases on the Japanese body politic had been exaggerated. The security relationship, he acknowledged in 1972, had survived relatively intact for two decades. But "the strain has been great," Kennan argued. Younger Japanese were increasingly alienated by the US military presence, and their political activism had occasionally stretched the limits of Japan's fledgling democracy. The long-term consequences of this were hard to predict, he observed, but "they could scarcely be good ones." Within a few years Kennan was again thinking in terms of addressing this dilemma by modifying the bilateral security treaty "to make it less offensive to Japanese opinion and clearer in its implications," and the US base structure to make it "less burdensome to Japan." Although by then he was ready to acknowledge that there was "no visible satisfactory alternative" for Tokyo to the US-Japan alliance, he remained uneasy about the asymmetry and room for disappointment in US and Japanese expectations of each other.[42]

Kennan's embrace of the alliance in spite of these concerns reflected his strong belief that US policy in East Asia under whatever circumstances needed to be centered on Japan—a core belief that dated from his initial reading of MacMurray's memorandum but was also inherent in the rationale for both the "reverse course" in occupation policy he had spearheaded and the offshore "security concept" he had proposed in 1948. "There can be no question," he wrote in 1977, "but that the cornerstone of American policy in the Far East should be Japan." He reaffirmed this in 2001, just four years before he died, writing that US "strategic interests in the entire north-Pacific region, for which we fought so hard in World War II, are dependent, as I see it, on the maintenance of a relationship of mutual confidence and alliance" with Japan.[43]

But Kennan never retreated from his insistence that the United States needed to be attentive to the "moral obligation" it inherited when it assumed responsibility for Japan after World War II. This was the obligation to deal respectably and fairly—not condescendingly—with the Japanese, and to acknowledge that Japan was a great power in its own right that would inevitably want and need to assert its independence. According to Kennan, Japan should continue to be the cornerstone of US policy in the Far East, but "not a passive cornerstone—rather, an active one, a talking one—a stone which often harbors a superior wisdom—a stone to be consulted, in some instances to be looked to for guidance, to be looked to sometimes even for leadership."[44] He offered the Japanese direct advice on how to exercise this role during a 1980 visit to Tokyo. Japan, he said, had "possibilities for greatness" and was uniquely equipped to exercise an international "usefulness of the highest order" because it had reached the "very top ranks of world powers" and had "the resources, the genius, the inventiveness, [and] the industriousness" to set an example for other countries. That example was of a prosperous and enterprising country that had the wisdom to avoid both defining national power and influence in military terms and embroiling itself in international conflicts. Accordingly, in a speech at the Tokyo International House, Kennan advised Japan not to "depart from the sound basis on which her defense posture has rested for these past 30 years" by pursuing offensive military capabilities, which would "tend to undermine" the US-Japan relationship—specifically reminding his audience that the security treaty did not oblige Washington to support offensive Japanese military operations. Kennan also warned that it would be the "most dreadful folly" for Japan to pursue nuclear weapons, observing that Hiroshima and Nagasaki had given the Japanese "a moral right superior to that of any other people to warn against the dangers of war in the modern age."[45]

Most fundamentally and strategically, Kennan said the "time has come" for Japan to "make her own judgments on the trend of world events" and "not hesitate to make her voice heard independently." She should do so not only with "those whom she cannot yet regard as friends" but also with "those to whom she had been accustomed to look for friendship and guidance and understanding"— implicitly but no doubt especially the United States. And in that regard, the Japanese should not "rely too extensively on the moods [and] the vagaries of opinion in other countries."[46] Kennan wrote in 1993 that Washington should be prepared to modify or even abandon the US military presence in Japan whenever Tokyo itself was inclined to do so. This was especially the case after the end of the Cold

War, which in Kennan's view eliminated "most of the original rationale for the existence of the present [US-Japan] defense arrangements"—except for the lingering problem of North Korea's nuclear ambitions.[47]

Kennan's encouragement to the Japanese to voice disagreements with US policy or about the bases was not always viewed as helpful in Washington. But he was nonetheless correct in identifying an underlying tension and fault line that would continue to complicate US-Japan relations. Although he may not have foreseen it in 1948, his own "reverse course" policy had helped plant the seeds of the prosperous and powerful Japan that would pose this dilemma for Washington decades later.

Revisiting Korea

In the years after the Korean War, Kennan reverted to his "fair-weather" position toward the US commitment to South Korea. During the 1960s and 1970s, he criticized successive governments in Seoul as repressive and as taking the US security umbrella for granted. Kennan especially viewed South Korea as a "dead weight" on US policy toward Japan because of what he saw as the South Koreans' unwillingness to accommodate themselves to Washington's primary need to focus its East Asian policy on Japan—which he flatly asserted was more important to the United States than Korea. By 1977, he was again advocating the gradual withdrawal of US military forces from Korea—albeit in consultation with its neighboring great powers—on the grounds that the region was sufficiently stable to allow it.[48]

Over the same time period, Kennan developed a somewhat revisionist view (revising his own long-standing assessment) on the strategic importance of Korea. In the 1964 speech in which he briefly acknowledged "containment" of China, he included South Korea among those areas where Washington needed to prevent the extension of Chinese Communist control: "those insular *and peninsular* [emphasis added] appendages of the Asiatic continent" that had survived intact after World War II and the Communist victory in China. Two years later, he reaffirmed his denial of a containment policy toward China, but nonetheless asserted that South Korea was among those areas where a Communist takeover would have been "irreconcilable" with Washington's postwar security commitments. And in 1970 he asserted that Korea was "important to us because it is vitally important to the security of Japan." This, Kennan professed, was the logic he had applied to US intervention in the Korean War in 1950. As we have seen, however, there was inconsistency at the time both in the logic he had used and in his advocacy of it: he had sometimes deemed South Korea strategically important, but usually not; and he had often insisted that letting it fall into a Communist sphere of influence was unacceptable—but he was sometimes prepared to let that happen if it did so in a way that was "gradual and inconspicuous."[49]

To his credit, Kennan anticipated that Washington would separately have problems with North Korea. In 1970, he observed that the regime there had "lost nothing, over [the] years, of its resentment over the frustration of its earlier effort of aggression," had retained a "burning hatred of us for standing in its way," and was militarizing and exuding hostility in ways that could easily fuel a crisis. Because of this risk, he wrote in 1977, "Korea represents one of the two most explosive and dangerous spots on our political map of the world," next to the Middle East.[50] The danger Kennan observed then was subsequently amplified by Pyongyang's pursuit of a nuclear weapons program.

The Legacy of Kennan's Southeast Asia Experience

Kennan never considered Southeast Asia itself to possess strategic importance to the United States. His consistent view was simply that it should be kept neutral—specifically, that it remain outside Communist control and thus unable to pose a danger to the United States. Paradoxically, even the Communist victory in Vietnam was consistent with this view inasmuch as Kennan's original defensive perimeter concept had dismissed the mainland of East Asia as expendable. Instead, his strategic concept had focused on the offshore islands and had paired the Philippines with Japan as a link that needed to be demilitarized and neutralized. Although Kennan retained this view for years thereafter, its efficacy—as with Japan—fell victim to the Korean War, which provided the rationale for Washington to sign the Mutual Defense Treaty with Manila in 1951, thereby ensuring a long-term US military presence. In the wake of the Vietnam War, he nonetheless tried to revive his earlier proposal for demilitarizing the Philippines by recommending the removal of the US military bases there on the grounds that the "original justification" for them had been "extensively undermined" and the US "involvement in Southeast Asia has been liquidated."[51]

This was another one of the very few areas in which Davies had a somewhat different perspective than Kennan. In the 1953 draft essay "Foreign Policy in the Long View," which he shared with Kennan and in which he—unlike Kennan—anticipated China's eventual emergence as an important strategic power, Davies also advocated a different operational approach to the defensive perimeter concept in Southeast Asia. He specifically anticipated the importance of the Philippines—and even some countries in mainland Southeast Asia—as forward-operating areas for the United States. Although he acknowledged the vulnerability of the Southeast Asian countries at the time, "the strategic significance of these states in the situation which we envisage for the future would be considerable."

> It would be through them that we would wish to exert pressure when necessary, on China, Russia and perhaps Japan. It would be from their territory, in part, that we might wish to intervene directly, when necessary, against one or several of the secondary powers in Asia. . . . [The Philippines would be particularly important in this respect, but Thailand, Malaya, and Burma] would also be a barrier to overland expansion southward and southwestward by China or Japan. . . . [In effect, the] avenue for projection of American strength would be, in addition to the direct course across the Arctic and North Pacific, across the Central Pacific to the Philippines and thence, as needed, to a continental lodgment in Thailand, Malaya, and Burma.[52]

Although some elements of Davies's vision were ultimately embraced by US military planners in the region, Kennan never subscribed to it. Instead, he retained his focus on demilitarizing and neutralizing Southeast Asia, based in part on his assessment of its marginal strategic importance. In his 1966 discourse on the relevance of containment to China and East Asia, he excluded not just Vietnam but the whole region. The countries of Southeast Asia were not in the same category as Japan or Korea because "they are not ones where we had, until recently at least, any specific commitment which bound us to their defense," and in any event even Soviet or Chinese Communist control of them would do "no irreparable damage, from the standpoint of our interests. . . . You can't draw blood from a stone; and no communists are going to make major military-industrial powers out of the Southeast Asian countries in any short space of time." Kennan added that the Sino-Soviet rift made it likely that any Southeast Asian Communist regime would more likely play Moscow and Beijing off each other than be a puppet of either. For those reasons, he dismissed any need for US military involvement in the region.[53]

Kennan reaffirmed this verdict in 1977, when he recommended that the United States retreat from Southeast Asia and focus instead on contemplating the lessons of Vietnam. Perhaps comparing it in his mind to what he—echoing both MacMurray and Davies—saw as the earlier ill-fated American infatuation with China, Kennan lamented the advocates of deep US engagement in Southeast Asia: "I find surprising the level of interest in the affairs of that area still manifested by portions of the American press and other media. Surely, if there are any peoples of which it may fairly be said that we have nothing to hope from them, it is the people of that unhappy region."[54] As with China, however, he was surprisingly shortsighted about the economic potential and strategic relevance of Southeast Asia.

Nonetheless, in the political realm Kennan was insightful and prescient in drawing a key lesson for the United States from his experience with Southeast Asia: the risks involved in dealing with mercurial friends and allies. In 1964 he highlighted one of the fundamental challenges inherent in the US competition with China for influence in the rest of East Asia, and Southeast Asia in particular:

> The weapons with which the Chinese are operating here are primarily the political reactions of the people of the threatened areas themselves; their inherited resentments, their fears, their weariness, and such error and prejudice among ourselves and their own regime as can be artificially pumped into their minds. And we, by the same token, have to struggle for control of this same weapon. We have to look to it, in fact, as the basis for our efforts. . . . It is vitally important to remember that we are working here with and through the reactions of people who are not under our power, and on whose loyalty and obedience we can lay no ultimate claim. . . . For this reason, I think we should be chary of ringing professions of determination and of brave resolutions to ourselves and to the world about what we propose to accomplish. . . . [For] our success depends on the collaboration of others for whom we cannot responsibly speak. . . . [The] main question has been not what we ourselves could do, but what we could assist and encourage others to do. We have had a great deal of loyal and effective collaboration in this effort. But we have found ourselves wedded, throughout, not just to the virtues of our associates in the threatened countries, but also to their weaknesses: to their domestic political ambitions, their inefficiencies, their blind spots, their internal rivalries and divisions, their ulterior commitments. We have found our way blocked, at one time or another, by short-sightedness, by timidity, by indifference, by misunderstanding, by deliberately inculcated error, by dislike of foreigners or anti-western prejudices, and above all, by the congenital tendency of people to respond to the efforts of outsiders towards their protection by slackening their own.[55]

Kennan added that these frustrations might have justified US withdrawal from the region if not for the probability that the consequences of doing so could be even worse. At the time, he was thinking primarily of South Vietnam and was still ambivalent about the rationale for the US military presence there. By the end of the Vietnam War, however, he had reassessed that balance sheet and advocated American military withdrawal and political retreat from Southeast Asia. Over the long term, a US strategic retreat from Southeast Asia would be neither feasible nor conducive to US interests. But Kennan's concern about the challenges and risks of relying on East Asian governments as vehicles for US policy in the region would remain a valid one.

Kennan and East Asia: The Balance Sheet

As this book has attempted to show, Kennan's overall approach to the Far East was based on a combination of his doctrine of containment, his defensive perimeter idea for applying that doctrine to the region, and—within that framework—his assessment of the relative strategic importance of those countries where the United States had interests at stake. In East Asia, Kennan applied containment in its strictest original sense: aimed exclusively at preventing the expansion of Soviet power and influence to areas vital to US interests or security. He discounted China in two respects: it was not strategically vital to US interests, and the expansion of Chinese Communism itself was not a major threat because China lacked the capacity for power projection—and whatever threat it might pose could be dealt with through the defensive perimeter concept. Indeed, in Kennan's view the entire mainland of East Asia was not strategically important to the United States. Its domination by Communism—either Soviet or Chinese—might or might not be inevitable, but this did not matter: if it occurred, it would be unfortunate but not catastrophic for the United States, which in any case could not afford to invest the resources and effort that would be necessary to prevent it from happening. Instead, Kennan believed that the United States should focus on the offshore islands as the forward line of US defense, and on that line to make a strong, stable, and self-sufficient Japan—the only strategically consequential power in East Asia—the cornerstone of US policy in the region. Such a Japan, combined with a forward US military presence based primarily on Okinawa, would deter the expansion of Soviet influence in East Asia, secure US interests there, and promote regional stability.

There were several flaws in this approach, many of which became apparent over time. The United States could not "renounce the idea that the mainland of Asia is a place where American purposes are to be realized or where Americans have some great role to play"—as Kennan advised as late as 1970.[56] His core judgment that China was strategically negligible, and that the United States could virtually ignore it, was never realistic. Although that may have appeared reasonable and even preferable at the end of the Chinese civil war, Kennan was injudicious in assuming that China under the Communists—or any other regime—would never be able to develop its economic base and military strength to a level that would require the United States to reckon with it. In his approach to China during the late 1940s and early 1950s, he had embraced too firmly MacMurray's dismissive attitude toward China a decade earlier. He then allowed both his frustration with policy direction and his emotions—especially in the wake of Davies's downfall—to cloud his judgment. Kennan held Chiang Kai-shek's regime beneath contempt, and his later assessment of the Chinese Communist leadership was similarly damning. He also remained scornful of those US constituencies and policymakers who advocated a deeper commitment to Chiang's regime—identifying them with their predecessors to whom MacMurray had attributed an ill-fated infatuation with China. Consequently, in his efforts to justify disengagement from China, Kennan frequently overstated his case: vilifying the Chinese, insisting that the United States have nothing to do with them, and rationalizing this by declaring China wholly expendable.

Some of Kennan's policies toward Japan, especially those involving Japanese security, were also unrealistic. He supported the demilitarization and neutralization of Japan without examining closely how this could be either operationally or diplomatically realized. He eventually retreated when confronted with the views of the US military establishment, the absence of Soviet receptivity to the neutralization option, and the consequences of the Korean War. In the meantime, he urged that Japan be allowed to develop a self-defense force, even though this appeared inconsistent with the concept of demilitarization and was certain to cause concern among Japan's neighbors.

In these and other areas, Kennan's approach to East Asia often reflected his disregard for domestic political or diplomatic realities. Although he recognized that US disengagement from China was staunchly opposed by many in Congress and much of the public, his underlying attitude—which became typical of his overall approach to foreign policymaking—was essentially that the uninformed or those with parochial interests should not be allowed to obstruct what he considered to be good policy and strategic pragmatism. He was similarly inclined to dismiss the political considerations that made it difficult for Washington to demilitarize Japan, to surrender South Korea to its fate, or to separate the United States from the European colonial powers' problems in Southeast Asia.

As has been seen, Kennan's approach to the region also occasionally revealed ethnocentrism or selective memory, both of which clouded some of his judgments. His condescending and subtly racist attitudes toward East Asian populations almost certainly influenced his persistently dismissive view of their developmental potential and strategic relevance, and thus hampered the objectivity of his assessment of US strategic interests and possibilities in the region. In addition, Kennan sometimes forgot or "misremembered" his role in policy decisions that were ill conceived or ill fated, such as his strong support for a US withdrawal from Korea before 1950; and he later claimed more consistency in his thinking about the utility of US military bases in the Philippines or Japan than was apparent during the same period.

Perhaps most importantly, Kennan's strategic framework for East Asia—essentially the defensive perimeter concept—suffered early on from inconsistency and ambiguity. He was never able to fully reconcile his view that the mainland of Asia was strategically expendable with his belief that US credibility and prestige needed to be protected against the appearance of acquiescence to Communist aggression. This was especially evident in Korea, where his support of US military intervention in 1950 reversed his earlier dismissal of South Korea's importance—a view to which he later returned. But it was also reflected in his approach to Vietnam, where he originally declared it strategically insignificant but then supported US military involvement—until the loss of US prestige there became irretrievable. Kennan was by no means alone in having no good formula for resolving this perennial dilemma in US foreign policy, but his vulnerability to falling victim to it highlights the limits on his diehard adherence to realpolitik. In the end, these inherent dilemmas in his defensive perimeter concept contributed to its short shelf life.

Despite these flaws and inconsistencies, Kennan's core East Asia policies were remarkably influential where they were followed, and were proved remarkably prescient where they were not. The former occurred primarily when Kennan was working for Marshall, who largely relied on the PPS to make policy, and the latter occurred primarily when he was working for Acheson, who did not.

In China, Kennan was a central proponent and agent of the policy of minimal aid and gradual disengagement that Truman adopted in 1948, on Marshall's recommendation. He was probably the most vocal advocate of the idea that Washington should adopt a wait-and-see attitude and not commit itself further in China—which is what Marshall chose to do. Moreover, Kennan originated the idea for the China White Paper, which provided the rationale for the disengagement policy even if it did not wholly succeed politically.

Kennan's influence in the case of Japan was indisputable and profound. He personally seized the initiative in conceptualizing and advocating a new approach to occupation policy, and in shepherding it through to approval by the National Security Council and the president. The "reverse course" that he thus orchestrated established the foundation on which postwar Japan was rebuilt, both politically and economically. And his strategic framework for the region, notwithstanding its ambiguities and short shelf life, helped establish the blueprint for Japan's incorporation into the US strategic posture in East Asia.

Korea, on the other hand, provides the most vivid example of a case in which Kennan's policy advice in East Asia was overruled—with severe consequences. His was one of many voices that supported the US withdrawal from Korea before 1950, and the subsequent decision to intervene militarily after the North Korean invasion. But Kennan was almost alone in warning of the dangers of crossing the 38th Parallel with US military forces. The validity of his fears was subsequently borne out, and he was later called on to help Washington deal with the consequences.

Similarly, Kennan's advice with respect to Indochina was largely ignored but later vindicated. He warned Washington not to identify itself with the European colonial powers' efforts to reassert their control in Southeast Asia, or to commit US resources in support of those efforts. Despite Kennan's counsel and that of others, the United States assumed a political and military obligation in Indochina that led to the protracted failure of the Vietnam War—thus validating Kennan's advice of fifteen years earlier.

Over the course of his involvement in East Asian affairs, Kennan was not always right—and when he was right, it was not always at the right time or for the right reasons. But he almost always focused on the right questions—the same questions that have resonated ever since in US relations with East Asia. Kennan understood that one of the key challenges was recognizing and acknowledging the real and potential limits on US interests, influence, and leverage in the region. He anticipated the risk of miscalculating Washington's capacity to drive events and ensure compliance with its strategic preferences in the Far East. He also anticipated the problem of dealing with East Asian governments—even and especially friendly ones—whose interests would never be wholly identical to Washington's, whose nationalism would often chafe under perceived US pressure or a US military presence, and whose comfort with and confidence in US engagement in the region could be fickle.

At its core, Kennan's strategic approach to East Asia implicitly recognized that the US role there after World War II was a historical anomaly, the rationale for which, and the sustainability of which, almost certainly could not be perpetual. He grappled throughout his professional career and thereafter with the question of how the United States should posture itself to deal with this reality. We are still grappling with the same dilemma.

Notes

INTRODUCTION

1. Kennan to Acheson, 21 August 1950, in US Department of State, *Foreign Relations of the United States*, 1950, vol. 7 (Washington, DC: Government Printing Office, 1976), 624. Hereafter, volumes in this series will be cited as *FRUS* with year and volume number.

2. Ibid., 625.

3. Kennan to Acheson, 23 August 1950, Dean Acheson Papers, Box 66, "August 1950" folder, Harry S. Truman Library, Independence, MO.

4. Wilson Miscamble, "George Kennan: A Life in the Foreign Service," *Foreign Service Journal* 81, no. 2 (February 2004): 29.

5. John Lewis Gaddis, *George F. Kennan: An American Life* (New York: Penguin Press, 2011), 298.

6. The most detailed account of Kennan's appointment by Marshall is contained in the enclosure to a 9 February 1953 letter from Kennan to Marshall, in "Documents Loaned to Dr. Forrest Pogue by George Kennan," February 1959, Verifax #358, George C. Marshall Research Foundation, Lexington, VA. See also Kennan's *Memoirs 1925–1950* (New York: Pantheon Books, 1967), 294–95, 313, 325–27; and the account in Gaddis, *George F. Kennan*, 228–30, 252–53.

1. ENCOUNTERS WITH EAST ASIA

1. George F. Kennan letter to author, 18 October 1993; George F. Kennan, *American Diplomacy*, Expanded ed. (Chicago: University of Chicago Press, 1984), 38.

2. George F. Kennan, *Memoirs 1925–1950* (New York: Pantheon Books, 1967), 8. See Frederick F. Travis, "The Kennan-Russel Anti-Tsarist Propaganda Campaign among Russian Prisoners of War in Japan, 1904–1905," *Russian Review* 40, no. 3 (July 1981): 263–77. The elder Kennan, best known for his book *Siberia and the Exile System* (1891), also wrote *E. H. Harriman's Far Eastern Plans* (1917), about the US railroad magnate's pursuit of investments in China.

3. See William Bullitt to John MacMurray, 14 December 1933, John Van Antwerp MacMurray Collection, Box 135, Seeley G. Mudd Manuscript Library, Princeton, NJ.

4. The MacMurray memorandum was first published as *How the Peace Was Lost: The 1935 Memorandum: Developments Affecting American Policy in the Far East: Prepared for the State Department by John Van Antwerp MacMurray*, ed. Arthur Waldron (Stanford, CA: Hoover Institution Press, Stanford University, 1992). Waldron's introduction and annotation provide a detailed analysis of the historical context of the memorandum.

5. Demaree Bess to John MacMurray, 1 November 1950, MacMurray Collection, Box 200; Philip Sprouse to W. Walton Butterworth, 16 January 1948, "MacMurray Report" folder, Records of the Office of Chinese Affairs, 1944–50, Department of State Records (Record Group 59), National Archives, Washington, DC; Max Bishop to Philip Jessup, 16 August 1949, ibid.; Philip Sprouse to Livingston Merchant, 21 February 1950, ibid.; Kennan to MacMurray, 19 September 1950, George F. Kennan Papers, Box 29, Folder 1, Seeley G. Mudd Manuscript Library, Princeton, NJ (hereafter "Kennan Papers" with box and folder where applicable); Kennan letter to author, 18 October 1993.

6. The Washington Conference of 1921–22 produced a series of treaties that imposed limits on naval construction by the major powers, clarified the territorial possessions of the powers in the Far East, and attempted to codify the US Open Door policy of ensuring China's sovereignty and territorial integrity. MacMurray had attended the conference as a legal adviser and was an expert on China's treaty obligations, having compiled and edited three volumes of *Treaties and Agreements with and concerning China* in 1921 and 1929.

7. Text of "Treaty between the United States of America, Belgium, the British Empire, China, France, Italy, Japan, the Netherlands, and Portugal, Signed at Washington February 6, 1922," *FRUS* 1922, 1:279.

8. MacMurray, *How the Peace Was Lost*, 83.

9. Ibid., 125. MacMurray's attitudes toward the Chinese were almost certainly reinforced by the earlier and similarly frustrating experience of his father-in-law, legal scholar Frank J. Goodnow, who had served as an adviser to the Chinese government during the years 1913–15. See Jedidiah Kroncke, "An Early Tragedy of Comparative Constitutionalism: Frank Goodnow and the Chinese Republic," *Pacific Rim Law & Policy Journal* 21, no. 3 (June 2012): 533–90. I am grateful to Professor Mark Elliott for drawing my attention to MacMurray's connection to Goodnow.

10. MacMurray, *How the Peace Was Lost*, 129–30.

11. Ibid., 62, 132, 134.

12. Ibid., 129, 131–32, 134–35.

13. See Waldron's discussion in MacMurray, *How the Peace Was Lost*, 39–54.

14. Kennan to MacMurray, 19 September 1950, Kennan Papers, Box 29, Folder 1. Kennan played a substantial role in drawing attention to MacMurray's memorandum; he suggested its publication to MacMurray and requested his permission to quote it. Buoyed by the attention Kennan drew to the memorandum, MacMurray tried without success to have it published. See Kennan to MacMurray, 19 March 1951, Kennan Papers, Box 29; MacMurray to Kennan, 26 February 1954, ibid.; Herbert S. Bailey to MacMurray, 4 June 1954, MacMurray Collection, Box 201.

15. Kennan note to John Paton Davies, undated, John Paton Davies Papers, Box 3, Folder "Correspondence 1982–1991," Harry S. Truman Library, Independence, MO (hereafter "Davies Papers" with box and folder where applicable). Kennan's reference is to the "Memorandum on the Present State of British Relations with France and Germany" written by British diplomat Sir Eyre Crowe, in which Crowe assessed Germany's expansionist ambitions and advised London to resist them. Many historians consider the memorandum a prescient warning of World War I.

16. See Kennan, *American Diplomacy*, 51; Kennan lecture, "International Situation," Princeton Graduate School, 25 April 1951, Kennan Papers, Box 300, Folder 4.

17. Kennan, *American Diplomacy*, 34, 46.

18. Ibid., 54.

19. See Warren I. Cohen, *America's Response to China: A History of Sino-American Relations*, 4th ed. (New York: Columbia University Press, 2000), 39–50, 89–97. The strategic rationale for the US war with Japan is chronicled in Waldo Heinrichs, *Threshold of War: Franklin D. Roosevelt and American Entry into World War II* (New York: Oxford University Press, 1988), 96–99, 118–45; and David Reynolds, *From Munich to Pearl Harbor: Roosevelt's America and the Origins of the Second World War* (Chicago: Ivan R. Dee, 2001), 58–62, 87–92, 139–44, 159–66. I am grateful to an anonymous reviewer for highlighting the ideas in this paragraph.

20. Kennan letter to author, 18 October 1993.

21. See E. J. Kahn Jr., *The China Hands: America's Foreign Service Officers and What Befell Them* (New York: Viking Press, 1975); and Paul Gordon Lauren, ed., *The China Hands' Legacy: Ethics and Diplomacy* (Boulder, CO: Westview Press, 1987).

22. See John Paton Davies Jr., *China Hand: An Autobiography* (Philadelphia: University of Pennsylvania Press, 2012); John Paton Davies Jr., *Dragon by the Tail: American, British, Japanese, and Russian Encounters with China and One Another* (New York: W. W. Norton, 1972); and the chapter he contributed to Lauren, *The China Hands' Legacy*, 37–57.

23. Davies, *China Hand*, 45.

24. Davies memorandum, "American Policy in Asia," 19 February 1944, Davies Papers, Box 11, Folder "Chronology 1942–1944" (2 of 3).

25. Davies memorandum, "The Need for Flexibility in American Policy toward China," 30 August 1944, ibid.

26. Davies memorandum, 7 November 1944, *FRUS* 1944, 6:669–71.

27. Davies memorandum, 15 November 1944, ibid., 695–96.

28. Ibid.

29. Davies, *China Hand*, 224, 232–33.

30. Ibid., 227, 229–30. Kennan later recorded his own view of Hurley's role as mediator between the CCP and the KMT: "I have no doubt that General Hurley deserves well of the opinion of posterity for his previous service as a lawyer, a soldier, and a politician," but Kennan ridiculed "the very suggestion that this leathery and picturesque product of the Choctaw Indian Territory in Oklahoma, with his violent personal prejudices, his sanguine disposition, and his fondness for uttering Indian war whoops at parties, should have been just the man to undertake the delicate task of reconciling the political ambitions of Mao and Chiang in a country where, so far as I am aware, he had never lived and of which he knew next to nothing." George F. Kennan, *Russia and the West under Lenin and Stalin* (New York: Mentor Books, 1960), 375.

31. Lauren, *The China Hands' Legacy*, 45–48.

32. Davies, *China Hand*, 239.

33. Davies, *Dragon by the Tail*, 184.

34. Davies, *China Hand*, 246.

35. Davies, *Dragon by the Tail*, 390; Davies, *China Hand*, 246.

36. Kennan, *Memoirs 1925–1950*, 239.

37. Davies to Harriman, 15 April 1945, *FRUS* 1945, 7:336–37.

38. Hurley to James Byrnes, 17 April 1945, ibid., 338–40.

39. Kennan, *Memoirs 1925–1950*, 237; Davies, *Dragon by the Tail*, 395.

40. Kennan to Harriman, 23 April 1945, *FRUS* 1945, 7:343.

41. Ibid., 343–44. This assessment of Moscow's flexibility and opportunism in dealing with developments in China was reinforced in other analyses Davies prepared later in 1945. Davies, *China Hand*, 259–61.

42. Kennan to Byrnes, 10 January 1946, *FRUS* 1946, 9:118–19.

43. Ibid., 119.

44. Dean Acheson, *Present at the Creation: My Years in the State Department* (New York: W. W. Norton, 1969), 203.

45. Butterworth to Donald Zagoria, 22 February 1974, W. Walton Butterworth Papers, Box 1, George C. Marshall Research Foundation, Lexington, VA.

46. Davies, *Dragon by the Tail*, 420; Davies, *China Hand*, 271.

47. Kennan, *Memoirs 1925–1950*, 294–95.

48. The article was published under the pseudonym "X" ostensibly because of Kennan's government position, but its authorship was soon widely known. See John L. Gaddis, *George F. Kennan: An American Life* (New York: Penguin Press, 2011), 251, 258–62.

49. Kennan, "Comments on the National Security Problem," 28 March 1947, in Giles D. Harlow and George C. Maerz, eds., *Measures Short of War: The George F. Kennan Lectures at the National War College, 1946–47* (Washington, DC: National Defense University

Press, 1991), 168–70; "Problems of US Foreign Policy after Moscow," 6 May 1947, ibid., 198–99.

50. Ibid.

51. Kennan lecture at University of Virginia, "Russian-American Relations," 20 February 1947, Kennan Papers, Box 16.

52. Harlow and Maerz, *Measures Short of War*, 301–2.

53. Kennan presentation at National War College, "Current Political Affairs," 10 January 1947, in Harlow and Maerz, *Measures Short of War*, 94–99.

54. Ibid., 106–7.

55. Kennan to Acheson, 29 April 1947, Policy Planning Staff Records, Lot 64D563, Record Group 59, National Archives (hereafter NA), Washington, DC, Box 33, Chronological File, 1947 folder (hereafter "PPS Records" with box number and file and folder where applicable). Kennan quickly realized that the PPS would require a larger staff, which it acquired within a few weeks of its establishment on 5 May 1945. Gaddis, *George F. Kennan*, 266.

2. CHINA

1. John Paton Davies Jr., *China Hand: An Autobiography* (Philadelphia: University of Pennsylvania Press, 2012), 293–94.

2. Davies's assignment to the PPS officially began on 1 August 1947. Davies Papers, Box 1, Folder "Assignments, Promotions, and Travel."

3. Vincent to Marshall, 20 June 1947, *FRUS* 1947, 7:849.

4. See Marshall to John Leighton Stuart, 19 June 1947, ibid., 190; James Forrestal, diary entries for 23 and 26 June 1947, James V. Forrestal Diaries, Box 4, Seeley G. Mudd Manuscript Library, Princeton, NJ.

5. Kennan to Lovett, 23 June 1947, PPS Records, Box 13, China 1947 folder.

6. Ibid.

7. Marshall to Lovett, 2 July 1947, *FRUS* 1947, 7:635; Minutes of Meeting of the Secretaries of State, War, and Navy, 26 June 1947, ibid., 850–51.

8. For a full account of the Wedemeyer mission, see William Stueck, *The Wedemeyer Mission: American Politics and Foreign Policy during the Cold War* (Athens: University of Georgia Press, 1984).

9. Wedemeyer's report is reprinted in United States Department of State, *The China White Paper*, originally issued as *United States Relations with China, with Special Reference to the Period 1944–1949* (Stanford, CA: Stanford University Press, 1967), 2:764–814; the summary of its conclusions and recommendations is on pp. 773–74.

10. Minutes of PPS meetings, 14 and 21 October 1947, PPS Records, Box 32; *FRUS* 1947, 7:899–900. For Davies's first appearance in the PPS, see Minutes of PPS meeting, 28 July 1948, PPS Records, Box 32. In his autobiography, Davies said the PPS "would have been insignificant" without Kennan and attributed this to Marshall's reliance on him and Kennan's "exceptional ability to conceptualize and interpret international relations." According to Davies, the rest of the PPS "acted as a sounding board against which he played his ideas, and as critics, contributors and occasionally originators of policy papers" that Kennan would edit and then take final responsibility for. Davies, *China Hand*, 296–97.

11. Davies memorandum, 29 October 1947, PPS Records, Box 45, PPS members chronological file, Davies folder.

12. George F. Kennan, *Memoirs 1925–1950* (New York: Pantheon Books, 1967), 145. In 1968 Kennan recommended that Butterworth receive an award for his heroic role in rescuing fellow passengers from an airplane crash in Lisbon in February 1943. Kennan Papers, Box 7, Folder 9. Other correspondence shows that Kennan and Butterworth re-

mained close friends—and for a period Princeton neighbors—until the latter's death in 1975.

13. John Paton Davies Jr., telephone interview by author, Asheville, NC, 23 November 1993; Davies, *China Hand*, 297.

14. Kennan to Butterworth, 29 October 1947, PPS Records, Box 33, Chronological file.

15. Kennan to Marshall, 3/4 November 1947, PPS Records, Box 13, China 1947 folder.

16. Ibid.

17. Ibid.

18. Ibid.

19. Kennan diary entry, 27 January 1948, George F. Kennan, *The Kennan Diaries*, ed. Frank Costigliola (New York: W. W. Norton, 2014), 209–10.

20. Wilson D. Miscamble, *George F. Kennan and the Making of American Foreign Policy, 1947–1950* (Princeton, NJ: Princeton University Press, 1992), 220–22; Stueck, *Wedemeyer Mission*, 121; see also William Stueck, "The Marshall and Wedemeyer Missions: A Quadrilateral Perspective," in *Sino-American Relations 1945–1955: A Joint Reassessment of a Critical Decade*, ed. Harry Harding and Yuan Ming (Wilmington, DE: Scholarly Resources Books, 1989), 109.

21. Butterworth to Marshall, 24 January 1948, *FRUS* 1948, 8:459; Kennan to Marshall and Lovett, 26 January 1948, PPS Records, Box 33, Chronological file.

22. Davies, *China Hand*, 302.

23. Kennan to Marshall Carter, 10 February 1948, PPS Records, Box 13, China 1948 folder.

24. Forrestal assumed the position of secretary of defense on 17 September 1947, when the National Security Act of 26 July 1947 went into effect. The Department of Defense itself was not created until 10 August 1949.

25. United States Department of State, *China White Paper*, 1:380–84; Forrestal diary entry, 12 February 1948, Forrestal Diaries, Box 4.

26. PPS 13, "Resume of World Situation," 6 November 1947, in Anna Kasten Nelson, ed., *The State Department Policy Planning Staff Papers*, 3 vols. (New York: Garland Publishing, 1983), 1:135 (hereafter *PPS Papers* with volume number).

27. Kennan lecture at Navy Secretary's Council, "Problems of Far Eastern Policy," 14 January 1948, Kennan Papers, Box 17.

28. PPS 23, "Review of Current Trends: U.S. Foreign Policy," in *PPS Papers*, 2:121–22.

29. Ibid., 123.

30. Kennan to Butterworth, 15 January 1948, PPS Records, Box 13, China 1948 folder; Kennan to Sidney Souers, 26 January 1948, ibid.; George Butler to Marshall/Lovett, 27 July 1948, *FRUS* 1948, 8:122.

31. Minutes of PPS meetings, 10, 11, 13, 19, 26 February and 2, 8 March, PPS Records, Box 32. The scholars included John King Fairbank, Karl Wittfogel, Mary Wright, and former ambassador Nelson Johnson.

32. Davies to Melby, 1 March 1948, John F. Melby Papers, Box 3, China 1948 folder, Harry S. Truman Library, Independence, MO. Melby did not respond to Davies's letter until July, long after the PPS's first attempt at a China policy paper had been suspended; see Melby to Davies, 29 April 1948 and 13 July 1948, ibid.

33. NSC 6, *FRUS* 1948, 8:44–50; Marshall to Lovett, 7 April 1948, ibid., 52–53.

34. Kennan's trip to Japan is the focus of the next chapter. Marshall had suggested to Kennan that he take a side trip to China to get a "glimpse of the Chinese picture" before doing "any more work on Chinese matters." While in Tokyo, however, Kennan decided that "a preponderance of considerations" made a trip to China inadvisable; specifically, Kennan feared that the media might deliberately misinterpret his visit or that the Chinese

government might try to draw him into discussions of US policy—all while the China aid bill was pending in Congress. Kennan memorandum of conversation with Marshall, 19 February 1948, PPS Records, Box 29A, Japan 1948 folder; Marshall to Lovett, 10 March 1948, ibid.; Kennan, *Memoirs 1925–1950*, 404.

35. Lovett to Marshall, 15 April 1948, *FRUS* 1948, 8:55–56; Butler to Marshall/Lovett, 27 July 1948, ibid., 123; Minutes of PPS Meetings, 5 April 1948, PPS Records, Box 32.

36. During the interim, the administration grappled inconclusively with the question of what to do about the US military presence in the Chinese coastal city of Qingdao. Butterworth and Kennan participated in NSC deliberations on the subject, all of which were eventually subsumed into NSC action on overall China policy. See Butterworth to Marshall, 13 May 1948, *FRUS* 1948, 8:312; Minutes of PPS Meetings, 14, 21, 25 June and 1, 2 July, PPS Records, Box 32. For NSC deferral of the Qingdao issue, see Minutes of NSC Meeting #15, 15 July 1948, Harry S. Truman Papers, President's Secretary's Files (hereafter PSF), Box 204, Truman Library, Independence, MO.

37. Souers to NSC, 26 July 1948, *FRUS* 1948, 8:118–22.

38. Ibid.

39. Butler to Marshall/Lovett, 27 July 1948, *FRUS* 1948, 8:122–24.

40. Butterworth to Marshall, 27 July 1948, State Department Decimal Files, 893.00/7-2748, Microfilm Publication LM69, Reel 11, RG 59, NA.

41. JCS to Forrestal, 5 August 1948, *FRUS* 1948, 8:132–35. This document was circulated on 6 August as NSC 22/1.

42. Davies, *China Hand*, 309–10.

43. Stuart to Marshall, 10 August 1948, *FRUS* 1948, 7:405–8.

44. Ibid., 408–10.

45. Marshall to Stuart, 12 August 1948, ibid., 415.

46. Handwritten note by Marshall, 11 August 1948, attached to copy of Stuart to Marshall, 10 August 1948, PPS Records, Box 13, China 1948 folder.

47. Minutes of PPS Meetings, 12 August 1948, with Davies draft attached, PPS Records, Box 32.

48. Kennan to Marshall, 12 August 1948, PPS Records, Box 33, Chronological file.

49. Ibid.

50. Marshall to Stuart, 13 August 1948, *FRUS* 1948, 7:416.

51. Lovett/Marshall to Stuart, 26 October 1948, ibid., 517. For Stuart's pleas, see Lovett/Marshall to Stuart, 26 October 1948, 505–8; and United States Department of State, *China White Paper*, 1:285–86.

52. Davies interview with author, 23 November 1993; Minutes of PPS Meeting, 27 August 1948, PPS Records, Box 32. The full text of PPS 39, including Kennan's cover letter and annex, is in *PPS Papers*, 2:412–46.

53. George F. Kennan interview by Forrest Pogue, 17 February 1959, Pogue Oral History #128, George C. Marshall Research Foundation, Lexington, VA, 16 (hereafter Kennan/Pogue interview).

54. PPS 39, *PPS Papers*, 2:416. Compare this with MacMurray's verdict in 1935: "Little as we may relish admitting to ourselves the necessity of discarding a rather romantic conception of what the development of China has in store for the world, we must face the fact (or the probability so overwhelming that we must accept it as the basis of a working theory) that China has become, from our viewpoint, an almost negligible factor." John Van Antwerp MacMurray, *How the Peace Was Lost: The 1935 Memorandum: Developments Affecting American Policy in the Far East: Prepared for the State Department by John Van Antwerp MacMurray*, ed. Arthur Waldron (Stanford, CA: Hoover Institution Press, Stanford University, 1992), 132.

55. PPS 39, *PPS Papers*, 2:421.

56. Ibid.

57. Ibid., 424–26.

58. Ibid., 426–30.

59. Ibid., 431–32; Davies, *China Hand*, 303.

60. Marshall to Kennan, 18 September 1948, PPS Records, Box 13, China 1948 folder; NSC 34, 13 October 1948, ibid.; for the record of Butterworth's and Lovett's concurrence, see PPS Records, Box 45, PPS members chronological file, Davies folder.

61. "Draft Report by the National Security Council on United States Policy toward China," 2 November 1948, *FRUS* 1948, 8:185–87.

62. Butterworth to Lovett, 3 November 1948, *FRUS* 1948, 8:187–89.

63. Memorandum for the President on NSC Meeting #26, 3 November 1948, Truman Papers, PSF, Box 207.

64. Q&A session following "Estimate of the International Situation," lecture to National Military Establishment Joint Orientation Conference, 8 November 1948, Kennan Papers, Box 17.

65. Kennan, untitled draft, 16 November 1948, Kennan Papers, Box 23.

66. Ibid.

67. Ibid.

68. "Proposed Press Statement by Mr. Kennan," 17 November 1948, Records of the State Department Office of Chinese Affairs (1944–1950), Microfilm Publication C0012, Reel 11, RG 59, NA (hereafter "CA Records" with reel number).

69. PPS 39/1, "United States Policy toward China," *PPS Papers*, 2:447–51.

70. Ibid., 448.

71. Ibid., 449–51.

72. Davies later characterized the "no policy" charge as "in accord with the popular assumption that policy meant action. Don't just stand there. Do something!" His view, however—which Kennan shared—was that "policy also includes passages of inaction, watchful waiting or calculated aloofness." He also attributed the military's attitude to its view of the State Department as "soft on Chinese Communism and so a dupe, at best, of Moscow" and presumably its view of Davies himself, based on criticism circulated by Hurley, Wedemeyer, and other generals. Davies, *China Hand*, 306, 311.

73. Kennan to Marshall/Lovett, 24 November 1948, ibid., 447; Kennan to Lovett, 22 November 1948, PPS Records, Box 33, Chronological file.

74. Marshall memorandum, 24 November 1948, CA Records, Reel 11; PPS 45, "United States Policy toward China in the Light of the Current Situation," 26 November 1948, *PPS Papers*, 2:509–17.

75. PPS 45, *PPS Papers*, 2:511–15.

76. Ibid., 509–10, 516–17; Kennan to Marshall, 24 November 1948, PPS Records, Box 33, Chronological file.

77. PPS 45, *PPS Papers*, 2:510.

78. Oral history interview, John F. Melby, November 1986, Truman Library, 168; Davies interview with author, 23 November 1993. See also Melby speech, "The Making of a White Paper," date and place of delivery unknown, Melby Papers, Box 32, Truman Library, 2–3; and Robert P. Newman, "The Self-Inflicted Wound: The China White Paper of 1949," *Prologue* 14, no. 3 (Fall 1982): 142. For Kennan's own acknowledgment of his role in urging Marshall to publish a white paper on China, see Kennan/Pogue interview, George C. Marshall Research Foundation, 16.

79. Davies interview with author, 23 November 1993; Marshall to Lovett, 26 November 1948, *FRUS* 1948, 8:220; Marshall handwritten notes on copy of PPS 45, 26 November 1948, PPS Records, Box 13, China 1948 folder; Walter Millis, ed., *The Forrestal Diaries* (New York: Viking Press, 1951), 534.

80. Kennan to Souers, 26 November 1948, PPS Records, Box 13, China 1948 folder; Kennan to Marshall, 30 November 1948, ibid.; Kennan to Marshall, 7 December 1948, ibid.; Marshall Carter to Butterworth, 2 December 1948, CA Records, Reel 11.

81. Forrestal to Souers, 14 December 1948, *FRUS* 1948, 8:232; Butterworth to Lovett, 16 December 1948, ibid., 233; JCS to Forrestal, 16 December 1948, PPS Records, Box 13, China 1948 folder.

82. Minutes of NSC Meeting #30, 16 December 1948, Truman Papers, PSF, Box 205; Stuart to Marshall, 18 December 1948, *FRUS* 1948, 8:235; Lovett to NSC, 24 December 1948, PPS Records, Box 13, China 1948 folder.

83. Minutes of NSC Meeting #33, 3 February 1949, Truman Papers, PSF, Box 205; Memorandum for the President on NSC Meeting #33, Truman Papers, PSF, Box 220; Minutes of NSC Meeting #34, 17 February 1949, Truman Papers, PSF, Box 205; Memorandum for the President on NSC Meeting #34, Truman Papers, PSF, Box 220.

84. NSC 34/1, "United States Policy toward China," 11 January 1949, *FRUS* 1949, 9:474–75.

85. Davies later wrote that Acheson had borrowed this metaphor from him, after Davies used it during a session with the Department's China hands early in Acheson's tenure as secretary. Davies, *China Hand*, 311. Davies wrote separately that Acheson had "carried on Marshall's policy of futile, excruciating entanglement [with China], forced on both of them by congressional and public pressure." Unpublished, undated manuscript "Secretaries of States: Marshall to Rusk," Davies Papers, Box 6, Folder "Manuscripts, Aborted [Unpublished articles and notes]."

86. Memorandum for the President on NSC Meeting #33, 3 February 1949, Truman Papers, PSF, Box 220.

87. PPS 39/2, "United States Policy toward China," 25 February 1949, *PPS Papers*, 3:25–28. Kennan later acknowledged that until early 1949 he had believed "very wrongly" that the Communists would never take over all of China. Kennan, *Memoirs 1925–1950*, 374.

88. PPS 39/2, *PPS Papers*, 3:27.

89. Ibid.

90. Ibid., 28.

91. Memorandum for the President on NSC Meeting #35, 32 March 1949, Truman Papers, PSF, Box 220.

3. JAPAN

1. For MacMurray's original argument, see John Van Antwerp MacMurray, *How the Peace Was Lost: The 1935 Memorandum: Developments Affecting American Policy in the Far East: Prepared for the State Department by John Van Antwerp MacMurray*, ed. Arthur Waldron (Stanford, CA: Hoover Institution Press, Stanford University, 1992), 132–34. George F. Kennan, *American Diplomacy*, 47–52; Kennan lecture at Princeton Graduate School, "International Situation," 25 April 1951, Kennan Papers, Box 300, Folder 4; "Unfinished Paper," September 1951, Kennan Papers, Box 24, Folder 1-D-18.

2. Kennan, "Unused Draft for Statement on Vietnam," 1967, Kennan Papers, Box 27, Folder 1-E-25.

3. George F. Kennan, *Memoirs 1925–1950* (New York: Pantheon Books, 1967), 393; Wilson D. Miscamble, *George F. Kennan and the Making of American Foreign Policy, 1947–1950* (Princeton, NJ: Princeton University Press, 1992), 247.

4. An early but still comprehensive account of the peace treaty issue from its origins is Frederick S. Dunn, *Peace-Making and the Settlement with Japan* (Princeton, NJ: Princeton University Press, 1963).

5. Borton to Bohlen, 6 August 1947, *FRUS* 1947, 6:478; Minutes of PPS meeting, 7 August 1947, PPS Records, Box 32; Davies to Kennan, 11 August 1947, PPS Records, Box

29A, Japan 1947 folder; John Paton Davies Jr., *China Hand: An Autobiography* (Philadelphia: University of Pennsylvania Press, 2012), 297–98.

6. Kennan to Lovett, 12 August 1947, *FRUS* 1947, 6:480; Minutes of PPS meetings, 18 and 20 August 1947, PPS Records, Box 32.

7. Penfield to Kennan, 14 August 1947, State Department Decimal Files, 740.0011PW (Peace)/8-1447, Box 3513, RG 59, NA; Max Bishop to Penfield, 14 August 1947, *FRUS* 1947, 6:492–93.

8. See memorandum by Col. S. F. Griffith, 14 August 1947, PPS Records, Box 29A, Japan 1947 folder. This memorandum also reflects the frustration of senior military officers with MacArthur's unilateral call for an end to the occupation.

9. Kennan, *Memoirs 1925–1950*, 368; Davies draft memorandum, 8 September 1947, attached to Minutes of PPS meeting, 8 September, PPS Records, Box 32.

10. Davies draft memorandum, circa 20 August 1947, attached to Penfield to Davies, 25 August 1947, PPS Records, Box 29A, Japan 1947 folder.

11. Borton to Davies, 22 August 1947, ibid.; Penfield to Davies, 25 August 1947, ibid.

12. Gen. C. Schuyler to Kennan, 24 September 1947, ibid.; Forrest Sherman to Kennan, 24 September 1947, ibid.

13. Edwin Martin to Borton, 26 September 1947, State Department Decimal Files, 740.0011PW(Peace)/8-1447, Box 3514, RG 59, NA.

14. Butterworth to Lovett, 22 September 1947, *FRUS* 1947, 6:523.

15. Kennan, *Memoirs 1925–1950*, 376.

16. Ibid.

17. PPS 13, "Resume of World Situation," 6 November 1947, *PPS Papers*, 1:135.

18. Kennan letter to author, 18 October 1993.

19. PPS 10, "Results of Planning Staff Study of Questions Involved in the Japanese Peace Settlement," 14 October 1947, *PPS Papers*, 1:108.

20. Carlisle Humelsine to Marshall Carter, 16 October 1947, PPS Records, Box 29A, Japan 1947 folder; Humelsine to Kennan et al., 29 October 1947, ibid.; Borton to M. M. Hamilton, 28 October 1947, State Department Decimal Files, 740.00119PW/10-2847, Box 3930, RG 59, NA; Kennan, *Memoirs 1925–1950*, 377; Davies interview with author, 23 November 1993. FE skepticism about Kennan's initiative is further reflected in Robert A. Fearey to Hamilton, 18 November 1947, State Department Decimal Files, 740.0011PW (Peace)/11-1847, Box 3514, RG 59, NA.

21. See Michael Schaller, *The American Occupation of Japan: The Origins of the Cold War in Asia* (New York: Oxford University Press, 1985), 90–92; Howard B. Schonberger, *Aftermath of War: Americans and the Remaking of Japan* (Kent, OH: Kent State University Press, 1989), 141–42. See also Michael Schaller, "MacArthur's Japan: The View from Washington," *Diplomatic History* 10, no. 1 (Winter 1986): 12–14; Howard B. Schonberger, "The Japan Lobby in American Diplomacy, 1947–1952," *Pacific Historical Review* 46 (1977): 327–34; and William S. Borden, *The Pacific Alliance: United States Foreign Economic Policy and Japanese Trade Recovery, 1947–1955* (Madison: University of Wisconsin Press, 1984), 71–72.

22. James Forrestal, diary entries for 3, 11, and 13 March 1947, Forrestal Diaries, Box 3. See also James V. Forrestal, *The Forrestal Diaries*, ed. Walter Millis (New York: Viking Press, 1951), 255–56.

23. Martin to Hilldring, 12 March 1947, *FRUS* 1947, 6:184; Martin to Hilldring, 12 March 1947, State Department Decimal Files, 894.50/3-1247, Microfilm Publication LM105, Reel 21, RG 59, NA; Robert W. Barnett to Martin, 13 and 15 May 1947, 894.50/5-1347 and 5-1547, ibid.

24. Schaller, *Occupation of Japan*, 109; Schonberger, *Aftermath of War*, 64–65. On the zaibatsu, see Howard B. Schonberger, "Zaibatsu Dissolution and the American Restoration

of Japan," *Bulletin of Concerned Asian Scholars* 5, no. 2 (September 1973): 16–31; and Thomas A. Bisson, *Zaibatsu Dissolution in Japan* (Berkeley: University of California Press, 1954).

25. James Forrestal, diary entry for 19 June 1947, Forrestal Diaries, Box 4; Hilldring to State-Army-Navy-Air Force Coordinating Committee (SANACC), 22 July 1947, SWNCC/SANACC Records, Microfilm Publication LM54, Reel 31, SWNCC 381 Series, NA (hereafter SWNCC Records with reel number and series); Hilldring to Peterson, 23 July 1947, *FRUS* 1947, 6:265.

26. Oral history interview, Charles E. Saltzman, 28 June 1974, Truman Library, 16–17; Saltzman to Marshall/Lovett, 29 August 1947, State Department Decimal Files, 740.00119 Control (Japan), Box 3817, RG 59, NA.

27. Schonberger, "Japan Lobby in American Diplomacy," 331–33.

28. Schonberger, *Aftermath of War*, 161–66; T. N. Dupuy to General Lauris Norstad, "Report on Visit to Japan with Under Secretary of the Army," 6 October 1947, Records of the Undersecretary of the Army, Draper/Voorhees Project Decimal File 1947–1950 (hereafter Draper Japan file), Box 18, SAOUS 091 Japan (10-6-47), Washington National Records Center (hereafter WNRC), Suitland, MD.

29. Penfield to Saltzman, 11 September 1947, State Department Decimal Files, 740.00119 Control (Korea)/9-1147, Box 3827, RG 59, NA.

30. Schonberger, *Aftermath of War*, 166–67; SWNCC 384, "Economic Recovery of Japan," 3 October 1947, SWNCC Records, Reel 32, SWNCC 384 Series; Saltzman to SWNCC, 9 October 1947, *FRUS* 1947, 6:302; Saltzman to SANACC, 15 October 1947, SWNCC Records, Reel 31, SWNCC 381 Series; Minutes of 61st SANACC Meeting, 1 November 1947, ibid.

31. See Frank McCoy to Hilldring, 11 August 1947, State Department Decimal Files, 894.50/8-1147, Reel 21, RG 59, NA; Hilldring to McCoy, 15 August 1947, 894.50/8-1547, ibid.; Saltzman to McCoy, 8 September 1947, 894.50/9-847, ibid.

32. Saltzman to Draper, 12 November 1947, *FRUS* 1947, 6:313–14.

33. Ibid.

34. See Minutes of SANACC Meeting #61, 1 November 1947, SWNCC Records, Reel 31, SWNCC 381 Series; Minutes of SANACC Meeting #63, 15 January 1948, ibid.; Draper to SANACC, 19 December 1947, SWNCC Records, Reel 32, SWNCC 384 Series; Fearey to Allison, 5 December 1947, State Department Decimal Files, 894.50/12-547, Reel 21; Draper to Wisner, 12 December 1947, State Department Decimal Files, 894.50/12-1247, Reel 21, RG 59, NA; Barnett to Martin/Whitman, 8 January 1948, State Department Decimal Files, 894.50/1-848 [Butterworth's position], ibid.; Fearey to Penfield, 8 January 1948, State Department Decimal Files, 894.50/1-848 [FE and OE differences on 381/2, the State redraft], ibid.; Saltzman to SANACC, 14 January 1948, State Department Decimal Files, 894.50/1-1448 [rejection of SANACC 384/1 and counterproposal], ibid.

35. Schonberger, *Aftermath of War*, 75; James L. Kauffman, "A Lawyer's Report on Japan Attacks Plan to Run Occupation," *Newsweek*, 1 December 1947, 36–38.

36. Barnett to Martin/Whitman, 8 January 1948, State Department Decimal Files, 894.50/12-547, Microfilm Publication LM105, Reel 21, RG 59, NA.

37. Schaller, *Occupation of Japan*, 118–19; Schonberger, *Aftermath of War*, 175–76; "US Aims to Make Japan Self-Reliant Nation and Deterrent to Another War, Says Royall," *New York Times*, 7 January 1948, 18.

38. Minutes of SANACC Meeting #63, 15 January 1948, SWNCC Records, Reel 31, SWNCC 381 Series; Saltzman to Marshall, 22 January 1948, SWNCC Records, Reel 32, SWNCC 384 Series; SANACC to MacArthur, 23 January 1948, ibid.; McCoy statement to FEC, 21 January 1948, *FRUS* 1948, 6:654–55. Draper was willing to accept the watering down of the language in SWNCC 384 because he was eager to have a directive to MacArthur

in hand before pending congressional consideration of a Japanese aid program. Schaller, *Occupation of Japan*, 120; Schonberger, *Aftermath of War*, 176.

39. James Forrestal, diary entry for 31 October 1947, Forrestal Diaries, Box 4.

40. Ibid. Walter Millis, in his edited version of Forrestal's diary, noted the influence this conversation with Kennan had on Forrestal's thinking. In a letter to a colleague several weeks later, Forrestal said he had "recently discovered that some ex-OPA boys have been writing up laws for Japan which in certain respects impose state socialism on that country—which is a fine way to keep them permanently busted and would ultimately lead to economic anarchy." Kennan had identified SCAP personnel formerly associated with the Office of Price Administration (OPA) as the force behind MacArthur's economic program. See Forrestal, *Forrestal Diaries*, 328–29.

41. Forrestal to Royall, 1 November 1947, James V. Forrestal Papers, Box 76, Seeley G. Mudd Manuscript Library, Princeton, NJ.

42. Royall to Lovett, 16 December 1947, attachment to Borton to Penfield, 26 February 1948, State Department Decimal Files, 740.00119 Control (Japan)/2-2648, Box 3819, RG 59, NA; Minutes of NSC Meeting #4, 17 December 1947, Truman Papers, PSF, Box 203. Lovett's acknowledgment of Royall's proposal generated confusion within the State Department, where Saltzman and others feared that Lovett ran the risk of surrendering some of State's responsibility on Japan policy to the Army. Lovett later clarified that he thought the mission Royall had suggested would be devoted exclusively to "the zaibatsu problem." (See the Borton to Penfield letter cited above, and its attachment, Butterworth to Allison, 27 February 1948.) Indeed, Royall apparently was anticipating what later became Draper's second economic mission to Tokyo.

43. Kennan to Marshall/Lovett, 14 October 1947, handwritten addendum by Lovett, PPS Records, Box 29A, Japan 1947 folder.

44. Butterworth to Marshall, 31 December 1947, Records of the State Department Bureau of Far Eastern Affairs, Briefing Books and Reference Materials Maintained by the Office of Northeast Asian Affairs, Lot File 60D330, Microfilm Publication C0044 (hereafter "NEA Briefing Books"), Reel 9, "US Policy toward Japan: Formulation and Content 1948–1949" folder, RG 59, NA.

45. Davies to Kennan, 16 January 1948, PPS Records, Box 45, PPS members chronological file, Davies personal folder.

46. Butterworth to Marshall, 29 January 1948, NEA Briefing Books, Reel 9, RG 59, NA. Kennan's own sense of urgency was reinforced the following day, when he had lunch with someone who had just returned from Japan and who "told me some disturbing things about the influences behind our policies of extreme democratization and de-concentration of economic life in Japan." Kennan diary entry, 30 January 1948, George F. Kennan, *The Kennan Diaries*, ed. Frank Costigliola (New York: W. W. Norton, 2014), 211.

47. Ibid.; Humelsine to Kennan, 9 February 1948, PPS Records, Box 29A, Japan 1947 folder; draft of Kennan to Marshall/Lovett, 27 January 1948, PPS Records, Box 29A, Japan 1948 folder. Kennan later said that he did not have himself "particularly in mind" when he originally proposed the Tokyo mission in PPS 10. In his memoirs, he recalled only that the decision to send him was the result of oral discussions on Japan he had with Marshall subsequent to PPS 10. Kennan letter to author, 31 January 1994; Kennan, *Memoirs 1925–1950*, 377.

48. Kennan to Lovett, 17 February 1948, PPS Records, Box 29A, Japan 1948 folder; Kennan to Lovett, 24 February 1948, ibid.; Kennan to Penfield, 17 February 1948, ibid.

49. Kennan to Butterworth, 10 February 1948, ibid.; Saltzman to Kennan, 12 February 1948, ibid.; Kennan, *Memoirs 1925–1950*, 382–83; Kennan to Green, 10 February 1993, Kennan Papers, Box 75, Folder 3; GHQ Far Eastern Command memo, 27 February 1948, Record Group 5, Records of General Headquarters, Supreme Commander for the Allied

Powers 1945–1951, Series 1, Subseries 4, Box 32, "KEM-KH" folder, MacArthur Memorial Archives, Norfolk, VA (hereafter "SCAP Records" with series and subseries where applicable).

50. Marshall to MacArthur, 12 February 1948, PPS Records, Box 29A, Japan 1948 folder.

51. Kennan speculated that the two generals had been alienated as a result of "the enormous frictions of the wartime competition between the Pacific and European theaters for supplies and support." Kennan, *Memoirs 1925–1950*, 382.

52. Kennan memorandum of conversation with Marshall, 19 February 1948, PPS Records, Box 29A, Japan 1948 folder.

53. PPS 23, "Review of Current Trends: US Foreign Policy," *PPS Papers*, 2:123.

54. Ibid. Kennan provided a Japanese audience a brief personal account of his 1948 trip to Tokyo during a 1980 visit to Japan. Transcript of Kennan speech and interviews, Tokyo International House, 31 October 1980, Kennan Papers, Box 278, Folder 7.

55. Kennan, *Memoirs 1925–1950*, 382; Green interview with Charles Stuart Kennedy, Association for Diplomatic Studies and Training (ADST) Foreign Affairs Oral History Project, 1995, as cited in John Lewis Gaddis, *George F. Kennan: An American Life* (New York: Penguin Press), 301.

56. Marshall Green interview with Wilson Miscamble, 6 July 1978, quoted in Miscamble, *George F. Kennan*, 258–60; Marshall Green, telephone interview by author, 18 May 1993, Washington, DC. Kennan later claimed that during the trip to Japan, someone in Tokyo loaned him a book about US policy during the period of the Russo-Japanese War of 1904–05, which included a copy of a letter from the elder George Kennan to President Theodore Roosevelt. According to the younger Kennan, the letter featured "some of the very things that I had been saying to General MacArthur." Kennan interview, Tokyo International House, 31 October 1980, Kennan Papers, Box 278, Folder 7.

57. Kennan, *Memoirs 1925–1950*, 383–84. Kennan later prepared a short summary of MacArthur's comments at this luncheon and submitted it with his trip report and Japan policy paper. See "General MacArthur's Remarks at Lunch, March 1, 1948," *PPS Papers*, 2:184–86.

58. Michael Schaller, *Douglas MacArthur: The Far Eastern General* (New York: Oxford University Press, 1989), 150; Kennan, *Memoirs 1925–1950*, 383; Kennan/Pogue interview, George C. Marshall Research Foundation, side 1, 20.

59. Kennan to MacArthur, 2 March 1948, SCAP Records, Series 1, Subseries 4, Box 32, MacArthur Memorial Archives.

60. Green interview with author, 18 May 1993; Marshall Green, *Pacific Encounters* (Bethesda, MD: DACOR Press, 1997), 24–27. According to Green, Kennan "never understood the importance" of his Soviet briefing in facilitating a second meeting with MacArthur, but Kennan's own correspondence and memoirs indicate otherwise. See Kennan to Butterworth, 16 March 1948, PPS Records, Box 29A, Japan 1948 folder, and Kennan, *Memoirs 1925–1950*, 385. Green's recollection of the origins of the Kennan briefing, however, is probably more accurate than Kennan's. Whereas Green traced it to his discussions with Babcock, Kennan in his memoirs attributed it to a meeting he had with Willoughby the night before. I agree with Miscamble that Kennan's memory on this point probably was faulty, and that Willoughby's call on Kennan was more likely a response to the Soviet briefing, rather than its inspiration. Miscamble, *George F. Kennan*, 261–62; Green interview with author; Green interview with Kennedy, as cited in Gaddis, *George F. Kennan*, 302; Willoughby-Kennan correspondence, 1948–1950, in Selected Papers of Major General Charles A. Willoughby, 1943–1954, Record Group 23B, MacArthur Memorial Archives, Norfolk, VA, Box 1.

61. Kennan to MacArthur, 5 March 1948, SCAP Records, Series 3, Subseries 3, Box 107, Folder 2 ("Political Adviser to SCAP, Correspondence July 1947–March 1951"). A copy of this document is in PPS Records, Box 29A, Japan 1948 folder.

62. Kennan, *Memoirs 1925–1950*, 385–86; "Conversation between General of the Army MacArthur and Mr. George F. Kennan, March 5, 1948," *PPS Papers*, 2:188, 192–93.

63. Green interview with author, 18 May 1993; Kennan, *Memoirs 1925–1950*, 386; *PPS Papers*, 2:193.

64. Ibid., 190–95.

65. Ibid., 188–90.

66. Kennan, *Memoirs 1925–1950*, 386; *PPS Papers*, 2:196; Kennan to Butterworth, 9 March 1948, PPS Records, Box 29A, Japan 1948 folder; Kennan to Butterworth, 10 March 1948, ibid.; Kennan/Pogue interview, George C. Marshall Research Foundation, side 1, 21.

67. The origins of the Draper mission are discussed in Schonberger, *Aftermath of War*, 180–82. Royall to MacArthur, 25 February 1948, SCAP Records, Series 2, Box 77, "Royall Mission, February 1949" folder.

68. Wisner to Marshall, 16 March 1948, State Department Decimal Files, 740.00119 Control (Japan)/3-1648, Box 3819, RG 59, NA; Marshall to Kennan, 17 March 1948, State Department Decimal Files, 894.50/3-1748, Reel 21, RG 59, NA.

69. Kennan to Butterworth, 16 March 1948, PPS Records, Box 29A, Japan 1948 folder.

70. Kennan to Butterworth, 9 March 1948, ibid. Kennan shared similar impressions of MacArthur's entourage with a Japanese audience in 1980. Transcript of Kennan speech and interviews, Tokyo International House, 31 October 1980, Kennan Papers, Box 278, Folder 7.

71. Kennan to Butterworth, 16 March 1948, PPS Records, Box 29A, Japan 1948 folder. Although a commentary on the US occupation of Japan, this passage clearly reflects Kennan's creeping disillusionment with contemporary US society, which would become a recurring theme in his writings years later.

72. Theodore Cohen, *Remaking Japan: The American Occupation as New Deal*, ed. Herbert Passim (New York: Free Press, 1987), 411. The other members of the Johnston Committee were Paul Hoffman, soon to be administrator of the European Recovery Administration; Robert Loree, chairman of the National Foreign Trade Council; and Sidney Scheuer, head of the New York consulting firm of Scheuer and Company. Colonel Trevor Dupuy, then Draper's top policy aide, later corroborated Cohen's claim that this group had been "thrown together" and that the elderly Johnston was only nominally in charge. Dupuy interview by author, 20 June 1994, McLean, Virginia.

73. "Material for the Draper Group," 18 March 1948, Records of the Supreme Commander for the Allied Powers, Economic and Scientific Section, Office of the Chief, General Subject File 1945–1952, Record Group 331, Box 5977, "Draper Mission" folder, WNRC.

74. "Informal Summary of Conclusions of 21 March Conference on Japan," 21 March (amended 23 March) 1948, PPS Records, Box 29A, Japan 1948 folder.

75. This, according to historian Richard Finn, was Draper's typical modus operandi. Richard B. Finn, *Winners in Peace: MacArthur, Yoshida, and Postwar Japan* (Berkeley: University of California Press, 1992), 197–98.

76. "Informal Summary of Conclusions of 21 March Conference on Japan," 21 March (amended 23 March) 1948, PPS Records, Box 29A, Japan 1948 folder.

77. Ibid.

78. "Conversation between General of the Army MacArthur, Under Secretary of the Army Draper, and Mr. George F. Kennan, March 21, 1948," in *PPS Papers*, 2:200–201.

79. Ibid., 198–200.

80. PPS 28, 25 March 1948 (Kennan's first draft), is in *FRUS* 1948, 6:691–96. The accompanying memorandum of discussion is in *PPS Papers*, 2:203–43, where it is published along with PPS 28/2, 26 May 1948 (Kennan's final draft).

81. Ibid., 203.

82. *FRUS* 1948, 6:691.

83. *PPS Papers*, 2:204–5, 208–10.

84. Ibid., 210–17; *FRUS* 1948, 6:692–93.

85. *FRUS* 1948, 6:693; *PPS Papers*, 2:218–19.

86. *PPS Papers*, 219–20; *FRUS* 1948, 6:693.

87. *FRUS* 1948, 6:694; *PPS Papers*, 2:222–29.

88. *PPS Papers*, 2:232–35; *FRUS* 1948, 6:694–95. Kennan here failed to recognize, or at least to acknowledge, that other countries in the region would also be "producing goods" and diversifying their economies in the course of postwar reconstruction.

89. *PPS Papers*, 2:235.

90. Ibid.

91. Paul Nitze, *From Hiroshima to Glasnost: At the Center of Decision: A Memoir*, with Ann M. Smith and Steven L. Rearden (New York: Grove Weidenfeld, 1989), 85.

92. Kennan to Lovett, 25 March 1948, PPS Records, Box 29A, Japan 1948 folder.

93. Kennan, *Memoirs 1925–1950*, 404.

94. Allison to Butterworth, 29 March 1948, PPS Records, Box 29A, Japan 1948 folder; Borton to Hamilton, 30 March 1948, State Department Decimal Files, 740.00119PW/3-3048, Box 3930, RG 59, NA.

95. Thorp to Butterworth, 6 April 1948, *FRUS* 1948, 6:964–65; Saltzman to Butterworth, 9 April 1948, ibid., 727–36. Saltzman also disagreed with Kennan's recommendation that the occupation's reform programs be brought to a close, on the grounds that this proposal was based on an incorrect assumption "that reform and stability are inconsistent."

96. Butterworth to Lovett, 16 April 1948, NEA Briefing Books, Reel 9, RG 59, NA; Dupuy to Draper, 15 April 1948, Draper Japan file, Box 18, SAOUS 091 Japan, WNRC, Suitland, MD; Green to Butterworth, 7 April 1948, State Department Decimal Files, 711.90/4-748, Microfilm Publication C0045, Reel 21, RG 59, NA. The Army Department's copy of PPS 28/1 (which incorporated the minor changes made within State), dated 16 April, is in Draper Japan file, Box 18, SAOUS 091 Japan, WNRC.

97. Wedemeyer to Draper, 21 April 1948, Draper Japan file, ibid.; Schuyler to Butterworth, 28 April 1948, PPS Records, Box 29A, Japan 1948 folder.

98. Schuyler to Butterworth, 28 April 1948, ibid.

99. Allison to Butterworth, 12 May 1948, State Department Decimal Files, 740.00119 Control (Japan)/5-1248, Box 3819, RG 59, NA; Kennan to Butterworth, 4 May 1948, PPS Records, Box 29A, Japan 1948 folder.

100. "Report on the Economic Position and Prospects of Japan and Korea and the Measures Required to Improve Them," 26 April 1948 (released to the press on 19 May 1948), Records of the Supreme Commander for the Allied Powers, Economic and Scientific Section, Office of the Chief, General Subject File 1945–1952, Record Group 331, Box 5979, "Johnston Report" folder, WNRC.

101. Allison to Butterworth, 21 May 1948, State Department Decimal Files, 740.00119 Control (Japan)/5-2148, Box 3819, RG 59, NA.

102. Ibid.

103. Butterworth to Schuyler, 24 May 1948, State Department Decimal Files, 711.94/5-2448, Microfilm Publication LM137, Reel 1, RG 59, NA; Saltzman to Butterworth, 24 May 1948, ibid.; Saltzman to Lovett, 27 May 1948, State Department Decimal Files, 740.00119 PW/5-2748, Box 3930, RG 59, NA; Royall to Marshall, 26 May 1948, Draper Japan file, Box 18, SAOUS 091 Japan, WNRC; Lovett to Royall, 29 May 1948, ibid.

104. Butterworth to Kennan, 26 May 1948, PPS Records, Box 29A, Japan 1948 folder; Butler to Lovett/Marshall, cover letter for PPS 28/2, "Recommendations with Respect to US Policy toward Japan," 26 May 1948, *PPS Papers*, 2:175.

105. James Forrestal, diary entry for 30 April 1948, Forrestal Diaries, Box 4.

106. Lovett to Souers, 1 June 1948, PPS Records, Box 29A, Japan 1948 folder; Draper to MacArthur, 7 June 1948, ibid.

107. MacArthur to Draper, 12 June 1948, ibid.; Butterworth to Kennan, 29 June 1948, ibid.

108. Kennan lecture at National War College, "The Present Situation in Japan," 19 May 1948, Kennan Papers, Box 17, Folder 8. Here Kennan borrowed an idea he had earlier recorded in his diary. Kennan diary entry, 30 January 1948, *Kennan Diaries*, 211.

109. Green to Butterworth, 7 April 1948, State Department Decimal Files, 711.90/4-748, Microfilm Publication C0045, Reel 21, RG 59, NA; Kennan to Marshall/Lovett, 5 May 1948, State Department Decimal Files, 740.0011PW (Peace)/4-2748, Box 3514, RG 59, NA.

110. Memorandum of Conversation, 26 May 1948, State Department Decimal Files, 711.94/5-2648, Microfilm Publication LM137, Reel 1, RG 59, NA; Memoranda Prepared in the Canadian Department for External Affairs, 3 June 1948, *FRUS* 1948, 6:800–807.

111. Saltzman to Marshall, 5 June 1948, *FRUS* 1948, 6:973–77; Lovett to Souers, 18 June 1948, ibid., 977; Dupuy to P&OD, 2 August 1948, Draper Japan file, Box 18, SAOUS 091 Japan, WNRC; Saltzman to William McWilliams, 3 August 1948, State Department Decimal Files, 711.94/8-348, Microfilm Publication LM137, RG 59, NA; Kennan to McWilliams, 11 August 1948, PPS Records, Box 29A, Japan 1948 file.

112. Butterworth to Kennan, 22 July 1948, PPS Records, Box 29A, Japan 1948 folder; Butterworth to Lovett, 16 September 1948, State Department Decimal Files, 711.94/9-1648, Microfilm Publication LM137, RG 59, NA.

113. James S. Lay to the NSC, 24 September 1948, *FRUS* 1948, 6:853; Memorandum for the President on NSC Meeting #22, 1 October 1948, Truman Papers, PSF, Box 220; Minutes of NSC Meeting #22, 30 September 1948, Truman Papers, PSF, Box 204.

114. Minutes of NSC Meeting #23, 7 October 1948, Truman Papers, PSF, Box 204. NSC 13/2 is in *FRUS* 1948, 6:858–62.

115. Dunn, *Peace-Making and the Settlement with Japan*, 77.

116. Lovett to Souers, 26 October 1948, *FRUS* 1948, 6:876–78; Lovett to Souers, 28 October 1948, ibid., 879–80.

117. Saltzman to Kennan, 1 October 1948, PPS Records, Box 29A, Japan 1948 folder; Fearey to Butterworth, 14 October 1948, State Department Decimal Files, 740.00119 PW/10-1448, Box 3931, RG 59, NA.

118. The tortuous course of the deliberations on the reparations issue is evident in both State and Army records. See Fearey to Kennan, 19 October 1948, PPS Records, Box 29A, Japan 1948 folder; Lovett to Royall, 28 October 1948, ibid.; Allison to Kennan (with attachments), 24 November 1948, ibid.; Forrestal to Lovett, 26 October 1948, Draper Japan file, Box 21, SAOUS 387.6 Japan, WNRC; Lovett to Royall, 5 November 1948, Draper Japan file, Box 21, OSA 091 Japan; Memorandum for the Record, 22 November 1948, Draper Japan file, Box 21, SAOUS 387.6 Japan; Kennan to Draper, 23 November 1948, ibid. By mid-December, the State Department—unable to agree internally on its position—recognized that the ground was slipping out from under it. Kennan was personally disinclined to defend continued reparations deliveries, and MacArthur came out in favor of the Army's insistence that they be stopped. Nonetheless, months of additional wrangling ensued before the NSC in early May 1949 approved an amended version of NSC 13/2 (NSC 13/3) that effectively ended the reparations program by explicitly reducing the question "to the

status of a dead letter." See Bishop to Butterworth, 17 December 1948, *FRUS* 1948, 6:1064; Draper to Lovett, 18 December 1948, Draper Japan file, Box 18, SAOUS 091 Japan NSC 13/2; Kennan to Humelsine, 22 December 1948, State Department Decimal Files, 740.00119 PW/12-1848, Box 3932, RG 59, NA; Fearey to Davies, 2 May 1949, *FRUS* 1949, 7:727; NSC 13/3, 6 May 1949, ibid., 735.

119. Kennan to Fearey, 27 October 1948, PPS Records, Box 29A, Japan 1948 folder.

120. Kennan, *Memoirs 1925–1950*, 382.

121. Butterworth to Lovett, 27 October 1948, *FRUS* 1948, 6:878; Lovett to Royall, ibid., 890.

122. Lieutenant Colonel Milner to Colonel McNamara, 9 December 1948, Draper Japan file, Box 18, SAOUS 091 Japan NSC 13/2; "Informal Memorandum of Understanding between State and Army Departments concerning Implementation of NSC 13/2," 7 December 1948, ibid.

123. Butterworth to Lovett, 20 December 1948, *FRUS* 1948, 6:933.

124. Minutes of NSC Meeting #29, 10 December 1948, Truman Papers, PSF, Box 205; Memorandum for the President on NSC Meeting #29, 10 December 1948, Truman Papers, PSF, Box 220.

125. MacArthur to Draper, 18 December 1948, SCAP Records, Series 2, Box 75, "Messages concerning NSC 13/2" folder.

126. Draper to MacArthur, 26 December 1948, ibid.

127. Ibid. For evidence of State-Army cooperation in the response to MacArthur, see Butterworth to Lovett, 20 December 1948, *FRUS* 1948, 6:932; Bishop to Butterworth, 28 December 1948, ibid., 938–39; Lovett to Souers, 29 December 1948, PPS Records, Box 29A, Japan 1948 folder.

128. MacArthur to Draper, 26 December 1948, SCAP Records, Series 2, Box 75, "Messages concerning NSC 13/2" folder.

129. Kennan, *Memoirs 1925–1950*, 393. McCoy officially withdrew US support for FEC-230 on 9 December 1948; the following day, he delivered to the commission the text of the economic stabilization directive. *FRUS* 1948, 6:1056–60.

130. William S. Borden, *The Pacific Alliance: United States Foreign Economic Policy and Japanese Trade Recovery, 1947–1955* (Madison: University of Wisconsin Press, 1984), 92. For evidence of MacArthur's foot-dragging on implementation of NSC 13/2, see Fearey to Davies, 2 May 1949, *FRUS* 1949, 7:724–27; Butterworth to Webb, 19 May 1949, ibid., 752–54. Revisionist and post-revisionist historians have debated the drivers and impact of the reverse course, with its critics primarily asserting that it subordinated Japanese democracy to US "hegemonic" Cold War strategies. I agree with those who judge that this critique exaggerates the scope of the policy shifts, overlooks the domestic Japanese support for them, and oversimplifies the US motivations behind the reverse course. The record presented here shows that Kennan himself was clearly driven by a combination of strategic and economic goals, and saw them as inseparable. See Judith Munro-Leighton, "A Post-revisionist Scrutiny of America's Role in the Cold War in Asia, 1945–1950," *Journal of American-East Asian Relations* 1, no. 1 (Spring 1992): 88–92; Masami Kimura, "American Asia Experts, Liberal Internationalism, and the Occupation of Japan," *Journal of American-East Asian Relations* 21, no. 3 (2014): 248–53; and John Swenson-Wright, *Unequal Allies? United States Security and Alliance Policy toward Japan, 1945–1960* (Stanford, CA: Stanford University Press, 2005), 35–36.

131. John W. Dower, "A Rejoinder," *Pacific Historical Review* 57, no. 2 (May 1988): 207.

132. Schonberger, *Aftermath of War*, 161, 195, 197; Borden, *Pacific Alliance*, 80; Finn, *Winners in Peace*, 192; Schaller, *American Occupation of Japan*, 132; and Michael Schaller, "MacArthur's Japan: The View from Washington," *Diplomatic History* 10, no. 1 (Winter 1986): 15.

133. Bruce Cumings, "Japan's Position in the World System," in Andrew Gordon, ed., *Postwar Japan as History* (Berkeley: University of California Press, 1993), 39.

134. Schonberger, *Aftermath of War*, 190.

135. Paul H. Nitze, interview by author, 7 June 1994, Washington, DC; Borden, *Pacific Alliance*, 44.

136. *PPS Papers*, 2:232; Department of State, *Transcript of Round Table Discussion on American Policy toward China Held in the Department of State, October 6, 7, and 8, 1949* (Washington, DC: W. D. Bowles, 1951), 25, 37–38; Kennan letter to author, 31 January 1994; Davies interview with author, 23 November 1993. In 1967, Kennan wrote that Washington, prior to WWII, "should have encouraged the Japanese to pursue their own interests on the Asian mainland in preference to their seeking increased power and influence in the island world of the Western and Southwestern Pacific; and it should have been our concern to see to it that the requirements of the Japanese economy for the raw materials available in that island world should be satisfied easily, abundantly, and without friction in order that no feeling should arise among the Japanese of a need for an extension of their political authority to that area as a means of assuring access to raw materials." Kennan, "Unused Draft for Statement on Vietnam," 1967, Kennan Papers, Box 27, Folder 1-E-25. This echoed MacMurray's emphasis on the need for the United States to attend to Japan's legitimate economic interests in order to avoid a hostile Japanese pursuit of them.

137. Schonberger, *Aftermath of War*, 142; Kennan letter to author, 31 January 1994. See also Schonberger, "The Japan Lobby in American Diplomacy, 1947–1952," *Pacific Historical Review* 46 (1977): 327–59.

138. Schonberger, *Aftermath of War*, 168; Schaller, *American Occupation of Japan*, 132; Schaller, "MacArthur's Japan," 15. Colonel Charles Kades, the deputy chief of SCAP's Government Section, wrote in January 1949 that "the State Department is far stronger in molding policy for Japan than the Department of the Army." He added that "there is no doubt that Mr. Draper is far more influential in German than in Japanese affairs." Kades to General Courtney Whitney, 6 January 1949, Papers of Charles L. Kades, 1948–1951, Box 1, Record Group 33, MacArthur Memorial Archives, Norfolk, VA.

139. Kennan letter to author, 18 October 1993; Davies interview with author, 23 November 1993; Nitze interview with author, 7 June 1994; Green interview with author, 18 May 1993.

140. Oral History Interview, William H. Draper, January 1972, Truman Library, 56-8.

141. Dupuy interview with author, 20 June 1994. Schonberger also cited as evidence of Draper's influence on PPS 28 a brief note, presumably written by the undersecretary, that is attached to his copy of the Kennan paper in the archives. The substantive fragments of the note include "Get in thought of new instructions to US member FEC" and "Strengthen econ recovery objective." Minor changes subsequently were made to the relevant sections of the paper. Dupuy, however, later confirmed that the handwriting on the note was not Draper's but his, and suggested that the note had no particular significance. Schonberger, *Aftermath of War*, 195; cover note on copy of PPS 28/2, 25 May 1948, Draper Japan file, Box 18, SAOUS 091 Japan; Dupuy interview with author, 20 June 1994; "Informal Summary of Conclusions of 21 March Conference on Japan," 21 March (amended 23 March) 1948, PPS Records, Box 29A, Japan 1948 folder.

142. Gaddis, *George F. Kennan*, 303. Gaddis suggests that Kennan's account of his role in the "reverse course" was solipsistic and that the 1948 trip to Tokyo may not have been necessary because MacArthur was already under pressure to adjust occupation policies. Kennan was certainly capable of and even prone to solipsism. But I think the weight of the evidence clearly shows that MacArthur was impervious to that pressure until Kennan became the vehicle for and agent of a unified push from Washington: the White House,

State, and Defense all explicitly agreed that a high-level mission to Tokyo was necessary, and Kennan's trip achieved their collective purpose. Ibid., 306.

4. EBB TIDE

1. Kennan letter to author, 18 October 1993.

2. John Van Antwerp MacMurray, *How the Peace Was Lost: The 1935 Memorandum: "Developments Affecting American Policy in the Far East": Prepared for the State Department by John Van Antwerp MacMurray*, ed. Arthur Waldron (Stanford, CA: Hoover Institution Press, Stanford University, 1992), 132–35.

3. PPS 23, "Review of Current Trends in US Foreign Policy," 24 February 1948, *PPS Papers*, 2:121–23.

4. Kennan to Marshall, 14 March 1948, PPS Records, Box 29A, Japan 1948 folder.

5. Ibid.

6. Ibid. Kennan much later misremembered both MacArthur's and his own views regarding Okinawa. "If my memory is correct," Kennan wrote in 1997, MacArthur "did not think that it should be necessary for us to retain troops indefinitely either in Japan or on Okinawa." His memory was incorrect inasmuch as both the general and Kennan in 1948 argued for a long-term US military presence on Okinawa. Kennan to Robert Eldridge, 5 September 1997, Kennan Papers, Box 77, Folder 1.

7. See John Lewis Gaddis, "The Strategic Perspective: The Rise and Fall of the 'Defensive Perimeter' Concept, 1947–1951," in *Uncertain Years: Chinese-American Relations, 1947–1950*, ed. Dorothy Borg and Waldo Heinrichs (New York: Columbia University Press, 1980), 61–118. Gaddis also noted that Kennan's concept was actually focused more on "strongpoint" than on "perimeter" defense because it emphasized "not so much control as denial" to the Soviet Union of the key nodes of Japan and the Philippines. John Lewis Gaddis, *Strategies of Containment: A Critical Appraisal of American National Security Policy during the Cold War*, rev. and expanded ed. (New York: Oxford University Press, 2005), 57–63.

8. See Gaddis, *Strategies of Containment*, 75–76.

9. See George F. Kennan, *Memoirs 1925–1950* (New York: Pantheon Books, 1967), 313, 325–29; Dean Acheson, *Present at the Creation: My Years in the State Department* (New York: W. W. Norton, 1969), 215; Forrest C. Pogue, *George C. Marshall: Statesman, 1945–1959* (New York: Viking Press, 1987), 150–51.

10. Kennan, *Memoirs 1925–1950*, 345; Kennan memorandum, 4 November 1947, PPS Records, Box 33, Chronological file.

11. Kennan to Marshall, 24 August 1950, in "Documents Loaned to Dr. Forrest Pogue by George Kennan," February 1959, Verifax #358, George C. Marshall Research Foundation; Kennan, *Memoirs 1925–1950*, 345; Marshall to Kennan, 6 January 1948, in "Research Material: Kennan-Marshall Correspondence," C. Ben Wright Kennan Biography Project Papers, Box 7, Folder 8, George C. Marshall Research Foundation.

12. Kennan to Acheson, 3 January 1949, Acheson Papers, Box 64.

13. Acheson, *Present at the Creation*, 215.

14. Kennan/Pogue interview, George C. Marshall Research Foundation, 13; Kennan, *Memoirs 1925–1950*, 426. Kennan also held Acheson accountable for the fact that during his tenure as secretary "the Foreign Service was ruined and the excesses of the security system reached the high level they were to retain, unhappily, into the [Eisenhower] administration." Kennan to Norman Graebner, 16 May 1959, Kennan Papers, Box 31.

15. Charles E. Bohlen, *Witness to History 1929–1969* (New York: W. W. Norton, 1973), 298.

16. Kennan, *Memoirs 1925–1950*, 426–27.

17. Davies interview with author, 23 November 1993; oral history interview, Charles Burton Marshall, June 1989, Truman Library, 126; oral history interview, Edwin M. Martin, 6 July 1970, Truman Library, 20.

18. Acheson, *Present at the Creation*, 347; Kennan, *Memoirs 1925–1950*, 427.

19. George F. Kennan, *The Kennan Diaries*, ed. Frank Costigliola (New York: W. W. Norton, 2014), 224, 236–37, 238; Kennan/Pogue interview, George C. Marshall Research Foundation, part 2, 12; Kennan, *Memoirs 1925–1950*, 465–66.

20. Kennan to Marshall, 14 March 1948, PPS Records, Box 29A, Japan 1948 folder; Kennan to Butterworth, 16 March 1948, ibid.

21. Minutes of PPS Meetings, 25 October and 15 November 1948, PPS Records, Box 32; NSC 37, "Strategic Value of Formosa," 1 December 1948, *FRUS* 1949, 9:261–62.

22. Minutes of PPS Meeting, 3 January 1949, PPS Records, Box 32; Butler to Lovett, 6 January 1949, PPS Records, Box 13, China 1949 folder.

23. Minutes of NSC Meeting #31, 6 January 1949, Truman Papers, PSF, Box 205; Memorandum for the President on NSC Meeting #31, Truman Papers, PSF, Box 220.

24. Butterworth to Lovett, 13 January 1949, PPS Records, Box 13, China 1949 folder; Draft of Davies memo, 7 January 1949, PPS Records, Box 45, PPS members chronological file, Davies folder; Lovett to Truman, 14 January 1949, *FRUS* 1949, 9:265–66.

25. NSC 37/1, "Draft Report by the National Security Council on the Position of the United States with Respect to Formosa," 19 January 1949, ibid., 271–74.

26. Ibid., 272, 274–75.

27. Butterworth to Acheson, 2 February 1949, ibid., 279–80; Minutes of NSC Meeting #33, 3 February 1949, Truman Papers, PSF, Box 205; Memorandum for the President on NSC Meeting #33, Truman Papers, PSF, Box 220; Souers to Acheson, 4 February 1949, *FRUS* 1949, 9:283.

28. NSC 37/3, "The Strategic Importance of Formosa," 10 February 1949, *FRUS* 1949, 9:284–86; NSC 37/4, "The Current Position of the United States with Respect to Formosa," 18 February 1949, ibid., 288–89; NSC 37/5, "Supplementary Measures with Respect to Formosa," 1 March 1949, ibid., 290–92.

29. Minutes of NSC Meeting #35, 3 March 1949, Truman Papers, PSF, Box 205; Memorandum for the President on NSC Meeting #35, Truman Papers, PSF, Box 220.

30. Johnson to Souers, 2 April 1949, *FRUS* 1949, 9:307–8. A comprehensive discussion of this period is central to David M. Finkelstein, *Washington's Taiwan Dilemma 1949–1950: From Abandonment to Salvation* (Annapolis, MD: US Naval Institute Press, 1993).

31. Merchant to Butterworth, 24 May 1949, *FRUS* 1949, 9:337–40.

32. Butterworth to Rusk, 9 June 1949, ibid., 346–50.

33. Merchant to Butterworth, 15 June 1949, CA Records, Reel 14; Minutes of PPS Meetings, 15, 17, 27 June 1949, PPS Records, Box 32.

34. Kennan letter to author, 18 October 1993; George F. Kennan, *Russia and the West under Lenin and Stalin* (New York: Mentor Books, 1960), 377. Here, too, Kennan was channeling MacMurray, who referred to "the leadership of Chiang Kai-shek—who possesses all the traditional Chinese capacity for compromise and wrangling and intrigue, but is unique among modern Chinese politicians in his ability to discern what he wants, make decisions and resolutely act upon them." MacMurray, *How the Peace Was Lost*, 92.

35. Davies interview with author, 23 November 1993.

36. Davies draft memorandum, "US Policy toward Formosa," 21 June 1949, PPS Records, Box 45, PPS members chronological file, Davies folder.

37. Davies memo, 22 June 1949, ibid.

38. PPS 53, Annex A, "A Possible Course of Action with Respect to Formosa and the Pescadores," 23 June 1949, *PPS Papers*, 3:67–74.

39. Kennan to Davies et al., 20 June 1949, PPS Records, Box 33, Chronological file.

40. Ibid.

41. PPS 53, "United States Policy toward Formosa and the Pescadores," 6 July 1949, *PPS Papers*, 3:63–66.

42. Ibid., 65.

43. Ibid., 65–66.

44. Walter Isaacson and Evan Thomas, *The Wise Men: Six Friends and the World They Made* (New York: Simon & Schuster, 1986), 477; Warren I. Cohen, "Acheson, His Advisers, and China, 1949–50," in *Uncertain Years: Chinese-American Relations, 1947–1950*, ed. Dorothy Borg and Waldo Heinrichs (New York: Columbia University Press, 1980), 25; Nancy Bernkopf Tucker, *Patterns in the Dust: Chinese-American Relations and the Recognition Controversy, 1949–1950* (New York: Columbia University Press, 1983), 200; David A. Mayers, *George Kennan and the Dilemmas of US Foreign Policy* (New York: Oxford University Press, 1988), 177; John L. Gaddis, *George F. Kennan: An American Life* (New York: Penguin Press, 2011), 357, 727.

45. Robert L. Messer, "Roosevelt, Truman, and China: An Overview," in *Sino-American Relations 1945–1955: A Joint Reassessment of a Critical Decade*, ed. Harry Harding and Yuan Ming (Wilmington, DE: Scholarly Resources Books, 1989), 74.

46. Finkelstein, *Washington's Taiwan Dilemma 1949–1950*, 181.

47. Secretary's Daily Meeting, 29 July 1949, Summaries of the Secretary's Daily Meetings, 1949–1952, Office of the Executive Secretariat, Records of the Secretary of State 1944–1953, Lot 53D443, RG 59, NA, Box 1 (hereafter "Secretary's Daily Meeting").

48. Rusk draft memo, 28 July 1949, PPS Records, Box 13, China 1949 folder; Kennan to Rusk et al., 29 July 1949, ibid.; NSC 37/6, "Current Position of the US with Respect to Formosa," 4 August 1949, *FRUS* 1949, 9:369–71; NSC 37/7, "The Position of the United States with Respect to Formosa," 17 August 1949, ibid., 376–78.

49. NSC 37/8, "Position of the United States with Respect to Formosa," 6 October 1949, *FRUS* 1949, 9:392–97; memo by Charlton Ogburn, "Decisions Reached by Consensus at the Meetings with the Secretary and the Consultants on the Far East," 2 November 1949, ibid., 160; Kennan to Rusk, 6 October 1949, PPS Records, Box 13, China 1949 folder; Kennan, *Kennan Diaries*, 227.

50. "Transcript of Presentation" by Kennan at "Q" Building, 14 October 1949, Kennan Papers, Box 17. In 1984, Kennan received an inquiry from a historian about his potential knowledge of or involvement in a plot during 1949–50 to assassinate Chiang Kai-shek. Kennan consulted with Davies, noting that he had no such knowledge. Davies's "imprecise recollection" was that there had been some discussion within the State Department of "the desirability of Chiang's being replaced" by a subordinate that was well respected by the US military, but the idea went nowhere and "I do not recall any suggestion of assassination." However, he added, "God knows what OPC [the covert Office of Policy Coordination, later part of the CIA] may have been up to." Although Kennan had ties to the CIA and had in fact played a role in the development of a US capability for covert political operations, if there had been an OPC plot against Chiang, it is plausible that Kennan would have had no knowledge of it and probably would have opposed it. He almost certainly would have agreed with Davies's view that assassination of Chiang "probably would have been followed by turmoil [on Taiwan]. This we did not want." Kennan to Davies, 6 December 1984, and Davies to Kennan, 12 December 1984, Kennan Papers, Box 10, Folder 12 "Davies, John Paton, Jr."

51. Marshall Carter to Bromley K. Smith, 11 February 1949, *FRUS* 1949, 8:123–24; Secretary's Daily Meeting, 8 March 1949.

52. Acheson, *Present at the Creation*, 302; see also transcript of Acheson comments during Princeton Seminars, 22–23 July 1953, Acheson Papers, Box 89, 581–87. Informal

work on the China White Paper apparently began in March 1949; according to John Melby, the first officer Butterworth assigned to the project, "there was no formal directive" that initiated it. See *FRUS* 1949, 9:1365; Melby, "The Making of a White Paper," Melby Papers, Box 32; oral history interview, John Melby, November 1986, Truman Library, 167–73; Robert P. Newman, "The Self-Inflicted Wound: The China White Paper of 1949," *Prologue* 14, no. 3 (Fall 1982): 141–56; Philip Sprouse to Butterworth, 25 July 1971, Butterworth Papers, Box 1.

53. Kennan to Acheson, 28 June 1949, PPS Records, Box 45, PPS members chronological file, Davies folder. A handwritten note on this memo says it was "communicated orally" by Kennan.

54. Secretary's Daily Meeting, 30 June 1949.

55. Secretary's Daily Meeting, 1 July 1949.

56. Kennan to Jessup et al., 29 July 1949, PPS Records, Box 13, China 1949 folder; Minutes of PPS Meeting, 1 August 1949, PPS Records, Box 32; "Points Suggested for Consideration: Meeting in Mr. Kennan's Office," 18 August 1949, State Department Decimal Files, 890.00/8-1849, Microfilm Publication C0045, Reel 3, RG 59, NA; Butterworth to Jessup, 18 August 1949, ibid. Kennan and Davies also appear to have retreated from a substantial role on the China White Paper. John Melby later asserted that Kennan considered it "the greatest state document ever produced by the American government," but this characterization by Kennan has not been corroborated. Nancy Bernkopf Tucker, ed., *China Confidential: American Diplomats and Sino-American Relations, 1945–1996* (New York: Columbia University Press, 2001), 62.

57. Memorandum by James Webb on meeting with Truman, 3 October 1949, PPS Records, Box 13, China 1949 folder.

58. Kennan was skeptical that the "proper staff work" had been done to make the conference a success; in particular, he thought it politically advisable to invite some critics of the administration's China policy—persons whose "hostility is mixed with some degree of intelligence if possible." Kennan was upset when told that he was to replace Jessup as the host of the conference because Jessup would be preoccupied in New York by the UN General Assembly (UNGA) session; Kennan, who had hoped to be at the UNGA himself, suggested that the conference be canceled. In the end, Kennan attended only the first half-day of the conference, and Jessup joined it on the second day. Kennan to Francis Russell, 20 September 1949, PPS Records, Box 13, China 1949 folder; Secretary's Daily Meeting, 4 October 1949.

59. Memorandum by Gerald Stryker, 2 November 1949, *FRUS* 1949, 9:156. For a full record of the "China Roundtable" conference, see Department of State, *Transcript of Round Table Discussion on American Policy toward China Held in the Department of State, October 6, 7, and 8, 1949* (Washington, DC: W. D. Bowles, 1951).

60. Secretary's Daily Meeting, 17 October 1949; "Meeting of the Secretary and the Consultants on the Far East," 26 October 1949, attachment to Charles Ogburn to Rusk, 17 November 1949, State Department Decimal Files, 890.00/11-1749, Microfilm Publication C0045, Reel 3, RG 59, NA.

61. Ogburn memorandum, "Decisions Reached by Consensus at the Meetings with the Secretary and the Consultants on the Far East," 2 November 1949, *FRUS* 1949, 9:161.

62. Ward previously had been accused of spying and held incommunicado by the Communists since November 1948.

63. Davies interview with author, 23 November 1993. Miscamble inaccurately suggests that the memo was written by Kennan himself and reflects a divergence of views between Kennan and Davies. Miscamble, *George F. Kennan*, 240. Kennan, for his part, did not recall any substantial disagreement with Davies on China policy. Kennan letter to author, 31 January 1994.

64. "Mr. Ward, the Russians, and Recognition," 17 November 1949, PPS Records, Box 45, PPS members chronological files, Davies folder; Kennan to Rusk, 17 November 1949, PPS Records, Box 33, Chronological files.

65. Kennan was dismissive of the administration's efforts to seek international pressure on the Chinese Communists to release Ward. On 21 November he wrote in his diary: "To my mind, this is a good example of how we should not behave. The Chinese Communists are under no obligation to us. It is our own fault that we left our Consul there when the place was taken by the Communists. . . . If we were prepared to behave like a great power, we would treat it as a bilateral issue and not make ourselves ridiculous by asking a lot of weaker powers to assist us in solving it." Kennan, *Kennan Diaries*, 238.

66. Kennan to Acheson, 6 January 1950, *FRUS* 1950, 1:132.

67. Historian Gordon Chang has shown that there were ongoing discussions within the Truman administration about the desirability of separating the Chinese Communists from Moscow, and many suggestions as to how this might be done, but there was never a "consistent and unified" plan of action. This was especially true in 1949 and 1950 (when Kennan and Davies were still involved) because the Communists' victory in China and subsequent alliance with Moscow, and the outbreak of the Korean War, convinced most observers in Washington that splitting the Communist bloc was a faint, long-term hope. Chang indicates that these attitudes and obstacles persisted well into the Eisenhower administration. Gordon H. Chang, *Friends and Enemies: The United States, China, and the Soviet Union, 1948–1972* (Stanford, CA: Stanford University Press, 1990). See also David Allan Mayers, *Cracking the Monolith: US Policy against the Sino-Soviet Alliance, 1949–1955* (Baton Rouge: Louisiana State University Press, 1986).

68. Davies memorandum, 15 April 1945, *FRUS* 1945, 7:336–37; Kennan to Byrnes, 10 January 1946, *FRUS* 1946, 9:118–19.

69. Kennan to Lovett, 23 June 1947, PPS Records, Box 13, China 1947 folder; Kennan lecture to Navy Secretary's Council, "Problems of Far Eastern Policy," 14 January 1948, Kennan Papers, Box 17.

70. Draft paper by Davies, 11 August 1948, attached to minutes of PPS Meeting of 12 August 1948, PPS Records, Box 32.

71. PPS 39, "United States Policy toward China," 7 September 1949, *PPS Papers*, 2:422–24, 430.

72. Kennan to Davies, 25 January 1949, PPS Records, Box 45, PPS members chronological file, Davies folder.

73. PPS 39/2, "United States Policy toward China," 25 February 1949, *PPS Papers*, 3:26, 28.

74. United States Department of State, *The China White Paper*, originally issued as *United States Relations with China, with Special Reference to the Period 1944–1949* (Stanford, CA: Stanford University Press, 1967), 1:xvi. Gaddis notes that there is no indication that Kennan or Davies objected to this characterization. This may have been a reflection of their growing marginalization within Acheson's circle of advisers on China, and thus their inattention to the preparation, contents, and political purposes of the Letter of Transmittal. Gaddis, *George F. Kennan*, 357.

75. United States Department of State, *China White Paper*, 1:xvi.

76. Kennan lecture to Joint Civilian Orientation Conference, 19 September 1949, Kennan Papers, Box 17, Folder 28. See also similar comments by Kennan during a presentation at the CIA, 14 October 1949, Kennan Papers, Box 17, Folder 29.

77. "Meeting of the Secretary and the Consultants on the Far East," 26 October 1949, attachment to Ogburn to Rusk, 17 November 1949, State Department Decimal Files, 890.00/11-1749, Microfilm Publication C0045, Reel 3, RG 59, NA.

78. Minutes of PPS Meeting, 11 January 1950, PPS Records, Box 32. Kennan repeated this theme at another Pentagon Orientation Conference, 17 April 1950, Kennan Papers, Box 18, Folder 1-C-7.

79. Davies interview with author, 23 November 1993; Davies to Nitze, 2 February 1950, *FRUS* 1950, 6:305–6.

5. PRELUDE TO THE KOREAN WAR

1. Kennan to Butterworth, 6 June 1949, State Department Decimal Files, 711.90/6-649, Microfilm Publication C0045, Reel 21, RG 59, NA.

2. The inclusion of Siam (Thailand) and Malaya among areas where "the Communists probably can be denied supremacy" may have reflected a PPS assessment that both countries were low priorities for either the Chinese or Soviet Communists. It is unlikely that Kennan would have advocated a substantial US containment effort in either country.

3. Acheson to Jessup, 18 July 1949, in Philip C. Jessup, *The Birth of Nations* (New York: Columbia University Press, 1974), 29.

4. Davies memorandum, "Suggested Course of Action in East and South Asia," 7 July 1949, *FRUS* 1949, 7:1148–51.

5. Secretary's Daily Meeting, 28 June 1948; Kennan to Webb et al., *FRUS* 1949, 7:1147.

6. Secretary's Daily Meetings, 11 and 22 July 1949; Rusk draft memorandum, 16 July 1949, State Department Decimal Files, 890.00/7-1649, Microfilm Publication C0045, Reel 3, RG 59, NA. Ironically, Jessup himself later wrote that it was the PPS—and Davies's "Suggested Course of Action" memo in particular—that was "responsible for focusing attention in the Department on the need for a vigorous Asian policy." In his own recommendations to Acheson, Jessup borrowed from Davies both the idea that "dramatic" action was needed in East Asia and several of Davies's specific suggestions. He also incorporated suggestions from a separate PPS paper on Southeast Asia (discussed below) that Davies had completed earlier in the year. Jessup, *Birth of Nations*, 24–26; Jessup to Rusk, 12 July 1949, *FRUS* 1949, 7:1153–54; Jessup et al. to Acheson, ibid., 1193–94.

7. Kennan lecture at NWC, "The Present Situation in Japan," 19 May 1948, Kennan Papers, Box 17, Folder 8.

8. Kennan lecture at NWC, "Contemporary Problems of Foreign Policy," 17 December 1948, Kennan Papers, Box 17, Folder 11.

9. Butterworth to Webb, 19 May 1949, *FRUS* 1949, 7:752–54; Souers to Johnson (and attachments), 24 May 1949, PPS Records, Box 29A, Japan 1949 folder.

10. NSC 44, "Limited Military Armament for Japan," 11 March 1949, PPS Records, Box 29A, Japan 1949 folder; Souers to the NSC, 27 April 1949, ibid.

11. Kennan lecture at Joint Civilian Orientation Conference No. 3, "An Estimate of the International Situation," Pentagon, 13 June 1949, Kennan Papers, Box 17, Folder 26; Kennan lecture at Joint Civilian Orientation Conference No. 4, Pentagon, 19 September 1949, Kennan Papers, Box 17, Folder 28.

12. NSC 49, "Current Strategic Evaluation of the US Security Needs in Japan," 15 June 1949, PPS Records, Box 29A, Japan 1949 folder.

13. Davies memorandum, "Suggested Course of Action for East and South Asia," 7 July 1949, *FRUS* 1949, 7:1147–51; Davies to Kennan, 8 July 1949, PPS Records, Box 45, PPS members chronological file, Davies folder; Rusk memorandum, 16 July 1949, State Department Decimal Files, 890/7-1649, Microfilm Publication C0045, Reel 3, RG 59, NA; Charles W. Yost to Jessup, 16 July 1949, ibid.; Kennan interview, 3 March 1967, John Foster Dulles Oral History Project, Seeley G. Mudd Manuscript Library, Princeton, NJ; Kennan, *Memoirs 1925–1950*, 394–95.

14. NSC 13/3, 6 May 1949, *FRUS* 1949, 7:730.

15. MacArthur to Acheson, 16 June 1949, ibid., 780.

16. MacArthur to Kennan, 16 June 1949, SCAP Records, Series 1, Subseries 4, Box 3, 1949 folder. Kennan's response, dated 29 June 1949, is in *FRUS* 1949, 7:793–94.

17. Acheson to MacArthur, 9 September 1949, *FRUS* 1949, 7:850.

18. Cloyce K. Huston memorandum of conversation with MacArthur, 16 July 1949, ibid., 806; Sebald to Butterworth, 26 July 1949, ibid., 810–11; Sebald to Acheson, 20 August 1949, ibid., 830–31.

19. Kennan to Acheson, 13 July 1949, ibid., 799.

20. Memorandum of conversation (Dening, Butterworth, et al.), 9 September 1949, ibid., 853–54; memorandum of conversation (Bevin, Acheson, et al.), 13 September 1949, ibid., 858–59; Acheson memorandum of conversation with Truman, 16 September 1949, ibid., 860.

21. The National Military Establishment became the Department of Defense on 10 August 1949, under amendments to the National Security Act of 1947.

22. Memorandum of conversation (Bevin, Acheson, et al.), 13 September 1949, *FRUS* 1949, 7:859.

23. Minutes of PPS meetings, 8 and 28 September 1949, PPS Records, Box 32.

24. "Department of State Comments on Current Strategic Evaluation of U.S. Security Needs in Japan (NSC 49)," 30 September 1949, *PPS Papers*, 3:183–86. Two days earlier Kennan had recorded in his diary: "I cannot agree that we should insist on a Japanese promise to be democratic and to observe human rights when I know that we have no serious intention of insisting that they live up to such a promise once they have signed it." Kennan diary entry, 28 September 1949, Kennan, *Kennan Diaries*, 227.

25. *PPS Papers*, 3:186; Fearey to Allison, 14 October 1949, *FRUS* 1949, 7:877–78; Butterworth to Sebald, 4 November 1949, ibid., 894–95.

26. Dean Acheson, *Present at the Creation: My Years in the State Department* (New York: W. W. Norton, 1969), 430.

27. Acheson/Voorhees memorandum of conversation, 15 December 1949, Acheson Papers, Box 65, December 1949 folder, Truman Library; Johnson to Acheson, 23 December 1949 (attached is Joint Chiefs of Staff to Johnson, 22 December 1949), *FRUS* 1949, 7:922–23.

28. Bradley/Acheson memorandum of conversation, 24 December 1949, *FRUS* 1949, 7:924–26; Acheson to Sir Oliver Franks, 24 December 1949, ibid., 927–29; Acheson/Franks memorandum of conversation, 24 December 1949, ibid., 929–30.

29. Memorandum of conversation on "Japanese Peace Treaty," 24 April 1950, Acheson Papers, Box 66, April 1950 folder.

30. Acheson, *Present at the Creation*, 431.

31. Ibid., 432–33.

32. Huston memorandum of conversation with MacArthur, 16 July 1949, *FRUS* 1949, 7:806; Sebald memorandum of conversation with MacArthur, 21 September 1949, ibid., 862; Fearey memorandum of conversation, 2 November 1949, ibid., 890–92; Sebald memorandum of conversation with MacArthur, 6 April 1950, PPS Records, Box 29A, Japan 1947–1953 folder.

33. Jessup to Acheson, 10 January 1950, *FRUS* 1950, 6:1115.

34. Butterworth memorandum of conversation with MacArthur, 5 February 1950, ibid., 1133–34.

35. MacArthur, "Memorandum on the Peace Treaty Problem," 14 June 1950, ibid., 1213–21.

36. Ibid., 1220.

37. MacArthur, "Memorandum on Concept Governing Security in Post-War Japan," 23 June 1950, ibid., 1227–28.

38. Davies paper, "American Policy in Asia," 19 February 1944, Davies Papers, Box 11, Folder "Chronological File 1942–1945" (2 of 3).

39. For the French prehistory of the American role in Vietnam, see especially Fredrik Logevall, *Embers of War: The Fall of an Empire and the Making of America's Vietnam* (New York: Random House, 2012); Andrew Rotter, *The Path to Vietnam: Origins of the American Commitment to Southeast Asia* (Ithaca, NY: Cornell University Press, 1987), 84–102; and Stanley Karnow, *Vietnam: A History*, revised and updated ed., (New York: Penguin Books, 1991), 146–75.

40. Kennan presentation at NWC, "Current Political Affairs," 10 January 1947, in *Measures Short of War: The George F. Kennan Lectures at the National War College, 1946–47*, ed. Giles D. Harlow and George C. Maerz (Washington, DC: National Defense University Press, 1991), 94–99, 106–7.

41. See Walter Hixson, *George F. Kennan: Cold War Iconoclast* (New York: Columbia University Press, 1989), 8, 70; Anders Stephanson, *Kennan and the Art of Foreign Policy* (Cambridge, MA: Harvard University Press, 1989), 157–59; David Allan Mayers, *George Kennan and the Dilemmas of US Foreign Policy* (New York: Oxford University Press), 271–74; and Wilson Miscamble, *George F. Kennan and the Making of American Foreign Policy, 1947–1950* (Princeton, NJ: Princeton University Press), 316–17.

42. Kennan presentation at Navy Secretary's Council, "Problems of Far Eastern Policy," 14 January 1948, Kennan Papers, Box 17.

43. PPS 23, "Resume of World Situation," 24 February 1948, *PPS Papers*, 2:121–22.

44. Kennan to Butterworth, 16 March 1948, PPS Records, Box 29A, Japan 1948 folder.

45. Kennan lecture at NWC, "United States Foreign Policy," 11 October 1948, Kennan Papers, Box 17.

46. PPS 13, "Resume of World Situation," 6 November 1947, *PPS Papers*, 1:132, 136.

47. PPS 23, "Resume of World Situation," 24 February 1948, *PPS Papers*, 2:121–22.

48. Ibid., 123.

49. Kennan to Marshall, 14 March 1948, PPS Records, Box 29A, Japan 1948 folder.

50. Ibid.

51. Ibid. Kennan reinforced this view two months later in a message to Butterworth that recommended a withdrawal of US forces from the Philippines "unless the record can be clearly established that they are there at the unsolicited request of the Philippine Government." He said Washington should not "tolerate a situation where the members of the Philippine Government whisper to us that they think it is a good thing that our forces should be there but they do not dare say so domestically for political reasons." Kennan to Butterworth, 13 May 1948, *PPS Papers*, Box 21, Folder "Philippines."

52. Kennan to Marshall, 14 March 1948, PPS Records, Box 29A, Japan 1948 folder.

53. Carleton Savage to Ruth Shipley, 24 May 1948, PPS Records, Box 33, Chronological file.

54. Davies interview with author, 23 November 1993; John Paton Davies Jr., *China Hand: An Autobiography* (Philadelphia: University of Pennsylvania Press, 2012), 316–19.

55. PPS minutes of meetings, 8 July and 2 August 1948, PPS Records, Box 32; Davies draft memo, 3 August 1949, PPS Records, Box 45, PPS members chronological file, Davies personal folder.

56. Davies, *China Hand*, 318; Davies interview with author, 23 November 1993.

57. PPS minutes of meetings, 30 August, 24 November, 14 and 16 December 1948, PPS Records, Box 32.

58. Kennan to Marshall/Lovett, 17 December 1948, PPS Records, Box 18, Indonesia folder. This document has a penciled notation by Kennan reading "Done orally."

59. Ibid.

60. Kennan lecture at NWC, 21 December 1948, Kennan Papers, Box 17, Folder 18; PPS minutes of meeting, 22 December 1948, PPS Records, Box 32.

61. Savage to various offices, 28 February 1948, State Department Decimal Files, 711.90/2-2849, Microfilm Publication C0045, Reel 21, RG 59, NA; Jessup to Kennan, 1 March 1949, Records of the Philippine and Southeast Asia Division, Lot File 54D190, Microfilm Publication C0014, Reel 6, "Southeast Asia-1949-US Policy" folder, RG 59, NA (hereafter "SEA Records" with reel number and folder).

62. Logevall, *Embers of War*, 211; Rotter, *Path to Vietnam*, 91–92; Karnow, *Vietnam: A History*, 187–91.

63. PPS minutes of meetings, 3, 7, 23, 25, 29, 31 March 1949, PPS Records, Box 32; Savage to Charles Reed, 25 March 1949, SEA Records, Reel 6, "Southeast Asia-1949-US Policy" folder, RG 59, NA; Reed to Allison, 31 March 1949, ibid.

64. PPS 51, "United States Policy toward Southeast Asia," 29 March 1949, *PPS Papers*, 3:32–59.

65. Ibid., 34–35.

66. Ibid., 37.

67. Ibid., 38–40.

68. Ibid., 40–43.

69. Ibid., 45–49. The Philippines was acknowledged as "a major asset to the United States" politically because it was a successful colonial model in the region and was one of the only countries there with "leaders practiced in the exercise of responsible power." But "the quality of the republic has not . . . thus far been tested" because Manila was economically and militarily dependent on Washington. Ibid., 36–37, 51.

70. Ibid., 44.

71. Ibid., 52–54.

72. Ibid., 54; Davies interview with author, 23 November 1993; Kennan letter to author, 31 January 1994. See Michael Schaller, "Securing the Great Crescent: Occupied Japan and the Origins of Containment in Southeast Asia," *Journal of American History* 69, no. 2 (September 1982), 392–414. Schaller highlights the linkage between PPS 51 and the "reverse course" in Japan: the promotion of economic integration between Southeast Asia and Japan. This linkage is also cited in Robert M. Blum, *Drawing the Line: The Origin of the American Containment Policy in East Asia* (New York: W. W. Norton, 1982), 113. However, both accounts show that this goal—as noted earlier—was more central to the thinking of economic policymakers than it was to Kennan and Davies.

73. Kennan to Acheson/Webb, 1 April 1949, State Department Decimal Files, 711.90/4-149, Microfilm Publication C0045, Reel 21, RG 59, NA; Blum, *Drawing the Line*, 114; Butterworth to Reed, 6 April 1949, State Department Decimal Files, 890.00/4-649, Microfilm Publication C0045, Reel 3, RG 59, NA.

74. PPS minutes of meeting, 2 May 1949, PPS Records, Box 32; Butterworth to Webb, 15 May 1949, SEA Records, Reel 6, "Southeast Asia-1949-US Policy" folder, RG 59, NA.

75. Kennan to Acheson, 19 May 1949, *PPS Papers*, 3:32.

76. Acheson, *Present at the Creation*, 293, 301.

77. Office of the Secretary to Butterworth/Rusk/Kennan, 1 July 1949, SEA Records, Reel 6, "Southeast Asia-US Policy" folder, RG 59, NA. PPS 51 was redesignated NSC 51 by the NSC.

78. Kennan to Rusk/Bohlen, 5 July 1949, PPS Records, Box 33, Chronological file.

79. Secretary's Daily Meeting, 11 July 1949, RG 59, NA.

80. Rusk to Thomas H. Lockett (Manila), 26 July 1949, *FRUS* 1949, Vol. 7, Part 2, 1176. The same text was subsequently sent to Jakarta and Paris; see William Lacey to Charles Livengood (Jakarta), 19 July 1949, SEA Records, Reel 6, "Southeast Asia-US Policy" folder; Lacey to David Bruce (Paris), 2 August 1949, ibid.

81. Davies, *China Hand*, 319; Davies interview with author, 23 November 1993.

82. Blum, *Drawing the Line*, 113, 124.

83. Michael Schaller, *The American Occupation of Japan: The Origins of the Cold War in Asia* (New York: Oxford University Press, 1985), 159.

84. PPS 51, 29 March 1949, *PPS Papers*, 3:56.

85. Ogburn memorandum of conversation, 17 May 1949, *FRUS* 1949, 7:27–28.

86. Kennan to Butterworth, 6 June 1949, State Department Decimal Files, 711.90/6-649, Microfilm Publication C0045, Reel 21, RG 59, NA; Kennan lecture at National Military Establishment Joint Civilian Orientation Conference, "An Estimate of the International Situation," 13 June 1949, Kennan Papers, Box 17, Folder 26.

87. Davies memo, "Suggested Course of Action in East and South Asia," 7 July 1949, PPS Records, Box 33, Chronological file.

88. Jessup to Rusk, 12 July 1949, *FRUS* 1949, 7:1153–54; Jessup/Case/Fosdick to Acheson, 29 August 1949, ibid., 1194.

89. Rotter, *Path to Vietnam*, 109–19, 186–90; Ogburn memorandum, "Decisions Reached by Consensus at the Meetings with the Secretary and the Consultants on the Far East," 2 November 1949, CA Records, Reel 12, "1949: US Policy towards China and the Far East" folder, RG 59, NA; Acheson/Truman memorandum of conversation, 17 October 1949, Acheson Papers, Box 65, October-November 1949 folder; Acheson/Truman memorandum of conversation, 17 November 1949, ibid.

90. See Logevall, *Embers of War*, 229–33; Rotter, *Path to Vietnam*, 168–72, 179–85, 197–98, 200–201; Melvyn P. Leffler, *A Preponderance of Power: National Security, the Truman Administration, and the Cold War* (Stanford, CA: Stanford University Press, 1992), 338–40, 380–83; Blum, *Drawing the Line*, 125, 144, 153; and Acheson, *Present at the Creation*, 671–73.

91. Acheson, *Present at the Creation*, 673.

92. Kennan lecture at Joint Civilian Orientation Conference #4, 19 September 1949, Kennan Papers, Box 17, Folder 28.

93. Ibid.

94. Kennan to Acheson, 6 January 1950, *FRUS* 1950, 1:131, 137. In this background paper Kennan renewed his concerns about the Philippines, where "recent months have witnessed political and economic deterioration on a scale so serious as to raise [the] question [of] whether [the] republic can cope successfully with [the] responsibilities of independence without extensive outside guidance. Responsibility now lies with [the] Filipinos. They will have to make suggestions. We will not force US guidance on them. But we must be sure [that the] present instability does not create too favorable opportunities for communist penetration. We could not remain indifferent to such [a] development." Ibid., 131.

95. Ibid., 132.

96. Ibid., 131; Kennan lecture at Pentagon Orientation Conference, 17 April 1950, Kennan Papers, Box 18, Folder 1-C-7.

97. Kennan to Butterworth, 6 June 1949, State Department Decimal Files, 711.90/6-649, Microfilm Publication C0045, Reel 21, RG 59, NA.

98. Kennan, *Memoirs 1925–1950*, 484.

99. Forrestal to Marshall, 26 September 1947, *FRUS* 1947, 6:817–18.

100. Kennan to Butterworth, 24 September 1947, PPS Records, Box 33, Chronological file; also in *FRUS* 1947, 6:814.

101. Butterworth to Lovett, 1 October 1947, *FRUS* 1947, 6:820–21; Kennan to Lovett, 1 October 1949, attached to Forrestal to Marshall, 26 September 1947, State Department Decimal File, 740.00119 Control (Korea)/9-2647, Box 3827, RG 59, NA. Other attachments to this memorandum (Carlisle Humelsine to Kennan, 29 September 1947, ibid.; Humelsine to Lovett, 29 September 1947, ibid.) indicate that Lovett, in response to a recommendation

from Saltzman, requested that the PPS prepare a study of the Korea issue. It was subsequently decided that the results of the 29 September meeting in Marshall's office made such a paper unnecessary.

102. PPS 13, "Resume of World Situation," 6 November 1947, *PPS Papers*, 1:135.

103. Kennan lecture for Council of Secretary of the Navy John Sullivan, "Problems of Far Eastern Policy," 14 January 1948, Kennan Papers, Box 299, Folder 3.

104. In January 1948, the Soviet Union had denied entry into North Korea of a UN commission empowered to implement plans for elections aimed at reunifying the peninsula. The UN responded by scheduling elections in South Korea alone in May 1948. These elections, Kennan believed, were certain to raise tensions on the peninsula and make the US presence there even more problematic. Kennan to Marshall, 14 March 1948, PPS Records, Box 29A, Japan 1948 folder.

105. NSC 8, "Report by the National Security Council on the Position of the United States with Respect to Korea," 2 April 1948, *FRUS* 1948, 6:1164–69.

106. Butterworth memorandum, 17 August 1948, ibid., 1276–79; Lovett to Marshall, 5 November 1948, ibid., 1319; Bishop to Butterworth, 17 December 1948, ibid., 1337–40; Butterworth to Lovett, 10 January 1949, State Department Decimal Files, 740.00119 Control (Korea)/1-1049, Box 3829, RG 59, NA; Souers to the NSC, 17 January 1949, 740.00119 Control (Korea)/1-2549, ibid.

107. NSC 8/2, "Position of the United States with Respect to Korea," 22 March 1949, *FRUS* 1949, 7:969–78.

108. Minutes of NSC Meeting #36, 22 March 1949, Truman Papers, PSF, Box 205.

109. Kennan, *Memoirs 1925–1950*, 484–85; Kennan to Vera Michaels Dean, 3 January 1956, Kennan Papers, Box 31, Folder 2-B-1956; Kennan to Allen S. Whiting, 20 October 1960, Kennan Papers, Box 31, Folder 2-B-1960; Kennan remarks in transcript of Princeton seminar, 13–14 February 1954, Acheson Papers, Box 90, Folder 1, 1189–90.

110. Ronald McGlothlen, *Controlling the Waves: Dean Acheson and U.S. Foreign Policy in Asia* (New York: W. W. Norton, 1993), 71; Hixson, *George F. Kennan: Cold War Iconoclast*, 102.

111. Quoted in Acheson, *Present at the Creation*, 357.

112. Ibid., 357–58.

113. See John Lewis Gaddis, "The Rise and Fall of the 'Defensive Perimeter' Concept," in *Uncertain Years: Chinese-American Relations, 1947–1950* (New York: Columbia University Press, 1980), ed. Dorothy Borg and Waldo Heinrichs; and Chapter 14, "'The Speech': Achesonian Deterrence at the Press Club," in *The Origins of the Korean War*, ed. Bruce Cumings, vol. 2, *The Roaring of the Cataract 1947–50* (Princeton, NJ: Princeton University Press, 1990), 408–38.

114. Kennan diary entry, 8 January 1950, *Kennan Diaries*, 240; "Unused draft of speech for delivery by the Secretary of State," 8 January 1950, Kennan Papers, Box 24, Folder 1-D-0; Cumings, *Origins of the Korean War*, 2:421.

115. Kennan to Allen S. Whiting, 20 October 1960, Kennan Papers, Box 30, Folder 2-B-1960.

116. PPS 39/1, "United States Policy toward China," 24 November 1948, *PPS Papers*, 2:448.

117. PPS 13, "Resume of World Situation," 6 November 1947, *PPS Papers*, 1:135.

118. Blum, *Drawing the Line*, 168–77, provides a concise bureaucratic history of NSC 48. The State Department's objections to the paper are outlined in Stephen C. Brown to Sprouse, 24 October 1949, CA Records, Microfilm Publication C0012, Reel 13, RG 59, NA; Allison to Butterworth, 29 November 1949, State Department Decimal Files, 711.90/11-2949, Microfilm Publication C0045, Reel 21, RG 59, NA; Butterworth to Rusk, 20 December 1949, ibid.

119. Kennan to Rusk, 2 November 1949, PPS Records, Box 26, "Asia 1948–1951" folder.

120. Livingston T. Merchant to Allison, 2 December 1949, State Department Decimal Files, 711.90/11-2449, Microfilm Publication C0045, Reel 21, RG 59.

121. NSC 48/1, "The Position of the United States with Respect to Asia," 23 December 1949, reprinted in Thomas H. Etzold and John Lewis Gaddis, eds., *Containment: Documents on American Policy and Strategy, 1945–1950* (New York: Columbia University Press, 1978), 253. The "Conclusions" section of NSC 48/1 was later amended by the NSC, redesignated NSC 48/2, and approved by the president on 30 December 1949. NSC 48/2 is reprinted in Etzold and Gaddis, *Containment*, 269–76, and also appears in *FRUS 1949*, 7:1215–20.

122. Etzold and Gaddis, *Containment*, 256–57, 273–74.

123. Ibid., 273–75.

124. Ibid., 255.

125. Ibid., 272.

126. Minutes of NSC Meeting #50, 29 December 1949, Truman Papers, PSF, Box 207.

127. Etzold and Gaddis, *Containment*, 263.

128. Ibid., 264.

129. Ibid., 275.

130. Ibid., 255–56, 272–73.

131. Ibid., 259–60. Compare with PPS 51, 29 March 1949, *PPS Papers*, 3:36–42.

132. Etzold and Gaddis, *Containment*, 275. The only two substantial portions of NSC 48 that do not show measurable evidence of Kennan's influence are the paper's detailed discussion of the economic considerations underlying US policy in East Asia, and its recommendation that Washington actively support the formation of regional associations and collective security arrangements. This merely reflects issues on which Kennan had little interest or involvement. As shown earlier, he was never preoccupied with the economic factors involved with his strategic policy proposals; he simply left the details of implementation to more technically qualified policymakers. The issue of regional associations in East Asia appears to have gained currency only in mid-1949, when Jessup and the Consultants adopted it as one of their ideas. Kennan does not appear to have expressed a strong interest in the issue one way or the other.

6. KOREA

1. Kennan to Joseph G. Whelan, 3 July 1959, Kennan Papers, Box 31, Folder 2-B-1959.

2. George F. Kennan, *Memoirs 1925–1950* (New York: Pantheon Books, 1967), 496.

3. Ibid., 485; oral history interview, Charles Burton Marshall, June 1989, Truman Library, 70; Nitze interview with author, 7 June 1994.

4. John Lewis Gaddis, *George F. Kennan: An American Life* (New York: Penguin Press, 2011), 396; Dean Acheson, *Present at the Creation: My Years in the State Department* (New York: W. W. Norton, 1969), 402–5.

5. Kennan, *Memoirs 1925–1950*, 490.

6. Ibid., 486.

7. Ibid. Truman was then living in Blair House while the White House underwent renovations and redecorating.

8. Kennan, *Memoirs 1925–1950*, 486.

9. Memorandum of Blair House Conversation on "Korean Situation," 25 June 1950, Acheson Papers, Box 66, May–June 1950 folder.

10. Kennan to Acheson, "Possible Further Communist Initiatives in the Light of the Korean Situation," 26 June 1950, Kennan Papers, Box 24, Folder 1-D-10. This document

was marked "Not used—overtaken by events" on 27 June 1950 by Dorothy Hessman, Kennan's secretary. A copy is in PPS Records, Box 34, Chronological file.

11. Kennan diary entry, 26 June 1950, George F. Kennan, *The Kennan Diaries*, ed. Frank Costigliola (New York: W. W. Norton, 2014), 250. Kennan added that he thought it "of historical significance" that Acheson's subsequent support for US military intervention was not something "pressed upon him by the military leaders."

12. Memorandum of Second Blair House Conversation on "Korean Situation," 26 June 1950, Acheson Papers, Box 66, May–June 1950 folder; Acheson, *Present at the Creation*, 407–8.

13. Kennan draft memorandum, 27 June 1950, and attachments (Jessup to Kennan, 27 June 1950, and Hessman to files, 28 June 1950), PPS Records, Box 20, Korea 1950 folder. Kennan's original draft is in Kennan Papers, Box 24, Folder 1-D-11.

14. Kennan draft memorandum, 27 June 1950, PPS Records, Box 20, Korea 1950 folder.

15. Kennan diary entry, 27 June 1950, *Kennan Diaries*, 252–53.

16. "Meeting of the NSC in the Cabinet Room at the White House," 28 June 1950, Acheson Papers, Box 66, May-June 1950 folder.

17. Acheson memorandum of conversation with Johnson, 29 June 1950, ibid. A brief memorandum from Jessup to Acheson the following day, clarifying the minutes of the 25 June Blair House meeting, suggests that Acheson was interested in setting the record straight on how the military-related decisions at that meeting had been made. Jessup to Acheson, 30 June 1950, ibid.

18. Memoranda of Conversation of NSC Consultants' meetings, 29 June 1950, *FRUS 1950*, 1:324–30.

19. Davies draft memorandum, 29 June 1950, Davies Papers, Box 5, Folder "Korea."

20. Kennan diary entries, 29 and 30 June 1950, *Kennan Diaries*, 255–57.

21. Kennan to Jessup/Matthews, 30 June 1950, PPS Records, Box 20, Korea 1950 folder. Kennan's original 30 June draft is in Kennan Papers, Box 24, Folder 1-D-12. The NSC version, NSC 73, is in *FRUS 1950*, 1:331–38.

22. On 29 and 30 June, Truman and the "Blair House group" decided to expand US naval and air involvement in the war and ultimately to commit ground forces. Acheson, *Present at the Creation*, 411–13.

23. "Estimate: Possible Further Danger Points in Light of Korean Situation," Kennan Papers, Box 24, Folder 1-D-12. Although he thought the evidence suggested otherwise, Kennan acknowledged the possibility that Moscow was in fact preparing for war with the United States. If this were the case, he speculated, the Soviets would probably wait until the United States was at its weakest—for example, following a collapse in South Korea—and then attack, not where the West might expect it and was well prepared, such as in Iran or the Balkans, but across the central European front, "in order to derive a maximum advantage of surprise." Ibid.

24. Charles E. Bohlen, *Witness to History 1929–1969* (New York: W. W. Norton, 1973), 292; Kennan, *Memoirs 1925–1950*, 497; Frederick E. Nolting memorandum of conversation, 30 June 1950, *FRUS 1950*, 7:258. Kennan had coordinated his 30 June draft with Bohlen, who worked out of the PPS while in Washington during the summer of 1950. Kennan to Jessup/Matthews, 30 June 1950, PPS Records, Box 20, Korea 1950 folder.

25. Kennan comment in transcript of Princeton Seminar, 13–14 February 1954, Acheson Papers, Box 90, Folder 2, 1318.

26. Nitze to Acheson, 11 July 1950, State Department Decimal Files, 795.00/7-1050, Microfilm Publication LM81, Reel 2, RG 59, NA; Jessup to Acheson, 11 July 1950, ibid.

27. Secretary's Daily Meeting, 11 July 1950, Box 1, RG 59, NA.

28. Ibid.

29. Memorandum for the President on NSC Meeting #66, 25 August 1950, Truman Papers, PSF, Box 220. See also Minutes of NSC Meeting #63, 3 August 1950, Truman Papers, PSF, Box 208; Minutes of NSC Meeting #64, 10 August 1950, ibid.; and Secretary's Daily Meeting, 22 August 1950, RG 59, NA. Much of the paper trail on Kennan's ill-fated draft is in PPS Records, Box 70, "NSC 73—US Actions in Light of Korean Situation June–November 1950" folder.

30. Kennan to Acheson, 8 August 1950, PPS Records, Box 34, Chronological file.

31. Ibid.

32. Kennan to Acheson, 14 August 1950, *FRUS* 1950, 7:574–76.

33. Ibid.

34. Webb memorandum of conversation with Truman, 17 August 1950, PPS Records, Box 20, Korea 1950 folder; Kennan to Webb, 21 August 1950, State Department Decimal Files, 795.00/8-2150, Microfilm Publication LM81, Reel 5, RG 59, NA; Matthews to James Burns, 15 August 1950, State Department Decimal Files 795.00/8-1550, ibid. Another message, Webb to Truman, 21 August 1950, was withdrawn from the latter file for security reasons; presumably it was Webb's passage to Truman of Kennan's message that there was no evidence the Soviets were supplying the North Koreans through Rashin.

35. Kennan, *Memoirs 1925–1950*, 499. See also Kennan to Acheson, 26 May 1951, Acheson Papers, Box 77, "May 1951" folder.

36. Kennan diary entry, 12 July 1950, *Kennan Diaries*, 261; also cited in Kennan, *Memoirs 1925–1950*, 499.

37. Kennan to Acheson, 21 August 1950, *FRUS* 1950, 7:625–26; Kennan to Acheson, 23 August 1950, Acheson Papers, Box 66, "August 1950" folder.

38. Kennan to Acheson, 21 August 1950, *FRUS* 1950, 7:627.

39. Kennan diary entry, 14 August 1950, *Kennan Diaries*, 269–70; quoted in Kennan, *Memoirs 1925–1950*, 500.

40. Ibid.

41. Acheson, *Present at the Creation*, 446; Kennan to Acheson, 21 August 1950, *FRUS* 1950, 7:623fn.

42. *FRUS* 1950, 7:625.

43. Ibid.; Kennan diary entry, 27 June 1950, *Kennan Diaries*, 252–53.

44. Gaddis, *George F. Kennan*, 396–97.

45. Kennan diary entry, 23 January 1952, *Kennan Diaries*, 308.

46. Multiple historians and international relations theorists have highlighted this dilemma—which was not unique to Kennan—between maintaining US credibility and upholding a narrowly interests-based approach to foreign policy. See Russell D. Buhite, "Major Interests: American Policy toward China, Taiwan, and Korea, 1945–1950," *Pacific Historical Review* 47, no. 3 (August 1978): 425–51; Walter L. Hixson, "Containment on the Perimeter: George F. Kennan and Vietnam," *Diplomatic History* 12, no. 2 (Spring 1988): 149–63; Judith Munro-Leighton, "A Postrevisionist Scrutiny of America's Role in the Cold War in Asia, 1945–1950," *Journal of American-East Asian Relations* 1, no. 1 (Spring 1992): 73–98. Buhite attributes the different US responses to regional crises to the distinction between "vital," "major," and "peripheral" interests—with "major" interests being "those which, in the opinion of American policy makers at a given time, may affect the national well-being to a considerable degree, and may [thus] require the expenditure of 'substantial' resources" that otherwise might not be considered. In the case of Korea, Kennan may have considered US credibility a valid "major" interest by this definition; but he does not appear to have acknowledged or articulated such a category of US interests. Buhite, "Major Interests," 427.

47. William Whitney Stueck Jr., *The Road to Confrontation: American Policy toward China and Korea, 1947–1950* (Chapel Hill: University of North Carolina Press, 1981),

29–30, 109–10; John Lewis Gaddis, *Strategies of Containment: A Critical Appraisal of American National Security Policy during the Cold War*, rev. and expanded ed. (New York: Oxford University Press, 1987), 107.

48. Kennan, *Memoirs 1925–1950*, 487; Kennan, *Kennan Diaries*, 252–53. See also Glenn D. Paige, *The Korean Decision: June 24–30, 1950* (New York: Free Press, 1968), 191–92.

49. Kennan diary entry, 28 June 1950, *Kennan Diaries*, 253–55.

50. Ibid.

51. Ibid.

52. Minutes of NSC Consultants meeting, 29 June 1950, *FRUS* 1950, 1:326, 328; Kennan, *Memoirs 1925–1950*, 488–89.

53. Kennan, *Memoirs 1925–1950*, 490–91; Acheson, *Present at the Creation*, 419, 451.

54. Bohlen, *Witness to History 1929–1969*, 292–93.

55. Feis to Acheson, 14 July 1950, State Department Decimal Files, 795.00/7-1550, Microfilm Publication LM81, Reel 2, RG 59, NA; Secretary's Daily Meeting, 14 July 1950, RG 59, NA.

56. Dulles to Nitze, 14 July 1950, PPS Records, Box 20, Korea 1950 folder.

57. Allison to Rusk, 15 July 1950, *FRUS* 1950, 7:393–95.

58. Kennan diary entry, 21 July 1950, *Kennan Diaries*, 265; quoted in Kennan, *Memoirs 1925–1950*, 488.

59. Lay to NSC members, 17 July 1950, PPS Records, Box 20, Korea 1950 folder; Rusk to various State offices, 22 July 1950, State Department Decimal Files, 795.00/7-2250, Microfilm Publication LM81, Reel 4, RG 59, NA.

60. PPS draft memorandum, 22 July 1950, *FRUS* 1950, 7:449–54. This document was drafted by PPS officer George Butler, but it clearly was a corporate product to which Kennan and Bohlen were key contributors. Acheson himself associated the resistance to crossing the 38th Parallel with "Paul Nitze's Policy Planning Staff, influenced by George Kennan's views." Acheson, *Present at the Creation*, 451.

61. Allison to Nitze, 24 July 1950, *FRUS* 1950, 7:458–59.

62. Ibid., 460–61.

63. Ibid. This memo helps explain Davies's description of Allison as "the fire-eater" on the subject of the 38th Parallel. In his memoirs, Allison offers a much more benign account of his role in the debate. He allows only that "at one point I was asked my opinion" (whereas the record shows that Rusk specifically assigned him responsibility for supervising State's work on the issue) and that he merely "took the position that such a crossing should not arbitrarily be precluded." Allison blamed subsequent events on the fact that MacArthur "took matters into his own hands." Davies interview with author, 23 November 1993; John M. Allison, *Ambassador from the Prairie* (Boston: Houghton Mifflin Company, 1973), 153.

64. Paul H. Nitze, *From Hiroshima to Glasnost: At the Center of Decision: A Memoir* (New York: Grove Weidenfeld, 1989), 106–7.

65. PPS draft memorandum, 25 July 1950, *FRUS* 1950, 7:469–73.

66. Allison to Rusk, 27 July 1950, *FRUS* 1950, 7:480–81; Memo to files on Undersecretary's meeting, 28 July 1950, ibid., 486.

67. Dulles to Nitze, 1 August 1950, ibid., 514.

68. Stueck, *Road to Confrontation*, 205; Kennan, *Memoirs 1925–1950*, 496; Kennan, *Kennan Diaries*, 269. Kennan's position on China's membership in the UN will be addressed in the next chapter.

69. Kennan to Acheson, 8 August 1950, PPS Records, Box 34, Chronological file; Kennan to Acheson, 14 August 1950, *FRUS* 1950, 7:574.

70. Kennan to Acheson, 21 August 1950, *FRUS* 1950, 7:624.

71. "Background Press Conference," 22 August 1950, Kennan Papers, Box 18, Folder 1-C-9. In early November 1950, after the UN had authorized crossing the 38th Parallel and MacArthur had done so, Kennan gave the *New York Times* correspondent who attended this press conference permission to cite his views on the subject. Kennan subsequently was extremely upset at the way the *Times* characterized his views and considered writing a response but eventually let the matter drop. See "Correspondence, November 1950, concerning press report of GFK's alleged views on policy in Korea," Kennan Papers, Box 24, Folder 1-D-15; Philip Watts/William McWilliams to Webb, 30 November 1950, PPS Records, Box 34, Chronological file.

72. Bishop to Jessup, 24 August 1950, *FRUS* 1950, 7:641.

73. NSC 81, "US Courses of Action in Korea," 1 September 1950, *FRUS* 1950, 7:685–93.

74. Ibid.; Acheson memorandum on NSC meeting, 7 September 1950, ibid., 705; JCS to Johnson, 7 September 1950, ibid., 707; Memorandum for the President on NSC Meeting #67, 7 September 1950, Truman Papers, PSF, Box 220; NSC 81/1, 9 September 1950, *FRUS* 1950, 7:712–21. For some of the prehistory of NSC 81, focusing on the various papers that were subsumed into it, see Butler to Allison, 15 August 1950, ibid., 582; Walter P. McConaughy to Jessup, 24 August 1950, ibid., 641.

75. James L. Stokesbury, *A Short History of the Korean War* (New York: William Morrow, 1988), 65–78, 81, 87; Clay Blair, *The Forgotten War: America in Korea 1950–1953* (New York: Doubleday, 1987), 270–94, 327, 333–36; Acheson, *Present at the Creation*, 452–55.

76. Acheson, *Present at the Creation*, 454.

77. Stokesbury, *A Short History*, 91–94, 98–100; Blair, *The Forgotten War*, 363–64, 432–68; Acheson, *Present at the Creation*, 462–63, 469–71.

78. During the autumn of 1950, Davies—still at the PPS after Kennan's departure—drafted a series of memos that assessed the possibility of Chinese intervention. Like Kennan and others in Washington, he consistently saw Chinese actions as subordinate to Soviet decisions. For example, on 22 September he speculated that Moscow might be pressing the Chinese to aid the North Koreans. After the Chinese intervention became apparent, he wrote on 7 November that "it is to be assumed that the Kremlin is actively egging China on" but that it could not be assumed that Moscow "was able easily to persuade the Chinese." Ten days later, Davies still referred to the attack as "the Kremlin's Korean adventure" and assessed that the Chinese intervened as agents of Moscow, but he acknowledged the possibility of Sino-Soviet fault lines: "The North Koreans having collapsed, [Moscow] has succeeded in transferring primary responsibility to the Chinese. Whether this was achieved by orders which were obediently obeyed, by coercion, by concessions or whether the Kremlin may even have had to restrain Peiping, we do not know." Davies memos, 22 September 1950, *FRUS* 1950, 7:753–55; 7 November 1950, ibid., 1078–85; and 17 November 1950, ibid., 1178–82 (also in Davies Papers, Box 5, Folder "Korea").

79. George F. Kennan, *Memoirs 1950–1963* (New York: Pantheon Books, 1972), 25.

80. Kennan to Anne O'Hare McCormick, 15 November 1950, Kennan Papers, Box 29, 1950 folder. This letter, which Kennan drafted in response to a 13 November column by McCormick in the *New York Times*, noted that "we can only conjecture" what prompted the Chinese to act: "It was probably a mixture of several factors, among which Communist discipline, a real concern about US intentions, and possibly some material Russian bribes in the form of concessions in Manchuria, may all have played a part." In any event, a notation on the letter reads "The original was never sent."

81. Kennan, *Memoirs 1950–1963*, 16; Bohlen, *Witness to History 1929–1969*, 294–95; Kennan, *Kennan Diaries*, 272; Kennan/Pogue interview, George C. Marshall Research Library, side 2, 4.

82. Quoted in Wilson Miscamble, *George F. Kennan and the Making of American Foreign Policy, 1947–1950* (Princeton, NJ: Princeton University Press, 1992), 328.

83. Kennan diary entry, 3 December 1950, as quoted in Kennan, *Memoirs 1950–1963*, 27.

84. Ibid.; Sheppard memorandum of conversation, 3 December 1950, *FRUS* 1950, 7:1336–39.

85. Kennan, *Memoirs 1950–1963*, 27–28.

86. Kennan memorandum, 3 December 1950, PPS Records, Box 20, Korea 1950 folder.

87. Reprinted in Kennan, *Memoirs 1950–1963*, 31, and in Acheson, *Present at the Creation*, 476.

88. Acheson, *Present at the Creation*, 476; Lucius D. Battle memorandum of conversation, 4 December 1950, *FRUS* 1950, 7:1345–47; Kennan, *Memoirs 1950–1963*, 31–32. Acheson read Kennan's 4 December 1950 personal note to an audience at an academic conference in 1954, describing its contents as having been "profoundly true." See transcript of Princeton Seminar, 13–14 February 1954, Acheson Papers, Box 90, Folder 1, 1258–59.

89. Acheson memorandum of telephone conversation with Marshall, 4 December 1950, Acheson Papers, Box 66, December 1950 folder; Kennan, *Kennan Diaries*, 272–75.

90. Hessman to Battle, 6 December 1950 (forwarding Kennan's notes on 4 December meeting with Marshall), Acheson Papers, Box 66, December 1950 folder; Kennan, *Memoirs 1950–1963*, 32–33; Acheson, *Present at the Creation*, 477; Forrest C. Pogue, *George C. Marshall: Statesman, 1945–1959* (New York: Viking Press, 1987), 467–68.

91. Kennan, *Memoirs 1950–1963*, 33, 37–38; Kennan/Pogue interview, George C. Marshall Research Library, side 2, pp. 3, 5 (pp. 3–9 contain Kennan's full account of his role in December 1950).

92. Dean Rusk, telephone interview by author, 5 July 1994, Athens, GA.

93. Acheson, *Present at the Creation*, 482.

94. Kennan to Bohlen, 5 December 1950, Kennan Papers, Box 29, 1950 folder; Kennan, *Memoirs 1950–1963*, 34.

95. Kennan to Nitze, 6 January 1950, PPS Records, Box 48, PPS members chronological file, Kennan folder.

96. Ibid.

97. Reinhardt to Acheson, 17 March 1951, *FRUS* 1951, 6:241–43.

98. Corrigan/Cory memorandum of conversation, 3 May 1951, ibid., 401–7.

99. Davies memo, 24 March 1951, ibid., 1607–8.

100. Davies to Nitze, 8 May 1951, *FRUS* 1951, 6: 421–22.

101. "Memorandum by George F. Kennan concerning Events from May 18 to May 25, 1951," nd, ibid., 460–61.

102. Kennan to Matthews (on second meeting with Malik), nd, ibid., 507–11. The events leading up to Kennan's first meeting with Malik are contained in "Memorandum by George F. Kennan concerning Events from May 18 to May 25, 1951," nd, ibid., 460–61, and Kennan to Tsarapkin, 26 May 1951, ibid., 462. The first meeting itself is summarized in Kennan to Matthews, 31 May 1951, ibid., 483–86, and in Kennan, *Kennan Diaries*, 287–90. The second meeting is summarized in Kennan, *Kennan Diaries*, 290–94.

103. Kennan to Acheson, 20 June 1951, *FRUS* 1951, 6:536–38; copied in Kennan, *Kennan Diaries*, 294–99.

104. Malik speech, 23 June 1950, *FRUS* 1951, 7:546–47; Acheson, *Present at the Creation*, 533–34; Stokesbury, *A Short History*, 138–39; Blair, *The Forgotten War*, 924–25, 932–33.

105. Kennan, *Memoirs 1950–1963*, 37.

106. Ibid., 38.

107. "Unfinished paper," September 1951, Kennan Papers, Box 24, Folder 1-D-18; Kennan, *Memoirs 1950–1963*, 39–53.

108. Ten years later, Kennan wrote that he believed Moscow had probably not informed Beijing in any detail about Soviet efforts to build up the North Korean army, and that the Chinese probably had "little, if any, prior warning" when the invasion began. Kennan to Allen Whiting, 20 October 1960, Kennan Papers, Box 31, Folder 2-B-1960.

7. AFTERMATH OF KOREA

1. Kennan to Acheson, 21 August 1950, *FRUS* 1950, 7:624.

2. "Transcript of Presentation Held in Room 1276, 'Q' Building," 14 October 1949, Kennan Papers, Box 17, Folder 29.

3. Maxwell M. Hamilton/Allison to Dulles, 10 July 1950, *FRUS* 1950, 6:1238.

4. Kennan to Dulles, 20 July 1950, PPS Records, Box 29A, Japan 1950 folder.

5. Kennan to Rusk, 18 July 1950, PPS Records, Box 29A, Japan 1950 folder; George F. Kennan interview, 3 March 1967, John Foster Dulles Oral History Project, Seeley G. Mudd Manuscript Library, Princeton, NJ; Nitze to McWilliams, 26 July 1950, PPS Records, Box 29A, Japan 1950 folder; PPS memorandum, "Assumption by Japan of a Greater Measure of Responsibility for Its Own Security, Both Internal and External," 26 July 1950, *FRUS* 1950, 6:1255–57. For Dulles's proposal, see Dulles to Nitze, 20 July 1950, ibid., 1246–48. On 20 July Kennan recorded in his diary that he had emphasized to Acheson the need to put Japan (and Germany) "on a fully independent footing, able to carry on successfully without us." George F. Kennan, *The Kennan Diaries*, ed. Frank Costigliola (New York: W. W. Norton, 2014), 264.

6. Dulles to Willard L. Thorp et al., 9 August 1950, *FRUS* 1950, 6:1267–70.

7. Kennan interview, 3 March 1967, Dulles Oral History Project, Princeton.

8. Kennan to Dulles, 21 August 1950, *FRUS* 1950, 6:1276–78.

9. George F. Kennan, *Memoirs 1925–1950* (New York: Pantheon Books, 1967), 496; Kennan diary entry, 31 July 1950, *Kennan Diaries*, 269; Kennan interview, 3 March 1967, Dulles Oral History Project, Princeton.

10. Kennan to Acheson, 21 August 1950, PPS Records, Box 26, Asia 1948–1951 folder. This memorandum is also in *FRUS* 1950, 7:623–28.

11. Kennan to Acheson, 21 August 1950, PPS Records, Box 26, Asia 1948–1951 folder.

12. Ibid.; Kennan to Acheson, 23 August 1950, Acheson Papers, Box 66, August 1950 folder; Dean Acheson, *Present at the Creation: My Years in the State Department* (New York: W. W. Norton, 1969), 446.

13. For the final exchange of interagency correspondence that led to the peace treaty decision, see *FRUS* 1950, 6:1278–96.

14. Davies had been among the first to suggest a two-treaty solution, in August 1947. Davies draft memorandum, nd (circa 20 August 1947), attached to Penfield to Davies, 25 August 1947, PPS Records, Box 29A, Japan 1947 folder.

15. Kennan, *Memoirs 1925–1950*, 395–96, 498; Acheson, *Present at the Creation*, 429–30.

16. George F. Kennan, *Memoirs 1950–1963* (New York: Pantheon Books, 1972), 41–42, 45–46.

17. See Kennan's speech to Pittsburgh Foreign Policy Association, 3 May 1956, reprinted in *US News & World Report*, 29 June 1956, 74; Kennan to C. Brayton Wilbur, 30 July 1956, Kennan Papers, Box 31, Folder 2-B-1956; Kennan to Joseph G. Whelan, 3 July 1959, Kennan Papers, Box 31, Folder 2-B-1959; George F. Kennan, "Japanese Security and American Policy," *Foreign Affairs* 43, no. 1 (October 1964): 14.

18. Kennan to Joseph G. Whelan, 3 July 1959, Kennan Papers, Box 31, Folder 2-B-1959.

19. Acheson, *Present at the Creation*, 429; Sebald memorandum of conversation with MacArthur, 21 September 1949, *FRUS* 1949, 7:862; Fearey memorandum of conversation, 2 November 1949, ibid., 891.

20. Kennan to Marshall, 14 March 1948, PPS Records, Box 29A, Japan 1948 folder; PPS 28, *FRUS* 1948, 6:692; Kennan to Acheson, 6 January 1950, *FRUS* 1950, 1:130; Nitze to Dulles, 27 July 1950, PPS Records, Box 34, Chronological files; Kennan to Acheson, 21 August 1950, PPS Records, Box 26, Asia 1948–1951 folder. Kennan's ambiguity on the neutralization idea during this period is also reflected in his National War College lecture "The Present Situation in Japan," 18 May 1948, Kennan Papers, Box 17, Folder 8; Joint Civilian Orientation Conference lecture at the Pentagon, 13 September 1949, Kennan Papers, Box 17, Folder 28; "Transcript of Presentation Held in Room 1276, 'Q' Building," 14 October 1949, Kennan Papers, Box 17, Folder 29.

21. Kennan's desire that Washington pursue a Soviet guarantee of Japanese neutrality was also inconsistent with a suggestion he made in mid-1949 that after World War II the United States should have accepted "a re-entry of Japanese influence and activity into Korea and Manchuria" as a counterweight to Soviet influence there. In later years he occasionally returned to the idea of a neutralized Japan, claiming in 1980 that he had been "right in my belief that the best solution in northeastern Asia would have been a neutralized and demilitarized Japan," and in 1984 that "we should have stuck to [MacArthur's] principle" in this regard. But he appeared by then to have forgotten the inconsistencies and impracticability of both MacArthur's and his own thinking during 1948–50. Kennan to Jessup/Rusk, 8 September 1949, PPS Records, Box 13, China 1949 folder; Kennan, "Japanese Security and American Policy," 27; Kennan, "Unused Draft for Statement on Vietnam," 1967, Kennan Papers, Box 27, Folder 1-E-25; Kennan diary entry, 22 May 1980, *Kennan Diaries*, 526; George F. Kennan, *American Diplomacy*, expanded ed. (Chicago: University of Chicago Press, 1984), 170.

22. PPS 51, "United States Policy toward Southeast Asia," 29 March 1949, *PPS Papers*, 3:39.

23. Robert M. Blum, *Drawing the Line: The Origin of the American Containment Policy in East Asia* (New York: W. W. Norton, 1982), 113, 124–25, 177, 199, 214; Andrew J. Rotter, *The Path to Vietnam: Origins of the American Commitment to Southeast Asia* (Ithaca, NY: Cornell University Press, 1987), 116, 122, 135–36, 197–200; Thomas H. Etzold and John Lewis Gaddis, eds., *Containment: Documents on American Policy and Strategy, 1945–1950* (New York: Columbia University Press, 1978), 276.

24. Blum, *Drawing the Line*, 214; Michael Schaller, *The American Occupation of Japan: The Origins of the Cold War in Asia* (New York: Oxford University Press, 1985), 159.

25. PPS memorandum, "United States Policy toward Indochina in the Light of Recent Developments," 16 August 1950, *FRUS* 1950, 6:857. A draft of this paper contained in the PPS records indicates that Davies was its author. Davies draft, 16 August 1950, PPS Records, Box 37, "Record copies" folder.

26. PPS memorandum, 16 August 1950, *FRUS* 1950, 6:858.

27. Kennan to Acheson, 21 August 1950, *FRUS* 1950, 7:623–28.

28. Ibid., 624–25.

29. John Paton Davies Jr., *China Hand: An Autobiography* (Philadelphia: University of Pennsylvania Press, 2012), 319.

30. Kennan diary entry, 17 July 1950, *Kennan Diaries*, 263; Kennan to Acheson, 17 July 1950, *FRUS* 1950, 6:380–81.

31. Bohlen to Rusk, 22 July 1950, PPS Records, Box 34, Chronological file; Secretary's Daily Meeting, 25 July 1950.

32. Kennan diary entry, 22–23 April 1952, *Kennan Diaries*, 312.

33. Kennan, *Memoirs 1925–1950*, 492–94; Kennan diary entry, 17 July 1950, *Kennan Diaries*, 262–63.

34. Kennan diary entry, 28 July 1950, *Kennan Diaries*, 267–68.

35. Ibid.

36. Kennan, *Memoirs 1925–1950*, 492–95; Kennan interview, 3 March 1967, Dulles Oral History Project, Princeton; Kennan diary entry, 17 July 1950, *Kennan Diaries*, 263. This was the occasion on which Kennan learned that Dulles had referred to him as "a very dangerous man" because of Kennan's support for Chinese Communist membership in the UN and opposition to US military action north of the 38th Parallel in Korea. Kennan, *Memoirs 1925–1950*, 496; Kennan diary entry, 31 July 1950, *Kennan Diaries*, 269.

37. Gordon Chang notes that the Eisenhower administration later conducted some covert operations—the details of which remain classified—in Tibet and northern China to "impair relations between the USSR and Communist China." Gordon Chang, *Friends and Enemies: The United States, China, and the Soviet Union, 1948–1972* (Stanford, CA: Stanford University Press, 1990), 100–101.

38. Davies interview with author, 23 November 1993; Kennan to Rusk, 7 November 1949, PPS Records, Box 33, Chronological files.

39. Davies interview with author, 23 November 1993. The details of Davies's plan, inasmuch as they are publicly available, are included in John W. Finney, "The Long Trial of John Paton Davies," *New York Times Magazine*, 31 August 1969, 7–9, 23–28, 35; "The Strange Case of John P. Davies," *US News and World Report*, 11 December 1953, 26–32, 106–17; and E. J. Kahn Jr., *The China Hands: America's Foreign Service Officers and What Befell Them* (New York: Viking Press, 1975), 244–45.

40. Conrad E. Snow to Davies, 27 June 1951, Kennan Papers, Box 10, Folder 13. This folder also contains Davies's written response to the charges, supporting documents, and "Personal History." A copy of the Snow letter is also in PPS Records, Box 45, PPS members chronological file, Davies 1951–1953 folder, which also contains numerous documents relevant to Davies's loyalty investigation. For a detailed account of the case against Davies, see especially Finney, "The Long Trial of John Paton Davies," and "The Strange Case of John P. Davies," *US News and World Report*. Davies's memoir, *China Hand*, which was incomplete at his death, contains only the beginning of the story and a brief account of his dismissal from the State Department; its epilogue by historian Bruce Cumings fills in some of the details and Davies's life in retirement. Davies, *China Hand*, 3–7, 322–38.

41. Davies interview with author, 23 November 1993.

42. Kennan to Conrad E. Snow, 21 June 1951, Kennan Papers, Box 10, Folder 13. Kennan had written similarly glowing personnel evaluations for Davies as his supervisor on the PPS, describing him as "extremely industrious, enthusiastic about his work, and irreproachably loyal to his superiors and his subordinates" and "one of the most brilliant and competent officers of the [Foreign] Service in political matters." Kennan, "Annual Efficiency Report" on Davies, 12 November 1948, Davies Papers, Box 7, Folder "Personnel Records." Paul Nitze, when he succeeded Kennan as director of the PPS, followed suit in an evaluation written after Davies came under fire: "My respect for his character is unqualified. My confidence in his patriotism is unconditional. . . . His intellectual contributions have been indispensable in shaping the national policy throughout his period of work with us. Invariably they have served to strengthen and improve policies in the direction of fulfillment of the national interest. His discretion has been exceptional. I know of no one more trustworthy than he in guarding secrets of national policy." Nitze to Elbridge Durbrow, 11 August 1951, ibid.

43. Davies to Kennan, 6 July 1951, Kennan Papers, Box 10, Folder 13; Kennan to Arthur Schlesinger Jr., 20 February 1952, Davies Papers, Box 4, Folder "Kennan, George F."

44. Kennan to Davies, 26 January 1952, Davies Papers, Box 4, Folder "Kennan, George F."

45. Kennan to Arthur Schlesinger Jr., 20 February 1952, ibid.; Kennan to Nitze, 26 July 1952, with attached draft of Kennan to Acheson, 25 July 1952, Kennan Papers, Box 29, Folder 5.

46. Kennan to William Schaufele Jr., 4 June 1996, Kennan Papers, Box 76, Folder 8.

47. Kennan to Davies, 28 January 1953, Kennan Papers, Box 29, Folder 7.

48. Kennan to Arthur Schlesinger Jr., 20 February 1952; Kennan to Davies, 10 March 1953; Kennan to Davies, 29 November 1953; all in Davies Papers, Box 4, Folder "Kennan, George F."

49. Apparent summary of Kennan-Davies phone conversation, 23 November 1953; undated copy of Kennan telegram to Davies; Kennan to Davies, 14 December 1953; all in Davies Papers, Box 4, Folder "Kennan, George F." This folder also contains several other items related to Kennan's public defense of Davies. His letter appeared in the *New York Times* on 17 December 1953. During this period, Kennan declined requests from other State Department China Hands to support them publicly on the grounds that his relationship with Davies was unique because the charges against him—particularly regarding the CIA plan—involved his work directly for Kennan in the PPS. Kennan to O. Edmund Clubb, 26 October 1953, Kennan Papers, Box 8, Folder 10; Kennan to John Melby, nd, ibid., Box 31, Folder 2.

50. Kennan to Davies, 11 January 1954, Davies Papers, Box 4, Folder "Kennan, George F."

51. Davies, *China Hand*, 6.

52. See the Bruce Cumings epilogue in Davies, *China Hand*, 333–35; Finney, "The Long Trial of John Paton Davies"; and David Halberstam, *The Best and the Brightest*, 2nd ed. (New York: Random House, 1972), 379–92. In January 1969, Davies was symbolically rehabilitated when the State Department issued him a security clearance to serve as a consultant for the Arms Control and Disarmament Agency. Kennan on that occasion wrote another letter to the *New York Times* saying that the clearing of Davies's name "corrects in at least the formal sense what was certainly one of the most inexcusable of the injustices committed upon Government servants and others during the so-called 'McCarthy' period. . . . This belated correction will not restore to the public life of the country the decade and a half of the services of a talented, dedicated and wholly patriotic Foreign Service officer that were forfeited as a consequence of it. But if it will help to engender in American public opinion a more incisive revulsion at the spectacle of political figures playing fast and loose with the reputations of others for the sake of political gain, and if the memory of it will inspire the Department of State to a somewhat greater sense of loyalty toward its own personnel, then perhaps the anguish caused not just to an innocent man but to family and friends as well by this breaking of an honorable career will have served some useful purpose. Mr. Davies, in any case, deserves highest praise for the dignity and restraint with which he has borne a long and wholly undeserved injustice." *New York Times*, 15 January 1969, 1; ibid., 22 January 1969, 46.

53. Kennan to William Schaufele Jr., 4 June 1996, Kennan Papers, Box 76, Folder 8; Richard D. Challener interview with Kennan, 1967, John Foster Dulles Oral History project, in *Interviews with George F. Kennan*, ed. T. Christopher Jespersen (Jackson: University Press of Mississippi, 2002), 124. Kennan's own account of the Davies case and his role in it is in *Memoirs 1950–1963*, 200–214.

8. VIETNAM

1. Kennan lecture, "Background of Present World Situation," Haverford College, Haverford, PA, 19 April 1955, Kennan Papers, Box 19, Folder 1-C-50.

2. Kennan to Jose Smole, 15 February 1962, Kennan Papers, Box 31, Folder 2-B-1962.

3. Ibid.

4. "A Fresh Look at Our China Policy," *New York Times Magazine*, 22 November 1964, 147; Kennan to Muste, 4 January 1965, in "An Exchange: A Policy for the Far East," *Liberation*, April 1965, 10.

5. Kennan to Muste, 19 February 1965, "An Exchange," 10.

6. Ibid., 11; Kennan to Roger Hagen, 11 December 1964, Kennan Papers, Box 31, Folder 2-B-1964.

7. This theme, and the evolution of Kennan's thinking about the Vietnam War, is addressed in Walter L. Hixson, "Containment on the Perimeter: George F. Kennan and Vietnam," *Diplomatic History* 12, no. 2 (Spring 1988): 149–63.

8. Kennan diary entry, 7 February 1965, George F. Kennan, *The Kennan Diaries*, ed. Frank Costigliola (New York: W. W. Norton, 2014), 431; Kennan lecture, "Some Lessons of American Diplomatic History," Ripon College, Ripon, WI, 11 February 1965, Kennan Papers, Box 21, Folder 1-C-139.

9. Kennan to William Sloane Coffin Jr., 27 August 1965, Kennan Papers, Box 31, Folder 2-B-1965.

10. George F. Kennan, "Dilemma in Vietnam," *New York Times*, 12 December 1965, E-1.

11. Ibid., E-2.

12. Ibid.

13. *New York Times*, 11 February 1966, 2. Oddly, Kennan's diary makes no mention of his Senate appearance. Kennan, *Kennan Diaries*, 439.

14. "Kennan on Vietnam," *New Republic*, 26 February 1966, 20–21. This article is a transcript of Kennan's testimony before the Senate Foreign Relations Committee.

15. Gavin made his proposal in a letter published in the February 1966 issue of *Harper's Magazine*.

16. "Kennan on Vietnam," 21, 25, 29.

17. Ibid., 25.

18. Ibid., 20.

19. Ibid., 22, 30.

20. *New York Times*, 28 February 1966, 9.

21. *New York Times*, 12 February 1966, 8.

22. Kennan to Llewellyn Thompson, 5 April 1966, Kennan Papers, Box 31, Folder 2-B-1966.

23. "Kennan on Vietnam," 26.

24. Ibid.

25. Kennan lecture, "Containment: Russia and China," Denison University, Granville, OH, 9 February 1966, Kennan Papers, Box 263, Folder 6.

26. Ibid.

27. Kennan to Emmet John Hughes, 31 May 1966, Kennan Papers, Box 31, Folder 2-B-1966.

28. "Kennan Urges Policy of War Moderation," *New York Times*, 25 September 1966, E-11.

29. Kennan "dinner talk" at Woodrow Wilson School, 5 November 1966, Kennan Papers, Box 22, Folder 1-C-152. Kennan had given lip service to the idea of neutralizing Vietnam in early May 1966, arguing that Soviet or Chinese Communist control there would be acceptable as long as there was no "utilization of South Vietnam territory by the dominant Communist power for military purposes." Nobody, he thought, "could make of that territory more than what its population, resources, and customs already make it . . . and that means that no one . . . could make them a serious threat to the United States." Kennan to Klaus Knorr, 3 May 1966, Kennan Papers, Box 31, Folder 2-B-1966.

30. "Why Stay in Vietnam?," *New Republic*, 11 February 1967, 9; "US Policy in Asia—as Two Ex-Envoys See It," *US News & World Report*, 13 February 1967, 19–20; Kennan to John Crocker, 9 November 1967, Kennan Papers, Box 31, Folder 2-B-1967.

31. Kennan to Arthur Schlesinger Jr., 17 October 1967, Kennan Papers, Box 31, Folder 2-B-1967.

32. Ibid. Kennan was unaware of the level to which the Chinese were in fact involved in Vietnam. Beijing provided large amounts of military aid and over 300,000 support troops to Vietnam during the mid-1960s. See Qiang Zhai, *China and the Vietnam Wars, 1950–1975* (Chapel Hill: University of North Carolina Press, 2000).

33. Kennan to Schlesinger, 17 October 1967, Kennan Papers, Box 31, Folder 2-B-1967.

34. Ibid.

35. Ibid.

36. Ibid.

37. "Introducing Eugene McCarthy," *New York Review of Books* 10, no. 7 (11 April 1968): 14–15. Also available at http://www.nybooks.com/articles/1968/04/11/introducing-eugene-mccarthy/.

38. *US News & World Report*, 17 June 1968, 68. This article is an edited transcript of a speech by Kennan entitled "America after Vietnam," which was delivered in Williamsburg, VA, on 1 June 1968. The full text of the speech and various published versions of it are in Kennan Papers, Box 14, Folder 1-B-160.

39. "Kennan Urges a Speedy Withdrawal," *New York Times*, 10 November 1969, 3.

40. Hixson, "Containment on the Perimeter," 150.

41. In this respect, Hixson correctly recognized the "elusive and contradictory nature of Kennan's positions on Vietnam." Ibid., 162.

42. Kennan lecture, "Beyond Vietnam," Denison University, Granville, OH, 10 February 1970, Kennan Papers, Box 304, Folder 20.

43. Kennan diary entry, 10 May 1972, *Kennan Diaries*, 473–74.

44. "A Special Supplement: The Meaning of Vietnam," *New York Review of Books* 22, no. 10 (12 June 1975): 28. Also available at http://www.nybooks.com/articles/1975/06/12/a-special-supplement-the-meaning-of-vietnam/; George F. Kennan, *The Cloud of Danger: Current Realities of American Foreign Policy* (Boston: Little, Brown, 1977), 95. Earlier in 1975, Kennan had expressed similar sentiments to historian John Lukacs: "So far as Indochina is concerned, I think our people have taken leave of their senses. There is now nothing for us to do but to retire, keep our mouth shut, and try to live it down." John Lukacs, ed., *Through the History of the Cold War: The Correspondence of George F. Kennan and John Lukacs* (Philadelphia: University of Pennsylvania Press, 2010), 60.

CONCLUSION

1. George F. Kennan, *Russia and the West under Lenin and Stalin* (New York: Mentor Books, 1960), 260–61.

2. Kennan to Walter Lippman, 6 April 1948, Kennan Papers, Box 17, Folder 7. This letter is marked "Not Sent."

3. Kennan speech, "Russian and American Interests in East Asia," American Historical Association, Seattle, WA, 8 September 1960, Kennan Papers, Box 302, Folder 16; George F. Kennan, "The Sources of Soviet Conduct," *Foreign Affairs* 25, no. 4 (July 1947): 566–82.

4. Kennan speech, "The United States and the Problem of China," State Bar of California, 1 October 1964, Kennan Papers, Box 269, Folder 29.

5. Ibid.; George F. Kennan, *Memoirs 1925–1950* (New York: Pantheon Books, 1967), 367.

6. Kennan lecture, "Containment: Russia and China," Denison University, Granville, OH, 9 February 1966, Kennan Papers, Box 263, Folder 6. Kennan allowed one possible exception to his judgment that China posed no threat sufficient to make it the target of containment: Chinese development of a long-range nuclear strike capability. But he rejected the idea that this would justify a preventive strike on China, and instead emphasized the priority of nuclear arms control negotiations.

7. Kennan interview, *Bill Moyers' Journal*, 30 January 1973, Kennan Papers, Box 271, Folder 8.

8. Kennan speech, "The United States and the Problem of China," State Bar of California, 1 October 1964, Kennan Papers, Box 269, Folder 29.

9. Kennan presentation at Central Intelligence Agency, 14 October 1949, Kennan Papers, Box 17, Folder 29; "Unfinished Paper," September 1951, Kennan Papers, Box 24, Folder 1-D-18; *New York Herald Tribune*, 21 September 1958, 1, 6; Kennan lecture at Phillips Andover Academy, 8 October 1958, Kennan Papers, Box 19, Folder 1-C-79; Kennan to Walter Lippman, 18 October 1960, Kennan Papers, Box 30, Folder 2-B-1960; George F. Kennan, "Reflections on the Walgreen Lectures," in *American Diplomacy*, expanded ed. (Chicago: University of Chicago Press, 1984), 165.

10. Kennan to Arnold Wolfers, 28 May 1956, Kennan Papers, Box 31, Folder 2-B-1956.

11. Kennan speech, "Russian and American Interests in East Asia," American Historical Association, Seattle, WA, 8 September 1960, Kennan Papers, Box 302, Folder 16; Kennan speech, "The United States and the Problem of China," State Bar of California, 1 October 1964, ibid., Box 269, Folder 29; George F. Kennan, "A Fresh Look at Our China Policy," *New York Times Magazine*, 22 November 1964, 27, 140–47.

12. Kennan diary entry, 25 November 1996, George F. Kennan, *The Kennan Diaries*, ed. Frank Costigliola (New York: W. W. Norton, 2014), 653; Kennan speech, Denison University, Granville, OH, 10 February 1970, Kennan Papers, Box 304, Folder 20; George F. Kennan, *Memoirs 1950–1963* (New York: Pantheon Books, 1972), 54.

13. Kennan, *Memoirs 1950–1963*, 54–56; Kennan lecture, "Beyond Vietnam," Denison University, Granville, OH, 10 February 1970, Kennan Papers, Box 304, Folder 20.

14. Richard Ullman, "The US and the World: An Interview with George Kennan," *New York Review of Books* 46, no. 13 (12 August 1999): 6. See also Kennan diary entry, 25 November 1996, *Kennan Diaries*, 653.

15. Kennan, *Memoirs 1950–1963*, 56; Kennan to Arnold Wolfers, 28 May 1956, Kennan Papers, Box 31, Folder 2-B-1956. Kennan privately attributed some of his impressions of China's way of dealing with foreigners to a classic history of the Opium War by a British colonial official and historian: Maurice Collis, *Foreign Mud: Being an Account of the Opium Imbroglio at Canton in the 1830s and the Anglo-Chinese War That Followed* (London: Faber and Faber Limited, 1946); Kennan considered this "one of the finest books ever written in the field of diplomatic history." Kennan to Harold Hochschild, 1 February 1965, Kennan Papers, Box 31, Folder 2-B-1965.

16. Kennan, *Memoirs 1950–1963*, 57.

17. Kennan to Wolfers, 28 May 1956, Kennan Papers, Box 31, Folder 2-B-1956; Kennan lecture, "International Situation," Princeton Graduate School, 25 April 1951, Kennan Papers, Box 300, Folder 4; Kennan, *American Diplomacy*, 165.

18. Kennan speech, "Russian and American Interests in East Asia," American Historical Association, Seattle, WA, 8 September 1960, Kennan Papers, Box 302, Folder 16.

19. Kennan lecture at Pentagon Orientation Conference, 17 April 1950, Kennan Papers, Box 18, Folder 1-C-7; "Unfinished Paper," September 1951, Kennan Papers, Box 24, Folder 1-D-18; Kennan to Wolfers, 28 May 1956, Kennan Papers, Box 31, Folder 2-B-1956.

20. "Unused Material Written for Possible Use in *Memoirs*, Volume II," 1970, Kennan Papers, Box 27, Folder 1-E-28.

21. Kennan to Harold Hochschild, 6 October 1964, Kennan Papers, Box 31, Folder 2-B-1964; Kennan, "A Fresh Look at Our China Policy"; Kennan to Nitze, 6 January 1951, PPS Records, Box 48, PPS members chronological file, Kennan folder. In 1964 Kennan commented that UN membership "confers certain rights and duties, relating to the good order and conduct of the international community" and judged it "hard to believe that the regime in Peking qualifies under these standards." At the same time, he speculated that the Chinese Communist regime might nonetheless "soon be accorded wide diplomatic recognition and be at least offered the possibility" of UN membership, and that "we Americans will have to accommodate ourselves in one way or another." Kennan speech, "The United States and the Problem of China," State Bar of California, 1 October 1964, Kennan Papers, Box 269, Folder 29; Kennan to Roger Hagan, 11 December 1964, Kennan Papers, Box 31, Folder 2-B-1964.

22. Kennan speech, "Russian and American Interests in East Asia," American Historical Association, Seattle, WA, 8 September 1960, Kennan Papers, Box 302, Folder 16.

23. Kennan, interview by Robert J. Moskin, *Look*, 19 November 1963, in George F. Kennan, *Interviews with George F. Kennan*, ed. T. Christopher Jespersen, 45 (Jackson: University of Mississippi Press, 2002); Kennan, *Kennan Diaries*, 405; Kennan speech, "The United States and the Communist Giants," Princeton University, 25 February 1965, Kennan Papers, Box 262, Folder 5; Kennan lecture, "Beyond Vietnam," Denison University, Granville, OH, 10 February 1970, Kennan Papers, Box 304, Folder 20.

24. George F. Kennan, "The Nixon Visit to Peking," draft article for The Observer, February 1972, Kennan Papers, Box 270, Folder 8.

25. Kennan interview, *Bill Moyers' Journal*, 30 January 1973, Kennan Papers, Box 271, Folder 8; George F. Kennan, *The Cloud of Danger: Current Realities of American Foreign Policy* (Boston: Little, Brown, 1977), 103.

26. Kennan, *Cloud of Danger*, 106.

27. Ibid., 102–5; Kennan speech, "Russian and American Interests in East Asia," American Historical Association, Seattle, WA, 8 September 1960, Kennan Papers, Box 302, Folder 16; Kennan lecture, "Containment: Russia and China," Denison University, Granville, OH, 9 February 1966, Kennan Papers, Box 263, Folder 6.

28. Kennan diary entry, 25 November 1996, *Kennan Diaries*, 653–54.

29. Ibid. On the subject of human rights in China, Kennan said in a 1999 interview that "it really is in ill grace for us to be talking down to them and saying, by implication, 'you ought to learn to govern yourselves as we do.' . . . Let people be what they are, and treat them accordingly." Ullman, "The US and the World: An Interview with George Kennan," 6.

30. Kennan to Anders Stephanson, 3 April 1997, Kennan Papers, Box 77, Folder 4.

31. Kennan to Donald Rumsfeld, 22 February 2001, Kennan Papers, Box 77, Folder 4.

32. Kennan diary entry, 25 July 1950, *Kennan Diaries*, 267; Kennan lecture, "International Situation," Princeton Graduate School, 25 April 1951, Kennan Papers, Box 300, Folder 4; "Unfinished Paper," September 1951, Kennan Papers, Box 24, Folder 1-D-18; Kennan letter to Walt Rostow, 28 May 1956, Kennan Papers, Box 31, Folder 2-B-1956; Kennan speech, "Russian and American Interests in East Asia," American Historical Association, Seattle, WA, 8 September 1960, Kennan Papers, Box 302, Folder 16; Kennan, *Interviews with George F. Kennan*, 45; Kennan speech, "The United States and the Problem of China," State Bar of California, 1 October 1964, Kennan Papers, Box 269, Folder 29; Kennan lecture, "Containment: Russia and China," Denison University, Granville, OH, 9 February 1966, Kennan Papers, Box 263, Folder 6; Kennan lecture, "Beyond Vietnam," Denison University, Granville, OH, 10 February 1970, Kennan Papers, Box 304, Folder 20.

33. Davies to Kennan, 2 October 1953, and Kennan to Davies, 26 October 1953, Kennan Papers, Box 10, Folder 12.

34. Kennan appears not to have absorbed Richard Nixon's oft-quoted observation in 1967 that "we simply cannot afford to leave China forever outside the family of nations, there to nurture its fantasies, cherish its hates and threaten its neighbors." Richard M. Nixon, "Asia after Vietnam," *Foreign Affairs*, October 1967, 121.

35. Kennan to Davies, 8 January 1998, Kennan Papers, Box 10, Folder 12. Kennan similarly told an interviewer two years earlier: "I can't vouch for the Chinese, because I don't know anything about China." Kennan interview, NewsHour with Jim Lehrer, 16 April 1996. Kennan never saw China firsthand until he made his first and only visit there in October 1980. On an excursion to the city of Hangzhou, he was impressed by the sunrise over West Lake: "The whole scene was so unbelievably Chinese, in the sense of its resemblance to the scenes from Chinese paintings, that one was quite startled. One does not expect places these days really to look like what they are supposed to look like." George F. Kennan, *Sketches from a Life* (New York: Pantheon Books, 1989), 303.

36. Quoted in Kennan, *Memoirs 1950–1963*, 53.

37. Kennan speech to Pittsburgh Foreign Policy Association, 3 May 1956, *US News & World Report*, 29 June 1956, 74–75; Kennan to John Allison, 28 May 1956, Kennan Papers, Box 31, Folder 2-B-1956.

38. Kennan speech, "Russian and American Interests in East Asia," American Historical Association, Seattle, WA, 8 September 1960, Kennan Papers, Box 302, Folder 16.

39. George F. Kennan, "Japanese Security and American Policy," *Foreign Affairs* 43, no. 1 (October 1964): 22. In this article, Kennan also tried to refute what he described as the original rationale for the security treaty, including the notion that Japan during 1949–50 was "seriously threatened with invasion or with overt military intimidation from the Communist mainland of Asia." In this regard, however, he was exaggerating the nature of the threat as perceived at the time and overlooking his own focus then on Japan's vulnerability to Communist subversion—which was one of the central drivers of the "reverse course." Ibid., 15–16.

40. Ibid., 25; Kennan to McGeorge Bundy, 18 November 1964, Kennan Papers, Box 31, Folder 2-B-1964.

41. Kennan, "Japanese Security and American Policy," 25–27. Kennan's article, as Gaddis notes, alarmed the US ambassador in Tokyo, who "urgently arranged a rebuttal" in a speech by Assistant Secretary of State William Bundy that rejected any rationale for reconsidering or altering US-Japan security arrangements. Bundy later said the episode reinforced the view in Washington that Kennan knew little about East Asia. See John Lewis Gaddis, *George F. Kennan: An American Life* (New York: Penguin Press, 2011), 584–85; Bundy speech, "Progress and Problems in East Asia: An American Viewpoint," 29 September 1964, *Department of State Bulletin* 51, no. 1321 (19 October 1964): 536.

42. Kennan, *Memoirs 1950–1963*, 53; Kennan, "Critique of Mr. Wakaizumi's paper," 8 October 1975, Kennan Papers, Box 306, Folder 13.

43. Kennan, *Cloud of Danger*, 107; Kennan to Donald Rumsfeld, 22 February 2001, Kennan Papers, Box 77, Folder 4.

44. Kennan, *Cloud of Danger*, 110.

45. Transcript of Kennan speech and interviews, Tokyo International House, 31 October 1980, Kennan Papers, Box 278, Folder 7.

46. Ibid.

47. George F. Kennan, *Around the Cragged Hill: A Personal and Political Philosophy* (New York: W. W. Norton, 1993), 195.

48. Kennan, "Japanese Security and American Policy," 17–20; Kennan, *Cloud of Danger*, 111–13.

49. Kennan speech, "The United States and the Problem of China," State Bar of California, 1 October 1964, Kennan Papers, Box 269, Folder 29; Kennan lecture, "Containment: Russia and China," Denison University, Granville, OH, 9 February 1966, ibid., Box 263, Folder 6; Kennan lecture, "Beyond Vietnam," Denison University, Granville, OH, 10 February 1970, ibid., Box 304, Folder 20.

50. Kennan, "Beyond Vietnam"; Kennan, *Cloud of Danger*, 111.

51. Kennan speech, "Russian and American Interests in East Asia," American Historical Association, Seattle, WA, 8 September 1960, Kennan Papers, Box 302, Folder 16; Kennan speech, "The United States and the Problem of China," State Bar of California, 1 October 1964, ibid., Box 269, Folder 29; Kennan, *Cloud of Danger*, 97. Kennan's momentary attention to the strategic importance of Indonesia during 1948–49 also appears to have ended after the Dutch recognition of Indonesian independence in December 1949.

52. Davies to Kennan, 2 October 1953, Kennan Papers, Box 10, Folder 12.

53. Kennan lecture, "Containment: Russia and China," Denison University, Granville, OH, 9 February 1966, Kennan Papers, Box 263, Folder 6.

54. Kennan, *Cloud of Danger*, 94–95.

55. Kennan speech, "The United States and the Problem of China," State Bar of California, 1 October 1964, Kennan Papers, Box 269, Folder 29.

56. Kennan lecture, "Beyond Vietnam," Denison University, Granville, OH, 10 February 1970, Kennan Papers, Box 304, Folder 20.

Bibliography

ARCHIVAL AND MANUSCRIPT COLLECTIONS

National Archives, Washington, DC
    Department of State Records (Record Group 59)
        Central Decimal Files
        Records of Ambassador at Large Philip C. Jessup, 1946–1952
        Records of the Office of Chinese Affairs, 1944–1950
        Records of the Office of Northeast Asian Affairs
        Records of the Office of the Executive Secretariat
        Records of the Office of the Assistant Secretary of State for Occupied Areas,
            1946–1949
        Records of the Philippine and Southeast Asia Division
        Records of the Policy Planning Staff
    Records of the State-War-Navy Coordinating Committee
    Records of the State-Army-Navy-Air Force Coordinating Committee
Washington National Records Center, Suitland, Maryland
    Undersecretary of the Army (Draper/Voorhees) Project Decimal File, 1947–1950
      (Record Group 335)
    Records of the Supreme Commander for the Allied Powers, 1945–1952 (Record
      Group 331)
Seeley G. Mudd Manuscript Library, Princeton, NJ
    John Foster Dulles Oral History Project
    James V. Forrestal Diaries and Papers
    George F. Kennan Papers
    John Van Antwerp MacMurray Collection
Harry S. Truman Library, Independence, MO
    President's Secretary's Files
    Dean Acheson Papers
    John M. Allison Papers
    John Paton Davies Jr. Papers
    John F. Melby Papers
    John Stewart Service and Charles E. Rhetts Papers
    Sidney W. Souers Papers
    Oral Histories: W. Walton Butterworth, O. Edmund Clubb, William H. Draper,
      U. Alexis Johnson, Robert A. Lovett, Charles Burton Marshall, Edwin M.
      Martin, John Melby, Paul H. Nitze, Arthur A. Ringwalt, Charles E. Saltzman,
      John Stewart Service, Philip D. Sprouse
George C. Marshall Research Foundation, Lexington, VA
    W. Walton Butterworth Papers
    Forrest C. Pogue Materials
    C. Ben Wright Kennan Biography Project Papers
MacArthur Memorial Archives, Norfolk, VA
    Records of General Headquarters, Supreme Commander for the Allied Powers,
      1945–1951 (Record Group 5)

Papers of Charles L. Kades, 1948–1951 (Record Group 33)
Selected Papers of Major General Charles A. Willoughby, USA, 1943–1954
(Record Group 23B)

PUBLISHED GOVERNMENT DOCUMENTS

Cole, Alice C., Alfred Goldberg, Samuel A. Tucker, and Rudolph A. Winnacker, eds. *The Department of Defense: Documents on Establishment and Organization 1944–1978.* Washington, DC: Office of the Secretary of Defense, Historical Office, 1978.

Etzold, Thomas H., and John Lewis Gaddis, eds. *Containment: Documents on American Policy and Strategy, 1945–1950.* New York: Columbia University Press, 1978.

MacMurray, John Van Antwerp. *How the Peace Was Lost: The 1935 Memorandum: Developments Affecting American Policy in the Far East: Prepared for the State Department by John Van Antwerp MacMurray.* Edited and with an introduction by Arthur Waldron. Stanford, CA: Hoover Institution Press, Stanford University, 1992.

Nelson, Anna Kasten, ed. *The State Department Policy Planning Staff Papers.* 3 vols. New York: Garland Publishing, 1983.

United States Department of State. *The China White Paper*, originally issued as *United States Relations with China, with Special Reference to the Period 1944–1949.* 2 vols. Stanford, CA: Stanford University Press, 1967.

——. *Foreign Relations of the United States.* Vols. 1944–1951. Washington, DC: Government Printing Office, 1965–83.

——. *Transcript of Round Table Discussion on American Policy toward China Held in the Department of State, October 6, 7, and 8, 1949.* Washington, DC: W. D. Bowles, 1951.

United States National Intelligence Council. *Tracking the Dragon: National Intelligence Estimates on China during the Era of Mao, 1948–1976.* Washington, DC: Government Printing Office, 2004.

United States Senate. *Informal Meeting with George F. Kennan: Hearing before the Committee on Foreign Relations.* Eighty Sixth Congress, First Session, 12 May 1959.

PERSONAL CORRESPONDENCE

Davies, John Paton, Jr., to author, 12 June 1993
Davies, John Paton, Jr., to author, 1 November 1998
Kennan, George F. to author, 18 October 1993
Kennan, George F. to author, 31 January 1994
Kennan, George F. to author, 24 October 1995

INTERVIEWS

Davies, John Paton, Jr. Telephone interview by author, 23 November 1993, Asheville, NC.
Dupuy, Trevor N. Interview by author, 20 June 1994, McLean, VA.
Green, Marshall. Telephone interview by author, 18 May 1993, Washington, DC.
Nitze, Paul H. Interview by author, 7 June 1994, Washington, DC.
Rusk, Dean. Telephone interview by author, 5 July 1994, Athens, GA.

PUBLISHED MEMOIRS AND DIARIES

Acheson, Dean. *Present at the Creation: My Years in the State Department.* New York: W. W. Norton, 1969.

Allison, John M. *Ambassador from the Prairie, or Allison Wonderland.* Boston: Houghton Mifflin, 1973.

Bohlen, Charles E. *Witness to History 1929–1969.* New York: W. W. Norton, 1973.

Davies, John Paton, Jr. *China Hand: An Autobiography*. Philadelphia: University of Pennsylvania Press, 2012.

——. "The China Hands in Practice: The Personal Experience." In *The China Hands' Legacy: Ethics and Diplomacy*, edited by Paul Gordon Lauren, 37–57. Boulder, CO: Westview Press, 1987.

——. *Dragon by the Tail: American, British, Japanese, and Russian Encounters with China and One Another*. New York: W. W. Norton, 1972.

Forrestal, James V. *The Forrestal Diaries*. Edited by Walter Millis. New York: Viking Press, 1951.

Green, Marshall. *Pacific Encounters: Recollections and Humor*. Bethesda, MD: DACOR Press, 1997.

Green, Marshall, John H. Holdridge, and William N. Stokes. *War and Peace with China: First-Hand Experiences in the Foreign Service of the United States*. Bethesda, MD: DACOR Press, 1994.

Jessup, Philip C. *The Birth of Nations*. New York: Columbia University Press, 1974.

Kennan, George F. *Around the Cragged Hill: A Personal and Political Philosophy*. New York: W. W. Norton, 1993.

——. *At a Century's Ending: Reflections 1982–1995*. New York: W. W. Norton, 1996.

——. *Interviews with George F. Kennan*. Edited by T. Christopher Jespersen. Jackson: University Press of Mississippi, 2002.

——. *The Kennan Diaries*. Edited by Frank Costigliola. New York: W. W. Norton, 2014.

——. *Memoirs 1925–1950*. New York: Pantheon Books, 1967.

——. *Memoirs 1950–1963*. New York: Pantheon Books, 1972.

——. *Sketches from a Life*. New York: Pantheon Books, 1989.

MacArthur, Douglas. *Reminiscences*. New York: McGraw-Hill, 1964.

Melby, John F. *The Mandate of Heaven*. Toronto: University of Toronto Press, 1968.

——. "Vietnam—1950." *Diplomatic History* 6, no. 1 (1982): 97–109.

Nitze, Paul H. *From Hiroshima to Glasnost: At the Center of Decision, A Memoir*. With Ann M. Smith and Steven L. Rearden. New York: Grove Weidenfeld, 1989.

——. *Tension between Opposites: Reflections on the Practice and Theory of Politics*. New York: Charles Scribner's Sons, 1993.

Rusk, Dean. *As I Saw It*. As told to Richard Rusk. Edited by Daniel S. Papp. New York: W. W. Norton, 1990.

Willoughby, Charles A., and John Chamberlain. *MacArthur 1941–1951: Victory in the Pacific*. London: William Heinemann, 1956.

BOOKS

Ambrose, Stephen E. *Rise to Globalism: American Foreign Policy since 1938*. 5th rev. ed. New York: Penguin Books, 1988.

Anderson, David L. *Imperialism and Idealism: American Diplomats in China, 1861–1898*. Bloomington: Indiana University Press, 1985.

Beisner, Robert L. *Dean Acheson: A Life in the Cold War*. Oxford: Oxford University Press, 2006.

Bernstein, Richard. *China 1945: Mao's Revolution and America's Fateful Choice*. New York: Alfred A. Knopf, 2014.

Bird, Kai, and Martin Sherwin. *American Prometheus: The Triumph and Tragedy of J. Robert Oppenheimer*. New York: Vintage Books, 2006.

Bisson, Thomas A. *Zaibatsu Dissolution in Japan*. Berkeley: University of California Press, 1954.

Blair, Clay. *The Forgotten War: America in Korea 1950–1953*. New York: Doubleday, 1987.

Blum, Robert. *The United States and China in World Affairs*. Edited by A. Doak Barnett. New York: McGraw-Hill, 1966.

Blum, Robert M. *Drawing the Line: The Origin of the American Containment Policy in East Asia*. New York: W. W. Norton, 1982.

Borden, William S. *The Pacific Alliance: United States Foreign Economic Policy and Japanese Trade Recovery, 1947–1955*. Madison: University of Wisconsin Press, 1984.

Borg, Dorothy. *The United States and the Far Eastern Crisis of 1933–1938*. Cambridge, MA: Harvard University Press, 1964.

Borg, Dorothy, and Waldo Heinrichs, eds. *Uncertain Years: Chinese-American Relations, 1947–1950*. New York: Columbia University Press, 1980.

Brinkley, Douglas. *Dean Acheson: The Cold War Years 1953–71*. New Haven, CT: Yale University Press, 1992.

Buckley, Roger. *US-Japan Alliance Diplomacy, 1945–1990*. Cambridge: Cambridge University Press, 1992.

Buhite, Russell. *Soviet-American Relations in Asia, 1945–1954*. Norman: University of Oklahoma Press, 1981.

Cha, Victor D. *Powerplay: The Origins of the American Alliance System in Asia*. Princeton, NJ: Princeton University Press, 2016.

Chace, James. *Acheson: The Secretary of State Who Created the American World*. New York: Simon & Schuster, 1998.

Chang, Gordon H. *Friends and Enemies: The United States, China, and the Soviet Union, 1948–1972*. Stanford, CA: Stanford University Press, 1990.

Chay, Jongsuk. *Unequal Partners in Peace and War: The Republic of Korea and the United States, 1948–1953*. Westport, CT: Praeger, 2002.

Chen Jian. *China's Road to the Korean War*. New York: Columbia University Press, 1994.

——. *Mao's China and the Cold War*. Chapel Hill: University of North Carolina Press, 2001.

Christensen, Thomas J. *The China Challenge: Shaping the Choices of a Rising Power*. New York: W. W. Norton, 2015.

——. *Useful Adversaries: Grand Strategy, Domestic Mobilization, and Sino-American Conflict, 1947–1958*. Princeton, NJ: Princeton University Press, 1996.

——. *Worse Than a Monolith: Alliance Politics and Problems of Coercive Diplomacy in Asia*. Princeton, NJ: Princeton University Press, 2011.

Cohen, Theodore. *Remaking Japan: The American Occupation as New Deal*. Edited by Herbert Passin. New York: Free Press, 1987.

Cohen, Warren I. *America's Response to China: A History of Sino-American Relations*. 4th ed. New York: Columbia University Press, 2000.

——. *East Asia at the Center: Four Thousand Years of Engagement with the World*. New York: Columbia University Press, 2000.

Collis, Maurice. *Foreign Mud: Being an Account of the Opium Imbroglio at Canton in the 1830s and the Anglo-Chinese War That Followed*. London: Faber and Faber, 1946.

Congdon, Lee. *George Kennan: A Writing Life*. Wilmington, DE: ISI Books, 2008.

Cumings, Bruce, ed. *Child of Conflict: The Korean-American Relationship, 1943–1953*. Seattle: University of Washington Press, 1983.

——. *The Origins of the Korean War*. Vol. 1, *Liberation and the Emergence of Separate Regimes 1945–1947*. Princeton, NJ: Princeton University Press, 1981.

——. *The Origins of the Korean War*. Vol. 2, *The Roaring of the Cataract 1947–1950*. Princeton, NJ: Princeton University Press, 1990.

——. *Parallax Visions: Making Sense of American–East Asian Relations at the End of the Century*. Durham, NC: Duke University Press, 1999.

Dobbs, Charles M. *The United States and East Asia since 1945*. Lewiston, NY: Edwin Mellen Press, 1990.

Dower, John W. *Embracing Defeat: Japan in the Wake of World War II*. New York: W. W. Norton, 1999.

———. *Empire and Aftermath: Yoshida Shigeru and the Japanese Experience, 1878–1954*. Cambridge, MA: Harvard University Press, 1988.

Duiker, William J. *U.S. Containment Policy and the Conflict in Indochina*. Stanford, CA: Stanford University Press, 1994.

Dunn, Frederick S. *Peace-Making and the Settlement with Japan*. Princeton, NJ: Princeton University Press, 1963.

Eastman, Lloyd E. *The Abortive Revolution: China under Nationalist Rule, 1927–1937*. Cambridge, MA: Harvard University Press, 1974.

Fairbank, John K. *China: A New History*. Cambridge, MA: Harvard University Press, 1992.

———. *The Great Chinese Revolution, 1800–1985*. New York: Harper & Row, 1986.

———. *The United States and China*. 4th ed., enlarged. Cambridge, MA: Harvard University Press, 1983.

Fairbank, John K., Edwin O. Reischauer, and Albert M. Craig. *East Asia: Tradition and Transformation*. Boston: Houghton Mifflin, 1978.

Fearey, Robert A. *The Occupation of Japan: Second Phase: 1948–1950*. Westport, CT: Greenwood Press, 1950.

Feis, Herbert. *The China Tangle: The American Effort in China from Pearl Harbor to the Marshall Mission*. Princeton, NJ: Princeton University Press, 1953.

———. *The Road to Pearl Harbor*. Princeton, NJ: Princeton University Press, 1950.

Ferguson, Niall. *Colossus: The Price of America's Empire*. New York: Penguin Press, 2004.

Finkelstein, David M. *Washington's Taiwan Dilemma, 1949–1950: From Abandonment to Salvation*. Fairfax, VA: George Mason University Press, 1993.

Finn, Richard B. *Winners in Peace: MacArthur, Yoshida, and Postwar Japan*. Berkeley: University of California Press, 1992.

Fitzgerald, Frances. *Fire in the Lake: The Vietnamese and the Americans in Vietnam*. New York: Random House, 1972.

Forsberg, Aaron. *America and the Japanese Miracle: The Cold War Context of Japan's Postwar Economic Revival, 1950–1960*. Chapel Hill: University of North Carolina Press, 2000.

Franklin, Laurel. *George F. Kennan: An Annotated Bibliography*. Westport, CT: Greenwood Press, 1997.

Gaddis, John Lewis. *George F. Kennan: An American Life*. New York: Penguin Press, 2011.

———. *The Long Peace: Inquiries into the History of the Cold War*. New York: Oxford University Press, 1987.

———. *Strategies of Containment: A Critical Appraisal of American National Security Policy during the Cold War*. Rev. and expanded ed. New York: Oxford University Press, 2005.

———. *The United States and the End of the Cold War: Implications, Reconsiderations, Provocations*. Oxford: Oxford University Press, 1992.

———. *The United States and the Origins of the Cold War, 1941–1947*. New York: Columbia University Press, 1972.

———. *We Now Know: Rethinking Cold War History*. Oxford: Oxford University Press, 1997.

Garver, John W. *The Sino-American Alliance: Nationalist China and American Cold War Strategy in Asia*. Armonk, NY: M. E. Sharpe, 1997.

Gellman, Barton. *Contending with Kennan: Toward a Philosophy of American Power*. New York: Praeger, 1984.

Gilpin, Robert. *War and Change in World Politics*. Cambridge: Cambridge University Press, 1981.

Goldstein, Avery. *Rising to the Challenge: China's Grand Strategy and International Security*. Stanford, CA: Stanford University Press, 2005.

Goncharov, Sergei N., John W. Lewis, and Xue Litai. *Uncertain Partners: Stalin, Mao, and the Korean War*. Stanford, CA: Stanford University Press, 1993.

Gordon, Andrew, ed. *Postwar Japan as History*. Berkeley: University of California Press, 1993.

Grasso, June M. *Truman's Two-China Policy, 1948–1950*. Armonk, NY: M. E. Sharpe, 1987.

Green, Michael J. *By More Than Providence: Grand Strategy and American Power in the Asia Pacific since 1783*. New York: Columbia University Press, 2017.

Gries, Peter Hays. *China's New Nationalism: Pride, Politics, and Diplomacy*. Berkeley: University of California Press, 2004.

Halberstam, David. *The Best and the Brightest*. 2nd ed. New York: Random House, 1972.

Han Suyin. *Eldest Son: Zhou Enlai and the Making of Modern China, 1898–1976*. London: Pimlico, 1994.

Harding, Harry, and Yuan Ming, eds. *Sino-American Relations 1945–1955: A Joint Reassessment of a Critical Decade*. Wilmington, DE: Scholarly Resources Books, 1989.

Harlow, Giles D., and George C. Maerz, eds. *Measures Short of War: The George F. Kennan Lectures at the National War College, 1946–47*. Washington, DC: National Defense University Press, 1991.

Harries, Meirion, and Susie Harries. *Sheathing the Sword: The Demilitarization of Japan*. New York: Macmillan, 1987.

Heinrichs, Waldo. *Threshold of War: Franklin D. Roosevelt and American Entry into World War II*. New York: Oxford University Press, 1988.

Herman, Arthur. *Douglas MacArthur: American Warrior*. New York: Random House, 2016.

Herring, George C. *From Colony to Superpower: U.S. Foreign Relations since 1776*. Oxford: Oxford University Press, 2008.

Hess, Gary R. *The United States' Emergence as a Southeast Asian Power, 1940–1950*. New York: Columbia University Press, 1987.

——. *Vietnam and the United States: Origins and Legacy of War*. Boston: Twayne Publishers, 1990.

Hixson, Walter L. *George F. Kennan: Cold War Iconoclast*. New York: Columbia University Press, 1989.

Hogan, Michael J., ed. *The End of the Cold War: Its Meaning and Implications*. Cambridge: Cambridge University Press, 1992.

Holsti, K. J. *International Politics: A Framework for Analysis*. 5th ed. Englewood Cliffs, NJ: Prentice Hall, 1988.

Hotta, Eri. *Japan 1941: Countdown to Infamy*. New York: Alfred A. Knopf, 2013.

Iriye, Akira. *Across the Pacific: An Inner History of American-East Asian Relations*. New York: Harcourt, Brace & World, 1967.

——. *China and Japan in the Global Setting*. Cambridge, MA: Harvard University Press, 1992.

——. *The Cold War in Asia: A Historical Introduction*. Englewood Cliffs, NJ: Prentice-Hall, 1974.

Isaacson, Walter, and Evan Thomas. *The Wise Men: Six Friends and the World They Made*. New York: Simon & Schuster, 1986.

James, D. Clayton. *The Years of MacArthur, Vol. III: Triumph and Disaster 1945–1964*. Boston: Houghton Mifflin, 1985.

Jensen, Kenneth M., ed. *Origins of the Cold War: The Novikov, Kennan, and Roberts "Long Telegrams" of 1946*. Washington, DC: United States Institute of Peace Press, 1993.

Jespersen, T. Christopher. *American Images of China, 1931–1949*. Stanford, CA: Stanford University Press, 1996.

Johnston, Alastair Iain. *Cultural Realism: Strategic Culture and Grand Strategy in Chinese History*. Princeton, NJ: Princeton University Press, 1995.

Kahn, E. J., Jr. *The China Hands: America's Foreign Service Officers and What Befell Them*. New York: Viking Press, 1975.

Karnow, Stanley. *In Our Image: America's Empire in the Philippines*. New York: Random House, 1989.

——. *Vietnam: A History*. Rev. and updated ed. New York: Penguin Books, 1991.

Kaufman, Victor S. *Confronting Communism: U.S. and British Policies toward China*. Columbia: University of Missouri Press, 2001.

Kennan, George. *E. H. Harriman's Far Eastern Plans*. Garden City, NY: Country Life Press, 1917.

Kennan, George F. *American Diplomacy*. Expanded ed. Chicago: University of Chicago Press, 1984.

——. *The Cloud of Danger: Current Realities of American Foreign Policy*. Boston: Little, Brown, 1977.

——. *The Decision to Intervene*. Princeton, NJ: Princeton University Press, 1958.

——. *The Fateful Alliance: France, Russia, and the Coming of the First World War*. New York: Pantheon Books, 1984.

——. *The Nuclear Delusion: Soviet-American Relations in the Atomic Age*. New York: Pantheon Books, 1983.

——. *Russia and the West under Lenin and Stalin*. New York: Mentor Books, 1960.

——. *Russia Leaves the War*. Princeton, NJ: Princeton University Press, 1956.

Kennan, George F., and John Lukacs. *George F. Kennan and the Origins of Containment, 1944–1946: The Kennan-Lukacs Correspondence*. Columbia: University of Missouri Press, 1997.

Kim, Seung-yong. *American Diplomacy and Strategy toward Korea and Northeast Asia, 1882–1950 and After: Perception of Polarity and the US Commitment to a Periphery*. New York: Palgrave Macmillan, 2009.

Kingsbury, Damien. *Southeast Asia: A Political Profile*. 2nd ed. Melbourne, Australia: Oxford University Press, 2005.

Kissinger, Henry. *On China*. New York: Penguin Press, 2011.

——. *World Order*. New York: Penguin Press, 2014.

Koen, Ross Y. *The China Lobby in American Politics*. Edited by Richard C. Kagan. New York: Octagon Books, 1974.

LaFeber, Walter. *The Clash: A History of US-Japan Relations*. New York: W. W. Norton, 1997.

Lampton, David M. *Same Bed, Different Dreams: Managing U.S.-China Relations, 1989–2000*. Berkeley: University of California Press, 2001.

Lauren, Paul Gordon, ed. *The China Hands' Legacy: Ethics and Diplomacy*. Boulder, CO: Westview Press, 1987.

Lee, Steven Hugh. *Outposts of Empire: Korea, Vietnam, and the Origins of the Cold War in Asia, 1949–1954*. Montreal: McGill-Queen's University Press, 1995.

Leffler, Melvyn P. *For the Soul of Mankind: The United States, the Soviet Union, and the Cold War*. New York: Hill and Wang, 2007.

——. *A Preponderance of Power: National Security, the Truman Administration, and the Cold War*. Stanford, CA: Stanford University Press, 1992.

Li, Laura Tyson. *Madame Chiang Kai-shek: China's Eternal First Lady*. New York: Atlantic Monthly Press, 2006.

Lieberthal, Kenneth. *Governing China: From Revolution through Reform*. New York: W. W. Norton, 1995.

Lilley, James. *China Hands: Nine Decades of Adventure, Espionage, and Diplomacy in Asia.* With Jeffrey Lilley. New York: Public Affairs, 2004.

Logevall, Fredrik. *Choosing War: The Lost Chance for Peace and the Escalation of War in Vietnam.* Berkeley: University of California Press, 1999.

——. *Embers of War: The Fall of an Empire and the Making of America's Vietnam.* New York: Random House, 2012.

——. *Origins of the Vietnam War.* London: Pearson Education, 2001.

Lowe, Peter. *Containing the Cold War in East Asia: British Policies towards Japan, China, and Korea, 1948–1953.* Manchester: Manchester University Press, 1997.

——. *Contending with Nationalism and Communism: British Policy towards Southeast Asia, 1945–65.* London: Palgrave Macmillan, 2009.

Lukacs, John. *George Kennan: A Study of Character.* New Haven, CT: Yale University Press, 2007.

——, ed. *Through the History of the Cold War: The Correspondence of George F. Kennan and John Lukacs.* Philadelphia: University of Pennsylvania Press, 2010.

Lyman, Robert. *Among the Headhunters: An Extraordinary World War II Story of Survival in the Burmese Jungle.* Boston: Da Capo Press, 2016.

MacFarquhar, Roderick. *Origins of the Cultural Revolution I: Contradictions among the People, 1956–1957.* New York: Columbia University Press, 1974.

——. *Origins of the Cultural Revolution II: The Great Leap Forward, 1958–1960.* New York: Columbia University Press, 1983.

——. *Origins of the Cultural Revolution III: The Coming of the Cataclysm, 1961–1966.* New York: Columbia University Press, 1997.

MacFarquhar, Roderick, and Michael Schoenhals. *Mao's Last Revolution.* Cambridge, MA: Harvard University Press, 2006.

MacMillan, Margaret. *Nixon and Mao: The Week That Changed the World.* New York: Random House, 2007.

——. *Paris 1919: Six Months That Changed the World.* New York: Random House, 2001.

MacMurray, John V. A., ed. *Treaties and Agreements With and Concerning China, 1894–1919.* 2 vols. Washington, DC: Carnegie Endowment for International Peace, 1921.

——. *Treaties and Agreements with and concerning China, 1919–1929.* Washington, DC: Carnegie Endowment for International Peace, 1929.

Manchester, William. *American Caesar: Douglas MacArthur, 1880–1964.* Boston: Little, Brown, 1978.

Mann, James. *About Face: A History of America's Curious Relationship with China, from Nixon to Clinton.* New York: Alfred A. Knopf, 1999.

Matray, James Irving. *The Reluctant Crusade: American Foreign Policy in Korea, 1941–1950.* Honolulu: University of Hawaii Press, 1985.

May, Ernest R. *The Truman Administration and China, 1945–1949.* Edited by Harold M. Hyman. Philadelphia: J. B. Lippincott, 1975.

Mayers, David Allan. *Cracking the Monolith: U.S. Policy against the Sino-Soviet Alliance, 1949–1955.* Baton Rouge: Louisiana State University Press, 1986.

——. *George Kennan and the Dilemmas of US Foreign Policy.* New York: Oxford University Press, 1988.

McCullough, David. *Truman.* New York: Simon & Schuster, 1992.

McGlothlen, Ronald. *Controlling the Waves: Dean Acheson and U.S. Foreign Policy in Asia.* New York: W. W. Norton, 1993.

McLellan, David S. *Dean Acheson: The State Department Years.* New York: Dodd, Mead, 1976.

McMahon, Robert J. *The Limits of Empire: The United States and Southeast Asia since World War II.* New York: Columbia University Press, 1999.

Mead, Walter Russell. *Special Providence: American Foreign Policy and How It Changed the World*. New York: Alfred A. Knopf, 2001.

Mercer, Jonathan. *Reputation and International Politics*. Ithaca, NY: Cornell University Press, 1996.

Milne, David. *Worldmaking: The Art and Science of American Diplomacy*. New York: Farrar, Straus and Giroux, 2015.

Miscamble, Wilson. *George F. Kennan and the Making of American Foreign Policy, 1947–1950*. Princeton, NJ: Princeton University Press, 1992.

——. *The Most Controversial Decision: Truman, the Atomic Bombs, and the Defeat of Japan*. Cambridge, MA: Cambridge University Press, 2011.

Mitter, Rana. *Forgotten Ally: China's World War II, 1937–1945*. Boston: Houghton Mifflin Harcourt, 2013.

Morgenthau, Hans J. *Politics among Nations: The Struggle for Power and Peace*. 5th ed., rev. New York: Alfred A. Knopf, 1978.

Morris, Seymour, Jr. *Supreme Commander: MacArthur's Triumph in Japan*. New York: HarperCollins, 2014.

Nagai, Yonosuke, and Akira Iriye, eds. *Origins of the Cold War in Asia*. New York: Columbia University Press, 1977.

Nathan, Andrew J., and Robert S. Ross. *The Great Wall and the Empty Fortress: China's Search for Security*. New York: W. W. Norton, 1997.

Nugent, Walter. *Habits of Empire: A History of American Expansionism*. New York: Alfred A. Knopf, 2008.

Paige, Glenn D. *The Korean Decision: June 24–30, 1950*. New York: Free Press, 1968.

Patterson, James T. *Grand Expectations: The United States 1945–1974*. New York: Oxford University Press, 1996.

Peck, James. *Washington's China: The National Security World, the Cold War, and the Origins of Globalism*. Amherst: University of Massachusetts Press, 2006.

Pogue, Forrest C. *George C. Marshall: Statesman, 1945–1959*. New York: Viking Press, 1987.

Press, Daryl G. *Calculating Credibility: How Leaders Assess Military Threats*. Ithaca, NY: Cornell University Press, 2005.

Purifoy, Lewis McCarroll. *Harry Truman's China Policy: McCarthyism and the Diplomacy of Hysteria, 1947–1951*. New York: New Viewpoints, 1976.

Pyle, Kenneth B. *Japan Rising: The Resurgence of Japanese Power and Purpose*. New York: Public Affairs, 2007.

Qiang Zhai. *China and the Vietnam Wars, 1950–1975*. Chapel Hill: University of North Carolina Press, 2000.

Qing, Simei. *From Allies to Enemies: Visions of Modernity, Identity, and US-China Diplomacy, 1945–1960*. Cambridge, MA: Harvard University Press, 2007.

Reischauer, Edwin O. *The Japanese*. Cambridge, MA: Harvard University Press, 1977.

Reynolds, David. *From Munich to Pearl Harbor: Roosevelt's America and the Origins of the Second World War*. Chicago: Ivan R. Dee, 2001.

——. *The Long Shadow: The Legacies of the Great War in the Twentieth Century*. New York: W. W. Norton, 2014.

Ross, Robert S. *Negotiating Cooperation: The United States and China, 1969–1989*. Stanford, CA: Stanford University Press, 1995.

Rotter, Andrew J. *The Path to Vietnam: Origins of the American Commitment to Southeast Asia*. Ithaca, NY: Cornell University Press, 1987.

Russell, Richard L. *George F. Kennan's Strategic Thought: The Making of an American Political Realist*. Westport, CT: Praeger, 1999.

Samuels, Richard J. *Rich Nation, Strong Army: National Security and the Technological Transformation of Japan*. Ithaca, NY: Cornell University Press, 1994.

——. *Securing Japan: Tokyo's Grand Strategy and the Future of East Asia*. Ithaca, NY: Cornell University Press, 2007.

Schaller, Michael. *Altered States: The United States and Japan since the Occupation*. New York: Oxford University Press, 1997.

——. *The American Occupation of Japan: The Origins of the Cold War in Asia*. New York: Oxford University Press, 1985.

——. *Douglas MacArthur: The Far Eastern General*. New York: Oxford University Press, 1989.

——. *The United States and China: Into the Twenty-First Century*. 3rd ed. New York: Oxford University Press, 2002.

Schell, Orville, and John Delury. *Wealth and Power: China's Long March to the Twenty-First Century*. New York: Random House, 2013.

Schonberger, Howard B. *Aftermath of War: Americans and the Remaking of Japan, 1945–1952*. Kent, OH: Kent State University Press, 1989.

Shirk, Susan L. *China: Fragile Superpower*. New York: Oxford University Press, 2007.

Simmons, Robert R. *The Strained Alliance: Peking, P'yongyang, Moscow, and the Politics of the Korean Civil War*. New York: Free Press, 1975.

Solomon, Richard H. *Chinese Negotiating Behavior: Pursuing Interests through "Old Friends"*. Washington, DC: United States Institute of Peace Press, 1999.

Spector, Ronald H. *Eagle against the Sun: The American War with Japan*. New York: Vintage Books, 1985.

Spence, Jonathan. *The Chan's Great Continent: China in Western Minds*. New York: W. W. Norton, 1998.

——. *Mao Zedong*. New York: Viking Penguin, 1999.

Steel, Ronald. *Walter Lippman and the American Century*. Boston: Little, Brown, 1980.

Stephanson, Anders. *Kennan and the Art of Foreign Policy*. Cambridge, MA: Harvard University Press, 1989.

Stokesbury, James L. *A Short History of the Korean War*. New York: William Morrow, 1988.

Stuart-Fox, Martin. *A Short History of China and Southeast Asia: Tribute, Trade and Influence*. Crows Nest NSW, Australia: Allen & Unwin, 2005.

Stueck, William Whitney, Jr. *The Road to Confrontation: American Policy toward China and Korea, 1947–1950*. Chapel Hill: University of North Carolina Press, 1981.

——. *The Wedemeyer Mission: American Politics and Foreign Policy during the Cold War*. Athens: University of Georgia Press, 1984.

Sugita, Yoneyuki. *Pitfall or Panacea: The Irony of US Power in Occupied Japan, 1945–1952*. New York: Routledge, 2003.

Swaine, Michael D., and Ashley J. Tellis. *Interpreting China's Grand Strategy: Past, Present, and Future*. Santa Monica, CA: Rand, 2000.

Swenson-Wright, John. *Unequal Allies? United States Security and Alliance Policy toward Japan, 1945–1960*. Stanford, CA: Stanford University Press, 2005.

Takemae, Eiji. *Inside GHQ: The Allied Occupation of Japan and Its Legacy*. Translated and adapted from the Japanese by Robert Rickets and Sebastian Swann. New York: Continuum, 2002.

Taylor, Jay. *The Generalissimo: Chiang Kai-shek and the Struggle for Modern China*. Cambridge, MA: Harvard University Press, 2011.

Thompson, Nicholas. *The Hawk and the Dove: Paul Nitze, George Kennan, and the History of the Cold War*. New York: Henry Holt, 2009.

Tsou, Tang. *America's Failure in China, 1951–1950*. Chicago: University of Chicago Press, 1963.

Tuchman, Barbara. *Stilwell and the American Experience in China, 1911–45*. New York: Grove Press, 1985.

Tucker, Nancy Bernkopf, ed. *China Confidential: American Diplomats and Sino-American Relations, 1945–1996*. New York: Columbia University Press, 2001.
——. *The China Threat: Memories, Myths, and Realities in the 1950s*. New York: Columbia University Press, 2012.
——. *Patterns in the Dust: Chinese-American Relations and the Recognition Controversy, 1949–1950*. New York: Columbia University Press, 1983.
Tyler, Patrick. *A Great Wall: Six Presidents and China*. New York: Public Affairs, 1999.
Unger, Debi, and Irwin Unger. *George Marshall: A Biography*. With Stanley Hirshson. New York: HarperCollins, 2014.
Vogel, Ezra F. *Deng Xiaoping and the Transformation of China*. Cambridge, MA: Harvard University Press, 2011.
Wang Gungwu. *The Chinese Overseas: From Earthbound China to the Quest for Autonomy*. Cambridge, MA: Harvard University Press, 2000.
Wang Zheng. *Never Forget National Humiliation: Historical Memory in Chinese Politics and Foreign Relations*. New York: Columbia University Press, 2012.
Whelan, Richard. *Drawing the Line: The Korean War, 1950–1953*. Boston: Little, Brown, 1990.
Whiting, Allen S. *China Crosses the Yalu: The Decision to Enter the Korean War*. New York: Macmillan, 1960.
Wray, Harry, and Hilary Conroy, ed. *Japan Examined: Perspectives on Modern Japanese History*. Honolulu: University of Hawaii Press, 1983.

ARTICLES

Beckham, Rhonda S. "George F. Kennan and the Rebuilding of Japan: The Second Phase of Occupation Policy." Master of arts thesis, Old Dominion University, December 1990.
Buhite, Russell. "Major Interests: American Policy toward China, Taiwan, and Korea, 1945–1950." *Pacific Historical Review* 47, no. 3 (August 1978): 425–51.
Cohen, Warren I. "US, China, and the Cold War in Asia, 1949–1979." *Centennial Review* 24, no. 2 (Spring 1980): 127–47.
Cumings, Bruce. "Japan's Position in the World System." In *Postwar Japan as History*. Edited by Andrew Gordon, 34–63. Berkeley: University of California Press, 1993.
——. "Kennan, Containment, Conciliation: The End of Cold War History." *Current History* 94, no. 595 (November 1995): 359–63.
Davies, John Paton, Jr. "Two Hundred Years of American Foreign Policy: America and East Asia." *Foreign Affairs* 55, no. 2 (January 1977): 368–94.
——. "The U.S. Invented the 'Imbalance of Power.'" *New York Times Magazine*, 7 December 1969, 50, 142–50.
Dore, R. P. "The Prestige Factor in International Affairs." *International Affairs* 51, no. 2 (April 1975): 190–207.
Dower, John W. "Occupied Japan and the American Lake." In *America's Asia: Dissenting Essays on Asian-American Relations*. Edited by Edward Friedman and Mark Selden, 146–206. New York: Random House, 1969.
——. "A Rejoinder." *Pacific Historical Review* 42, no. 2 (May 1988): 202–9.
Downey, Betsy. "In Which 'Mr. X' Goes to Asia: George Frost Kennan and Containment in China and Korea: 1947–1950." *Mid-America: An Historical Review* 72, no. 1 (January 1990): 71–89.
Doyle, Randall. "The Reluctant Heretic: George F. Kennan and the Vietnam War, 1950–1968." *Grand Valley Review* 27, no. 1 (2004): 54–83.

Etzold, Thomas H. "The Far East in American Strategy, 1948–1951." In *Aspects of Sino-American Relations since 1784*. Edited by Thomas Etzold, 102–26. New York: New Viewpoints, 1978.

Feaver, John H. "The China Aid Bill of 1948: Limited Assistance as a Cold War Strategy." *Diplomatic History* 5, no. 2 (Spring 1981): 107–20.

Finney, John W. "The Long Trial of John Paton Davies." *New York Times Magazine*, 31 August 1969, 7–9, 23–28, 35.

Foltos, Lester J. "The New Pacific Barrier: America's Search for Security in the Pacific, 1945–47." *Diplomatic History* 13, no. 3 (1989): 317–42.

Herring, George C. "The Truman Administration and the Restoration of French Sovereignty in Indochina." *Diplomatic History* 1, no. 2 (1977): 97–117.

Hixson, Walter L. "Containment on the Perimeter: George F. Kennan and Vietnam." *Diplomatic History* 12, no. 2 (Spring 1988): 149–63.

Hunt, Michael H. "Beijing and the Korean Crisis, June 1950–June 1951." *Political Science Quarterly* 107, no. 3 (Autumn 1992): 453–78.

Igarashi, Takeshi. "The Ordeal of the Containment Policy: George Kennan and the Redirection of American Occupation Policy for Japan." Unpublished paper prepared for Japan Seminar, University of Maryland, College Park, MD, 28 February 1981.

Izumikawa, Yasuhiro. "To Coerce or Reward? Theorizing Wedge Strategies in Alliance Politics." *Security Studies* 22, no. 3 (2013): 498–531.

Joshi, Shashank. "Honor in International Relations." Working Paper No. 2008-0146, Weatherhead Center for International Affairs, Harvard University, Cambridge, MA, December 2008.

Kennan, George F. "A Fresh Look at Our China Policy." *New York Times Magazine*, 22 November 1964, 27, 140–47.

——. "Japanese Security and American Policy." *Foreign Affairs* 43, no. 1 (October 1964): 14–28.

——. "Let Peace Not Die of Neglect." *New York Times Magazine*, 25 February 1951, 10, 38–41.

——. "The Sources of Soviet Conduct." *Foreign Affairs* 25, no. 4 (July 1947): 566–82.

Kim, Seung-yong. "American Elites' Strategic Thinking toward Korea: From Kennan to Brzezinski." *Diplomacy & Statecraft* 12, no. 1 (March 2001): 185–212.

Kimura, Masami. "American Asia Experts, Liberal Internationalism, and the Occupation of Japan: Transcending Cold War Politics and Historiography." *Journal of American-East Asian Relations* 21 (2014): 246–77.

Kramer, Mark, ed. "Forum: George F. Kennan and the Cold War: Perspectives on John Gaddis's Biography." *Journal of Cold War Studies* 15, no. 4 (Fall 2013): 153–245.

Kroncke, Jedidiah. "An Early Tragedy of Comparative Constitutionalism: Frank Goodnow and the Chinese Republic." *Pacific Rim Law & Policy Journal* 21, no. 3 (June 2012): 533–90.

Leary, William M., and William Stueck. "The Chennault Plan to Save China: US Containment in Asia and the Origins of the CIA's Aerial Empire, 1949–1950." *Diplomatic History* 8, no. 4 (1984): 349–64.

Logevall, Fredrik. "Bernath Lecture: A Critique of Containment." *Diplomatic History* 28, no. 4 (September 2004): 473–99.

Lucas, Scott, and Kaeten Mistry. "Illusions of Coherence: George F. Kennan, US Strategy and Political Warfare in the Early Cold War, 1946–1950." *Diplomatic History* 33, no. 1 (2009): 39–66.

Maddux, Thomas, and Diane Labrosse, eds. "H-Diplo Roundtable Review on John Lewis Gaddis, *George F. Kennan: An American Life.*" *H-Diplo Roundtable Reviews* 13, no. 24 (16 April 2012): 1–51.

Mao, Lin. "China and the Escalation of the Vietnam War: The First Years of the Johnson Administration." *Journal of Cold War Studies* 11, no. 2 (Spring 2009): 35–69.

McLean, David. "American Nationalism, the China Myth, and the Truman Doctrine: The Question of Accommodation with Peking, 1949–50." *Diplomatic History* 10, no. 1 (Winter 1986): 25–42.

Miscamble, Wilson. "George Kennan: A Life in the Foreign Service." *Foreign Service Journal* 81, no. 2 (February 2004): 22–34.

Moore, Ray A. "The Occupation of Japan as History: Some Recent Research." *Monumenta Nipponica* 36, no. 3 (Autumn 1981): 317–28.

Munro-Leighton, Judith. "A Postrevisionist Scrutiny of America's Role in the Cold War in Asia, 1945–1950." *Journal of American-East Asian Relations* 1, no. 1 (Spring 1992): 73–98.

Muste, A. J., and George F. Kennan. "An Exchange: A Policy for the Far East." *Liberation*, April 1965, 6–24.

Newman, Robert P. "The Self-Inflicted Wound: The China White Paper of 1949." *Prologue* 14, no. 3 (Fall 1982): 141–56.

Nixon, Richard M. "Asia After Vietnam," *Foreign Affairs* 46, no. 1 (October 1967): 111–25.

Press, Daryl G. "The Credibility of Power: Assessing Threats during the 'Appeasement' Crises of the 1930s." *International Security* 29, no. 3 (Winter 2004/5): 136–69.

Rintz, William A. "The Failure of the China White Paper." *Constructing the Past* 11, no. 1, article 8 (2009): 76–84.

Schaller, Michael. "Consul General O. Edmund Clubb, John P. Davies, and the 'Inevitability' of Conflict between the United States and China, 1949–50: A Comment and New Documentation." *Diplomatic History* 9, no. 2 (1985): 149–60.

——. "MacArthur's Japan: The View from Washington." *Diplomatic History* 10, no. 1 (Winter 1986): 1–23.

——. "Securing the Great Crescent: Occupied Japan and the Origins of Containment in Southeast Asia." *Journal of American History* 69, no. 2 (September 1982): 392–414.

Schonberger, Howard B. "The Japan Lobby in American Diplomacy, 1947–1952." *Pacific Historical Review* 46 (1977): 327–59.

——. "A Rejoinder." *Pacific Historical Review* 42, no. 2 (May 1988): 209–18.

——. "US Policy in Postwar Japan: The Retreat from Liberalism." *Science & Society* 46, no. 1 (Spring 1982): 39–59.

——. "Zaibatsu Dissolution and the American Restoration of Japan." *Bulletin of Concerned Asian Scholars* 5, no. 2 (September 1973): 16–31.

Shibayama, Futoshi. "U.S. Strategic Debates over the Defense of Japan: Lessons for the Twenty-First Century." *Journal of American-East Asian Relations* 9, nos. 1–2 (Spring–Summer 2000): 29–54.

Travis, Frederick F. "The Kennan-Russel Anti-Tsarist Propaganda Campaign among Russian Prisoners of War in Japan, 1904–1905." *Russian Review* 40, no. 3 (July 1981): 263–77.

Ullman, Richard. "The US and the World: An Interview with George Kennan." *New York Review of Books* 46, no. 13 (12 August 1999): 4–6. Also available at http://www.nybooks.com/articles/1999/08/12/the-us-and-the-world-an-interview-with-george-kenn/.

US News and World Report. "The Strange Case of John Paton Davies." 11 December 1953, 26–32, 106–17.

Whelan, Joseph G. "George Kennan and His Influence on American Foreign Policy." *Virginia Quarterly Review* 35, no. 2 (Spring 1959): 196–220.

Williams, Justin, Sr. "American Democratization Policy for Occupied Japan: Correcting the Revisionist Version." *Pacific Historical Review* 42, no. 2 (May 1988): 179–202.

Wood, Steve. "Prestige in World Politics: History, Theory, and Expression." *International Politics* 50, no. 3 (March 2013): 387–411.

Index

Note: Page numbers in italics indicate illustrations.